W9-CLD-207

Jack the Ripper

An Encyclopedia

Jack the Ripper

An Encyclopedia

John J. Eddleston

ABC-CLIO
Santa Barbara, California
Denver, Colorado
Oxford, England

Maps by Jill M. O. Looper

Library of Congress Cataloging-in-Publication Data
Eddleston, John J., 1952–
Jack the Ripper: An encyclopedia / John J. Eddleston.
p. cm.
Includes bibliographical references and index.
ISBN 1-57607-414-5 (hardcover: alk. paper) — 1-57607-547-8 (e-book)
1. Jack the Ripper. 2. Serial murders—England—London—History—19th century. 3. Serial murderers—England—London—History—19th century. 4. Whitechapel (London, England)—History. I. Title.
HV6535.G6 L6532 2001
364.15'23'092—dc21 2001004226
CIP

07 06 05 04 03 02 01 10 9 8 7 6 5 4 3 2 1

ABC-CLIO, Inc.
130 Cremona Drive, P.O. Box 1911
Santa Barbara, California 93116-1911

This book is printed on acid-free paper ∞.
Manufactured in the United States of America

Contents

Preface

Jack the Ripper! The very name conjures images of dark London streets, swirling fog, and a figure in the shadows waiting to claim his next victim. For this we have to thank the film industry, which, it appears, has never let the facts of the Ripper crimes get in the way of a good story. This mystique is not the prerogative of film alone, for many writers too have perpetuated myths, errors, sloppy research, and downright invention. The truth is that none of the murders took place in a fog—but much of the writing on this subject has created a literary fog that has obscured the truth for more than 100 years.

There are, of course, some excellent books on the subject. Most notable among these are Philip Sugden's *The Complete History of Jack the Ripper* and the exceptional *The Jack the Ripper A–Z* by Paul Begg, Martin Fido, and Keith Skinner, but neither of these volumes approaches the subject as this encyclopedia does. The first does not cover all the possible victims and suspects, and the second, by definition, has the entries for each particular crime divided throughout the book.

In this encyclopedia I have attempted to start by telling the stories of each crime, followed by my own thoughts regarding which are most likely to be attributable to Jack. In the next three sections I list the witnesses, the police, and others who played a part. Also included are a chronology, descriptions of the killer, a discussion of some of the more important so-called Ripper communications, and details of the myths and errors usually perpetuated by those who are unfamiliar with good research. Finally, I cover the suspects, review the literature to date, give some resources, and summarize my own thoughts on the killer. Wherever possible, the entries are cross-referenced so that the student new to the subject may easily find all the information he or she requires.

I hope I do not fall into the trap that many previous writers have. Many, it seems, decide who the Ripper was and then write a book detailing how this particular individual may be "proven" to be the killer. My own opinion is that the best books simply give the facts, review the evidence, and then, if possible, give an opinion as to who Jack *might* have been.

The "Summary" section, as I have said, gives my own opinion, but it is important to realize that I am *not* stating categorically that this man was Jack. I am merely saying that of the hundred and more candidates I have looked at, this man is the only one who I can believe might have wielded the knife in those gas-lit East London streets.

There will, of course, be other books on this subject. There will, I have no doubt, be other candidates suggested in the future, and I eagerly look forward to the first full-length work "proving" that the killer was none other than Queen Victoria herself, dressed in shabby clothes she had borrowed from a servant and a deerstalker hat that Prince Albert once wore at Balmoral. There are books out there now that are almost as ludicrous in their conclusions.

I would not be arrogant enough to suggest that my work on this subject will grant me a place among such names as Philip Sugden, Paul Begg, Martin Fido, Keith Skinner, Richard Whittington-Egan, James Tully, William Beadle, and the like, all of whom are first-class researchers and brilliant writers. I hope only that this book may be viewed by the general public interested in these brutal unsolved murders as a trustworthy, accurate, and interesting work that may be relied upon to give the facts and that will not, like so many others, perpetuate myths.

Perhaps, at last, the fog will begin to clear.

John J. Eddleston
West Sussex, England

A Note on Terminology

Names

Many of those who lived in the Whitechapel area used two or more names, usually with the intention of obscuring their identity in encounters with the police. Once arrested for, say, drunkenness, a person would have a record. On future occasions he or she would often give a different name so that his or her previous convictions would remain undetected. This is one reason that more than one version is given of the names of many people mentioned in the narratives of the crimes, though in some cases alternative versions were created by garbled reporting at the time.

Numbering of Floors

There is a basic difference in how the floors of buildings are numbered in Britain and the United Sates. In the United States, the street-level floor of a building is referred to as the first floor, and thereafter floors are numbered upward: second, third, fourth, and so on.

In Britain, the street-level floor is called the ground floor, the next one up is the first floor, and the floors are then numbered upward: second, third, etc. This means that what is called the fourth floor in the United States would be called the third floor in Britain.

Throughout this book, the American convention is used. For instance, when I refer to Martha Tabram's body being discovered on the second floor of George Yard Buildings, the location would have been described as the first floor in British reports of the time.

Money

Although Britain now has a decimal currency with 100 new pennies to the pound, in 1888 it had a different system with 240 pennies to the pound. For clarity, a brief outline of the currency system of the day is given here under the names of particular coins.

Farthing—4 to the penny, so 960 to the pound
Halfpenny—2 to the penny, so 480 to the pound
Penny—240 to the pound

All three coins were made of bronze. There were even smaller fractions of the farthing, but they need not concern us.

Threepence—as the name suggests, worth 3 pennies. There were 80 to the pound.
Sixpence—known affectionately as a *tanner.* There were 40 to the pound.
Shilling—also known as a *bob.* Twenty shillings made up 1 pound, and there were 12 pennies in 1 shilling.
Florin—a 2-shilling piece also known as *two bob.* There were 10 to the pound.
Half a crown—a coin worth 2 shillings and sixpence that is the equivalent of 30 pennies. There were 8 to the pound.
Crown—A 5-shilling piece worth 60 pennies. Four crowns made up 1 pound.

All the coins from the threepence to the crown were made of silver.

Sovereign—a coin worth 1 pound
Guinea—a coin worth 1 pound and 1 shilling, or 21 shillings

These two coins were made of gold and would seldom have been seen in the East End of London.

How to Use This Book

The book is divided into 14 sections, each covering in detail an aspect of the crimes.

The first section, "The Victims" outlines the stories of all possible victims of Jack the Ripper together with what is known of each woman's life. This information is gleaned from press reports, original documents now held in the British Public Record Office, inquest reports, and other such sources. This section is not cross-referenced because other sections are all related to this one. The section is organized chronologically.

The next three sections cover "The Witnesses," "The Police," and "Others Who Played a Part." These short summary entries are organized alphabetically and cross-referenced to other sections. Links to the entries in "The Victims" are given in boldface.

The fifth section is the "Chronology," which is a summary of the events, placed here for ease of reference in relation to the four preceding sections.

The next two sections try to bring us a little closer to the killer known as Jack the Ripper. The sixth section, "Descriptions," summarizes all the principal descriptions of men seen with the victims. In the seventh section, "Letters and Correspondence," I look at various communications purporting to come from the killer, assessing their potential validity and summarizing the results. These two sections are arranged chronologically.

The eighth section, "Miscellaneous," ties up some of the loose ends in discussing various items connected with the crimes and with research since the time of the murders. It is organized alphabetically.

There are, as already mentioned, many fundamental errors that have been perpetuated in other volumes over the years. For the five so-called canonical murders, many of these are listed in the ninth section, "Myths and Errors." Some of the most persistent myths are examined in detail. This section is followed by "Locations," which describes the main streets, public houses, lodging houses, and the like in the area where the murders occurred.

In the eleventh section, "Suspects," I examine over 140 of the men suggested as the killer. Each suspect is given a rating as to probability, and many are discussed in detail in order to explain that rating. The section is organized alphabetically and is followed by the "Literature" section, in which all of the books and films on the Ripper crimes are listed, many with annotations.

The thirteenth section, "Resources," points the serious student to the files that contain primary information on the murders, correspondence, and other details about some of the people involved.

The book ends with the "Summary" section, which outlines my own thoughts on who the killer might have been.

I hope the reader finds this volume a valuable addition to the available literature.

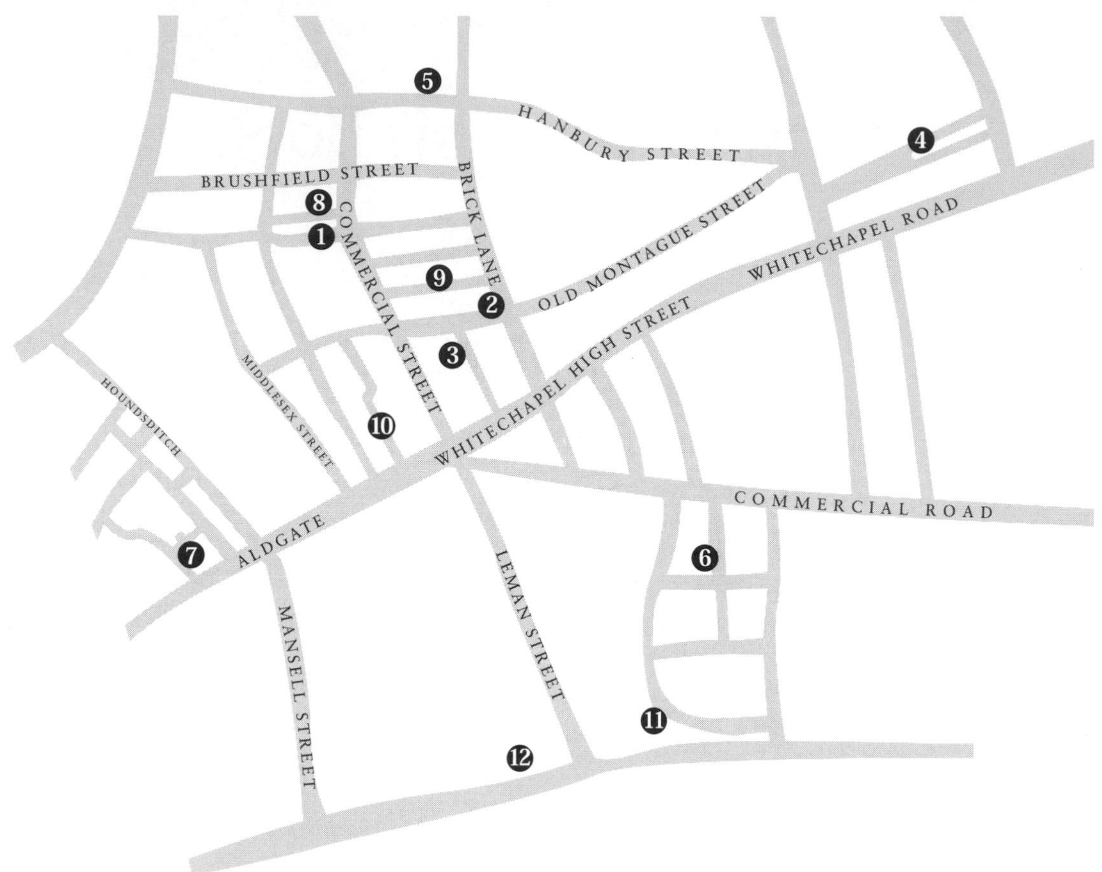

1. Annie Millwood
2. Emma Elizabeth Smith
3. Martha Tabram
4. Mary Ann Nichols
5. Annie Chapman
6. Elizabeth Stride
7. Catherine Eddowes
8. Mary Jane Kelly
9. Annie Farmer
10. Alice McKenzie
11. Pinchin Street torso
12. Frances Coles

A general map of the Whitechapel and Spitalfields area showing the sites of various attacks attributed to Jack the Ripper

I

The Victims

As with all other aspects of the Jack the Ripper case, there are disagreements as to precisely how many victims the killer finally claimed. Most writers agree that Mary Ann Nichols, Annie Chapman, and Catherine Eddowes were murdered by the same hand. The vast majority also include Mary Jane Kelly, though some claim that she might have been killed by someone else who used the Ripper murders to disguise his crime. There is some dispute over whether Elizabeth Stride was a Ripper victim and even more argument over Martha Tabram. As for the rest, they have been included or omitted in other works depending on which particular theory a writer is trying to push.

In this section, *all* the possible East End victims are included, in chronological order. The women covered and the dates upon which they were attacked are:

- Fairy Fay—Monday, 26 December 1887
- Annie Millwood—Saturday, 25 February 1888
- Ada Wilson—Wednesday, 28 March 1888
- Emma Elizabeth Smith—Tuesday, 3 April 1888
- Martha Tabram—Tuesday, 7 August 1888
- Mary Ann Nichols—Friday, 31 August 1888
- Annie Chapman—Saturday, 8 September 1888
- Susan Ward—ca. Saturday, 15 September 1888
- Elizabeth Stride—Sunday, 30 September 1888
- Catherine Eddowes—Sunday, 30 September 1888
- The Whitehall Mystery—ca. Wednesday, 3 October 1888
- Mary Jane Kelly—Friday, 9 November 1888
- Annie Farmer—Tuesday, 20 November 1888
- Rose Mylett—Thursday, 20 December 1888
- Elizabeth Jackson—ca. Tuesday, 4 June 1889
- Alice McKenzie—Wednesday, 17 July 1889
- The Pinchin Street Torso—ca. Sunday, 8 September 1889
- Frances Coles—Friday, 13 February 1891

Other victims, such as Carrie Brown, are only ever included to suit a particular theory. Such "victims" are referred to in the "Miscellaneous" section.

A summary at the end of this section details my thoughts upon which victims may properly be placed at Jack's door.

Fairy Fay

Monday, 26 December 1887

Once the press of the day had determined that a series of murders had occurred, it was necessary to decide precisely which victims formed part of that series. The more victims there were, the more sensational the case. This approach, plus newspaper inaccuracies and confusion, led to the inclusion of Fairy Fay in the list as Jack's first victim.

The suggestion that there had been a murder in 1887 was first made in a broadsheet titled "Lines on the Terrible Tragedy in Whitechapel," which was published in early September 1888. This sheet referred to victims such as Annie Millwood and Ada Wilson but also referred to an earlier victim who had died "twelve months ago."

Soon afterward this suggestion was picked up by the *Daily Telegraph,* and in its issues of 10 and 11 September the story of the first victim was fleshed out. Now a date was given: 26 December, and a location: somewhere around Osborn Street and Wentworth Street.

It is telling that the articles in the *Telegraph* stated that this particular victim had been killed by means of a stick, or possibly an iron bar, thrust into her body. It went on to say that the unfortunate woman had never been identified.

According to the records, no crime of this nature occurred on this date, so it is clear that the *Telegraph* articles had garbled an account of the death of Emma Elizabeth Smith, who had been attacked in the early-morning hours following a Bank Holiday, Easter Monday, which fell on 2 April 1888. Emma had been attacked by three youths in Osborn Street, and the writers of the articles had merely mistaken the date of the public holiday. However, the story had now entered the public consciousness and continued to be expanded upon.

On 12 November 1888, W. A. Hunter, Member of Parliament for Aberdeen North, asked in the House of Commons whether the Home Secretary had considered extending a pardon to any accomplices the killer might have had in earlier murders, especially in the case of the crime that had taken place the previous Christmas. Again, this incident shows that the actual crime referred to was the attack upon Emma Smith. This question was repeated in the House on 23 November, by which time Annie Farmer had been added to the list of those attacked.

Despite this transparent confusion, stories of this first unnamed victim continued. In 1910 Dr. Lyttleton Stewart Forbes Winslow published his memoirs, *Recollections of Forty Years,* which embroidered the story still further, and finally, on 29 October 1950, Terence Robertson wrote an article titled "Madman Who Murdered Nine Women" for the popular newspaper *Reynolds News.* Robertson gave the victim a name, Fairy Fay, and stated that she had been attacked while taking a shortcut home from a public house in Mitre Square.

In fact, it is obvious that Fairy Fay never existed. Jack the Ripper did not claim his first victim on Boxing Night in 1887, and all references to this supposed crime are in fact distorted stories of the murder of Emma Elizabeth Smith.

Suggestions for further reading:

Begg, Paul, Martin Fido, and Keith Skinner. *The Jack the Ripper A–Z.* Headline, 1996.

Sugden, Philip. *The Complete History of Jack the Ripper.* Robinson Publishing, 1994.

Annie Millwood

Saturday, 25 February 1888

Thirty-eight-year-old Annie was admitted to the Whitechapel Workhouse Infirmary at 5 P.M. on the evening of 25 February 1888, suffering from a number of knife wounds in the legs and lower torso.

A resident of a lodging house at 8 White's Row, Annie was the widow of a soldier named Richard Millwood. She explained to the police that she had been attacked by a man who had drawn a clasp knife from his pocket. He was a complete stranger to her, and there seemed to be no witnesses to the attack.

White's Row as it is today. This is the street where Annie Millwood lodged and where she was found on 25 February 1888. Admitted to the hospital, Annie died the following month. (Yvonne Berger)

In due course Annie recovered from her injuries, and she was discharged to the South Grove Workhouse almost a month later, on 21 March. Ten days later, however, on 31 March, she was at the back of the building when she collapsed. This time there was no recovery, and Annie Millwood was pronounced dead.

The inquest was held on 5 April before Coroner Wynne Edwin Baxter, and after various medical witnesses testified, a verdict was returned that Annie had died from "a sudden effusion into the pericardium from the rupture of the left pulmonary artery through ulceration." In effect, she died not as a result of her injuries but from natural causes.

Suggestions for further reading:

Begg, Paul, Martin Fido, and Keith Skinner. *The Jack the Ripper A–Z.* Headline, 1996.

Hinton, Bob. *From Hell . . . The Jack the Ripper Mystery.* Old Bakehouse Publications, 1998.

Jakubowski, Maxim, and Nathan Braund. *The Mammoth Book of Jack the Ripper.* Robinson Publishing, 1999.

Sugden, Philip. *The Complete History of Jack the Ripper.* Robinson Publishing, 1994.

Ada Wilson

Wednesday, 28 March 1888

Ada Wilson, a woman who described herself as a seamstress (a term often used by Victorians as a euphemism for a prostitute), was about to retire for the night at her home at 9 Maidman Street, Burdett Road, Mile End. It was about 2:30 A.M. on 28 March, and just as Ada was checking that the house was secure, there was a knock on the front door.

Upon opening the door, Ada saw a man who was about 30 years old. He had a sunburned face and a fair mustache and was about 5 feet 6 inches tall. He wore light-colored trousers, a dark coat, and a wideawake hat (a soft felt hat with a low crown and wide brim). Immediately he demanded money from Ada and added that if she did not at once produce the cash, she had but a few moments to live.

Ada indignantly refused to hand over any money, whereupon the stranger reached into his pocket, drew out a clasp knife, and plunged it twice into her throat. Fortunately for Ada, her screams of anguish brought neighbors rushing to her aid, and her attacker was fortunate to escape. Her neighbors sought medical assistance, and Dr. Wheeler of Mile End Road attended Ada at her house and bandaged her wounds, after which he ordered that she be taken to the London Hospital.

For some time it was believed that Ada had little chance of survival, but she proved to be a tenacious woman and eventually made a full recovery. She was released from the hospital on 27 April.

There was a witness to the attack, and as a result the assailant was almost captured. Rose Bierman, another resident of 9 Maidman Street, reported that she had heard terrible screams and upon running downstairs had seen Mrs. Wilson, who was only partially dressed, wringing her hands and crying, "Stop that man for cutting my throat! He has stabbed me." Only then did Rose notice a young, fair man rush to the front door and let himself out. After he had escaped, Rose ran out, found two constables outside the Royal Hotel, and told them what had happened.

As in the case of Fairy Fay, once a series of crimes had been suggested, the press looked for all possible cases of assault that might have some similarities, however slight, to the canonical murders. This approach caused Ada Wilson's name to be added to the list of Jack the Ripper's victims, though in fact the attack on her appeared to be a simple case of robbery gone wrong rather than an attempt at murder.

Suggestions for further reading:

Begg, Paul, Martin Fido, and Keith Skinner. *The Jack the Ripper A–Z*. Headline, 1996.

Hinton, Bob. *From Hell . . . The Jack the Ripper Mystery*. Old Bakehouse Publications, 1998.

Jakubowski, Maxim, and Nathan Braund. *The Mammoth Book of Jack the Ripper*. Robinson Publishing, 1999.

Sugden, Philip. *The Complete History of Jack the Ripper*. Robinson Publishing, 1994.

Emma Elizabeth Smith

Tuesday, 3 April 1888

Monday, 2 April 1888, was a Bank Holiday, and at about 7 P.M. that day Emma Elizabeth Smith, a 45-year-old widow with two children, left the common lodging house where she lived, 18 George Street, Spitalfields, and spent most of the evening in and around Whitechapel High Street and the area to the east, almost certainly soliciting.

At 12:15 A.M. on 3 April Emma was seen by Margaret Hayes, a fellow lodger at George Street. At that time Emma was talking to a man of medium height who wore a dark suit and a white silk handkerchief around his throat. The two were on the corner of Farrance Street and Burdett Road, in Limehouse. There is no suggestion that this man played any part in the events of later that day.

According to the story that Emma herself would later tell, she was wending her way home at around 1:30 A.M. and was just passing St. Mary's Church when she noticed three men coming toward her. Concerned, Emma crossed the road so she wouldn't have to pass the men, but they began to follow her, and in Osborn Street they attacked, robbed, and raped her.

Sometime between 2 A.M. and 3 A.M., Emma arrived back at her lodgings. It was obvious that she had been badly beaten. Her face was bruised, and her

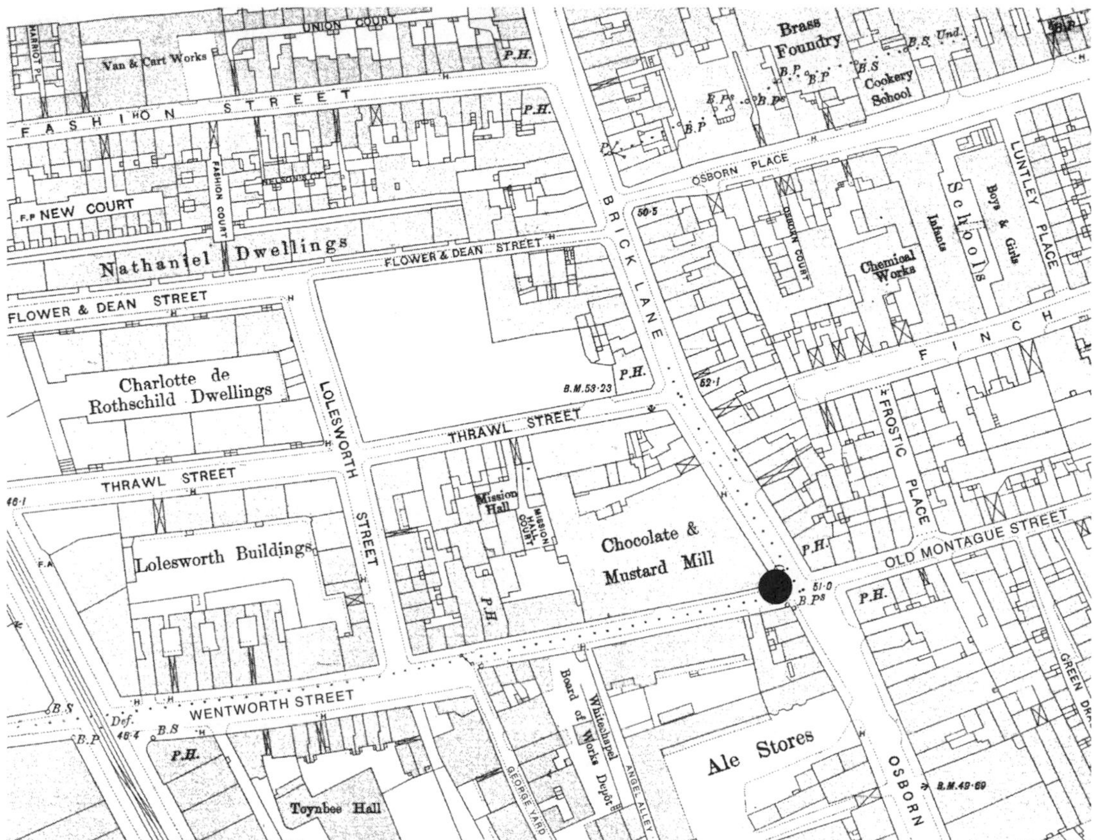

The location of the attack upon Emma Elizabeth Smith

right ear had been almost torn off. She also complained about pains in the lower groin, so the deputy keeper of the lodging house, Mary Russell, took Emma to the London Hospital, where she was attended to by the house surgeon, Dr. George Haslip. Haslip determined that in addition to her other injuries, Emma had also had a blunt object, possibly a stick, inserted forcibly into her vagina, causing a tear in the perineum.

On the way to the hospital, as Emma and Mary Russell had passed Taylor Brothers Mustard and Cocoa Mill on the corner of Brick Lane and Wentworth Street, Emma had pointed out that the mill was opposite to where she had been attacked. She mumbled a story of three men, the youngest of whom was only 18 or 19 years old. At the hospital Emma did not respond to treatment. She soon fell into a coma and died, from peritonitis, at 9 A.M. on Wednesday, 4 April.

The police investigating the case noted that there had been three men involved and that the principal motive appeared to be robbery. Though no arrests were made, it was believed that one of the gangs in the area had been responsible—possibly the Old Nichol gang, so named because its base of operations was around Old Nichol Street at the top of Brick Lane.

Suggestions for further reading:

Begg, Paul, Martin Fido, and Keith Skinner. *The Jack the Ripper A–Z*. Headline, 1996.

Hinton, Bob. *From Hell . . . The Jack the Ripper Mystery*. Old Bakehouse Publications, 1998.

Jakubowski, Maxim, and Nathan Braund. *The Mammoth Book of Jack the Ripper*. Robinson Publishing, 1999.

Sugden, Philip. *The Complete History of Jack the Ripper.* Robinson Publishing, 1994.

Martha Tabram
Tuesday, 7 August 1888

John Saunders Reeves, a dockside laborer, had to be at work early. That was why he left his home at 37 George Yard Buildings, George Yard, at 4:45 A.M. on 7 August. However, on this particular date John Reeves would be delayed, for as he walked down the stairs he found the body of a woman on the second-floor landing.

By this time it was already getting light, so Reeves could plainly see that the woman lay on her back in a pool of blood. Her clothing was disarranged and her legs open, and it was clear that she had been the victim of some kind of attack. Reeves ran into the street, found a policeman, Constable Thomas Barrett, and told Barrett of his grim discovery. Barrett and Reeves returned to George Yard Buildings, where Barrett, noticing that the woman's skirts had been pushed up, concluded that there had been recent intimacy and that the woman had possibly been the victim of a sexual attack.

Barrett sent for a doctor, and at 5:30 A.M. Dr. Timothy Robert Killeen of 68 Brick Lane arrived at the scene. He pronounced the woman dead, and his initial examination showed that she had been stabbed 39 times. He concluded that she had been dead for approximately three hours, putting the time of her death at about 2:30 A.M. Dr. Killeen ordered the removal of the body to the Workhouse Infirmary mortuary in Old Montague Street, where he would perform the postmortem.

George Yard as it is today. Martha Tabram was murdered on a landing of a building that stood at the top left, about where the white building is now. She was stabbed 39 times early on the morning of 7 August 1888. (Yvonne Berger)

Martha Tabram met her death on a landing of the marked building. Note that Angel Alley, where Mary Ann Connolly took her soldier, runs parallel and to the east.

Constable Barrett played a greater part than just being the first police officer on the scene. The investigation was led by Detective Inspector Edmund Reid, and Barrett told him that at 2 A.M. on the morning of 7 August he had seen a soldier loitering in Wentworth Street, which ran along the north end of George Yard. Barrett had questioned the man, who said he was waiting for "a chum who had gone with a girl." The constable was able to give a reasonably detailed description of this soldier, stating that he was aged 22 to 26, 5 feet 9 or 10 inches tall, with a fair complexion, dark hair, and a small dark-brown mustache turned up at the ends. He was wearing one good-conduct badge on his tunic.

As a result of this report, Inspector Reid took Constable Barrett to the Tower of London, where troops were stationed, that same day. There Barrett was able to view a number of prisoners who were being detained in the guardroom, presumably for various offenses committed over the Bank Holiday of 6 August. Barrett failed to pick anyone out, but it was arranged that he would be taken back to the Tower the next day, when he would be able to view all soldiers who had been absent from duty on 6 August.

Meanwhile, also on 7 August, Inspector Reid made a number of inquiries of people who lived in George Yard Buildings, including Joseph and Elizabeth Mahoney, who lived at 47 George Yard Buildings. They had been out enjoying themselves on Bank Holiday Monday and had returned home at 1:40 A.M.

Joseph had stayed in for the rest of the night, but Elizabeth had gone out again almost immediately to buy their supper from a chandler's shop in Thrawl Street. By the time she had returned home, it was 1:50 A.M. Neither she nor Joseph had seen anything on the stairs, and they had not been disturbed by noises or screams during the night.

Alfred George Crow, a carman, lived at 35 George Yard Buildings. It had been 3 A.M. on the 7th when he had returned home, and as he had passed the spot where the body of the woman would later be discovered, he had seen someone lying on the landing. He had taken no notice because it was quite common to find someone the worse for drink sleeping it off on the stairs. He went on home and went to bed, and he too heard nothing to disturb his rest during the remainder of the night. Inspector Reid believed that Crow had seen the woman's body, leading to the conclusion that she had been killed sometime between 2 and 4:50 A.M., when the body was found. This time frame agreed with the findings of Dr. Killeen, who said the woman had died at about 2:30 A.M.

Francis Hewitt, the superintendent of George Yard Buildings, lived just 12 feet from where the body had lain. He had heard nothing at all during the night. His wife did report hearing a single cry of "Murder," but this had come early in the evening, well before the time when the woman must have been attacked.

On Wednesday, 8 August, Constable Barrett was taken back to the Tower. Inspector Reid stressed the importance of the visit and told Barrett to be very careful. A number of men were paraded for his review, and Barrett walked slowly down the line before picking one man out. He was asked if he were sure in his identification, whereupon he looked again and chose a second man who was standing six or seven positions away from the first. Both soldiers were then escorted to the orderly room.

Immediately Barrett admitted that he had made a mistake with the first man. Only after he had picked him out had the constable realized that the man wore medal ribbons, whereas the soldier he had seen in Wentworth Street had had none. That soldier was then allowed to go without even having his name taken.

The second soldier was Private John Leary, and he denied being anywhere near the scene of the crime on the night of 6–7 August. Leary explained that he and another man, Private Law, had gone out together that night. They had traveled to Brixton, where they drank until the pubs closed. Before leaving the public house, Leary went to relieve himself, and when he came out Law had already gone, so he set off to walk through Battersea and Chelsea on his way back to the barracks. From Chelsea he walked past Charing Cross and into the Strand, where he saw Law again. By then it was 4:30 A.M., and the two friends walked on to Billingsgate, where they had a final drink before getting back to their barracks at 6 A.M. When Private Law was interviewed he confirmed this story in every detail, and Leary was dismissed.

A description of the dead woman was issued, stating that she was aged about 37, 5 feet 3 inches tall, with dark hair and a dark complexion. At the time of her death she was wearing a dark-green skirt, a brown petticoat, a long black jacket, brown stockings, a black bonnet, and side-sprung boots. All her clothing was described as "old."

The inquest opened at 2 P.M. on Thursday, 9 August, at the Working Lad's Institute in Whitechapel Road. The coroner for the district, Wynne Edwin Baxter, was on holiday in Scandinavia, so the task of chairing the proceedings fell to his deputy, George Collier. By this time there had been three identifications of the dead woman, but all these witnesses had given different names: the most likely was Martha Turner, but none had yet been conclusive.

Only a few witnesses were called. Elizabeth Mahoney told of her and her husband's movements and confirmed that she did not believe there had been a body on the stairs at the time she retired. Alfred Crow spoke of seeing someone lying on the landing when he returned home, and he was followed by John Saunders Reeves, who had actually found the body.

The next witness was Constable Barrett, and he was followed by Dr. Killeen. The doctor had completed his postmortem, and he now gave the court his report. There were a total of 22 stab wounds to the trunk; the left lung had been penetrated in five places and the right lung in two. The heart, which was rather fatty, had been penetrated once. All the other internal organs appeared to be healthy, but the liver had been penetrated five times, the spleen twice, and the stomach six times. There was one wound in the lower body, and there was no evidence of a struggle. (The doctor did not mention the other wounds to the victim's throat and legs.)

A number of writers have placed words and testimony in Dr. Killeen's mouth. His findings have been grossly misquoted, and it is time to set the record straight. Dr. Killeen did not state that the killer was ambidextrous. He found one wound that *might* have been inflicted by a left-handed person, but all the others were inflicted by someone wielding a weapon with the right hand. Nor did he say that the killer had used a bayonet or a surgical knife. He did say that one of the wounds appeared to have been inflicted by a different weapon than the rest. This wound, on the breastbone, had come from some long, strong instrument, *possibly* a bayonet or a dagger. All the other wounds could have been inflicted by an ordinary penknife. Finally, there is no truth in the assertion that Dr. Killeen said that the killer demonstrated surgical skill, and he did not say that the killer had known how and where to cut.

After these witnesses had been heard, Collier adjourned the inquest for two weeks in the hope that in that intervening period the police would be able to put a name to the unfortunate woman.

In fact, the police did not have to wait very long. That same day a prostitute named Mary Ann Connolly, also known as Pearly Poll, walked into the Commercial Street Police Station and said she knew who the dead woman was. The name she gave for the victim was Emma Turner, and Mary Ann went on to say that on the night of 6 August she and Emma had been in the company of two soldiers from 10 until 11:45 P.M. The four had been drinking in various public houses, and at 11:45 P.M. they had separated, Mary Ann going with the corporal up Angel Alley and Emma going with the private up George Yard, so that business could be transacted. That was the last Mary Ann had seen of her friend. Arrangements were immediately made for Mary Ann to visit the Tower the next day in order to identify the two soldiers.

That same evening, at 11:45 P.M., Corporal Benjamin returned to his barracks at the Tower. He had been on official leave on 6 August and was supposed to have returned that same evening. He had failed to do so, and now his clothing and bayonet were carefully examined for traces of blood. None could be found, and Benjamin explained that he had been staying with his father at the Canbury Hotel, Kingston-upon-Thames. The story was checked and shown to be true.

The parade at the Tower for the benefit of Mary Ann Connolly was arranged for 11 A.M. on 10 August, but Mary Ann failed to appear. She could not be found that day or the next, having decided to visit her cousin, Mrs. Shean, who lived at 4 Fuller's Court, Drury Lane. It was not until 12 August that she was traced by Sergeant Eli Caunter. A new arrangement was then made with the Tower.

The parade finally took place on 13 August, but Mary Ann failed to pick out anyone. Only now did she volunteer the information that the soldiers she and Emma had been with had worn white bands around their hats. This meant that they were Coldstream Guards, not Grenadiers, so yet another parade, this time at the Wellington Barracks, had to be arranged.

On 14 August a formal identification of the victim was finally made. Henry Samuel Tabram was a foreman furniture packer living at 6 River Terrace, East Greenwich, and he had read reports of the crime in the newspapers. These stories had given Tabram as one version of the dead woman's name, and Tabram visited the mortuary to investigate this possibility. He was able to say that the victim was his wife, Martha Tabram, from whom he had been separated for some 13 years. She had also been known as Martha Turner and Emma Turner.

Martha had been born Martha White, the daughter of Charles Samuel and Elisabeth White, at 17 Marshall Street, London Road, Southwark, on 10 May 1849, meaning that she was 39 when she died. She had four older siblings: Henry, Esther, Stephen, and Mary Ann. Her father had died suddenly in November 1865 when Martha was 16.

On 25 December 1869 Martha White had married Henry Tabram at the Trinity Church, Newington. The union produced two children: Frederick John, born in February 1871, and Charles Henry, born in December 1872. Martha was always very fond of drink, which led to innumerable arguments between her and Henry and finally to his leaving her in 1875, though he continued to maintain her to the tune of 12 shillings per week. In due course, Henry found that Martha was living with another man, so he reduced the payment to 2 shillings and sixpence per week.

This formal identification led to other information about Martha Tabram. Mary Bousfield, also apparently known under the alias of Mary Luckhurst, of 4 Star Place, Commercial Road, stated that she had known Martha as her lodger. Martha had called herself Martha Turner and had left with a man about six weeks before her death, still owing rent. This man was William Turner, who said he had lived with Martha, on and off, for about 10 years. They had parted from time to time because of Martha's drinking, and he was now living at the Victoria Working Men's Home on Commercial Street.

It was also on 14 August that the parade at Wellington Barracks was arranged, and it took place the following day, 15 August. Mary Ann Connolly attended and picked out two men, describing one as the corporal who had been with her and the other as the private who had been with "Emma," the name by which she had known Martha Tabram.

From the outset it was plain that Mary Ann's identification was incorrect. The "corporal" she picked out proved to be Private George, who had two good-conduct medals. He was able to prove that from 8 P.M. until 6 A.M. on the night of 6–7 August he had been with his wife at 120 Hammersmith Road. The other soldier, Private Skipper, had actually been in the barracks from 10:05 P.M. through the night on 6 August.

The inquest reopened, again before Deputy Coroner Collier, at 2 P.M. on 23 August. Henry Samuel Tabram gave evidence of his formal identification. He was followed by William Turner, who explained that he had lived with Martha until three weeks before her death. She had then moved to 19 George Street

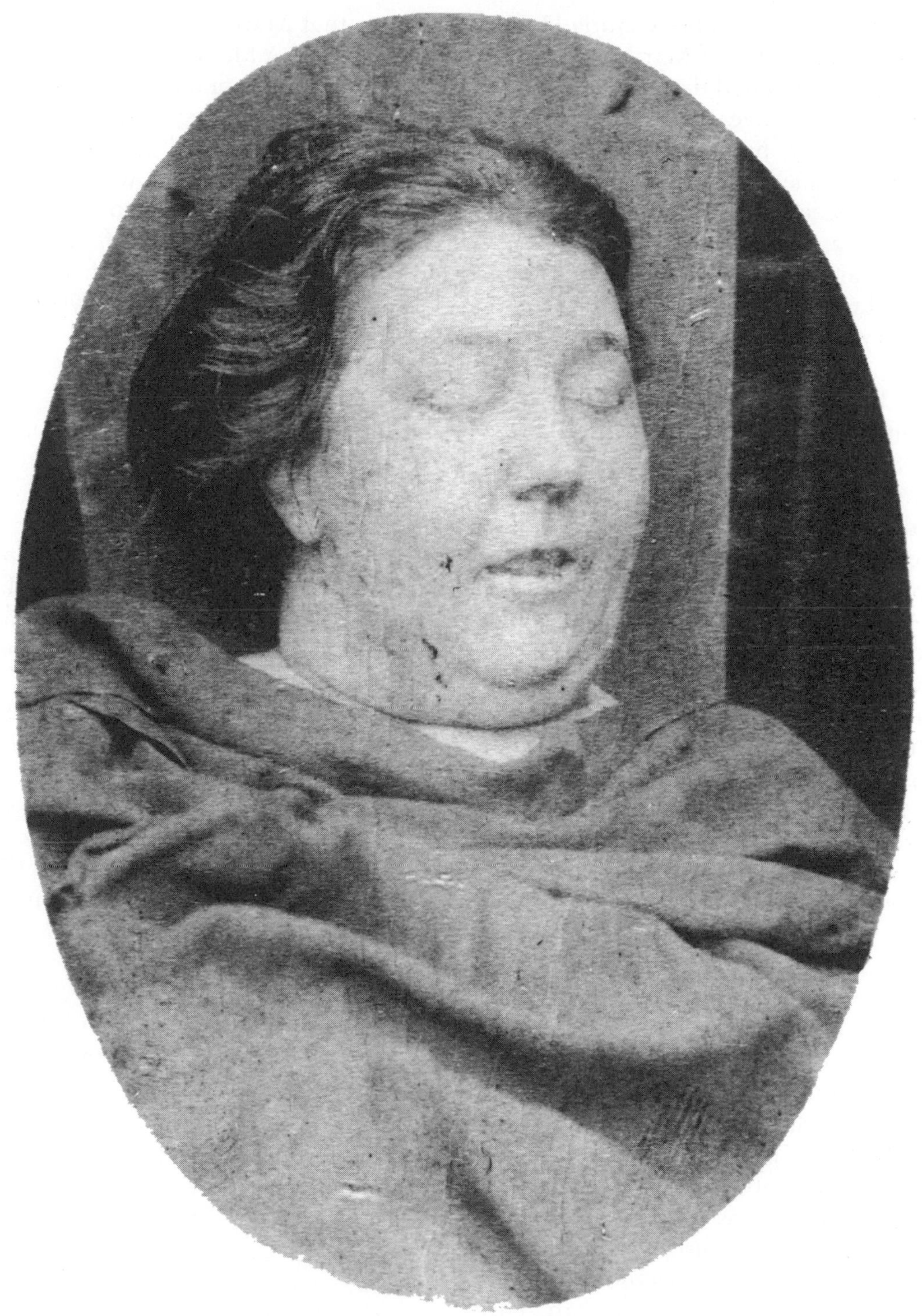

The body of Martha Tabram lying in the mortuary. Note that she looks much older than her 39 years, owing in no small part to the type of life she had led. Her body was formally identified by her estranged husband, Henry Samuel Tabram. (Public Record Office, London)

while he had gone to the Victoria Home. After giving details of Martha's drinking habits, Turner stated that the last time he had seen her alive was on Saturday, 4 August. They had met in Leadenhall Street, and she had appeared to be destitute. He believed she was trying to earn a living as a hawker and had given her 1 shilling and sixpence to buy some stock. He had never seen her alive again.

Mary Bousfield then confirmed that Martha and William Turner had lived with her at Star Place for a period of about four months. They had left about six weeks before Martha's death, owing some rent. One day, while Mary Bousfield was out, Martha had returned briefly and left behind the key to the room she had once rented.

Ann Morris was Martha's sister-in-law and lived at 23 Fisher Street, Cambridge Heath Road. She was able to add only that she had seen Martha outside the White Swan public house at 11 P.M. on 6 August. Martha had been arrested three times for annoying Ann and trying to obtain money from her. Indeed, on the last occasion Martha had received a sentence of seven days' hard labor.

One of the final witnesses was Mary Ann Connolly, who told of the encounter with the two soldiers. After a brief summing-up by the deputy coroner, the jury duly returned a verdict of "murder by some person or persons unknown."

Was Martha Tabram a victim of Jack the Ripper? There were certainly high-ranking police officers who later came to believe that she was, including Inspector Frederick George Abberline. Others have claimed that she was a victim of the soldier who took her up George Yard. This theory, however, may well be untenable. It must be remembered that Martha and the unidentified soldier went off together at 11:45 P.M. on 6 August. It is highly likely, according to the testimony of Elizabeth Mahoney, Alfred Crow, and Dr. Killeen, that Martha was not killed until around 2:30 A.M. on 7 August, giving her ample time to find another client.

It has also been suggested that Martha should not be included among the Ripper's victims because she was not mutilated and her throat was not cut. However, a report by Chief Inspector Swanson the following month (September 1888) stated that there were nine stab wounds to the throat, and there is also a report in the *Illustrated Police News* that reads in part, "she being throttled while held down." Finally, there is the sheer frenzy of the attack, which led to 39 separate wounds.

Twentieth-century psychological reports on the unidentified killer known as Jack the Ripper have assumed that Mary Ann Nichols was the first victim but also add that this was unlikely to have been his first attack. Serial killers do not always perfect their "technique" in their first attack. It is quite possible that Jack claimed the life of Martha Tabram before he had perfected his throttling and cutthroat technique. This is especially true if credence may be given to the *Illustrated Police News* report, which, unfortunately, cannot be verified from other, more reliable sources.

Suggestions for further reading:

Begg, Paul, Martin Fido, and Keith Skinner. *The Jack the Ripper A–Z*. Headline, 1996.

Hinton, Bob. *From Hell . . . The Jack the Ripper Mystery.* Old Bakehouse Publications, 1998.

Jakubowski, Maxim, and Nathan Braund. *The Mammoth Book of Jack the Ripper.* Robinson Publishing, 1999.

PRO Files MEPO 3/140. Available on microfilm at the Public Record Office, Kew.

Sugden, Philip. *The Complete History of Jack the Ripper.* Robinson Publishing, 1994.

Mary Ann Nichols

Friday, 31 August 1888

It was a few minutes before 3:40 A.M. on 31 August when Charles Cross, a car-

The spot where Mary Ann Nichols was murdered, as it is today. The small bushes stand on a spot that was once a stable yard with two large gates separating it from the street. Mary Ann's body lay on what is now the colored pavement, with her head pointing to the left and her feet pointing to the right, toward the large building, which was then a school and is now apartments. She was murdered during the early hours of 31 August 1888. (Yvonne Berger)

man, turned from Brady Street into Buck's Row, a dark road with terraced houses on the southern side and warehouses on the north. It ended with the looming presence of the Board School where Buck's Row joined Winthrop Street and widened considerably.

Cross walked on the northern side of the street, and as he reached the end of Buck's Row he noticed what he thought was a tarpaulin lying in the gateway to Brown's Stable Yard. He walked over to take a closer look and found that what he had actually seen was a woman lying on the ground. Before he could investigate further, Cross heard footsteps approaching from the direction of Brady Street.

Robert Paul was also a carman and, like Cross, was on his way to work. As he strolled down Buck's Row, Paul saw movement close to the Board School. As he drew nearer a man came toward him, tapped him on the shoulder, and said, "Come and look over here; there's a woman lying on the pavement."

Drunks lying in the streets were not an uncommon sight in this part of London, and Paul didn't really want to get involved, but nevertheless, he and Cross, the man who had spoken to him, drew closer to the still form.

The woman lay on her back with her head toward Brady Street, the direction from which both Cross and Paul had come. Her hands were down by her sides, her legs straight out and slightly apart, and her skirts raised. They probably thought that perhaps she wasn't drunk after all but had been the victim of some kind of attack, possibly a rape.

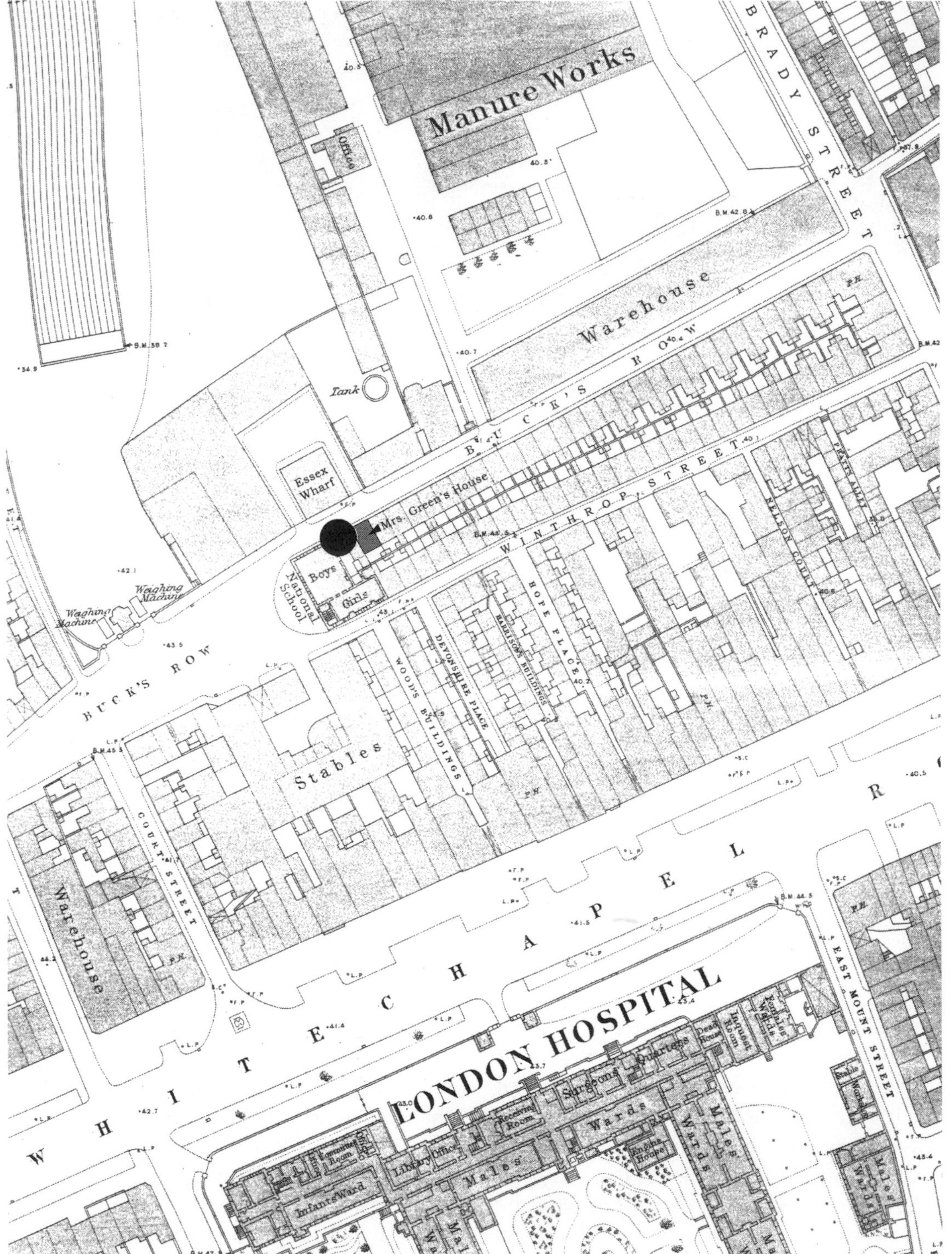

Buck's Row, where Mary Ann Nichols, believed by some to be the first Ripper victim, met her death on 31 August 1888

Cross touched the woman's hands, noticed that they were cold, and announced to Paul, "I believe she's dead." Paul too touched her face and hands. He confirmed that the woman's flesh was cold but, to be sure, crouched down and listened for any sounds of breathing. There were none, but as he brushed her breast Paul thought he might have noticed a slight movement. If she was breathing, then it was very shallowly.

Straightening up, Paul said, "I think she's breathing but very little if she is." He suggested they prop her up, but Cross would have none of this idea. After a brief discussion, the two men decided that, as they were already going to be late for work, the best idea would be to carry on to their respective places of employment but to tell the first policeman they saw what they had found. The only effort they made on behalf of the woman was to pull her skirts down a little in order to preserve her modesty.

Paul and Cross walked on toward Baker's Row. There, at the junction of Hanbury Street and Old Montague Street, they saw a policeman, Constable Jonas Mizen. Later there would be some dispute as to precisely what Paul and Cross said to the officer, but what is certain is that they went on to their work while Constable Mizen walked purposefully off toward Buck's Row.

Mizen was not the first policeman to find the stricken woman. Buck's Row was part of the beat of Constable John Neil, who had last walked down the street at around 3:15 A.M., when he had noticed nothing suspicious. Now, at 3:45 A.M., he walked eastward along Buck's Row toward the Board School. He was

A view down what was then Buck's Row toward the school building. To the left of the school was Buck's Row and the location of Mary Ann Nichols's murder. To the right was Winthrop Street. Past the "No Entry" sign, on the same side, is the narrow alleyway known as Wood's Buildings through which Jack may well have made his escape. (Yvonne Berger)

on the south side of the street when he saw the shape in front of the Brown's Stable Yard doors. Unlike Cross and Paul, Constable Neil had a lantern, and he now shone its light onto the still figure. Neil could see that the woman had been attacked because her throat had been cut, and blood still flowed slowly from the wound.

Constable Neil knew that a brother officer, Constable John Thain, had a beat that took him along Brady Street and the top of Buck's Row. Noticing that Thain was just passing, Neil flashed his lantern in order to obtain assistance. Thain rushed down Buck's Row and heard Neil call out, "Here's a woman has cut her throat; run at once for Dr. Llewellyn."

Thain ran off to fetch the doctor, leaving Neil alone with the woman. Soon afterward, however, Constable Mizen arrived, and Neil told him to fetch the ambulance and further assistance from Bethnal Green Police Station. Once again Neil was alone with the woman, and while waiting for assistance to arrive, he took a look around to see if he could find any clues to what might have happened.

Brown's Stable Yard was firmly closed and locked. Almost directly opposite where the woman lay was Essex Wharf, and Neil now rang the bell to determine whether the occupants might have seen or heard anything. The call was answered by Walter Purkiss, who appeared at a second-floor window. Neil asked him if he had heard anything, but Purkiss said he hadn't. Soon afterward Sergeant Kerby arrived on the scene, alerted by the other officers, and proceeded to knock on the door of the first terraced house, New Cottage, at 2 Buck's Row,

Wood's Buildings, looking from Whitechapel Road toward what was Winthrop Street and the school. If Jack was disturbed by the approach of Charles Cross, he may well have escaped by dashing around the school and running down this alleyway toward the point from which the photograph was taken. (Yvonne Berger)

next to where the woman's body lay. The house was occupied by Emma Green and her family of two daughters and a son. Like Walter Purkiss, Emma Green had heard nothing during the night. Meanwhile, Constable Neil was examining the roadway to see if he could find any marks of wheels where a cart might have dropped the woman. He found nothing.

At about 4 A.M., Dr. Rees Ralph Llewellyn, having been aroused by Constable Thain, arrived at Buck's Row. He made a quick examination of the woman and pronounced her dead. He too found that the woman's hands were cold but her legs were still warm, and he determined that she had not been dead more than half an hour, thus putting the earliest time of death at around 3:30 A.M. By now a small crowd of onlookers, including three men from Barber's Slaughter Yard in Winthrop Street, was starting to gather, so Dr. Llewellyn ordered that the body be moved to the mortuary, where he would make a more detailed examination later in the day.

The body was lifted onto the ambulance, and Constables Neil and Mizen, accompanied by Sergeant Kerby, took the woman to the mortuary in Old Montague Street while Constable Thain waited for more senior officers to arrive in Buck's Row. In due course Inspector John Spratling arrived, and Thain pointed out to him where the body had lain. Emma Green's son was just washing away the last of the blood from the pavement, but small signs of it could still be seen between the paving stones. Having satisfied himself that he could do no more in Buck's Row, Inspector Spratling went to the mortuary to view the body for himself and take down a description of the dead woman.

The mortuary was locked at that hour, and the woman's body still lay on the ambulance, which had been left in the yard. Inspector Spratling began to write down his description of the dead woman, and while he was doing so, Robert Mann, the mortuary keeper, arrived with the keys. The body was moved into the mortuary itself, and Spratling continued with his notes. Looking for marks on the woman's clothing, he lifted her skirts and discovered that she had been mutilated: her abdomen had been ripped open and her intestines exposed. Spratling immediately sent for Dr. Llewellyn, who returned to make a second examination. He would later tell the press, "I have seen many terrible cases but never such a brutal affair as this."

One of the first priorities was to identify the body. This process did not prove to be as difficult as one might imagine, though the woman carried no formal identification, and her few belongings—a comb, a white pocket handkerchief, and a piece of looking glass—gave no clue. Her clothing at first appeared to be undistinguished: a reddish-brown ulster with seven large brass buttons, a brown linsey (woollen) frock, a white chest flannel (a light cotton undergarment), two petticoats, a pair of stays, black ribbed woollen stockings, a pair of men's side-sprung boots (boots that fastened at the side), and a black straw bonnet trimmed with black velvet. However, a petticoat bore the mark "Lambeth Workhouse, P.R.," which indicated that at some time the woman had been a resident in that establishment.

Two women soon came forward to identify the body. Reports on the crime had spread throughout the district, which led to the news that a woman fitting the victim's description had been living at a lodging house at 18 Thrawl Street. Ellen Holland, another resident of that establishment, told the police that she knew the dead woman as Polly. The second witness, Mary Ann Monk, who was an inmate of the Lambeth Workhouse, viewed the body at 7:30 P.M. on

31 August and stated that the victim was Mary Ann Nichols. This identification enabled the police to trace Mary Ann's relatives, and on 1 September Edward Walker, Mary Ann's father, and William Nichols, her estranged husband, both confirmed the identification.

Mary Ann had been born in Dean Street, off Fetter Lane, on 26 August 1845, the daughter of Edward and Caroline Walker. On 16 January 1864 she had married William Nichols, a printer's machinist, the ceremony taking place at St. Bride's in Fleet Street. William and Mary Ann lodged briefly in Bouverie Street but soon went to live with her father at 131 Trafalgar Street, Walworth. They stayed there for some time, finally moving to new lodgings at 6D Peabody Buildings, Stamford Street, in 1874. They had five children: Edward John, born in 1866; Percy George in 1868; Alice Esther in 1870; Eliza Sarah in 1877; and Henry Alfred in 1879. In 1880 the marriage broke up with some bitterness, and William moved to 37 Coburg Road, Old Kent Road.

From this time, Mary Ann's movements are, for the most part, well known. Briefly, the timeline is as follows:

- 6 September 1880–31 May 1881—Lambeth Workhouse
- 31 May 1881–24 April 1882—Not known
- 24 April 1882–18 January 1883—Lambeth Workhouse
- 18–20 January 1883—Lambeth Workhouse Infirmary
- 20 January–24 March 1883—Lambeth Workhouse
- 24 March–21 May 1883—Living with her father
- 21 May–2 June 1883—Lambeth Workhouse
- 2 June 1883–25 October 1887—Living with Thomas Stuart Drew in York Mews, 15 York Street, Walworth
- 25 October 1887—St. Giles's Workhouse, Endell Street.
- 26 October–2 December 1887—Strand Workhouse, Edmonton
- 2–19 December 1887—Not known with certainty but possibly sleeping rough in Trafalgar Square. Mary Ann was found there when the area was cleared of homeless people.
- 19–29 December 1887—Lambeth Workhouse
- 29 December 1887–4 January 1888—Not known
- 4 January–16 April 1888—Mitcham Workhouse and Holborn Infirmary
- 16 April–12 May 1888—Lambeth Workhouse
- 12 May–12 July 1888—Working for Samuel and Sarah Cowdry
- 12 July–1 August 1888—Not known
- 1–2 August 1888—Gray's Inn Temporary Workhouse
- 2–24 August 1888—Lodging at 18 Thrawl Street
- 24–30 August 1888—Lodging at 56 Flower and Dean Street, a house known locally as the White House.

On the morning of 1 September, Dr. Llewellyn carried out a full postmortem on the body. Later that same day, the inquest opened at the Working Lad's Institute in Whitechapel Road before Wynne Edwin Baxter, the coroner for the South Eastern District of Middlesex. The jury, having been duly sworn in, was taken to view the body, which still lay in a shell in the mortuary. Upon the jurors' return to the Institute, the first witnesses were called.

Edward Walker, the dead woman's father, stated that his present residence was 16 Maidswood Road, Camberwell. He confirmed his identification of Mary Ann and added that he had not seen her for two years, the last occasion being on Saturday, 5 June 1886, at the funeral of his son, also named Edward, who had been

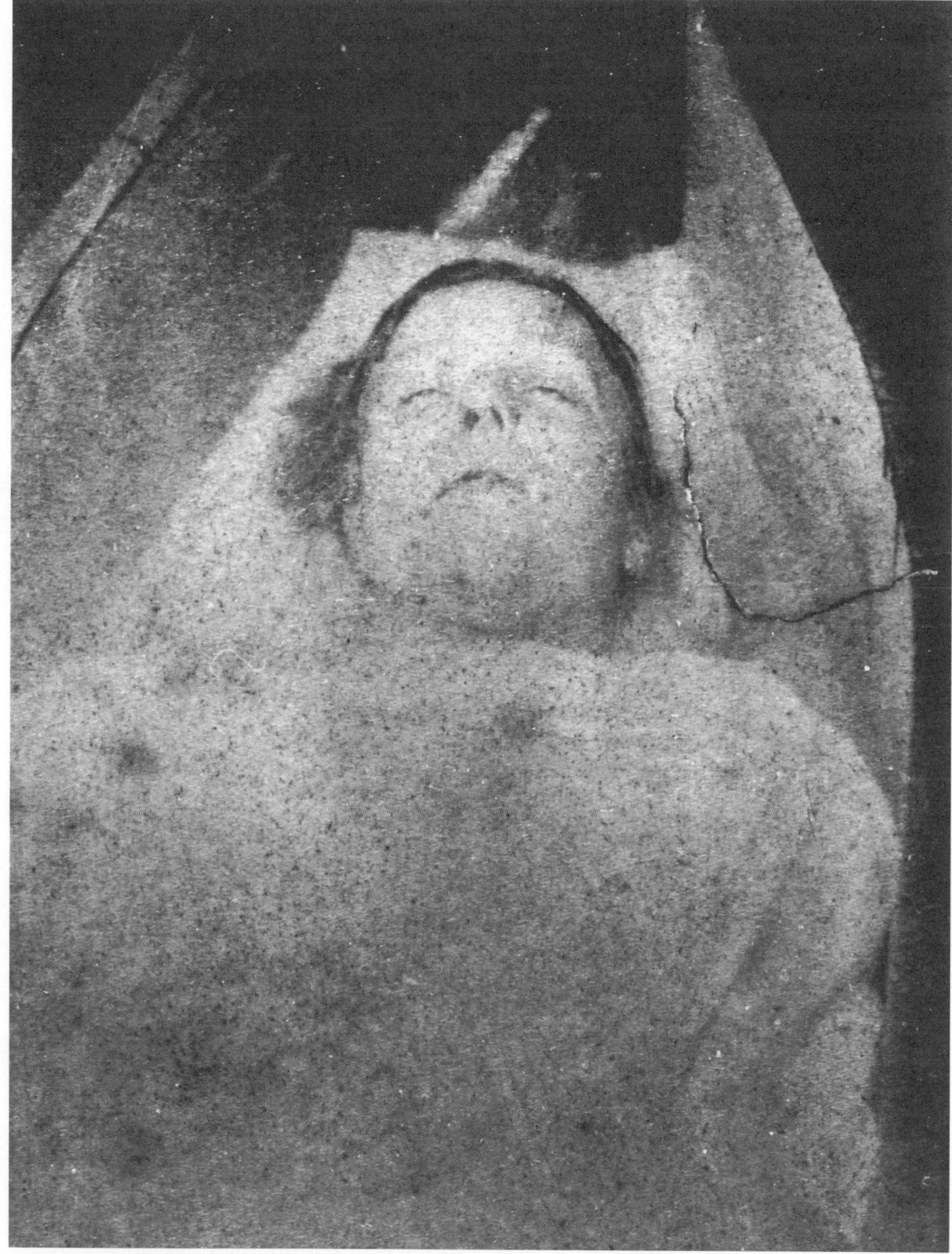

Mary Ann Nichols lying in a coffin shell at the mortuary. The photograph is of poor quality, but her general features can be plainly discerned. (Public Record Office, London)

burned to death in an accident with a paraffin lamp. Walker then went on to speak of the breakup of his daughter's marriage.

According to Walker, William Nichols had had an affair with the nurse who had attended Mary Ann during her last confinement. As a result of that affair, the couple had separated, with the eldest son, Edward John, going to live with his grandfather while the other four children remained with their father. Since that time William Nichols had had another child with the nurse.

Walker went on to confirm that Mary Ann had lived with him from March to May 1883 and that she was not a particularly sober woman. One night they had argued over her drinking habits, and the next morning she had left. He had certainly not turned her out into the streets. Although he had not seen Mary Ann for two years, he had received a letter from her around the previous Easter. It had been written from the home of Samuel and Sarah Cowdry of Ingleside, Rose Hill Road, Wandsworth, where Mary Ann had been employed as a domestic servant. The letter, which he still had, read:

> I just write to say you will be glad to know that I am settled in my new place, and going on all right up to now. My people went out yesterday, and have not returned, so I am left in charge. It is a grand place inside, with trees and gardens back and front.
>
> All this has been newly done up. They are teetotallers and religious, so I ought to get on. They are very nice people, and I have not too much to do. I hope you are all right and the boy has work. So goodbye for the present.

The letter was signed, "From yours truly, Polly," and carried a postscript: "Answer soon, please, and let me know how you are." Edward had replied to that letter, but Mary Ann had never contacted him again. He had not known that not long afterward, Sarah Cowdry had sent a postcard to the Lambeth Workhouse stating that Mary Ann had absconded from Ingleside, taking with her clothing to the value of 3 pounds, 10 shillings.

Edward Walker told the court that he was unable to say whether his daughter had been living with anyone recently, but he had heard that three or four years earlier she had been living with a man named Drew who lived in York Mews and had a shop in York Street. Finally, he knew that William Nichols had once been summoned to show why he should not contribute to his wife's upkeep, but the charge had been dismissed owing to the fact that Mary Ann had been living with another man. Later, when William himself gave evidence, it would be shown that this was not the entire truth.

The next witness was Constable John Neil, who spoke of his discovery of Mary Ann's body. He had been walking on the right-hand side of the street when he saw a figure lying in the street, by a gateway. Having shone his lantern upon it, he saw a woman lying with her left hand touching the gates of the stable yard. Blood was still oozing from a wound in her throat. Her eyes were wide open, and her arm was quite warm from the joints upward. Her bonnet was off her head and lying by her side, close to her left hand. At that point, Neil heard a fellow constable patrolling up Brady Street and signaled to him. When the other officer approached, Neil told him to "run at once for Dr. Llewellyn." Soon afterward Constable Mizen arrived and was sent to fetch the police ambulance, which was in reality little more than a handcart.

Constable Neil then described his rousing of Walter Purkiss at Essex Wharf and the arrival of Sergeant Kerby. After Dr. Llewellyn had said that the woman was dead, Neil had helped to lift the body onto the ambulance and afterward noticed a small patch of congealed blood where the body had lain. It was no more than 6 inches in diameter.

Neil had stayed at the mortuary with the body and was there when Inspector Spratling arrived. He saw the inspector writing a description of the woman and noticed the mutilations once her clothing had been lifted. Neil then spoke of the route his beat had taken, confirming that he had never been farther from the body's location than Baker's Row and the Whitechapel Road.

Dr. Llewellyn (whose name was given erroneously in some press reports as Henry) said that he was a surgeon practicing from 152 Whitechapel Road. At about 4 A.M. on Friday, 31 August, he had been called to Buck's Row, where he had found the dead woman lying on her back. She had severe injuries to her throat, and though her hands and wrists were cold, her lower extremities were quite warm. During his initial examination he noted that there was very little blood about the neck and no signs of a struggle having taken place. He estimated that she had been dead for no more than half an hour.

Before continuing with Dr. Llewellyn's evidence, an important point needs to be cleared up. In a report to the press, issued later on 1 September, the doctor stated that there was only a small pool of blood on the footway; he described it as "not more than would fill two wine glasses, or half a pint at the outside." This comment led to speculation that Mary Ann had been killed elsewhere and dumped in Buck's Row. Indeed, this notion is an important part of the Masonic Conspiracy theory. In fact, other witnesses, including Constables Neil, Mizen, and Thain, would state that a good deal of blood had been absorbed by Mary Ann's clothing and that her back appeared to be soaked in it, as Constable Neil's hands had been smeared when he helped lift the body onto the ambulance. Dr. Llewellyn and the police officers investigating the crime had little doubt that Mary Ann had met her death at the spot where her body was found.

Dr. Llewellyn, continuing his narrative, told of his being called out a second time by Inspector Spratling. He had gone immediately to the mortuary and there noted extensive abdominal mutilations. He then gave the details of his postmortem findings.

The body was that of a female 40 to 45 years of age. Her face was bruised, with one mark running along the lower part of the jaw on the right-hand side. This mark might have been caused either by a fist or by the pressure of a thumb. Another circular bruise was noted on the left-hand side, which might have been caused by the pressure of fingers.

On the left side of the neck, about 1 inch below the jaw, an incision commenced that was about 4 inches long and ran from a point immediately below the ear. A second cut, commencing on the same side, but an inch in front of the first cut and an inch below it, was a circular incision that terminated some 3 inches below the right jaw. This cut had completely severed all the tissues down to the vertebrae, and the carotid arteries on both sides of the neck had been severed. Dr. Llewellyn thought that both incisions had been made from left to right and that the knife used was "a strong-bladed knife, moderately sharp, and used with great violence." No blood was found on the breast or the front of the clothes.

Turning to the abdominal cuts, the doctor stated that there were no other injuries until the lower part of the abdomen. Some 2 or 3 inches from the left side was a very deep wound that ran in a jagged manner and cut through the tissues. There were also three or four other cuts, running downward on the right side, the knife again having been used violently. Dr. Llewellyn stated that the injuries might have been inflicted by a left-handed person and that they had all been inflicted with the same weapon. In response to questioning about the degree of medical knowledge exhibited by the killer, the doctor replied that he "must have had some rough anatomical knowledge, for he seemed to have attacked all the vital parts." He also stated that the crime could have been executed in four or five minutes, at which point the inquest was adjourned until Monday, 3 September.

Further examination of Dr. Llewellyn's testimony is necessary, as it has often been misquoted by other writers. The doctor initially believed that the assailant had attacked Mary Ann from in front. Probably using his right hand to stifle her cries, he wielded the knife in his left hand and used it to cut her throat. Later Llewellyn came to doubt this conjecture. There can be little doubt that Mary Ann's throat was not cut while she was standing, or there would almost certainly have been bloodstains on the front of her clothing. A more likely scenario is that she was either throttled or struck and placed on the ground by her killer, who then knelt or crouched at her right side, possibly facing toward Brady Street, and cut her throat from left to right so that any blood flow would be away from him. He then probably inflicted the mutilations by drawing the knife downward and toward himself, indicating that he was right-handed. There was evidence of throttling because Mary Ann's face was bruised and her tongue lacerated slightly.

The inquest reopened on 3 September, with Inspector Spratling as the first witness. Spratling stated that he had arrived at Buck's Row at 4:30 A.M. on 31 August. By then the body had been moved and two constables guarded the spot that was pointed out to him. At the time, the last of the blood was being washed away by one of Emma Green's sons. He then described his visit to the mortuary, his attempt to write down a description, his discovery of the abdominal mutilations, and his call to Dr. Llewellyn.

There was some dispute over precisely what happened next. The police held that instructions had been given that the body was to be left alone but that two mortuary attendants, Robert Mann and James Hatfield, had stripped and cleaned the body before the postmortem could take place. This point was now confirmed by Detective Sergeant Patrick Enright, who said in response to a question that he had given express instructions that the body was not to be touched. Continuing his evidence, Inspector Spratling then gave details of the clothing the dead woman had worn and pointed out that the stays she had worn were still fastened.

At the conclusion of his testimony, the inspector told the court he and Sergeant Godley had searched along the tracks of the East London and District Railway, and had also searched the Great Eastern Railway yard, but had found nothing. There had been a man on night duty at the gates of the Great Eastern yard, some 50 yards from the spot where the body had lain, but he had heard nothing. Neither had Emma Green and her family, or Walter Purkiss and his family. Finally, Barber's Horse Slaughterer's yard was 150 yards away from the body, the distance having been measured by walking around the Board School and into Winthrop Street. Three men had been working there throughout the night, and none of them had known anything of the crime until the discovery of the body.

Henry Tomkins was one of those three men, and he testified that he and his fellow workmen, James Mumford and Charles Brittain, had started work between 8 P.M. and 9 P.M. on Thursday, 30 August. At midnight he and Brittain had left the yard, not returning until around 1 A.M. Throughout the night the gates of the slaughter yard had been left open, and none of the men had heard anything until Constable Thain had come by to tell them about the body. This statement itself was open to question. When he came to give his own evidence, Thain would deny calling at the yard on his way to fetch Dr. Llewellyn, but Tomkins was adamant that the officer had left his cape there earlier that morning and had called to pick it up on the way to the surgery in Whitechapel Road.

Continuing his story, Tomkins stated that he and Mumford were the first to leave the slaughter yard and go to look at the body at around 4:15 A.M. They were followed a few minutes later by Brittain. At that time the doctor was there, along with three or four policemen. Tomkins stayed at the spot until the body was lifted onto the ambulance and taken away.

The next witness was Inspector Joseph Henry Helson, the officer in charge of the investigation, who said he had first heard of the murder at 6:45 A.M. on Friday, 31 August. He went to the mortuary, where he saw the body, which was still fully clothed. The inspector was present while the clothing was removed and noted that the bodice of the dress was buttoned down to the middle and the stays were still fastened. The abdominal mutilations were visible while the stays were still on, implying that the stays had been in position while these injuries were inflicted.

Constable Mizen was the next officer to give his testimony, and he told of the encounter with two men, Cross and Paul, putting the meeting at the junction of Baker's Row and Hanbury Street. According to Mizen, Cross had told him that he was wanted by a policeman in Buck's Row. Cross had said nothing about having found a woman or about a murder having been committed, and as Mizen walked off toward Buck's Row he saw the two men go off down Hanbury Street.

This story too was open to debate, for then Cross stepped into the witness box to give his version of events. He told the court of his discovery of Mary Ann's body and his encounter with the other man, Robert Paul, though at this stage Paul had not been traced and Cross did not know his name. Going off to find a policeman, they had encountered Constable Mizen, and Cross swore he had told the officer that they had found a woman lying on the pavement and had touched her hands and found them cold. He said he had told the constable that he thought she was either dead or drunk, while the other man had expressed his belief that she was dead. The constable had said, "All right," and walked off toward Buck's Row. He and the other man had continued into Hanbury Street, and he had seen his companion turn into Corbetts Court.

The time came for William Nichols, the dead woman's husband, to take the stand. He confirmed that he and Mary Ann had been separated for eight years but denied that the separation had anything to do with an affair between him and Mary Ann's nurse. He claimed they had parted because of his wife's drinking habits. However, William never actually denied that an affair had taken place between him and the nurse; he stated, "I have a certificate of my boy's birth two years after that." This comment refers to the birth of Henry Alfred in 1879, but it also implies that an affair did take place during Mary Ann's previous confinement, that of Eliza Sarah in 1877. William also confirmed that when he and Mary Ann had first parted, he had paid her an allowance of 5 shillings per week. Sometime in 1881 or 1882 he had discovered that she was living with another man and hence had stopped the payments. The Guardians of the Parish of Lambeth had then summoned him to show why he should not contribute to his wife's support, but when he explained that she was living with another man, the summons had been withdrawn. William ended his evidence by saying that he had not seen his wife for three years.

According to the press reports of the day, the next witness was Jane Oram, but her evidence was identical to that known to have been given by Ellen Holland. It is likely then that Jane Oram and Ellen Holland are one and the same and that their names were confused by the newspapers. Ellen lived at 18 Thrawl Street and stated that she and the dead woman had occupied the same bed for about six weeks, up to eight or ten days before Mary Ann's death. Indeed, it was Ellen who had identified the body.

Ellen had seen Mary Ann in the early hours of 31 August. She had gone to watch a large fire in the docks, and on her way home had met Mary Ann by accident at the corner of Osborn Street and Whitechapel Road. Based on their conversation, Ellen believed that Mary Ann had been staying at the White House, where men and women were allowed to share accommodations (some lodging houses were very strict about separating the sexes to discourage lewd behavior). . Mary Ann was very drunk, and Ellen tried to persuade her to come back with her to the lodging house in Thrawl Street. Mary Ann replied that she had no money for her bed, adding that she had earned it twice over that night but had drunk it away in the Frying Pan public house. Ellen was able to put the time of this meeting at 2:30 A.M. because the clock at St. Mary's struck as they were speaking. Soon afterward Ellen saw Mary Ann stagger off eastward along Whitechapel Road.

The final witness on 3 September was Mary Ann Monk, who merely confirmed that she had known Mary Ann as an inmate of the Lambeth Workhouse, at which point Baxter adjourned the proceedings for two weeks. He could not know that five days later another terrible murder, the subject of the next entry, would take place in Hanbury Street.

On Thursday, 6 September, Mary Ann Nichols was buried at Ilford Cemetery. Meanwhile, the police investigation proceeded apace, and the first suspect's name came into the frame. A weekly report, signed by Acting Superintendent Davies and dated 7 September, read in part, "A man named Pizer alias Leather Apron had been in the habit of illusing prostitutes in various parts of the Metropolis for some time past, and careful enquiries have been made to trace him, but without success." Perhaps more importantly, the report continued in the very next sentence, "There is no evidence against him at present. Enquiries are being continued."

A further report, also dated 7 September but signed this time by Inspector Helson, confirmed that the police were convinced that Mary Ann Nichols had met her death at the spot where her body was found. That report confirmed that Mary Ann had been seen in the Whitechapel Road at about 11 P.M. on 30 August and that she had been seen leaving the Frying Pan public house on Brick Lane at 12:30 A.M.. She had been seen again, at 1:20 A.M. inside the lodging house at 18 Thrawl Street, where the deputy keeper had asked her for the fourpence for her bed. Mary Ann had said that she had no money but was going back out to earn some. Her parting words were, "I'll soon get my doss money; see what a jolly bonnet I've got now." The final sighting was of course by Ellen Holland, at 2:30 A.M. This report too referred to Pizer and repeated that there was at present no evidence against him.

Nonetheless, John Pizer was arrested by Sergeant William Thick on Monday,

10 September. Details about Pizer are given in "The Suspects" section of this book, so suffice it to say here that he was released on 11 September and appeared at Annie Chapman's inquest the following day, 12 September.

The inquest on Mary Ann Nichols reopened on Monday, 17 September, with Dr. Llewellyn being recalled. In the meantime, Annie Chapman had met her death, and some of her internal organs had been removed and taken away by her killer. Dr. Llewellyn had reexamined Mary Ann and confirmed that no part of her viscera was missing.

Emma Green, who lived at 2 Buck's Row, next to where the body was found, was the next witness. She said that she had retired for the night at 11 P.M. on Thursday, 30 August. Both of her sons had already gone to bed, one at 9 P.M. and the other at 9:45. Her daughter had retired at the same time she had, and they both occupied the front room on the first floor. She had heard nothing until there was a knock at the door at about 4 A.M. on 31 August. She had thrown open the window and seen three or four constables and two or three other men. She could also see the body of the victim, but it was too dark to see exactly what had taken place. Questioned by one of the jurymen, Green confirmed that she was a light sleeper.

Walter Purkiss, who lived in Essex Wharf, almost opposite to where the body had lain, said that he lived in that house with his wife, family, and servant. Purkiss and his wife slept in the front room on the second floor, and they had both gone to bed at 11 P.M., or possibly 11:15. Purkiss had slept fitfully during the night and was awake between 1 A.M. and 2 A.M. His wife had been awake most of the night, but neither of them had heard a sound; they described the street as unusually quiet that night. When the police officer had awakened him, Purkiss had opened the window and looked out. He could see the body, the police, and some other men.

Patrick Mulshaw was a night watchman, and on the night of Mary Ann's death he had been guarding some sewage works in Winthrop Street at the back of the Working Lad's Institute. He had gone on duty at 4:45 P.M. on Thursday and had remained at his post until about 5:55 A.M. the next day. Mulshaw admitted that he had dozed during his watch but swore that he was not asleep between 3 and 4 A.M. During that time he had seen or heard nothing. Soon after that time a man had passed his position and said, "Watchman, old man, I believe somebody is murdered down the street."

Patrick had then walked down to Buck's Row and seen the body. The man who had spoken to him had not been traced. Finally, Patrick was able to say that he had seen no one about after midnight, but he had seen two constables, one of whom was Constable Neil.

Constable Thain then gave his testimony. His beat took him along Brady Street past the end of Buck's Row every 30 minutes. At 3:45 A.M. he had seen a signal from Constable Neil and had gone to offer his assistance. After speaking to Neil, Thain had gone for Dr. Llewellyn and accompanied the doctor back to Buck's Row. By the time they got there, there were a couple of workmen with Constable Neil. After the body had been removed, Thain had stayed to await Inspector Spratling. Thain ended by denying that he had taken his cape to the slaughter yard, though he admitted sending it there with a fellow officer. He stated that when he was sent for the doctor he did not call in at the yard to collect his cape and did not tell the workmen there about the body.

By now Robert Paul had been found, and he was the next to give evidence. He told of his walk down Buck's Row and of seeing a man standing in the middle of the road. As Paul drew nearer the other man tapped him on the shoulder and said, "Come and look at this woman here." After their cursory examination of the body the two men had gone off to find a policeman and had found one at the junction of Old Montague Street and Hanbury Street. By then it was not more than four minutes since they had left the body.

Robert Mann, an inmate of the Whitechapel Workhouse, was next. He was the man in charge of the mortuary and the keyholder of that building. There was much confusion over his evidence because Mann said he had received no instructions not to touch the body, which was in direct opposition to what the police had said. However, he was not a good witness, and Baxter informed the jury that Mann was subject to fits and hence "neither his memory nor statements are reliable."

James Hatfield, Mann's assistant at the mortuary, fared little better. He reported that Mary Ann had not been wearing stays, but when questioned further on the point he admitted that his memory was bad. It must be remembered that he and Mann were giving their evidence almost three weeks after the event.

After further evidence of police searches had been given by Inspector Spratling, a juryman commented that if a substantial reward had been offered by the Home Secretary after the murder of Martha Tabram in George Yard, then the two later murders might not have taken place. The inquiry was then adjourned until Saturday, 22 September.

On that final date, Baxter summed up the evidence that had been given. He began, though, by complaining that there was no proper Coroner's Court in Whitechapel and no public mortuary. He went on to describe Mary Ann's life and history. In the end he linked Mary Ann's death with that of Annie Chapman, suggesting that it was possible that in Mary Ann's case the killer might have sought to possess certain of the dead woman's organs but had been disturbed in his quest by Cross's arrival on the scene. The jury returned the only verdict it could: "murder by some person or persons unknown."

A couple of points should be mentioned in order to pin down the time of Mary Ann Nichols's death as accurately as possible. Certain factors such as the warmth of the upper arms and the blood still flowing from the throat wounds indicate that the murder took place just a few minutes before Charles Cross found the body. It is possible, therefore, that the killer saw Cross turn into Buck's Row from Brady Street and made good his escape in the shadows, putting the time of the attack upon Mary Ann at around 3:35 A.M.

Suggestions for further reading:

Begg, Paul, Martin Fido, and Keith Skinner. *The Jack the Ripper A–Z*. Headline, 1996.

Hinton, Bob. *From Hell . . . The Jack the Ripper Mystery*. Old Bakehouse Publications, 1998.

Jakubowski, Maxim, and Nathan Braund. *The Mammoth Book of Jack the Ripper*. Robinson Publishing, 1999.

PRO Files MEPO 3/140. Available on microfilm at the Public Record Office, Kew.

Sugden, Philip. *The Complete History of Jack the Ripper*. Robinson Publishing, 1994.

Annie Chapman

Saturday, 8 September 1888

A total of 17 souls lived in the house at 29 Hanbury Street. Facing the street at the front was a cat's-meat shop run by Harriet Hardiman, who slept in the shop with her 16-year-old son. There was one other room on the ground floor, at the back, which was used by Amelia Richardson to cook her food and hold regular weekly prayer meetings. Richardson and her 14-year-old grandson, Thomas, actually slept in the front room on the second floor, above the shop. She also used a cellar, access to which was through the backyard, from which she ran a packing-case business. Also living on the second floor, at the back, was Mr. Walker, a maker of tennis boots. He shared the room with his retarded adult son, Alfred.

The front room on the third floor was occupied by Mr. Thompson, a carman, his wife, and their adopted daughter. The third-floor back room was home to Mr. and Mrs. Copsey, who made cigars. The house also boasted an attic, at the front of which lived another carman, John Davis, with his wife and three sons. Finally, also in the attic but at the rear of the house lived Sarah Cox, a widow.

At 3:30 A.M. on 8 September, Thompson left the house to go to his work at Goodson's of Brick Lane. As he left the house he was heard by Amelia Richardson and called out "Good morning" as he passed her room.

Just over an hour later John Richardson, Amelia's son, who lived at 2 John Street, called in at number 29. John was a porter at Spitalfields Market but also helped his mother in her packing-case business. It was around 4:45 or 4:50 A.M. when he came by, and it was already getting light. John checked the passageway that led from the street to the yard at the back. Occasionally people had been found sleeping rough there, but on this occasion the passageway was clear. While he was at number 29 John noted that one of his boots was hurting him, so he opened the door that led into the backyard, sat on the top step, and used his knife to trim some leather from the offending boot. He then left the house, having been there no more than three minutes or so. The back door closed itself, and John Richardson later swore that he had closed the front door behind him.

In fact, the house had two front doors. The one to the east opened directly into the shop, and the one next to it gave access to a passage some 20 or 25 feet long that led to the rest of the house and the yard. The occupants of the house used the latter door to come and go.

At 5:45 A.M., John Davis rose from his bed and started to get ready for work. By 6 A.M. he was heading downstairs, intending to go out into the yard. As he walked down the passageway he noticed that the front door that led out into Hanbury Street was wide open. There was nothing unusual in this, and John believed that it was just another ordinary work day until he pushed open the door that led into the yard.

Three stone steps led down into the yard, and a small recess lay between them and the fence to the left as one looked down into the yard. There lay the terribly mutilated body of a woman, with her head lying in the recess and pointing toward the house. Davis stepped back, recovered his composure somewhat, and ran out into Hanbury Street. As he stumbled into the street he saw two men: James Green and James Kent. These two worked for Joseph and Thomas Bayley, packing-case makers of 23a Hanbury Street whose business was known simply as Bayley's, and were waiting outside the workshop. At the same time Henry John Holland, a boxmaker, was walking down Hanbury Street on his way to work. Davis managed to gasp, "Men, come here!"

Kent, Green, and Holland all followed Davis down the passageway of number 29. At the back door they all looked down at the body, but only Holland actually ventured down the three stone steps. He did not touch the body and went back up the steps seconds later. The men went back into Hanbury Street and ran off to find a policeman, except James Kent, who felt in need of a stiff brandy to steady his nerves.

It was by now 6:10 A.M., and Inspector Joseph Chandler was on duty in Commer-

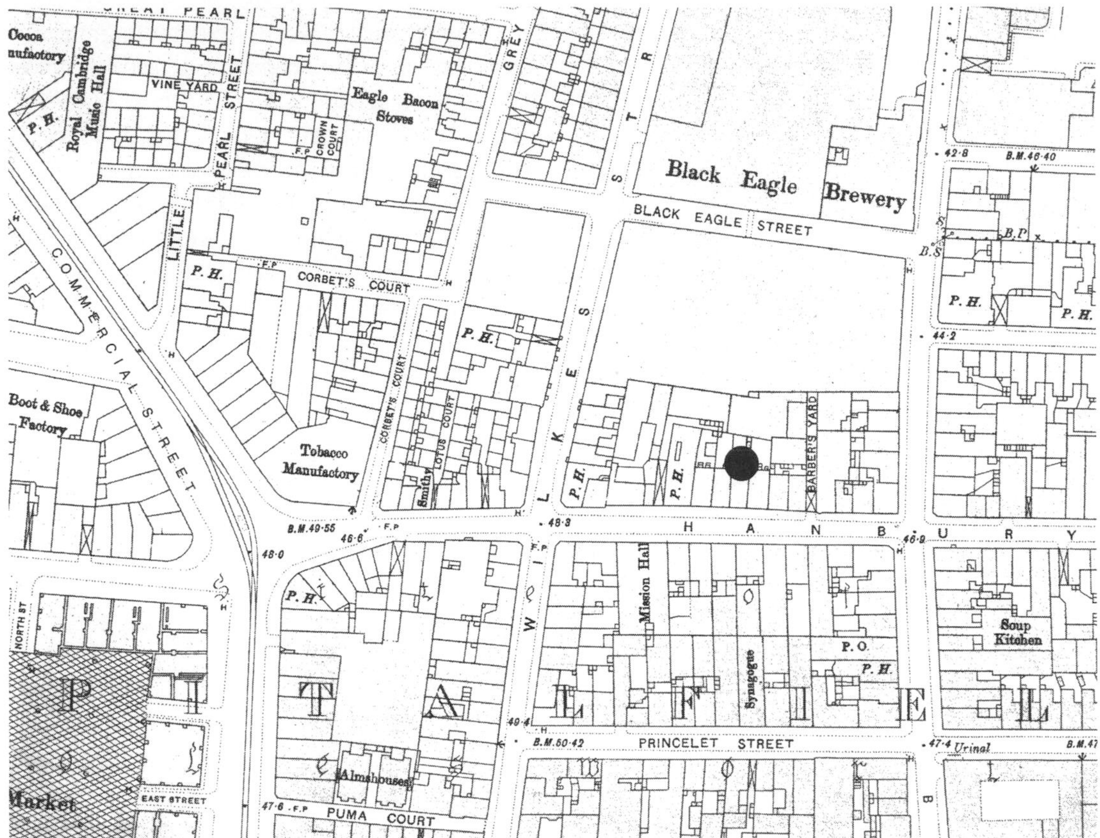

The back yard in Hanbury Street where Annie Chapman was brutally murdered. Albert Cadoche, who may have heard the murder taking place, lived in the house to the west.

cial Street, close to the corner of Hanbury Street, when he saw several men rushing toward him shouting, "Another woman has been murdered." The inspector immediately rushed to number 29. His narrative speaks for itself: "I at once proceeded to number 29 Hanbury Street and in the back yard found a woman lying on her back, dead, left arm resting on left breast, legs drawn up, abducted, small intestines and flap of the abdomen lying on right side, above right shoulder, attached by a cord with the rest of the intestines inside the body; two flaps of skin from the lower part of the abdomen lying in a large quantity of blood above the left shoulder; throat cut deeply from left and back in a jagged manner right around throat."

Inspector Chandler sent for Dr. George Bagster Phillips and for further assistance from the police station. Dr. Phillips arrived at 6:30 A.M., and his report was even more detailed than the inspector's:

> I found the body of the deceased lying in the yard on her back, on the left hand of the steps that lead from the passage. The head was about 6 inches in front of the level of the bottom step, and the feet were towards a shed at the end of the yard. The left arm was across the left breast, and the legs were drawn up, the feet resting on the ground and the knees turned outwards. The face was swollen and turned on the right side, and the tongue protruded from the front teeth, but not beyond the lips; it was much swollen. The small intestines, and other portions were lying on the right side of the body on the ground above the right shoulder, but attached.
>
> There was a large quantity of blood, with a part of the stomach above the left

> shoulder. The body was cold, except that there was a certain remaining heat, under the intestines, in the body. Stiffness of the limbs was not marked, but it was commencing. The throat was severed deeply. I noticed that the incision of the skin was jagged, and reached right around the neck.

Dr. Phillips believed that the woman had been dead for at least two hours, probably longer, thus putting his initial estimate of the time of death at 4:30 A.M.

The body was moved to the Whitechapel Mortuary, and Inspector Chandler then made a careful search of the yard. On the back wall of the house, close to where the woman's head had lain and about 18 inches from the ground, he found six patches of blood varying in size from a pencil point to a sixpenny piece. There were also smears of blood about 14 inches from the ground on the wooden paling that divided number 29 from the house next door.

Close to where the dead woman's feet had lain was a small piece of coarse muslin, a small tooth-comb (the type of comb worn in the hair), and a pocket comb in a paper case. Near where the woman's head had been lay a small portion of envelope containing two pills. The back of the envelope bore a seal and the words "Sussex Regiment" embossed in blue, and on the front was the letter "M" and lower still the letters "Sp," possibly the remaining part of a name and address. There was no stamp on the envelope, but it was postmarked, in red, "London, Aug 23, 1888."

One of the most enduring errors concerning the Ripper case has been the description of items found at this particular crime scene. Various writers have invented other articles that they say were found in the yard, having been deliberately placed there by the killer, including coins and brass rings. However, Inspector Chandler's report was methodical; he was the first officer on the scene and was an experienced officer with 15 years' background in the police force. His report makes no mention of any other items, and the logical conclusion is that there were no coins, no rings, and in fact no other items than those already listed.

After examining the yard, Inspector Chandler went to the mortuary and wrote down a description of the woman. This description, together with the publicity the case received, led to her rapid identification.

Amelia Palmer, who lived at 30 Dorset Street and had been a close friend of the victim, named the dead woman as Annie Chapman and stated that she had recently been living at Crossingham's lodging house at 35 Dorset Street. This identification was later confirmed by Timothy Donovan, the deputy at Crossingham's, who said Annie had lodged there for the past four months.

Annie Chapman was born Eliza Anne Smith in Paddington in 1841, but her parents, George Smith and Ruth Chapman, did not marry until 22 February 1842 at St. James Church, Paddington. Annie married John Chapman, a coachman, on 1 May 1869 at All Saints Church in Knightsbridge, and soon afterward the couple was living at 1 Brook Mews, Bayswater. They later moved to 17 South Bruton Mews, Berkeley Square, and in 1881 moved again to Clewer in Berkshire when John Chapman obtained employment as head coachman for a farm bailiff named Josiah Weeks.

John and Annie Chapman had three children. Emily Ruth was born on 25 June 1870, Annie Georgina on 5 June 1873, and John on 21 November 1880. The last child was unfortunately a cripple, and, even more tragically, Emily died of meningitis on 21 November 1882. Annie was rather too fond of drink, and this unfortunate proclivity led to a break-

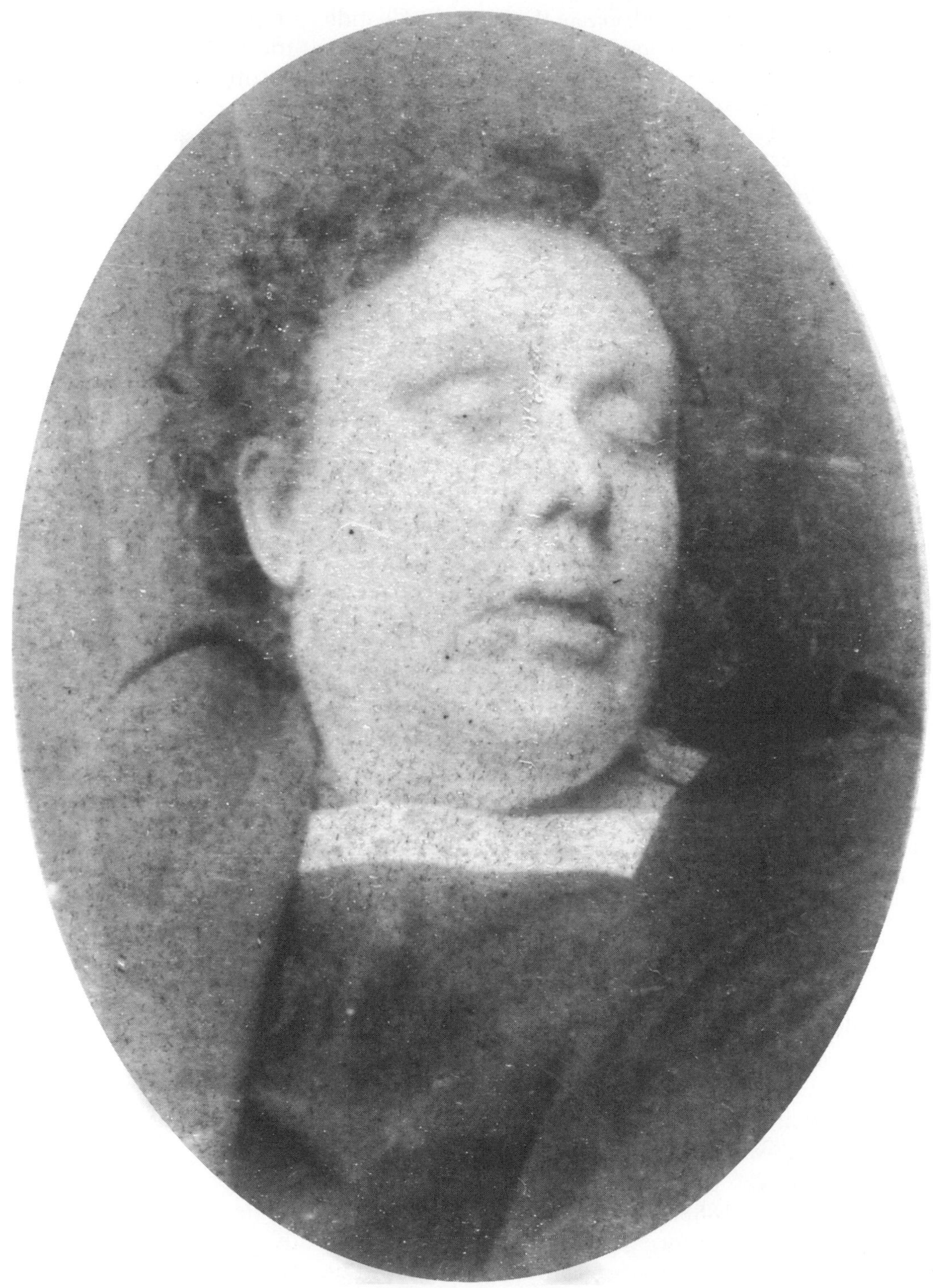

Annie Chapman lying dead in the mortuary. None of the terrible injuries inflicted upon her body can be seen. Annie was murdered on 8 September 1888, when she was 47 years old. She was ill at the time, and the postmortem showed that she would not have lived many more years even if she had not encountered Jack the Ripper. (Public Record Office, London)

down of the marriage around 1884. Soon afterward Annie moved to Spitalfields in London.

By 1886 Annie was lodging at 30 Dorset Street with a sievemaker, thus earning the local nickname "Annie Sivvy." After the separation, John Chapman allowed his wife an allowance of 10 shillings a week, but this allowance ended when he died on 25 December 1886. Very soon afterward Annie's relationship with the sievemaker ended, indicating that it had likely been her allowance that had kept them together in the first place.

At 8 A.M. on the morning of Monday, 10 September, Sgt. Thick finally captured John Pizer, alias Leather Apron, as described in the previous entry. Pizer had been staying at 22 Mulberry Street, and when the house was searched, five long-bladed knives were found. These, along with Pizer himself, were taken to Leman Street Police Station.

It was also on 10 September that the inquest on Annie Chapman opened before Coroner Wynne Edwin Baxter in the Alexandra Room of the Working Lad's Institute in Whitechapel Road.

John Davis spoke of finding the body on the morning of 8 September. The previous evening he had gone to bed at 8 P.M.. His last son had arrived home at 10:45 P.M., and none of the family had gone out again that night. John was awake from 3 A.M. until 5 A.M., when he managed to fall asleep for half an hour, but he heard the clock at Spitalfields Church strike 5:45 A.M. when he and his wife got up. Mrs. Davis made a cup of tea, and after drinking it John went down to the yard just as the church bell was striking the hour. After finding the body and telling his story to the men outside, John ran off to find a policeman and then returned to the house but did not enter it. He confirmed that he had not gone down into the yard at any time and had not touched the body. Finally, he testified that he and his family had lived in the house for only two weeks.

Amelia Palmer, whose name was incorrectly given in some newspaper reports as Farmer, spoke of her identification of the body. Amelia stated that she had seen the victim in Dorset Street on Monday, 3 September, at which time Annie had complained of feeling unwell. She had had a bruise on one temple and had said she had argued with another woman over a man known as Harry the Hawker. Amelia had seen Annie again the following day, this time near Spitalfields Church, and Annie had again said that she felt ill and had added that she was thinking of going to the casual ward to see if the people there could help her. Amelia had kindly given her friend 2 pennies and warned her not to spend the money on drink. The final meeting between the two women was at 5 P.M. on Friday, 7 September, again in Dorset Street, when Annie had said she felt too unwell to do anything but then countered with, "It's no good my giving way. I must pull myself together and go out and get some money or I shall have no lodgings."

Timothy Donovan, the deputy at Crossingham's, testified that he had seen Annie in the kitchen at the lodging house on Friday. She was still there at 1:45 A.M. on the 8 September, eating a baked potato, and he asked her for her doss money. She told him she had none but would be back soon. Annie then walked out into the street.

John Evans was the night watchman at Crossingham's, and he too saw Annie in the kitchen in the early hours of 8 September. She told him she had just had a pint of beer and had been to Vauxhall to see one of her sisters. After speaking to Donovan, Annie left the house, and Evans saw her walk up Little Paternoster Row toward Brushfield Street. After hearing Evans's evidence, Baxter adjourned the proceedings for two days.

On the following day, 11 September, John Pizer was released from custody because no evidence against him had been found. His viability as a suspect is discussed in the appropriate section of this book.

Also on 11 September another suspect came to the attention of the police. At 10 P.M. that day, Dr. Cowan of 10 Landseer Road and Dr. Crabb of Holloway Road went to the police to state that Jacob Isenschmid, a butcher who lived at 60 Mitford Road, had left his lodgings on several occasions and might possibly be connected with the crimes. Acting Superintendent McFadden went to the address given and there spoke to George Tyler, the occupier, who confirmed that Isenschmid's movements had been erratic and that he had been away from home at the times of the murders.

McFadden then went to see Mrs. Isenschmid, who said she had not seen her husband for two months but added that he was in the habit of carrying large butcher's knives with him. Convinced that this man warranted close attention, McFadden ordered Constable Cracknell to keep a watch on Isenschmid's home.

The inquest reopened on Wednesday, 12 September, and one of the early witnesses was Fountain Smith, a brother of the dead woman. He offered little evidence beyond stating that his sister had been 47 years old and that he had seen her shortly before her death, when he gave her 2 shillings.

James Kent, one of the men who worked for Bayley's in Hanbury Street, testified that he had left home at 6 A.M. on the day in question, getting to work about 6:10 A.M. His employer's gate was open, but while he was still waiting outside a man he now knew to be John Davis rushed up and appealed for assistance. Kent described how he and James Green had then gone to number 29, walked down the passageway, and stood at the top of the steps, from which they could plainly see the body. He said he noticed that the woman had a handkerchief of some kind around her throat and that her hands were bent with the palms upward. The sight distressed him so much that he had to leave the house and take some brandy. Shortly afterward he went to Bayley's to get a piece of canvas to throw over the body.

James Green said he had gotten to Bayley's about 5:50 A.M. He added little new testimony, merely confirming much of the evidence given by James Kent.

Amelia Richardson told the court that at around 6 A.M. on 8 September she had heard some commotion and noise in the passage, and her grandson, Thomas Richardson, had gone downstairs to investigate. He returned to say, "Oh, Grandmother, there is a woman murdered." She went down herself and saw the body. At that time there were police and some other men in the passage, which was quite crowded.

Mrs. Richardson said she had retired the previous night at 9:30 P.M. She had been awake for most of the night and was certainly wide awake at 3 A.M. After that she dozed fitfully and heard nothing apart from Mr. Thompson leaving the house about 3:30 A.M. She was sure she would have heard anyone going through the passage, but she hadn't heard a thing that Saturday.

Harriet Hardiman said she had gone to bed at 10:30 P.M. on 7 September. She woke at 6 A.M. when she heard footsteps in the passage. She too sent her son to investigate, and he came back and told her a woman had been killed in the yard.

John Richardson now gave his testimony and swore he had seen nothing when he trimmed his boot in the yard. It was suggested at the time that the open back door might well have obscured

Richardson's view; Dr. Phillips had estimated the time of death at 4:30 A.M., and if he were correct, then the body must have been lying in the yard when Richardson opened the door. In fact, it is highly unlikely that Annie was dead at this time; it is much more probable that the doctor was wrong. If we accept this scenario, then John Richardson's testimony narrows the time of death to some time after 4:55 A.M.

John Pizer, the man who had been suspected of the murder, was now called merely to show that he had been home at the time of the murder and had remained there until he was arrested by Sergeant Thick.

The final witness was Henry John Holland, who said that at 6:08 A.M. he was passing down Hanbury Street on his way to his place of work in Chiswell Street. As he passed number 29 an elderly man dashed out and cried, "Come and look in the backyard." Holland went through to the back door, saw the body, and stepped down into the yard to get a clearer look. He then went in search of a policeman and found one on duty in Spitalfields Market. That officer was unable to assist because he was on fixed-point duty and was unable to leave his post. This response so incensed Holland that later that day he made an official complaint at the police station in Commercial Street.

The next day, 13 September, the inquest began its third session, with Inspector Joseph Chandler as the first witness. He put the time he had noticed the men in Hanbury Street at 6:02 A.M. By the time he arrived at number 29 there were several people in the passage but none in the yard. After giving his report of what he had found in the yard, Inspector Chandler said he had sent for the doctor, the ambulance, and further police assistance. When other constables arrived he ordered them to remove all the people from the passageway.

After the body was moved, the inspector searched the yard, and in addition to the items already mentioned, he found a leather apron, which was wet, about two feet away from the water tap. At the time this discovery was believed to be a possible clue, but the apron was soon shown to belong to John Richardson. His mother had confirmed that she had found it in the cellar, rather green and moldy, and had washed it out and left it in the yard to dry.

The final portion of Chandler's evidence was confirmation that there was no sign of a struggle in the yard and that the back door opened outward, into the yard, on the left-hand side, the same side where the body had lain, so it was possible that John Richardson had missed seeing it when he opened the door.

Sergeant Edward Badham was one of the officers who had been sent to assist Inspector Chandler, but his only real contribution was to convey Annie Chapman's body to the mortuary on the police ambulance.

The time came for Dr. Phillips to outline the medical evidence. He described the scene upon his arrival and then spoke of his initial examination. There was a bruise on Annie's right temple, another on her upper eyelid, and two more on the top of her chest, but these appeared to not be fresh. There were more recent marks on Annie's face and jaw, from which the doctor deduced that the killer had seized her by the chin before her throat was cut. This and the protruding, swollen tongue indicated that Annie had been partially strangled before the wounds were inflicted. There were also the marks of one or more rings on Annie's ring finger, but an abrasion there suggested that the killer had wrenched these items from her.

The immediate cause of death had been the loss of blood from the throat wounds. The throat had been cut from left to right, and an attempt had been made to cut off Annie's head. Though the details of the injuries were not revealed in the press, an article in the *Lancet* of 29 September gave more detail: "The abdomen had been entirely laid open; the intestines, severed from their mesenteric attachments, had been lifted out of the body, and placed by the shoulder of the corpse; whilst from the pelvis the uterus and its appendages, with the upper portion of the vagina and the posterior two-thirds of the bladder had been entirely removed." The article went on to say that "the incisions were cleanly cut, avoiding the rectum, and dividing the vagina low enough to avoid injury to the cervix uteri."

Other parts of Dr. Phillips's testimony are controversial. He deduced that the killer was a medical expert or at least one who "had such knowledge of anatomical or pathological examinations as to be enabled to secure the pelvic organs with one sweep of a knife." However, as will become plain when future crimes are described, the killer need not have had any such anatomical knowledge. Though the concept was not clear at the time that the crimes were committed, with hindsight it seems that the Ripper was a trophy collector, and it is likely that all he sought was some organ from his victim. (This subject is discussed at length in the "Descriptions" section of this book.)

After brief testimony from Mary Elizabeth Simonds, a nurse at the Whitechapel Infirmary, to the effect that she and another woman named Frances Wright had undressed and washed the body at the mortuary, thc inquest was adjourned again until 19 September.

On 13 September the suspect Jacob Isenschmid was picked up and taken to Holloway Police Station. From there he was taken to the Infirmary at Fairfield Road Asylum, Bow, where he was certified as a dangerous lunatic.

The police were also following up the possible lead of the envelope found close to Annie's body. The crest was traced to the 1st Battalion of the Sussex Regiment at Farnborough, and this identification was confirmed by Captain Young of that regiment. He told the police that the men used this stationery to write letters home and that the envelopes could be purchased in the canteen. However, no men could be found who had written to an address in Spitalfields, and none of the men's handwriting matched the writing on the front of the envelope. The trail was confused even further when it was discovered that the stationery could also be bought over the counter in the Lynchford Road Post Office.

On 14 September Ted Stanley, who was also known as "the Pensioner," called at the Commercial Street Police Station. He had been mentioned at the inquest as a close friend of the dead woman, but up to this point the police had been unable to trace him. Stanley gave a satisfactory account of his movements and said he had last seen Annie on the corner of Brushfield Street on 2 September, at which time she was wearing two rings on one of her fingers.

On the same day yet another suspect, Edward McKenna, was arrested. He had been seen at Heath Street carrying a knife and was taken to the police station in Commercial Street. However, he was able to prove that he was at a lodging house in Brick Lane at the time Annie had likely met her death.

One final event also took place on 14 September: Annie Chapman was laid to rest in the Manor Park Cemetery. The ceremony was deliberately kept quiet, and only members of her family attended.

The "clue" of the torn envelope was laid to rest on 15 September, when William Stevens, a painter who lodged at Crossingham's and had known Annie, said that on Friday, 7 September, she came into the house and told him she had been to the hospital. She had with her a bottle of medicine, a bottle of lotion, and a box containing two pills. As she was showing him the box, it fell to pieces in Annie's hands, and she took the pills out, picked up a piece of envelope from the floor, and wrapped the pills in it.

On 19 September the inquest opened again. Details had already been given in press reports of an argument Annie was supposed to have had in Crossingham's lodging house some time before her death. Eliza Cooper, who had lodged at that same address for the past five months, said she had argued with Annie on the Tuesday (4 September) before the latter met her death. According to Eliza, the contretemps was about a piece of soap, but matters cooled down and they all went for a drink at the Britannia public house on the corner of Commercial and Dorset Streets. Here the argument flared up again, and Annie lashed out and slapped Eliza's face. Eliza retaliated by striking Annie in the left eye and on the chest.

Dr. Phillips was recalled to discuss the various bruises on Annie's body in light of Eliza Cooper's testimony. He confirmed that he had seen the old bruises but stated that there were scratches of recent origin about 2 inches below the lobe of one ear. He stated again his belief that Annie had been seized by the throat and that her killer seemed to display anatomical knowledge.

Two valuable witnesses appeared at the hearing on 19 September. The first was Elizabeth Darrell, sometimes referred to as Elizabeth Long. She lived at 32 Church Street, but on the morning of 8 September, at 5:30 A.M., she was walking down Hanbury Street on the same side as number 29, on her way to Spitalfields Market. Close to the shutters of that house she saw a man and a woman talking. The man had his back toward Brick Lane, and the woman faced Mrs. Darrell. Mrs. Darrell had seen the dead woman since and was sure that the woman she had seen was the same person. As she passed, Mrs. Darrell heard the man say, "Will you?" and the woman reply, "Yes." Though she never saw the man's face, Mrs. Darrell was able to give a partial description. He was dark, wore a brown deerstalker hat, and looked to be over 40. He had a shabby-genteel appearance, was a little taller than Annie, and appeared to be a foreigner. Since Annie Chapman had been five feet tall, this would put her companion at about 5 feet 2 inches.

The other valuable witness was Albert Cadoche (whose name sometimes appears as Cadosch), who lived next door to the murder scene at 27 Hanbury Street. On the morning that Annie's body was discovered, Albert rose at 5:15 A.M. and soon afterward went out into the yard. As he returned to his house he heard a voice say the one word "No." Three or four minutes later Albert was again in his yard and heard a sound as if something was falling against the fence, but he did not attempt to look over to next door to see what was going on. He heard no further noises and soon afterward left his house to go to work. He passed Spitalfields Church about 5:32 A.M.

Taken together and allowing for slight errors in the times given, if these two witnesses were telling the truth, and there is no reason to doubt them, then this information really pins down the time of the attack upon Annie to around 5:30 A.M. This time frame would indicate that the man seen outside number 29 by Mrs. Darrell was almost certainly the killer.

There was one further adjournment, to 26 September, on which date the coroner summed up the evidence before the jury returned the usual verdict. By now, the press was linking together four murders: those of Emma Smith, Martha Tabram, Mary Ann Nichols, and now Annie Chapman.

Suggestions for further reading:

Begg, Paul, Martin Fido, and Keith Skinner. *The Jack the Ripper A–Z.* Headline, 1996.

Hinton, Bob. *From Hell . . . The Jack the Ripper Mystery.* Old Bakehouse Publications, 1998.

Jakubowski, Maxim, and Nathan Braund. *The Mammoth Book of Jack the Ripper.* Robinson Publishing, 1999.

PRO Files MEPO 3/140. Available on microfilm at the Public Record Office, Kew.

Sugden, Philip. *The Complete History of Jack the Ripper.* Robinson Publishing, 1994.

Susan Ward

Ca. Saturday, 15 September 1888

On 3 October 1888 the *Daily Telegraph* carried a report that about 10 days earlier, around 23 September, a drunken prostitute had been attacked as she turned off Commercial Road. Fortunately for her, her screams scared the man off and she sustained only minor injuries to her arm.

In fact, the only person who was given treatment at the London Hospital during this period was a woman named Susan Ward, who was admitted on 15 September suffering from a cut upper arm, though there is no guarantee that her injury had been sustained on that same day. It did, however, fit the Ripper's pattern of attacking on or about weekends, and it has been suggested that this case was an unsuccessful attack on his part.

Suggestions for further reading:

Begg, Paul, Martin Fido, and Keith Skinner. *The Jack the Ripper A–Z.* Headline, 1996.

Elizabeth Stride

Sunday, 30 September 1888

Louis Diemschutz, a peddler in cheap jewelry, had spent most of Saturday, 29 September, selling his wares at the Westow Hill Market near Crystal Palace and was returning home in the early-morning hours of 30 September with the remaining unsold stock. In addition to his sales career, Louis was the steward of the International Workingmen's Educational Club at 40 Berner Street, which ran south from the Commercial Road, and he lived at that address with his wife, who helped him in the running of the club. Once he had returned his stock to the club building, Diemschutz planned to climb back onto his cart and drive the pony to his stables in George Yard.

Diemschutz turned his pony and cart from Commercial Road into Berner Street, noticing as he passed a tobacconist's shop that a clock in the window showed that the time was just about 1 A.M. A few seconds later he turned the cart toward the yard that divided the club from number 42. Guarding the entrance to the yard were two large wooden gates emblazoned with the names "W. Hindley, sack manufacturer, and A. Dutfield, van and cart builder." In fact, only Hindley now operated from the yard, Arthur Dutfield having moved on to Pinchin Street, but it was the latter gentlemen's business that had given the yard its name: Dutfield's Yard.

The two gates opened into the yard, and there was also a wicket doorway in the northernmost gate for access into the yard when the main gates were closed. However, tonight, as usual, the gates were thrown back against the side walls of the club building and number 42. There was little light in the yard except that cast down by the upper windows of the club, but Diemschutz knew the layout well enough and did not hesitate as he turned his pony into the entrance.

As the cart began to move into the yard, the pony shied toward the left, and, looking down, Diemschutz saw a dark shape lying on the ground to his right, close to the wall of the club. It was much too dark to see what the object was, and

Dutfield's Yard, where Elizabeth Stride was murdered. It was outside the Bee Hive that Louis Diemschutz told Edward Spooner about the murder.

Diemschutz's first instinct was to prod it and try to lift it with the handle of his whip. When this method didn't appear to work, he jumped down from the cart and struck a match to see what he had found. Though the flame flickered and died quickly in the wind, he saw that there was a human figure lying on the ground, and the fact that it wore a dress told him it was a woman.

Diemschutz's first thought was that the woman might be his wife, so he entered the club by the side entrance to look for her. Once he saw that she was safe, he told her and some club members who were standing nearby, "There's a woman lying in the yard, but I cannot say whether she's drunk or dead."

Diemschutz took a candle outside to get a better look, accompanied by a friend, Isaac M. Kozebrodsky. When they took a closer look, both men could plainly see that there was a good deal of blood around. It had flowed from where the woman lay almost to the side door of the club. Mrs. Diemschutz, standing at the door, saw this too and let out a scream, bringing more club members rushing out into the yard.

Louis Diemschutz and Isaac Kozebrodsky ran for the police. They turned right at the gates and headed south down Berner Street until they reached Fairclough Street. They then turned left into Fairclough Street, dashing past Providence Street, Brunswick Street, and Christian Street, and ran as far as Grove Street, all the while shouting loudly for the police. They saw no officer, so at Grove Street they turned and began to retrace their steps. As they passed the Bee Hive public house on the corner of Fairclough and Christian Streets they ran by a young man, Edward Spooner, and his lady friend, whom they had passed just moments before. Spooner stopped the two men and asked them what the matter was. Once they told him they had found a woman's body, he ran with them back to Dutfield's Yard.

By now there were a number of people gathered in the yard, and one of them struck a match. Spooner bent down and lifted the woman's chin, finding it slightly warm to the touch. He noticed that the woman's throat had been cut and that blood still flowed from the wound. About five minutes later two constables arrived and one took charge of the scene.

When Diemschutz and Kozebrodsky had turned right out of the gates, another member of the club, Morris Eagle, had also run for help, but he had turned left and run to the junction of Berner Street and Commercial Road. Turning right into Commercial Road, he had found Constable Henry Lamb with Reserve Constable Albert Collins between Batty Street and Christian Street, walking toward Berner Street. Those two officers had dashed back with Eagle. When they arrived at Dutfield's Yard, Lamb told his brother officer to fetch the doctor and Morris Eagle to run for help to the police station in Leman Street. As they left, Lamb placed his hand against the woman's face and found that it was slightly warm. He also held her wrist to see if he could detect a pulse but found none.

Constable Collins arrived at the surgery of Dr. Frederick William Blackwell of 100 Commercial Road between 1:05 A.M. and 1:10 A.M. While the doctor dressed and collected his things, he sent his assistant, Edward Johnston, back with Collins. They arrived at Dutfield's Yard at about 1:13 A.M., and Johnston's initial examination showed that the woman had an incision in her throat, which by now had stopped bleeding. Her body felt warm, with the exception of her hands, and Johnston now unfastened her blouse to see if her chest was also warm. He noted that her knees were closer to the club wall than her head and that her bonnet was lying on the ground 3 or 4 inches from her head. At about this time the gates to the yard were closed.

Dr. Blackwell arrived at the yard at 1:16 A.M., consulting his watch to confirm that time. He noted that the woman lay on her left side, close to and facing the right side of the passage, which was the club wall. Her feet were some nine feet from the gates and almost touched the wall. Dr. Blackwell also found her neck and chest quite warm and her legs and face slightly less so. Only her hands were cold.

The woman's right hand lay on her chest and was smeared inside and out with blood. This hand was open, but her left hand, lying on the ground, was partially closed. Upon examination, Dr. Blackwell found that this hand held a small packet of cachous wrapped in tissue paper, and some had spilled out onto the ground.

The woman's face was placid, with the mouth slightly open, and she wore a checked silk scarf around her neck. The bow was turned around to the left side and pulled very tight, possibly indicating that her assailant had grabbed it to pull her to the ground. There was a large incision in her neck that corresponded with the lower border of the scarf. Indeed, though Dr. Blackwell originally thought that the bottom edge of this scarf was frayed, he would later conclude that it had been cut when the killer drew his knife across the woman's throat. The single incision started on the left side of the neck and did not quite divide the vessels on that side. It then cut the windpipe in two and stopped at the right side, where the vessels were not cut. In Dr. Blackwell's opinion, the woman had been dead for 20 to 30 minutes, putting the time of death somewhere between 12:46 and 12:56 A.M.

Twenty or 30 minutes after Dr. Blackwell's arrival, the police surgeon, Dr. George Bagster Phillips, attended and after making his own examination estimated that the woman would have bled to death relatively slowly, taking about a minute and a half to die. This calculation would put the time of the actual attack somewhere between 12:44 and 12:54 A.M. This detail will prove to be important in my later explanation of the timetable.

Though the dead woman carried no identification, the police soon put a name to her, though even this would prove to be problematic owing to the evidence given by a woman called Mary Malcolm. However, when the inquest opened on Monday, 1 October, before Coroner Wynne Edwin Baxter in the Vestry Hall, Cable Street, the victim had tentatively been given a name: Elizabeth Stride.

Elizabeth was Swedish and had been born Elisabeth Gustafsdotter on 27 November 1843 in Torslanda, near Gothenburg. At the age of almost 17 she entered domestic service, but by March 1865 she had been registered by the police as a prostitute. She moved to London in February 1866, having previously given birth to a stillborn daughter in April 1865. On 7 March 1869 she married John Thomas Stride; her name was given on the marriage certificate as Elizabeth Gustifson. By the following year John Stride was running a coffee house at Upper North Street, Poplar, but in due course the marriage broke down and Elizabeth Stride began to invent a new past for herself. Perhaps her greatest lie, told to all and sundry, was that she had lost her husband and two of her children in the *Princess Alice* disaster, during which she claimed she had received injuries to the roof of her mouth. The *Princess Alice* was a pleasure steamer that collided with a steam collier on the river Thames on 3 September 1878. The pleasure boat went down, and 527 lives were lost, but the only instance of a fa-

The body of Elizabeth Stride in the mortuary. Many authors hold Elizabeth to have been the first victim on the night of the so-called double event of 30 September 1888. The only injury Elizabeth suffered was a cut throat, and it is possible that her killer was disturbed by the arrival of Louis Diemschutz and his horse and cart. (Public Record Office, London)

ther and two children dying was a man named Bell and his two sons. In fact, the truth about Elizabeth Stride was much more mundane: her husband died at the Poplar Union Workhouse on 24 October 1884, six years after the sinking of the *Princess Alice.*

What is known with accuracy is that Elizabeth herself was an inmate of the Poplar Union Workhouse in March 1877. She spent a brief period from 28 December 1881 to 4 January 1882 in the Whitechapel Infirmary, suffering from bronchitis, and that same year began lodging intermittently at 32 Flower and Dean Street. From 1885 onward she lived with a man named Michael Kidney. Beginning in mid-1888, she and Michael lived at 35 Devonshire Street, later moving to number 36. (Many authors have incorrectly named these latter addresses as Dorset Street. This error leads to many interesting possible connections with some of the other victims but has no basis in fact.)

The first witness at the 1 October inquest was William West, who described the layout of the club and the adjacent yard. West worked on a newspaper named *Der Arbeter Fraint* (The worker's friend), which was produced from offices in Dutfield's Yard. According to West, there was a front door to the club in Berner Street itself that led to a passage through the rest of the building. At the midpoint of this passage was a staircase that led to the second floor. There was also a window facing Berner Street. The front room on the ground floor of the club was used as a dining room, and behind this room was the kitchen, from which a door led directly into the yard. Behind the kitchen, but not actually connected to it because there was no way to pass into it from the kitchen, was the printing office of *Der Arbeter Fraint,* consisting of two rooms. The one actually adjoining the kitchen was the composing room, and the other was for the editor's use.

On the second floor of the club was a large room used for entertainments. It had three windows that faced the yard, and on Saturday night, 29 September, there had been a lively discussion titled "Why Jews Should Be Socialists." Ninety to 100 people had attended, and the meeting had broken up between 11:30 and midnight. Most people then left the club by the Berner Street door, but between 20 and 30 remained in the large room, and another dozen or so went downstairs.

Turning to Dutfield's Yard, West said that directly opposite the doorway of the kitchen were two water closets. To the left of the two wooden gates was a house occupied by two or three tenants that had three separate doors, all of which led into the yard. Opposite the gates were the workshops occupied by Messrs. Hindley and Co., and next to the workshops was a stable. There were only two exits from the yard: through the wooden gates or through the door that led into the club kitchen.

On Saturday West had been in the club until 9 P.M., when he went out briefly. He returned at 10:30 P.M. and at 12:30 A.M. on Sunday took some literature to the printing office. At that time he went into the yard by the kitchen door and returned to the club the same way. As he walked back to the club he noticed that the wooden gates were open and pushed back against the walls. Though he admitted he was rather nearsighted, West was sure he would have noticed anyone standing inside the gates, or the body of Elizabeth Stride had it been there at the time. Soon afterward West, his brother, and another club member named Louis Stanley left the club by the street door and went home, turning right and walking past the gates. The three men strolled together down Fairclough

Street and Grove Street as far as James Street.

The discussion at the club on the night of Saturday, 29 September, that West had referred to had been chaired by the next witness, Morris Eagle, who said that after the discussion broke up he left the club by the front door to escort his young lady home. It was then 11:45 P.M. Eagle returned at 12:35 A.M., and found the Berner Street door closed, so he walked through the gateway and into the club through the kitchen door. It was rather dark, and Eagle was unable to swear that there was nothing on the ground, though he doubted it.

When he went inside he heard a friend of his singing in Russian. Eagle went upstairs and joined his friend and had been there about 20 minutes when he heard that a woman had been found in the yard. Going outside, Eagle struck a match and saw her near the gates, lying in a pool of blood. He saw two men run for the police, going in the direction of Fairclough Street, so he turned the other way and headed for Commercial Road, where, at the corner of Grove Street, he found the two constables. He described how one of the constables later sent him to the police station to tell the inspector what had taken place.

Another witness was Joseph Lave, who had only recently arrived in London from the United States and was actually living, temporarily, at the Workingmen's Club. He testified that he had walked out into Berner Street to get some fresh air about 12:30 A.M. and had then walked into Dutfield's Yard itself. The yard was extremely dark, and Lave had to find his way by groping along the club wall. He swore that there was no body lying on the ground at that time and estimated that it was around 12:40 A.M. when he went back into the club.

The next witness was Louis Diemschutz, who told of his discovery of Elizabeth's body when he returned to the club at 1 A.M. on 30 September. He told of his search for a policeman and of meeting Edward Spooner in Fairclough Street. Soon after they had returned to Dutfield's Yard Morris Eagle had appeared with the two police constables. After Diemschutz's story had been told, the coroner adjourned the inquest until the following day.

On Tuesday, 2 October, the second day of the inquest, Constable Henry Lamb told his story. He estimated that he had been at the scene about 10 minutes before Dr. Blackwell arrived, putting the time of his own arrival at around 1:06 A.M. It was Constable Lamb who closed the gates, and he said that he had been able to do so without disturbing the position of Elizabeth Stride's body.

Once the gates were closed, Lamb saw that there were some men still in the yard, and he warned them to stay back in case they got blood on themselves and so drew suspicion. Later he went into the club and checked every room, finding another 15 or 20 people still inside. He also examined the water closets and the houses whose front doors led into Dutfield's Yard. He found nothing and confirmed that all the occupants of the cottages were in bed when he knocked on their doors. Finally, Lamb outlined details of his beat, stating that the closest it brought him to the murder scene was when he walked across the top of Berner Street on Commercial Road. He had passed that spot six to seven minutes before he was called to the scene.

The next witness was Edward Spooner, the man who had been standing outside the Bee Hive public house in Fairclough Street. He said he had arrived at Dutfield's Yard about five minutes before the two constables, which would put the time of his arrival, according to his own estimate, at just one minute past 1 A.M.

Spooner had helped Constable Lamb close the yard gates.

Next came a most contentious witness. Mary Malcolm lived at 50 Eagle Street, Red Lion Square, and she had viewed the body now lying in the mortuary and swore that it was that of her sister, Elizabeth Stokes, whom she said she recognized by a black mark on her leg. Malcolm went on to thoroughly assassinate her own sister's character, and indeed wasted a good deal of police time until the real Elizabeth Stokes appeared, alive and well.

The final witness on this second day was Dr. Frederick Blackwell, who gave details of the injury to Elizabeth's throat, the position of her body, and the cachous found in her left hand. The latter detail would be mentioned again in further hearings because there would be a great deal of supposition about Elizabeth Stride having had grapes or a grape stalk in her hand. Once again the hearing was adjourned until the following day, and on 3 October more evidence of Elizabeth's correct identity was given.

Elizabeth Tanner was the deputy keeper of the common lodging house at 32 Flower and Dean Street. She too had viewed the dead woman's body and said that it was a woman she had known as Long Liz for about six years. She knew that Liz was Swedish and had been told the story of her husband and children going down with the *Princess Alice*.

Elizabeth Tanner had last seen Long Liz at 6:30 P.M. on Saturday, 29 September, in the Queen's Head public house on Commercial Street, and again at 7 P.M. in the kitchen of the lodging house. The dead woman had been at the lodging house on both Thursday and Friday nights and on Saturday had cleaned Tanner's private rooms, for which she had been paid sixpence.

Catherine Lane was a fellow lodger at the house in Flower and Dean Street. She and her husband, Patrick, had lived there since 11 February and had known Long Liz for six or seven years. Catherine had spoken to Elizabeth on Thursday night, sometime between 10 and 11 A.M., and Elizabeth had told her that she had argued with her man and left him. Catherine also saw Elizabeth on Saturday, when the latter had cleaned Tanner's rooms, and the two women last met between 7 and 8 P.M. that same evening, in the kitchen of the lodging house.

Another lodger at 32 Flower and Dean Street was Charles Preston. He had lived there for 18 months and knew the dead woman as Long Liz. He had last seen her between 6 and 7 P.M. on Saturday, 29 September, in the kitchen. Preston too had heard the story of the *Princess Alice,* but he knew that Long Liz's surname was Stride and that her husband had once run a coffee stall in Upper North Street, Poplar.

The time had come for the man in Elizabeth's life to give his testimony. Michael Kidney was a waterside laborer who had lived with Elizabeth for three years. He denied that there had been any quarrel between them and said he had last seen her on Tuesday, 25 September, in Commercial Street as he was going to work. There had been no bad words between them, and he fully expected her to be there when he got home that night. He added that she had left him from time to time before, but it had always been because of drink. They had been apart a total of about five months in their three years together.

Kidney was obviously deeply upset at Elizabeth's demise. He said that if he had a force of detectives at his command he could catch the killer himself, but when pressed as to whether he had any concrete information that might lead to the apprehension of the man, Kidney had to admit he didn't know anything.

After Edward Johnston, Dr. Blackwell's assistant, had given his testimony,

Thomas Coram was called. Although he lived at 67 Plummers Road, Mile End, he had been visiting friends near Brady Street and was walking home along Whitechapel Road toward Aldgate at around 12:30 A.M. on 30 September. As he drew near number 253, he noticed a knife on the doorstep. There was a blood-stained handkerchief wrapped around the handle, but Coram did not touch it. Instead he pointed out the knife to a constable who was walking toward him.

That policeman was Constable Joseph Drage, who picked up the knife and saw that it was smothered in dried blood. He and Coram took the knife to Leman Street Police Station, and it was later handed over to Dr. Phillips for examination.

Dr. Phillips was then called to give his testimony both on that knife and on the death of Elizabeth Stride. Dr. Phillips and Dr. Blackwell had performed the postmortem on Monday, 1 October. In addition to the wound already described, the two doctors had found mud on the left side of the dead woman's face and a bluish discoloration over both shoulders, under her collarbone and on her chest. They inferred that these marks had been caused by the assailant seizing Elizabeth and forcing her down onto the ground, where he then cut her throat. Dr. Phillips also referred to the cachous that Elizabeth had held in her hand; he had also found some in the gutter that presumably had fallen from the tissue paper as her hand relaxed after the attack. Finally, he stated that although the knife found in Whitechapel Road might have caused the injuries, it was unlikely because it would have proved unwieldy.

This discussion of the knife was of course superfluous. It had been found at 12:30 A.M., and the medical evidence had shown that Elizabeth Stride had been attacked later than that. However, the issue was discussed at length, and the inquest was then adjourned again until Friday, 5 October.

When the inquest resumed, both doctors were recalled. Dr. Phillips was the first to give his testimony, and he stated that he had examined Elizabeth's body again and found no old injury to her mouth, thus laying to rest once and for all the story of the *Princess Alice* disaster. Dr. Phillips had also examined two handkerchiefs found in Elizabeth's possession and said that he believed the marks on the larger one were possibly fruit stains. He was certain that Elizabeth had not swallowed either the skin or seeds of grapes within many hours of her death. This point was confirmed by Dr. Blackwell.

The debate over the possibility of Elizabeth having eaten grapes had been fueled by a man who would not be called to the inquest to give evidence. Matthew Packer ran a greengrocer and fruiterer's shop from number 44 Berner Street. These premises were just south of the murder spot, separated from Dutfield's Yard only by one other house, number 42.

As a matter of routine, the police had spoken to every householder in Berner Street. At 9 A.M. on 30 September, Sergeant Stephen White had spoken to Matthew Packer, who said he had closed his shop at 12:30 A.M. on 30 September. Asked whether he had seen anything, he replied, "No, I saw no one standing about, neither did I see anyone go up the yard. I never saw anything suspicious or heard the slightest noise, and knew nothing about the murder until I heard of it this morning." Living in the same house were Mrs. Packer, Sarah Harrison, and Harry Douglas, and when Sergeant White spoke to them, they also said they had seen or heard nothing.

Matthew Packer, however, changed his story fairly rapidly. On 2 October two private detectives, Grand and Batchelor, who had been employed by the Whitechapel Vigilance Committee, spoke to Packer, who now swore that at 11:45 P.M. on 29 September he had sold half a pound of black grapes to a man and a woman who were standing outside his shop. He said the couple continued to loiter about the street for another half hour or so. Packer described the man as being middle-aged but then qualified the estimate to age 25 to 30. He described the man as about 5 feet 7 inches tall, stout, squarely built, and wearing a wideawake hat and dark clothes. The man had the appearance of a clerk.

Further inquiries about this story of the grapes led Grand and Batchelor to Mrs. Rosenfield and Miss Eva Harstein of 14 Berner Street. The two women claimed that on Sunday morning, after the body had been moved, they had noticed some white flower petals and a blood-stained grape stalk in Dutfield's Yard. The two detectives now visited the yard for themselves and amidst the rubbish there found a grape stalk. They decided to test the veracity of Packer's story by taking Packer to the mortuary in Golden Lane where the body of Catherine Eddowes (whose murder is described in the next entry) had been taken and asking if this was the woman he had seen in Berner Street. Packer replied that he had never seen her before in his life. They went on to the St. George's-in-the-East mortuary, where Elizabeth Stride lay.

The story of the grapes was made public by the *Evening News* on 4 October, causing Inspector Moore to ask Sergeant White to see Packer again. The sergeant visited number 44 once more, only to find that Matthew Packer was not there; his wife said two detectives had taken him to the mortuary to view the body. Sergeant White immediately went to St. George's-in-the-East and found Packer there with one of the detectives. Packer now confirmed that he had sold grapes to a man at around midnight; as he was speaking, the other detective came up and asked Packer to leave with them. At 4 P.M. that same day, Sergeant White again visited 44 Berner Street in time to see a hansom cab appear and take Packer to Scotland Yard to see Sir Charles Warren, commissioner of the Metropolitan Police.

What is to be made of Matthew Packer's story? It is true that he changed his tale to fit the facts of the case, though he managed to incorporate some errors, for example, stating that Elizabeth had worn a white flower pinned to her dress when in fact it had been a red one. It is possible that during his initial statement to Sergeant White, Packer forgot his grape-buying customer and only realized the significance of the incident later, but surely that is unlikely. What is certain is that eventually the police came to believe his testimony was unreliable, and Packer was not called to give evidence at the inquest.

Two other witnesses who might have given crucial testimony were not called before the inquest either. The first was Fanny Mortimer, who lived at 36 Berner Street. When she was interviewed by the police as part of their door-to-door inquiries, Mrs. Mortimer said she had been standing at her front door for most of the half hour from 12:30 until 1 A.M. She stated that she first went outside after hearing the measured tread of a policeman passing her house. Later testimony from the officer on the Berner Street beat would put this time at 12:30 A.M.

While she was at her door, Mrs. Mortimer saw no one except a man with a shiny black bag in his hand. Though some authors have seized on this sighting as a view of the archetypal Gentleman Jack killer, the man in fact was Leon Goldstein of 22 Christian Street, who reported to the Leman Street Police Station after the murder to say that he had passed down Berner Street after leaving a coffee house in Spectacle Alley. His shiny black bag had contained empty cigarette boxes.

Of more significance was the other witness, Israel Schwartz of 22 Ellen Street, Back Church Lane. He had made a statement to the police as early as 30 September indicating that he might have seen the murderer attack Elizabeth and that the killer might have had an accomplice.

According to Schwartz's statement, he had turned into Berner Street from Commercial Road at 12:45 A.M. on 30 September. As he drew closer to the entrance to Dutfield's Yard, Schwartz saw a man stop and speak to a woman who was standing in the gateway. Schwartz could not hear what was said between them, but the man tried to pull the woman into the street, turned her around, and threw her down onto the pavement. The woman screamed three times, and in order to avoid this scene, Schwartz crossed to the other side of the street. As he passed the couple Schwartz saw a second man lighting his pipe. The first man then called out, "Lipski," apparently addressing the man with the pipe, and Schwartz found himself being followed by the second man. Schwartz ran as far as the railway arch, by which time the man with the pipe had vanished.

Israel Schwartz was taken to view the body of Elizabeth Stride and swore that she was the woman he had seen in Berner Street. He went on to describe both men. The first one, the man who had thrown the woman down and later called out "Lipski," was aged about 30. He was 5 feet 5 inches tall with a fair complexion, dark hair, and a small brown mustache. He had a full face, was broad-shouldered, and wore a dark jacket and trousers. He also wore a black peaked cap and carried nothing in his hands.

The second man was a little older, about 35. He was 5 feet 11 inches tall with a fresh complexion, light brown hair, and a brown mustache. He wore a dark overcoat and an old black hard felt hat with a wide brim and, of course, had a pipe in his hand.

There was some discussion between various police officers as to why the first man had called out "Lipski." Israel Lipski was a Pole who had lived in the attic room of 16 Batty Street, which ran parallel to Berner Street. The room below Lipski's was home to a young married couple, Isaac and Miriam Angel, and on 28 June 1887 Miriam Angel and Israel Lipski were found in the house, both having been poisoned with nitric acid. Miriam died, but Lipski recovered and was subsequently charged with murder. He was tried at the Old Bailey, convicted, and hanged at Newgate Prison on 22 August 1887.

One possible interpretation was that the man had called out in the sense of "I am going to Lipski this woman," though this theory was never given any real credence. More widely accepted was the notion that the man with the pipe was named Lipski, so a search for a man with that name was launched, without success. It was also suggested that Schwartz might have misheard an instruction for the second man to follow Schwartz.

Inspector Abberline himself gave the most likely explanation. He knew that the term *Lipski* was used as a derogatory label for Jews, and Israel Schwartz had a Jewish appearance. Abberline believed that the man who called out had noticed Schwartz and was using the word to warn him off. It was likely that the man with the pipe was in the same position as Schwartz, an innocent bystander who had seen the assault and walked away to avoid trouble.

It is puzzling that Israel Schwartz was never called to testify at the inquest. The police gave the highest credence to his statements and believed there was a very good chance that he had seen Jack the Ripper. though that sobriquet had not yet been given to the nameless killer. One likely explanation is that the police wished to keep secret a man whom they believed to be a crucial witness.

To return to the 5 October inquest, the next witness was Sven Olsson, who was clerk to the Swedish Church in Princes Square. He had known the dead woman for 17 years but added little to the evidence beyond saying that she had registered with the church on 10 July 1868.

William Marshall lived at 64 Berner Street, and he too had viewed the body lying in the mortuary. He was sure it was a woman he had seen at 11:45 P.M. on 29 September. Marshall had gone to his front door at 11:30 P.M. and about fifteen minutes later noticed a man and a woman on the pavement between his house and the club but on the opposite side of the road. The couple was kissing, and he heard the man say, "You would say anything but your prayers." After this the couple walked up the street toward Packer's shop and Dutfield's Yard.

Marshall described the man as middle aged, about 5 feet 6 inches tall, rather stout, and looking like a clerk. He wore a small black coat, dark trousers, and a round cap with a small peak.

The next witness was James Brown of 35 Fairclough Street. At 12:45 A.M. he had left home to go to a chandler's shop for his supper. The shop was at the corner of Berner Street and Fairclough Street, and as Brown was crossing the road he saw a man and a woman standing together by the wall at the school that was opposite Dutfield's Yard. Brown was sure that the woman was Elizabeth Stride, and he heard her say to the man, "No, not tonight, some other night." The man was stout and about 5 feet 7 inches tall and wore a long coat that reached almost to his heels.

Another sighting of a man and a woman had been made by Constable William Smith, the officer whose beat took in Berner Street itself. Constable Smith began his testimony by giving details of his beat: It began at the corner of Jower's Walk and went down Commercial Road as far as Christian Street. From there he went down Christian Street and Fairclough Street as far as Grove Street, then back along Fairclough Street as far as Back Church Lane. From there he passed up Back Church Lane as far as Commercial Road, taking in all the interior streets such as Berner Street and Batty Street. Smith said he had last been in Berner Street at 12:30 or 12:35 A.M. on the 30th. This statement fixed the time that Mrs. Mortimer had gone to her front door.

On his 12:30 A.M. visit to Berner Street, Constable Smith had seen a man and a woman standing on the street across from Dutfield's Yard. The woman had a flower in her jacket, which indicated that she was Elizabeth. The man had a newspaper parcel in his hand about 18 inches long and 6 or 8 inches broad. He was 5 feet 7 inches tall and wore a hard felt deerstalker hat and dark clothes. He was about 28 years old and had no whiskers.

After the murder Constable Smith was not attracted to the scene of the crime by any commotion. Rather, he was on his normal beat, and as he turned into Berner Street at about 1 A.M. he saw a crowd of people outside the gates to Dutfield's Yard. Two policemen were already there, and after speaking to them, Smith went to fetch the police ambulance. As he was leaving, Dr. Blackwell's assistant, Edward Johnston, was just arriving.

Philip Kranz, the editor of *Der Arbeter Fraint,* was the next witness. He said he had been in the back room of the printing offices from 9 P.M. until he was told that a body had been found in the yard. During that time he heard no cry for help, but there was a good deal of singing coming from upstairs in the club, and it was possible that he simply didn't hear any sounds made by Elizabeth or her killer.

Detective Inspector Edmund Reid had arrived at Dutfield's Yard at 1:45 A.M. on the 30th, by which time Chief Inspector West, Inspector Pinhorn, and several other police officers were already in attendance. Dr. Blackwell and Dr. Phillips were also there, as were a number of bystanders. Inspector Reid ordered that every person's name and address be taken and that they all be examined for bloodstains. In all, 28 people were seen, questioned, and searched, but nothing related to the crime was found.

At 4:30 A.M. Elizabeth's body was moved to the mortuary in Cable Street, and Reid followed it there to take down a description. According to his notes, the dead woman was about 42 years old, 5 feet 2 inches tall with curly dark-brown hair. Her complexion was pale, her eyes were light gray, and her upper front teeth were missing. She wore a long black jacket trimmed with black fur, an old black skirt, a dark-brown velvet bodice, two light serge petticoats, a white chemise, a pair of white stockings, a black crepe bonnet, and a pair of side-sprung boots. Her jacket was decorated by a single red rose backed by a maidenhair fern. The only possessions found in her pockets were two handkerchiefs, a thimble, and a piece of wool on a card.

There was one final adjournment of the inquest to 23 October, when the verdict of "murder by some person or persons unknown" was announced. Just over two weeks earlier, on 6 October, the body of Elizabeth Stride had been laid to rest in a pauper's grave in the East London Cemetery.

Suggestions for further reading:

Begg, Paul, Martin Fido, and Keith Skinner. *The Jack the Ripper A–Z.* Headline, 1996.

Hinton, Bob. *From Hell . . . The Jack the Ripper Mystery.* Old Bakehouse Publications, 1998.

Jakubowski, Maxim, and Nathan Braund. *The Mammoth Book of Jack the Ripper.* Robinson Publishing, 1999.

PRO Files MEPO 3/140. Available on microfilm at the Public Record Office, Kew.

Sugden, Philip. *The Complete History of Jack the Ripper.* Robinson Publishing, 1994.

Catherine Eddowes
Sunday, 30 September 1888

At 1:30 A.M. on 30 September, Constable Edward Watkins's beat took him into Mitre Square in the City of London. Although close to the busy neighborhoods of Duke Street and Aldgate, the square was very quiet at night and poorly lit. There were only two lights in the square itself: one outside Kearley and Tongue's warehouse in the northwest corner, close to a passage that led to St. James's Place; the other on the wall at the entrance to Church Passage, which led into Duke Street. There was a third lamp outside the square, on the corner of Mitre Street, but it threw little light into Mitre Square itself because much of its glow was obstructed by Mr. Taylor's shop on the corner.

Few people lived or worked in the square. The only family living there was that of Constable Pearse. His home, number 3 Mitre Square, lay between an empty house and Kearley and Tongue's on one side and another warehouse, that of Williams and Co., on the other. There were three houses next to Taylor's shop, but these were all empty, and the shop itself was left locked up and deserted at night. The rest of the square consisted of warehouses that did have watchmen, but for the most part Mitre Square was empty, and that was just how Constable Watkins found it at 1:30 A.M.

After walking through the square and checking it carefully, Watkins left via St. James's Place. Turning right, he passed up Duke Street, which turned right upon itself. Watkins continued along Duke

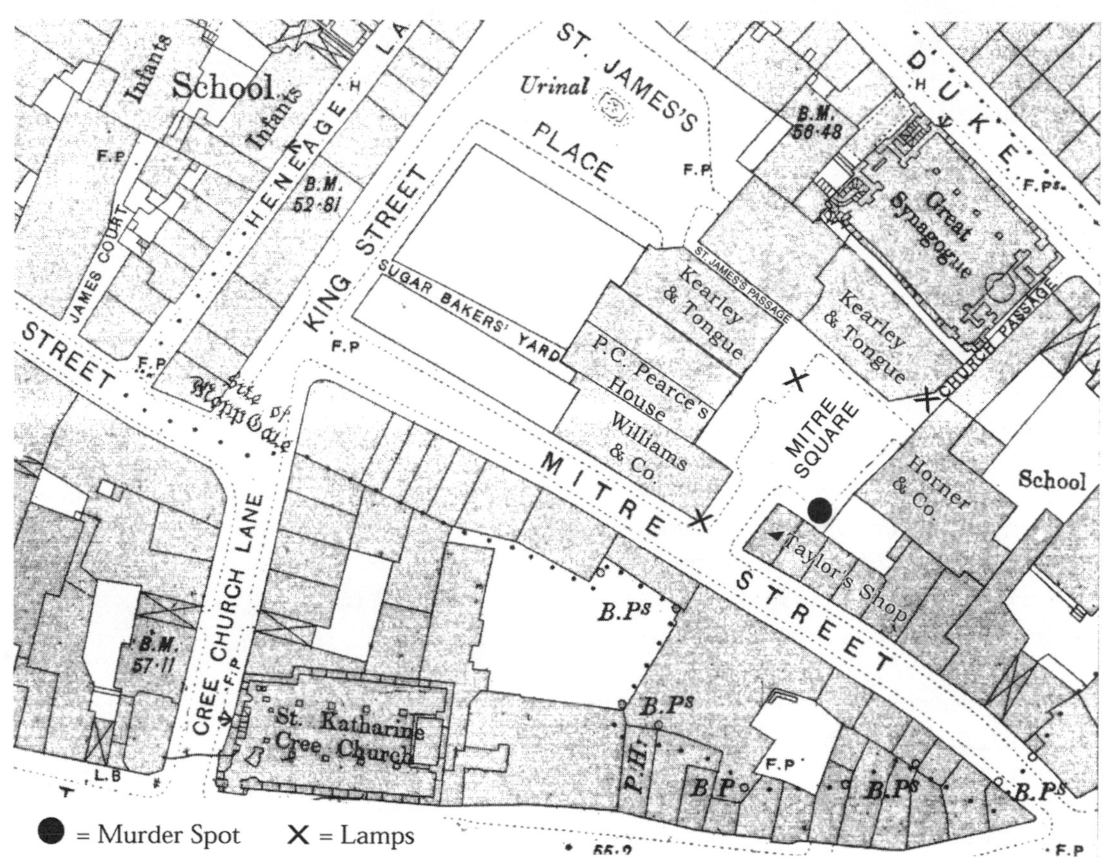

The corner of Mitre Square where Catherine Eddowes was butchered. It was at the top of Church Passage that she was seen by Joseph Lawende talking to a man who was almost certainly her killer.

Street and turned back toward St. James's Square, then walked down King Street and Creechurch Place, turning left at St. Katharine Cree Church into Leadenhall Street and then passing around into Mitre Street and back into Mitre Square. The entire beat took him about 14 minutes so that at 1:44 A.M. he was again turning into Mitre Square. This time the Square was not deserted, for in the southernmost corner, the darkest part of the place, lay the body of a woman clearly picked out by the lantern on Watkins's belt. She had been savagely mutilated.

Watkins ran across to Kearley and Tongue's warehouse, for he knew that the night watchman there, George James Morris, was a retired police officer. Watkins found the door to the warehouse ajar, pushed it open, and found Morris sweeping the steps that led down toward the door.

"For God's sake, mate, come to my assistance," cried Watkins.

"What's the matter?" asked Morris, to which Watkins replied, "Oh, dear, there's another woman cut to pieces."

Collecting his own lamp, Morris followed Watkins out into the square and looked at the woman's body. Then, while Watkins stood guard, Morris ran out through Mitre Street and turned left into Aldgate, all the while blowing his whistle to attract attention. He soon found two constables, James Thomas Holland and James Harvey, who had beats adjacent to Watkins's.

Constable Holland ran for medical assistance. The nearest surgery was that of

Dr. George William Sequeira at 34 Jewry Street, Aldgate, and by the time Holland had called that gentleman out it was 1:55 A.M. Dr. Sequeira reached Mitre Square soon afterward but didn't touch the body. It was plain that the poor woman was beyond all human aid, and he believed it would be better if the first detailed examination were made by the official police surgeon.

The holder of that office, Dr. Frederick Gordon Brown, arrived at the square at 2:18 A.M. Before this, at about 2:03 A.M., Inspector Edward Collard had arrived, having been alerted at Bishopsgate Police Station. Once Dr. Brown had made his examination, he ordered that the body be moved to the City Mortuary in Golden Lane.

Other officers had arrived on the scene by this time. At 1:58 A.M., three plainclothes detectives, Sergeant Robert Outram, Constable Daniel Halse, and Constable Edward Marriott, had been on the corner of Houndsditch and Aldgate High Street, having just been busy searching passageways and houses a few streets away as part of the police effort to trace the Whitechapel killer. Alerted to the fact that there had been a murder in Mitre Square, they ran to the spot and then set out in different directions to see if they could find the miscreant.

Only Constable Halse would later be called to give his testimony at the inquest. He left the square and traveled through Middlesex Street and on into Wentworth Street. There he saw two men; stopped them; and, satisfied with their explanation as to what they were doing at that time, allowed them to go on their way. From Wentworth Street he walked into Goulston Street, by which time it was after 2:15 A.M. Having found nothing, he returned to Mitre Square to report and to receive further instructions from his superiors.

When he reached the square, Halse received news that a discovery had been made, so he and another officer, Detective Constable Baxter Hunt, went immediately to Leman Street Police Station to find out more. They were directed to Goulston Street, where they spoke to Constable Alfred Long.

Constable Long's beat took him through 108–119 Wentworth Model Dwellings, close to the junction of Goulston Street and Wentworth Street, every half hour or so. At 2:20 A.M. he had seen nothing out of the ordinary, but at 2:55 A.M. he had spotted a piece of apron on the right-hand side of the open doorway. Just above the apron, written in white chalk on the black brick fascia, was a message that read:

> The Juwes are
> The men That
> Will not
> be Blamed
> for nothing

Long had left a fellow constable from a nearby beat to guard the writing while he took the piece of apron to Commercial Street Police Station. Other stations, including Leman Street, were notified of the find.

Halse now stayed with the graffito while Detective Hunt returned to Mitre Square to report to Inspector James McWilliam. The inspector ordered that the writing be photographed and sent Hunt back to Goulston Street with instructions that he and Halse should carry out a thorough search of the premises. The search revealed nothing, and the writing never was photographed. The erasure of what might have proved to be a crucial clue is discussed in the "Miscellaneous" section of this book. Suffice it to say here that Sir Charles Warren, the commissioner of the Metropolitan Police, and Superintendent Thomas Arnold, the head of H Division, agreed that the writing should be sponged from the wall,

Catherine Eddowes lying in the mortuary. She was certainly a victim of Jack the Ripper, and many believe her to be the second of two women he killed on the night of the so-called double event, 30 September 1888. Although her killer had but a few minutes to complete his work, Catherine was subjected to appalling mutilations. (Public Record Office, London)

and their decision was carried out at 5:30 A.M., despite Halse's objections.

The apron, meanwhile, had been handed over to Dr. Brown, and he took it to the Golden Lane mortuary to compare it with the clothing the dead woman was wearing. Inspector McWilliam was present when the garment was compared to a cut apron worn by the victim. The match was exact, even down to a seam that corresponded in both pieces. There could be no doubt that the killer had cut the piece of apron from the dead woman, probably used it to wipe his hands, and later discarded it in Goulston Street. If Constable Long was correct when he stated that he had not seen the apron at 2:20 A.M., then the murderer must have dropped it after that time, which seems to indicate that he was on the streets after the discovery of the body at 1:44 A.M. until at least 2:21 A.M.

Identifying the dead woman proved to be relatively simple. A mustard tin found near her body contained two pawn tickets for items pledged at the shop of Joseph Jones at 31 Church Street, Spitalfields. The pawned items turned out to be a man's flannel shirt, pledged on 31 August in the name of Emily Birrell of 52 Whites Row, and a pair of man's boots, pledged on 28 September in the name of Jane Kelly of 6 Dorset Street.

Police checks showed that both names and addresses were false, but the reports of these two items and the fact that the victim had the letters "T. C." tattooed in blue on her left forearm brought John Kelly, a laborer, to the Bishopsgate Police Station on 2 October.

Kelly said he believed the Mitre Square victim was a woman he had been living with for seven years, mostly at Cooney's lodging house at 55 Flower and Dean Street. Taken to view the body, Kelly confirmed the identification and said the woman was Kate Conway, who sometimes called herself by his surname, Kelly. With this name to work from, the police were able to establish that in fact the dead woman's correct name had been Catherine, or more commonly Kate, Eddowes.

Catherine Eddowes had been born to George and Catharine Eddowes in Wolverhampton on 14 April 1842. In December 1844, when Catherine was just two, the family moved to London and by 1851 was living at 35 West Street, Nelson Street, Bermondsey. Four years later, on 17 November 1855, Catherine's mother died and the large family was dispersed. Catherine was sent to live with an aunt, Elizabeth Eddowes, in Wolverhampton.

It seems that Kate was not happy with her aunt, for a few months later she ran away to Birmingham, where she moved in with another relative, an uncle, Thomas Eddowes. Not long afterward she met Thomas Conway, the man whose initials were tattooed on her arm, and they started living together.

Although Conway and Catherine never married, they stayed together until 1880, or perhaps 1881, and she bore him three children: a daughter, Annie, and two sons. The family came back to London, and it was there that the couple separated. Catherine met John Kelly at the Flower and Dean Street lodging house in 1881. She kept in touch with her daughter, whose married name was Phillips, for some time, but Catherine's constant demands for money created some friction between them. When Annie moved in 1886, she didn't bother to give her mother her new address. Consequently, by 1888 mother and daughter had not met for two years.

John Kelly was able to give the police further information about Catherine Eddowes. She had three sisters living in London. Two of these, Eliza Gold, who lived at 6 Thrawl Street, and Emma Jones of 20 Bridgewater Place, hadn't been friendly toward Catherine, again possibly owing to her habit of trying to borrow money. The third sister, Elizabeth Fisher of 33 Hatcliffe Street, Greenwich, had seen Catherine from time to time.

Referring to the events of the past few days, Kelly told the police that he and Catherine had spent much of the autumn in Hunton, near Maidstone, hop-picking. They had made some money, and Kelly had bought himself a new pair of boots. However, by Thursday, 27 September, they were back in London and had no money, meaning they couldn't afford their usual lodging house and had to sleep at the Casual Ward in Mile End.

On Friday, 28 September, Kelly managed to earn sixpence doing some laboring work. He gave fourpence to Catherine so she could have a single bed at Cooney's, Kelly himself having the intention of going back to Mile End, but Catherine wouldn't hear of it. She insisted that Kelly should have the bed and she would go to the Casual Ward, and after some discussion Kelly agreed rather reluctantly.

On Saturday, 30 September, Catherine and Kelly met again, still without much money to their names. Kelly announced that he would pawn his new boots. Catherine protested, but this time Kelly would not be moved, and the boots were exchanged at the pawnbroker's shop for 2 shillings and sixpence. The couple then had some breakfast at the Flower and Dean lodging house, bought some tea and sugar, and at 2 P.M. parted in Houndsditch, Catherine announcing that she intended to visit her daughter, Annie. One of the last things Kelly said to Catherine was a warning about the killer who was stalking the streets. Catherine replied, "Don't you fear for me. I'll take care of myself, and I shan't fall into his hands."

This conversation, or one very similar to it, was reported in different circumstances. A report in the *East London Observer* of 13 October refers to a supposed conversation between Catherine and the superintendent of the Casual Ward at Mile End. According to this article, Catherine commented that she and Kelly had returned from hop-picking because she believed she knew the identity of the killer and was going to claim the reward. Told that she might well become his next victim, Catherine replied, "Oh no fear of that." This report cannot be substantiated from any other source so must be said to be unreliable; yet some writers have claimed as a fact that Catherine Eddowes knew who the Ripper was. Those writers seem to have missed a rather obvious point: If Catherine did know the identity of the killer, then she must have met him, by accident or design, close to Mitre Square and then walked into that dark, secluded corner with him. This scenario is hardly likely, and it must be accepted that Catherine did not know who Jack the Ripper was.

When Catherine and Kelly parted in Houndsditch at 2 P.M. on 29 September she had no money, but she must have earned some in the next few hours because at 8:30 P.M. she was drunk and incapable. Constable Louis Robinson noticed a small crowd of people around 29 Aldgate High Street and, pushing his way through, found Catherine lying on the pavement. The constable picked her up and leaned her back against some shutters, but she slid sideways, so Robinson called over a fellow officer, Constable George Simmons, and together they took her to Bishopsgate Police Station. Of course, at this time neither officer knew the identity of the woman they had arrested. Upon their arrival at the station at 8:45 P.M., Catherine was asked her name and replied, "Nothing," so she was placed in a cell to recover. One hour later, at 9:45 P.M., Constable George Hutt came on duty and visited the cells several times during the next couple of hours to check on the prisoners.

By 11:45 P.M. Catherine was awake and singing softly to herself. By the time of the next check, at 12:30 A.M. on 30 September, she was asking when she would be allowed to leave, and Hutt told her, "Shortly." Catherine retorted, "I am capable of taking care of myself now." Less than half an hour later the desk officer, Sergeant James George Byfield, told Constable Hutt to see if any of the prisoners were fit to be discharged. That instruction led Hutt to unlock Catherine's cell and take her up to the office, where she asked him what time it was.

"Too late for you to get any more drink," replied Hutt, but Catherine persisted in asking the time and was then told that it was just on 1 o'clock. Catherine mused, "I shall get a damned fine hiding when I get home, then." Hutt responded, "And serve you right. You have no right to get drunk."

Asked for her name and address, Catherine said she was Mary Ann Kelly and lived at 6 Fashion Street. After this information was noted she was formally discharged, and Constable Hutt held the door open for her as she left. He watched her walk down the passage that led to the main street doors and asked her to pull them closed behind her. She shouted back, "All right. Good night, old cock," and Hutt noticed that she turned left, toward Houndsditch. It would later be said that Mitre Square was just eight minutes' walk away, meaning Catherine could have arrived there as early as 1:10 A.M.

It appears that Catherine was seen close to Mitre Square. After the murder a house-to-house inquiry brought three witnesses to the attention of the police: Joseph Lawende, Joseph Hyam Levy, and Harry Harris. These three men had spent the night of 29 September at the Imperial Club at 16–17 Duke's Place. They left about 1:30 A.M. on the 30th, and as they came into the street Lawende noticed a man and a woman standing at the corner of Church Passage, which led into Mitre Square.

For some reason that was never made plain, Levy seemed disturbed by the couple and remarked to his companions that he didn't like walking home alone when there were such people about. However, he did not take particular notice of the couple, for he was unable to offer any description of the man and woman, nor could Harris. Lawende did take a closer look and noticed that the woman, who had her back to him, was wearing a black jacket and bonnet and was quite small. She rested one hand on the man's chest, and their conversation was quiet. The man was facing Lawende, so Lawende's description of him was more detailed. According to later newspaper reports he was about 30 years old, 5 feet 7 or 8 inches tall and of medium build, with a fair complexion and mustache. He wore a pepper-and-salt loose jacket, a gray cloth cap with a peak, and a reddish neckerchief tied in a knot. Lawende thought he looked like a sailor.

Though he had not seen the woman's face, Lawende was later shown Catherine Eddowes's clothing and believed it was the same as that worn by the woman he had seen. If this is true, then we know that Catherine was alive, with a man, at the top of Church Passage at 1:35 A.M., and her body was found by Constable Watkins just nine minutes later. This means that the man Lawende saw must almost certainly have been the killer.

In fact, the time of the murder might well be narrowed down even further. Constable James Harvey had a beat that took him down Duke Street and along Church Passage. He did not actually go into Mitre Square but, having reached the junction of the square with Church Passage, turned and retraced his steps back into Duke Street. According to his reckoning he walked down Church Passage at 1:41 or 1:42 A.M., looked into the square, and saw nothing. How is this information to be explained?

In the first place, Harvey's timing is approximate. He guessed at the time he would have looked into Mitre Square by the time he passed the post office clock, which he said was about 1:28 or 1:29 A.M. Assuming, for the moment, that his timing was accurate, then when Harvey looked into Mitre Square Catherine Eddowes's body must have been lying in the far corner. Her killer might have still been there, hiding in the shadows. The corner where the murder took place was the darkest part of the square. An alternative explanation is that Catherine's body was lying in the dark and the killer had already made good his escape. However, this idea can be discounted because the minimum time required to inflict the mutilations, according to the medical evidence, would have been three minutes. So if Harvey did look into the square when he said he did, the killer must still have been there.

There is, however, a third possibility. Harvey was dismissed from the police on 1 July 1889 for reasons that are not known. This detail suggests that he was not the ideal police officer and hence may not have been as methodical in his duties as he should have been. Therefore, might another explanation be that Harvey skipped part of his beat in order to save himself a little time? Suppose Harvey patrolled the rather more public area of Duke Street but as he approached Church Passage, which had a light at the far end, all he did was look down the passage toward Mitre Square? After all, he knew that another officer, Constable Watkins, made a careful patrol of the square itself; surely all he had to worry about was Church Passage, and he could see down that plainly enough from Duke Street. Once the murder occurred, Harvey had no choice but to lie, saying he had walked down the passage at the time he was supposed to and had seen nothing in the square.

Whatever the truth of this incident, we can draw up a tentative timetable for the events leading to Catherine Eddowes's murder:

29 September

- 2 P.M.—She parts, penniless, from John Kelly in Houndsditch.
- 8:30 P.M.—She is arrested for being drunk in Aldgate High Street.
- 8:45 P.M.—She arrives at Bishopsgate Police Station.

30 September

- 1:02 A.M.— Catherine is released from the police station.
- 1:10 A.M.—The earliest time Catherine could have arrived at Mitre Square.
- 1:30 A.M.—Constable Watkins patrols Mitre Square and finds nothing.
- 1:30 A.M.—A woman believed to be Catherine is seen at the junction of Duke Street and Church Passage by Lawende and his friends.
- 1:40 A.M.—Latest possible time of death, according to Dr. Sequeira.
- 1:41 A.M.—The time Constable Harvey said he looked into Mitre Square.
- 1:44 A.M.—Constable Watkins finds Catherine's body.
- 2:20 A.M.—Constable Long patrols Wentworth Model Dwellings and finds nothing.
- 2:55 A.M.—Long finds the apron and the graffito.

The latter time seems to confuse many authors. Even if the Ripper had left the square by another route as Constable Watkins entered it through Mitre Street, he would still have been out of Mitre Square at 1:44 A.M. If we assume that Constable Long was diligent enough at

2:20 A.M. to have seen the apron had it been there, then the earliest it could have been deposited was 2:21 A.M. Does this time lapse mean that Jack walked the streets, carrying his trophies, for at least 37 minutes and possibly as long as 70 minutes if the apron was not left until 2:54 A.M.? Furthermore, does it prove that the Ripper's escape route from Mitre Square was northeast toward some hideaway? It is my opinion that it does not.

Is it not more reasonable to assume that the killer returned to his home or lodgings almost immediately after the Mitre Square murder? We know from the apron that he was probably stained with blood and fecal matter, so cleaning up would be a priority. Jack likely returned home, cleaned himself up, possibly changed his clothing, and then left home again, carrying nothing but the piece of apron. He discarded the scrap in the doorway, possibly also writing the message on the wall, sometime between 2:20 A.M. and 2:55 A.M. Why would he do so? His only reason would have been to throw the police off the scent by making them think that his base was to the northeast, possibly somewhere around Brick Lane. If this were the case, then his real base would probably have been relatively close to Goulston Street and Wentworth Street.

The inquest on Catherine Eddowes opened before Coroner Samuel Frederick Langham at the Golden Lane mortuary on 4 October, when most of the evidence was heard. There was only one adjournment, and the proceedings were concluded one week later, on 11 October.

The medical evidence was obviously crucially important. The postmortem had been conducted by Dr. Brown on Sunday, 30 September. Also present were Dr. Sequeira, Dr. William Sedgwick Saunders, and Dr. Phillips. I will consider each of the medical opinions in turn, beginning with Dr. Brown's findings as he entered Mitre Square at about 2:18 A.M. that Sunday. According to his notes taken at the time,

> the body was on its back; the head turned to the left shoulder; the arms by the sides of the body as if they had fallen there, both palms upwards, the fingers slightly bent; a thimble was lying off the finger on the right side; the clothes drawn up above the abdomen; the thighs were naked; left leg extended in a line with the body; the abdomen was exposed; right leg bent at the thigh and knee; the bonnet was at the back of the head; great disfigurement of face; the throat cut across; below the cut was a neckerchief; the upper part of the dress was pulled open a little way; the abdomen was all exposed; the intestines were drawn out to a large extent and placed over the right shoulder; they were smeared over with some feculant matter; a piece of about two feet was quite detached from the body and placed between the body and the left arm, apparently by design; the lobe and auricle of the right ear was cut obliquely through; there was a quantity of clotted blood on the pavement on the left side of the neck, round the shoulder and upper part of arm, and fluid blood serum which had flowed under the neck to the right shoulder, the pavement sloping in that direction; body was quite warm; no death stiffening had taken place; she must have been dead most likely within the half hour; we looked for superficial bruises and saw none; no blood on the skin of the abdomen or secretion of any kind on the thighs; no spurting of blood on the bricks or pavement around; no marks of blood below the middle of the body; several buttons were found in the clotted blood after the body was removed; there was no blood on the front of the clothes; there were no traces of recent connection.

When it came to the postmortem report, Dr. Brown was even more detailed.

> The throat was cut across to the extent of about six or seven inches. A superficial cut commenced about an inch and a half

below the lobe and about two and a half inches below and behind the left ear and extended across the throat to about three inches below the lobe of the right ear. The big muscle across the throat was divided through on the left side. The large vessels on the left side of the neck were severed. The larynx was severed below the vocal cord. All the deep structures were severed to the bone, the knife marking intervertebral cartilages. The sheath of the vessels on the right side was just opened. The carotid artery had a fine hole opening. The internal jugular vein was opened an inch and a half, not divided. The blood vessels contained clot. All these injuries were performed by a sharp instrument like a knife and pointed.

We examined the abdomen. The front walls were laid open from the breast bone to the pubes. The cut commenced opposite the ensiform cartilage. The incision went upwards, not penetrating the skin that was over the sternum. It then divided the ensiform cartilage. The knife must have cut obliquely at the expense of the front surface of that cartilage.

Behind this the liver was stabbed as if by the point of a sharp instrument. Below this was another incision into the liver of about two and a half inches, and below this the left lobe of the liver was slit through by a vertical cut. Two cuts were shewn by a jagging of the skin on the left side.

The abdominal walls were divided in the middle line to within quarter of an inch of the navel. The cut then took a horizontal course for two inches and a half towards the right side. It then divided round the navel on the left side and made a parallel incision to the former horizontal incision, leaving the navel on a tongue of skin. Attached to the navel was two and a half inches of the lower part of the rectus muscle on the left side of the abdomen. The incision then took an oblique direction to the right and was shelving. The incision went down the right side of the vagina and rectum for half an inch behind the rectum.

There was a stab of about an inch on the left groin. This was done by a pointed instrument. Below this was a cut of three inches going through all the tissues making a wound of the perineum about the same extent.

An inch below the crease of the thigh was a cut extending from the anterior spine of the ilium obliquely down the inner side of the left thigh and separating the left labium, forming a flap of skin up to the groin. The left rectus muscle was not detached.

There was a flap of skin formed from the right thigh attaching the right labium and extending up the spine of the ilium. The muscles on the right side inserted into the Poupart's ligament were cut through.

The skin was retracted through the whole of the cut in the abdomen, but the vessels were not clotted. Nor had there been any appreciable bleeding from the vessel. I draw the conclusion that the cut was made after death, and there would not be much blood on the murderer. The cut was made by someone on right side of body, kneeling below the middle of the body.

I removed the content of the stomach and placed it in a jar for further examination. There seemed very little in it in the way of food or fluid, but from the cut end partly digested farinaceous food escaped.

The intestines had been detached to a large extent from the mesentery. About two feet of the colon was cut away. The sigmoid flexure was invaginated into the rectum very tightly.

Right kidney pale, bloodless, with slight congestion of the base of the pyramids.

There was a cut from the upper part of the slit on the under surface of the liver to the left side, and another cut at right angles to this, which were about an inch and a half deep and two and a half inches long. Liver itself was healthy.

The gall bladder contained bile. The pancreas was cut but not through on the left side of the spinal column. Three and a half inches of the lower border of the spleen by half an inch was attached only to the peritoneum.

> The peritoneal lining was cut through on the left side and the left kidney carefully taken out and removed. The left renal artery was cut through. I should say that someone who knew the position of the kidney must have done it. The lining membrane over the uterus was cut through. The womb was cut through horizontally, leaving a stump of three quarters of an inch. The rest of the womb had been taken away with some of the ligaments. The vagina and cervix of the womb was uninjured.
>
> The bladder was healthy and uninjured, and contained three or four ounces of water. There was a tongue-like cut through the anterior wall of the abdominal aorta. The other organs were healthy. There were no indications of connection.
>
> The face was very much mutilated. There was a cut about quarter of an inch through the lower left eyelid dividing the structures completely through. The upper eyelid on that side, there was a scratch through the skin on the left upper eyelid near to the angle of the nose. The right eyelid was cut through to about half an inch. There was a deep cut over the bridge of the nose extending from the left border of the nasal bone down near to the angle of the jaw on the right side across the cheek. This cut went into the bone and divided all the structures of the cheek except the mucous membrane of the mouth. The tip of the nose was quite detached from the nose by an oblique cut from the bottom of the nasal bone to where the wings of the nose join on to the face. A cut from this divided the upper lip and extended through the substance of the gum over the right upper lateral incisor tooth. About half an inch from the top of the nose was another oblique cut. There was a cut on the right angle of the mouth, as if by the cut of a point of a knife. The cut extended an inch and a half parallel with lower lip. There was on each side of cheek a cut which peeled up the skin forming a triangular flap about an inch and a half. On the left cheek there were two abrasions of the epithelium. There was a little mud on the left cheek. Two slight abrasions of the epithelium under the left ear.

A number of questions were put to Dr. Brown. In reply he explained his opinion that the killer had inflicted the throat wound first, while Catherine was lying on the ground. The knife used was sharp and pointed and at least 6 inches long.

Referring to the degree of anatomical knowledge exhibited by the murderer, Dr. Brown said the killer showed considerable knowledge of the position of the various organs and how they might be removed but that someone used to cutting up animals would have this level of skill. He believed that the killer must have taken about five minutes over the murder and mutilations. Finally, turning to the piece of apron found in Goulston Street, Dr. Brown stated that it certainly had been cut from the apron Catherine Eddowes was wearing when she died.

Dr. Sequeira, the first medical practitioner on the scene, agreed with Dr. Brown's findings, but when asked about the murderer's surgical expertise, he stated that he saw no evidence of surgical skill whatsoever. Furthermore, he did not believe the killer was searching for any particular organ to remove but had merely happened to take away the kidney and part of the uterus.

The difference of opinion between these two doctors deserves a little more consideration. In his report to the inquest Dr. Brown based his assumption of even a slight degree of skill, such as that exhibited by a slaughterman, on the belief that Catherine's murderer had specifically sought to remove a kidney. If that were the case, then Brown's assumption would have been correct. However, if the Ripper merely sought to collect trophies, then any organ would suffice and Sequeira's opinion would carry greater weight. If we look at the

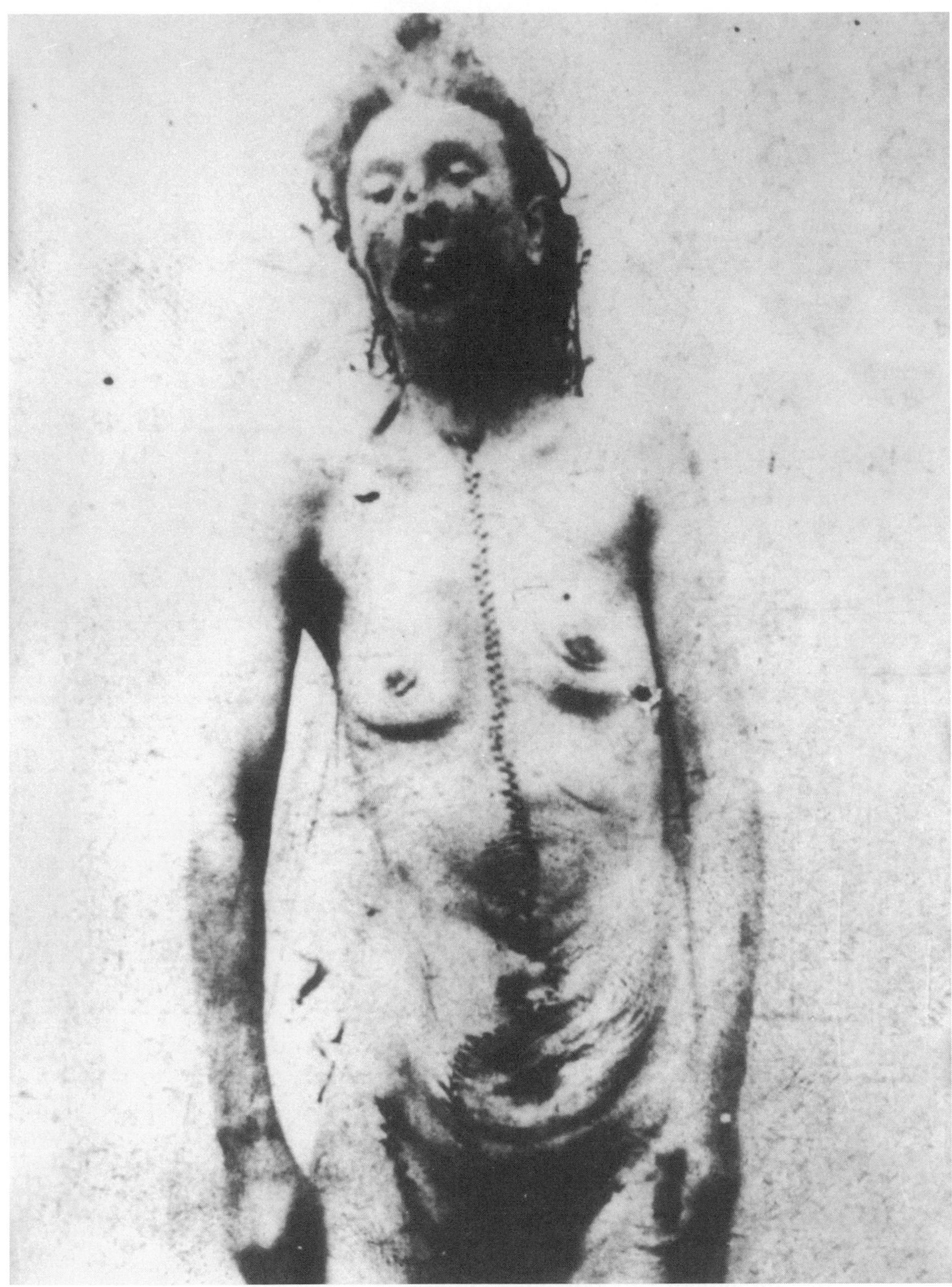

Another mortuary photograph of Catherine Eddowes. Her body was stitched following the postmortem and then hung upon pegs in the wall so that this picture could be taken. The stitching gives some indication of the ferocity of her wounds. One of her kidneys had been removed and taken away by her killer. (Public Record Office, London)

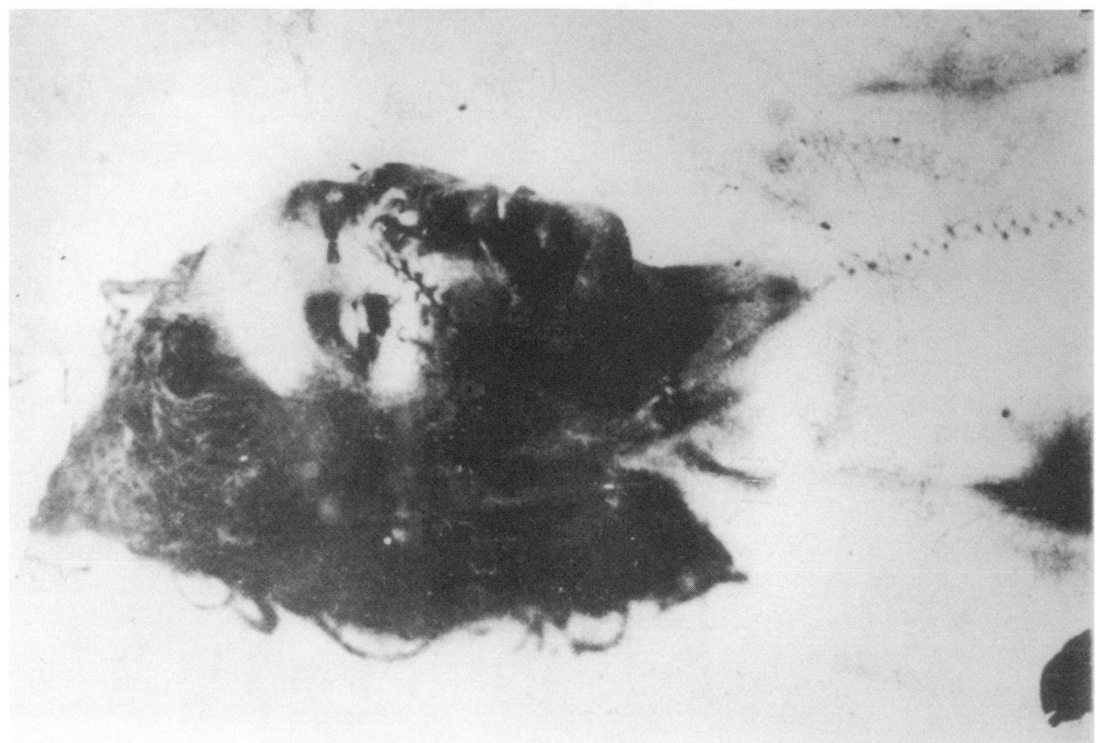

A close-up of Catherine Eddowes's face showing some of the mutilations after postmortem stitching. Catherine's killer cut off part of her apron, which he used to wipe his hands. This scrap was deposited in Goulston Street, close to a graffito that many authors have seen as a message from the killer. (Public Record Office, London)

one previous case in which organs had been removed, that of Annie Chapman, we see that the killer took totally different organs. This discrepancy indicates that Jack was nothing more than a trophy taker, in which case the level of his surgical skill may have been even less than Dr. Brown believed.

Dr. Saunders also gave evidence at the inquest, and he too believed that there was no evidence of surgical skill. He had examined Catherine's stomach contents for traces of any narcotic or drug that might have been used to render her senseless but had found nothing.

Dr. Phillips, the last of the four who had been at the postmortem, did not give evidence at the inquest, but a report from Chief Inspector Swanson gave Phillips's opinion. He too saw no degree of particular anatomical knowledge, but he believed that the killer might just as likely be a hunter, butcher, or slaughterman as a student of surgery. In short, according to the best medical evidence, Jack the Ripper appeared to have shown no special skills in his butchery of Catherine Eddowes. The final chapter of Catherine Eddowes's life took place on 8 October 1888, when she was laid to rest in the City of London Cemetery at Ilford. Crowds lined the streets, and hundreds gathered about the grave to see her body committed to the ground.

Suggestions for further reading:

Begg, Paul, Martin Fido, and Keith Skinner. *The Jack the Ripper A–Z*. Headline, 1996.

Hinton, Bob. *From Hell . . . The Jack the Ripper Mystery*. Old Bakehouse Publications, 1998.

Jakubowski, Maxim, and Nathan Braund. *The Mammoth Book of Jack the Ripper*. Robinson Publishing, 1999.

Sugden, Philip. *The Complete History of Jack the Ripper.* Robinson Publishing, 1994.

The Whitehall Mystery

Ca. Wednesday, 3 October 1888

On the morning of 3 October 1888, workmen reporting for duty on the site of the New Scotland Yard building on the Embankment found that during the previous night or early-morning hours someone had scaled the wooden palings around the area and deposited a body in one of the cellars. The body was in fact only the trunk of an adult female; her arms, legs, and hands had been cut off. The head and legs never turned up, but the arms were later found in the river Thames.

Though those investigating the East End murders never believed this crime had anything to do with the Whitechapel murders, the press seized on yet another murder to add to the growing catalog of crimes to be placed at Jack the Ripper's door. Like the Ripper crimes, this murder remains unsolved, but that is really the only thing it has in common with the other deaths. None of the typical mutilations were noted, beyond of course the dismemberment itself.

Suggestions for further reading:

Begg, Paul, Martin Fido, and Keith Skinner. *The Jack the Ripper A–Z.* Headline, 1996.

Mary Jane Kelly

Friday, 9 November 1888

By the beginning of November, many believed that the Ripper terror was over. The month of October had been a relatively quiet one, with only the horror of the kidney sent to George Lusk of the Whitechapel Vigilance Committee to disturb the peace. That situation was about to change in the most terrible of ways.

At 10:45 A.M. on 9 November, John McCarthy was in his chandler's shop at 27 Dorset Street, checking his accounts. McCarthy also owned 26 Dorset Street, which had been sectioned off into separate rooms, and a number of properties in Miller's Court, which ran between numbers 26 and 27. Most of his tenants paid their rent on time, but the books showed that one, Mary Jane Kelly, had run up arrears to the tune of 29 shillings. So McCarthy sent his assistant, Thomas Bowyer, to call on Mary and see whether he could get some money from her.

Mary Kelly lived at 13 Miller's Court. In effect, her lodging was the back room of 26 Dorset Street and was entered by means of the second door on the right, down the court. Bowyer walked down the narrow passageway, stopped at Mary's door, and knocked. There was no reply. He knocked a second time, but again there was no sound from within. It was the day of the Lord Mayor's Show, and Bowyer knew that Mary had expressed an interest in going to watch the parade. Perhaps she had already left, but Bowyer thought he would investigate further. Going further into the court, he turned to his right, where two windows from number 13 looked directly into Miller's Court. The windows were different sizes, the smallest one being closest to the edge of the wall. Two panes in this window were broken, and Bowyer reached in through one of these panes and pulled the curtain to one side so he could look into the room and determine whether Mary was really not at home.

The first thing Bowyer saw was what looked like two piles of flesh on a table. Then, as his eyes grew accustomed to the darkness inside the room, he also saw a body lying on the bed and a great deal of blood. Bowyer turned and ran back up the court to his employer's shop, where he gasped, "Governor, I knocked at the door and could not make anyone answer. I looked through the window and saw a lot of blood."

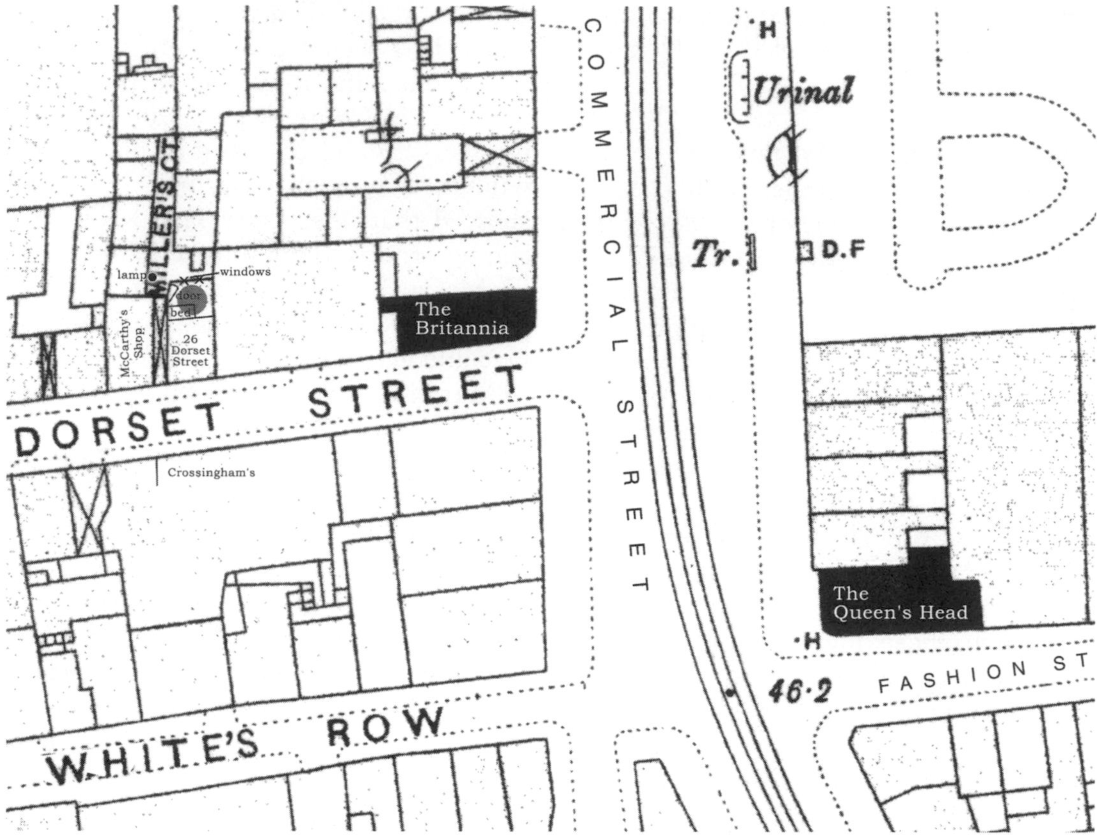

Miller's Court, Dorset Street. It was in the entry by the side of the lodging house opposite that George Hutchinson stood and was seen by Sarah Lewis.

John McCarthy went to see for himself, taking Bowyer back with him. Looking through the window and confronted by what Bowyer had described to him just a few minutes before, McCarthy told his assistant to run to the police station and fetch someone. Bowyer ran to Commercial Street Police Station and there blurted out his story to Inspector Walter Beck and Detective Walter Dew. Even as he was trying to make himself understood, his employer came into the police station and told the two officers what he and Bowyer had seen at Miller's Court. Soon all four men were hurrying back to the dark, narrow court. They reached number 13 just after 11 A.M. Once the two police officers had taken their turn at the window and seen the carnage inside, they sent for further help. At 11:15 A.M. Dr. George Bagster Phillips arrived and confirmed after his own view through the broken window that the body in the room was in such a state that it was beyond all aid. Fifteen minutes later, at 11:30 A.M., Inspector Abberline arrived, but the door to 13 Miller's Court was locked. The police believed that bloodhounds had been sent for, so they decided not to force an entry. This was largely because of Sir Charles Warren's pet theory on the use of bloodhounds and the officers at the scene awaiting his and the dogs' arrival. They did not know that Warren had already resigned. For hours the police and others merely stood around, waiting for something to happen.

At 1:30 P.M. Superintendent Thomas Arnold arrived and announced that the bloodhounds were not coming and that the door should be forced open immediately. John McCarthy armed himself with a pickaxe and smashed the door down. Dr. Phillips was the first man to enter the room, and as the door was pushed back it banged against a table that stood by the bed. The scene inside the small, dingy room was almost beyond belief, and it was clear that Jack the Ripper had struck yet again, this time indoors, where he could be secure in the knowledge that he would not be disturbed and could give full vent to his impulses. The body on the bed was unrecognizable as a human being and could only be identified as Mary Kelly by the eyes and hair.

The body was moved to Shoreditch Mortuary at 4 P.M., after which the windows of number 13 were boarded up and the front door padlocked shut. Two police officers stood guard at the entrance to the court to stop curious souls from trying to crowd down the court and take a look at the scene.

The following day, Saturday, 10 November, Inspector Abberline returned to 13 Miller's Court and made a careful search of the room. He paid special attention to the ashes in the grate, which appeared to have been the scene of a fierce blaze because the spout of a kettle had dropped off, the solder having melted. The inspector found that clothing had apparently been burned, possibly in order to give the killer the light he needed to complete his terrible work.

That same day the postmortem was carried out by Dr. Phillips, Dr. Thomas Bond, and Dr. Frederick Gordon Brown. Later that Saturday Dr. Phillips and Dr. Roderick Macdonald also visited 13 Miller's Court to sift through the grate ashes themselves, seeking any burnt human remains. This search would seem to contradict press reports that stated that no portion of the bodily organs were missing.

The inquest on Mary Jane Kelly opened at the Shoreditch Town Hall at 11 A.M. on Monday, 12 November, before Dr. Roderick Macdonald. Inspector Abberline began by escorting the jury to the mortuary to view the body and then to Miller's Court to see the scene of the crime. Once the jurors had returned to the Town Hall, the evidence began.

The first witness was Joseph Barnett, an unemployed market porter who had previously worked at Billingsgate and who had been Mary Kelly's longtime companion and lover. Barnett explained that he and Mary had first met in Commercial Street on Good Friday, 18 April 1887, at which time she was living at Cooley's lodging house in Thrawl Street. From the first moment they had gotten on well together and had agreed to meet again the following day. Once again they had enjoyed each other's company and had agreed to live together. They first shared a home in George Street, then lived in Little Paternoster Row off Dorset Street. After that they lived in Brick Lane, finally moving to 13 Miller's Court in early 1888.

The couple continued to live together at Miller's Court until 30 October, when they quarreled. According to Barnett the quarrel came about because Mary had allowed a homeless prostitute to move in with them. He had accepted this situation for a couple of days, but then they argued and he moved to a lodging house at New Street, Bishopsgate. He and Mary remained on good terms, however, and he visited her each day, usually giving her some money.

On the evening of 8 November, Barnett visited Mary Kelly at about 7:30 or 7:45 P.M. and stayed until about 8 P.M. When he first arrived a friend of hers, Lizzie Albrook, was there, but she soon left him alone with Mary. He apologized that he had no money to give her and said they were on good terms when they parted.

The story of Barnett's visit was confirmed by Maria Harvey, who was possibly Mary's closest friend. Harvey testified that she had slept at 13 Miller's Court on the nights of 5 and 6 November, after which she had found lodgings for herself at 3 New Court, also off Dorset Street. According to Harvey's testimony, she spent the afternoon of 8 November with Mary and was in Mary's room when Barnett called. Harvey then left so the couple could be alone and confirmed that the two seemed friendly with each other. The only discrepancy was that Harvey put the time of Barnett's arrival at about 6:55 P.M. She also said that she had left some clothing at Mary's room and that most of it was now missing, implying that her garments were among those burned in the grate.

There is some confusion over Maria Harvey's testimony, for press reports of the time make it clear that the woman who was in Mary's room when Joe Barnett called was in fact Lizzie Albrook. Other reports seem to confirm that Harvey actually spent the entire afternoon of 8 November with Kelly. Mary Kelly had called to visit Harvey at her room in New Court, and they had gone out drinking. They parted at about 7:30 P.M., and Harvey believed that Kelly was then heading toward Thrawl Street. It appears that in fact Mary Kelly then went home to Miller's Court, where she was joined by Lizzie Albrook, with Joe Barnett calling on her soon afterward.

Thomas Bowyer and John McCarthy told of their discovery of the body and, along with Joe Barnett, were also able to fill in the details of Mary Kelly's background. Though none of this story could be confirmed, Mary had told them and others that she had been born in Limerick, Ireland, but that her family had moved to Wales while she was still quite young. When she was 16 or so Mary had married a collier named Davies, but soon afterward he had been killed in the mines.

Mary said she had first come to London in 1884 and had begun working as a prostitute in a brothel in the West End. One of her clients had taken her to France, after which she began to call herself Marie Jeanette Kelly. After returning to London she took up with a man named Morganstone, who lived in Stepney. After that relationship ended she began living with Joe Fleming in Bethnal Green Road. In due course she moved to the East End, living first with a Mrs. Buki and later at Mrs. Carthy's at Breezer's Hill, Pennington Street. Little of this story can be demonstrated to be hard fact, and Mary may have invented much of it to give herself a more glamorous past. However, writer Bob Hinton has done some excellent research into Mary Kelly's history and has discovered a private hotel in Merthyr Tydfil that among its guests, in the 1881 census, listed a 16-year-old widow named Mary Davies.

So far the last sighting of Mary Kelly had been by Joe Barnett at around 8 P.M. on 8 November. Other witnesses were now called who could testify to Mary's movements later that day and into the next. Mary Ann Cox lived at 5 Miller's Court and had known the dead woman for about nine months. Mary Ann had been out soliciting in Commercial Street and returned to her room to warm herself about 11:45 P.M. on the 8th. As she turned into Dorset Street she saw Mary Kelly walking in front of her, in company with a man. At the time Mary Kelly seemed to be much the worse for drink, and as Mary Ann watched, the couple turned into Miller's Court.

By the time Cox reached the entrance to the court, Mary and her male friend were just going into Kelly's room. As she passed, Mary Ann called out, "Good night, Mary Jane," and Mary replied in kind, though with some difficulty owing to the drink, adding that she intended to have a song. Cox got a good look at the man because there was a light almost directly opposite the door. She described him as about 36 years old and 5 feet 5 inches tall. He was stout, with a fresh complexion but blotches on his face. He had a thick, carrotty mustache and was dressed in shabby dark clothes with a dark overcoat and a black billycock hat (a derby). He was carrying a quart can of beer. Cox heard Mary Kelly singing inside her room, "Only a violet I plucked from my mother's grave when a boy."

At midnight Cox went back out, returning to Miller's Court again at 1 A.M., at which time she heard Mary Kelly still singing inside her room. When Cox returned for the last time at 3 A.M., there was no light from the windows of number 13, and all was quiet. Throughout the rest of the night, Cox slept fitfully. She heard several men entering and leaving the court and finally heard someone leave at 5:45 A.M., though she could not say from which room.

Elizabeth Prater lived at 20 Miller's Court, the room immediately above Mary Kelly's. Prater returned to the court at about 1 A.M. on 9 November and stood for a time in the archway in Dorset Street, waiting for the man with whom she was living. When he did not appear, she went up to her room and finally retired for the night at about 1:30 A.M. She then slept for a few hours until awakened by her kitten walking across her throat. Very soon afterward she heard a cry of "Murder" (such cries were a daily occurrence in Whitechapel at the time, and people rarely took any notice). She had no idea what time it was but, because the lodging-house light was out, assumed that it was sometime after 4

The Ten Bells public house, where Mary Jane Kelly was a frequent customer. The Ten Bells briefly changed its name to the Jack the Ripper from 1976 to 1988. The interior contains some fascinating Ripper exhibits. (John Eddleston)

A close-up of the entrance to the Ten Bells public house. Mary Jane Kelly passed through this very door, and so might have Jack the Ripper! (John Eddleston)

A.M. At 5:30 A.M. Prater went out to the Ten Bells public house for a tot of rum. She then went back to her room and slept until 11 A.M.

That same cry of "Murder" may well have been heard by another witness, Sarah Lewis. Lewis lived at 29 Great Pearl Street but very early on the 9th had argued with her husband and walked out of the house. She decided she would stay with some friends, the Keylers, who lived at 2 Miller's Court. It was 2:30 A.M. as Lewis passed Christ Church; soon after this she was in Dorset Street, approaching the entrance to Miller's Court. She saw a man standing by the lodging house that was almost directly opposite the court. She described this man as not tall but stout and stated that he was wearing a black wideawake hat. As she looked at him, another young man with a woman passed along the street. The man near the lodging house appeared to be looking up the court as if waiting for someone to come out.

Inside the Keylers' room, Sarah Lewis slept in a chair until about 3:30 A.M., then she sat there awake until 5 A.M. Just before 4 A.M. she heard a single loud scream of "Murder," thus apparently confirming Prater's story. If both women were correct, this cry may have been Mary Kelly's last word, placing the time of the attack upon her at about 4 A.M. on the 9th.

Much more contentious was the testimony of Caroline Maxwell, who lived in Dorset Street. Though there was some difference between the medical evidence and that of Sarah Lewis and Elizabeth Prater, the general consensus was that Mary Kelly had been killed sometime in the early hours of 9 November. However, Maxwell claimed to have seen Mary Kelly after this time.

Maxwell had known Mary Kelly for only four months and had previously spoken to her only twice, but she stated that between 8 and 8:30 A.M. on the 9th she had seen Kelly standing on the corner of Miller's Court. The two women fell into conversation, and Kelly admitted that she was feeling the worse for drink and pointed out some vomit in the gutter that she said she had just produced. One hour after this, at about 9:30 A.M., Maxwell saw Kelly again, talking to a stout man in dark clothes outside the Britannia public house. This testimony has been seized upon by a number of authors who wish to extend the Masonic Conspiracy theory (discussed in the "Suspects" section) to claim that some kind of conspiracy existed and that someone other than Mary Kelly died in the room at 13 Miller's Court. A much more likely explanation is that Maxwell was mistaken about the date.

Dr. Phillips started the long-awaited medical evidence, but if the onlookers and gentlemen of the press were expecting a graphic illustration of the Ripper's latest atrocities, they were sadly disappointed. Phillips reported that the immediate cause of death was the severance of Mary's right carotid artery. Beyond that he would say only that he deduced that Mary had been attacked while lying at the far right side of the bed and that her body had subsequently been pulled from that side after death, probably so the killer could more easily inflict the other injuries. He placed the time of death somewhere between 4:45 and 5:45 A.M., which did not agree with the testimony of the two women who had heard the cry of "Murder." It must be remembered that there is no proof that this cry issued from Mary Kelly; on the other hand, it is also possible that various factors may indicate that the time of death was somewhat earlier. All we can infer with accuracy is that Mary Kelly died in the early hours of 9 November, possibly as early as 4 A.M., possibly as late as 5:45 A.M.

Spitalfields Church. It was this clock that Sarah Lewis used to time her arrival in Dorset Street. Soon afterward she saw a man standing in the entrance to a lodging house and looking up Miller's Court. That man was almost certainly George Hutchinson. (Yvonne Berger)

The only other witnesses were Inspector Beck, the first policeman at the scene, and Inspector Abberline, who reported on his searches of the premises and the fire grate. After this testimony the coroner told the jury he believed they might have enough information to return a verdict, which they duly did.

The conspiracy theorists have read much into the haste with which the inquest was concluded, deducing that the state was hiding something. This notion is pure nonsense. The only purpose of any inquest is to determine the cause and circumstances of death. It was plain that Mary Kelly was the victim of murder by some unknown person, and this conclusion was reflected in the verdict. A more likely reason for secrecy is that the police wished to prevent further sensationalist reports in the newspapers.

What then were the extent of Mary Kelly's injuries? Although no details were given at the inquest or in the newspapers, it is possible to piece together what occurred from Dr. Bond's notes, published in part in the *Lancet*. Dr. Bond had arrived at Miller's Court at 2 P.M. on 9 November while the body was still in situ. His notes, written on 10 November, read as follows:

> The body was lying naked in the middle of the bed, the shoulders flat, but the axis of the body inclined to the left side of the bed. The head was turned on the left cheek. The left arm was close to the body with the forearm flexed at a right angle and lying across the abdomen. The right arm was slightly abducted from the body and rested on the mattress, the elbow bent and the forearm supine with the fingers clenched. The legs were wide apart, the left thigh at right angles to the trunk and the right forming an obtuse angle with the pubes.
>
> The whole of the surface of the abdomen and thighs was removed and the abdominal cavity emptied of its viscera. The breasts were cut off, the arms mutilated by several jagged wounds and the face hacked beyond recognition of the features and the tissues of the neck were severed all round down to the bone. The viscera were found in various parts viz: the uterus and kidneys with one breast under the head, the other breast by the right foot, the liver between the feet, the intestines by the right side and the spleen by the left side of the body. The flaps removed from the abdomen and thighs were on a table.
>
> The bed clothing at the right corner was saturated with blood and on the floor beneath was a pool of blood covering about two feet square. The wall by the right side of the bed and in a line with the neck was marked by blood which had struck it in a number of separate splashes.
>
> The face was gashed in all directions, the nose, cheeks, eyebrows and ears being partly removed. The lips were blanched and cut by several incisions running obliquely down to the chin. There were also numerous cuts extending irregularly across all the features.
>
> The neck was cut through the skin and other tissues right down to the vertebra, the fifth and sixth being deeply notched. The skin cuts in the front of the neck showed distinct ecchymosis. The air passage was cut at the lower part of the larynx through the cricoid cartilage.
>
> Both breasts were removed by more or less circular incisions, the muscles down to the ribs being attached to the breasts. The intercostals between the fourth, fifth and sixth ribs were cut and the contents of the thorax visible through the openings.
>
> The skin and tissues of the abdomen from the costal arch to the pubes were removed in three large flaps. The right thigh was denuded in front to the bone, the flap of skin including the external organs of generation and part of the right buttock. The left thigh was stripped of skin, fascia and muscles as far as the knee.
>
> The left calf showed a long gash through the skin and tissues to the deep muscles and reaching from the knee to five inches above the ankle.

> Both arms and forearms had extensive and jagged wounds.
>
> The right thumb showed a small superficial incision about one inch long, with extravasation of blood in the skin and there were several abrasions on the back of the hand and forearm showing the same condition.
>
> On opening the thorax it was found that the right lung was minimally adherent by old firm adhesions. The lower part of the lung was broken and torn away.
>
> The left lung was intact; it was adherent at the apex and there were a few adhesions over the side. In the substances of the lung were several nodules of consolidation.
>
> The pericardium was open below and the heart absent.
>
> In the abdominal cavity was some partly digested food of fish and potatoes and similar food was found in the remains of the stomach attached to the intestines.

Dr. Bond made one error in his long report. Mary Kelly was not naked. The surviving photographs show that she was wearing a small chemise.

Crucially, Bond was of the opinion that the killer, though he had great coolness and daring and undoubtedly possessed much physical strength, showed no indication of specialized anatomical knowledge.

The inquest having been closed, and the few witnesses heard, one would think that this was the end of the matter, but one more crucial witness was yet to give his testimony. At 6 P.M. on 12 November, the same day that the inquest took place, a laborer named George Hutchinson walked into Commercial Street Police Station and said he wished to make a statement. That statement deserves reporting in full:

> About 2:00 A.M., 9th, I was coming by Thrawl Street, Commercial Street, and just before I got to Flower and Dean Street I met the murdered woman Kelly and she said to me "Hutchinson, will you lend me sixpence." I said "I can't, I have spent all my money going down to Romford." She said "Good morning, I must go and find some money." She went away towards Thrawl Street. A man coming in the opposite direction to Kelly tapped her on the shoulder and said something to her. They both burst out laughing. I heard her say "Alright" to him and the man said "You will be alright for what I have told you." He then placed his right hand around her shoulders. He also had a kind of a small parcel in his left hand, with a kind of a strap round it. I stood against the lamp of the Queens Head Public House and watched him. They both then came past me and the man hung down his head with his hat over his eyes. I stooped down and looked him in the face. He looked at me stern. They both went into Dorset Street. I followed them. They both stood at the corner of the court for about 3 minutes. He said something to her. She said "Alright my dear, come along, you will be comfortable." He then placed his arm on her shoulder and gave her a kiss. She said she had lost her handkerchief. He then pulled his handkerchief, a red one, out and gave it to her. They both then went up the court together. I then went to the court to see if I could see them but could not. I stood there for about three quarters of an hour to see if they came out. They did not so I went away.

On the original statement these words are followed by an empty line, after which the following was written: "Description: age about 34 or 35, height 5ft 6, complexion pale, dark eyes and eye lashes, slight moustache curled up each end and hair dark, very surley looking; dress, long dark coat, collar and cuffs trimmed astracan and a dark jacket under, light waistcoat, dark trousers, dark felt hat turned down in the middle, button boots and gaiters with white buttons, wore a very thick gold chain, white linen collar, black tie with horse shoe pin, respectable appear-

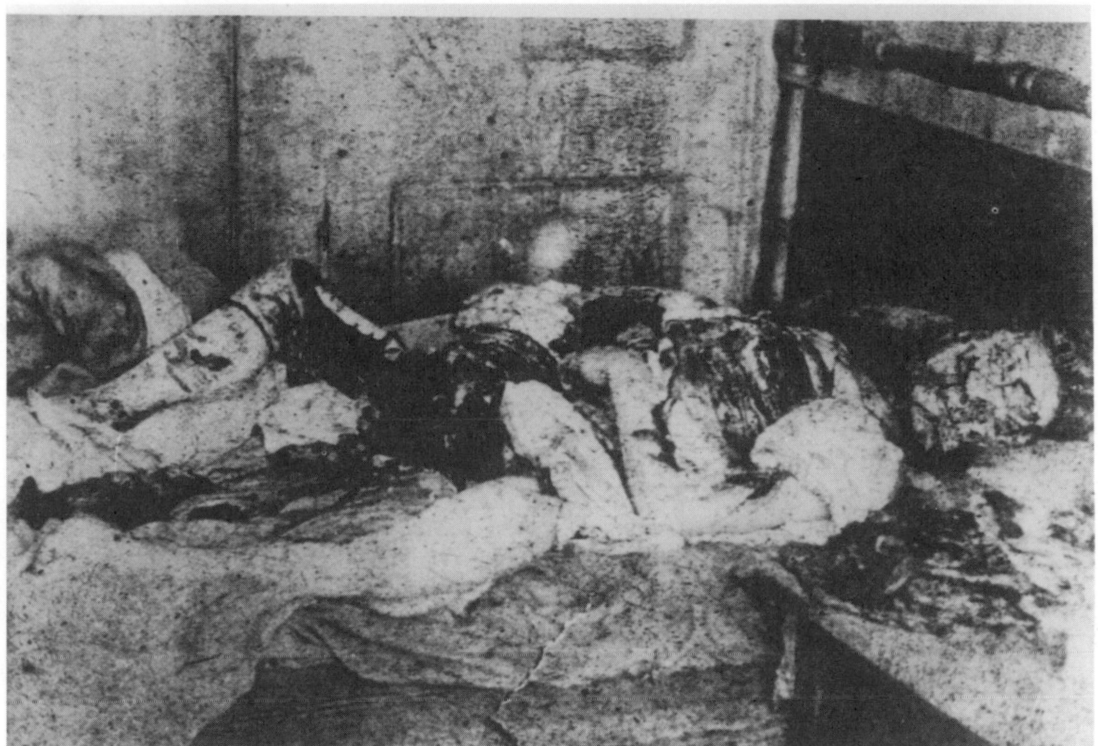

The body of Mary Jane Kelly lying on her bed on the afternoon of 9 November 1888. Parts of her body have been placed between her legs, under her head, and on the table, which can be seen at bottom right. Close scrutiny reveals marks on the wall above Mary's left hand that look like the letter M. *Some writers have claimed that this clue was deliberately placed in this awkward position as a clue to James Maybrick being the murderer.* (Public Record Office, London)

ance, walked very sharp, Jewish appearance. Can be identified."

In the entire statement, only two alterations were made to arrive at the final version quoted above. Initially Hutchinson referred to the public house where he was standing as the Ten Bells, but this name was crossed out and the Queen's Head substituted. Also, in his detailed description of the man, the word *dark* was originally placed before the words *slight moustache* and then crossed out.

The press soon found Hutchinson, and the following day, Tuesday, 13 November, he gave another statement to reporters that carried even more detail. In this he said,

> The man was about 5ft 6ins in height, and 34 or 35 years of age, with dark complexion and dark moustache, turned up at the ends. He was wearing a long dark coat, trimmed with astracan, a white collar, with black necktie, in which was affixed a horseshoe pin. He wore a pair of dark "spats" with light buttons over button boots, and displayed from his waistcoat a massive gold chain. His watch chain had a big seal, with a red stone, hanging from it. He had a heavy moustache curled up and dark eyes and bushy eyebrows. He had no side whiskers, and his chin was clean shaven. He looked like a foreigner.

Later, the same report continued,

> He carried a small parcel in his hand about 8in long, and it had a strap round it. He had it tightly grasped in his left hand. It looked as though it was covered in dark American cloth. He carried in his

> right hand, which he laid upon the woman's shoulder, a pair of brown kid gloves. One thing I noticed, and that was that he walked very softly. I believe that he lives in the neighbourhood, and I fancied that I saw him in Petticoat Lane on Sunday morning, but I was not certain.

Many students of the murders place great store on George Hutchinson's statement and description of the man he saw, especially because Inspector Abberline gave it credence and assigned two detectives to accompany Hutchinson on walks around the district to see if he could find the man. The statement is especially useful to those who wish to find a "gentleman" killer such as those involved in Royal or Masonic conspiracies. Can this theory, however, be treated with much confidence?

It may well be that Hutchinson lied about the man he saw. The reasons for this possibility are discussed in the "Suspects" section, but let us for a moment assume that he was telling the truth and that he saw Mary Kelly's well-dressed client at about 2 A.M. This testimony would dovetail neatly with that of Sarah Lewis, who saw a man standing opposite the court at 2:30 A.M., looking up the passageway as if waiting for someone to come out. We can then assume that the man she saw was Hutchinson, who would have left the spot about 15 minutes later. This evidence still would not necessarily make the client the murderer because the best opinion available puts Mary Kelly's death at some time between 4 and 5:45 A.M. The "gentleman" would have had to remain in Mary's room with her for at least two hours before he attacked her. Would it not be more reasonable to assume that Hutchinson's stern man completed his business with Mary and left some time after Hutchinson did, after which Mary would have had time to find another client?

One final drama remained to be played out: the funeral of the victim. It took place on Monday, 19 November, at St. Patrick's Roman Catholic Cemetery at Leytonstone, having been paid for by Henry Wilton, the verger of St. Leonard's Church in Shoreditch. Thousands lined the route to pay their last respects.

Suggestions for further reading:

Begg, Paul, Martin Fido, and Keith Skinner. *The Jack the Ripper A–Z*. Headline, 1996.

Hinton, Bob. *From Hell . . . The Jack the Ripper Mystery.* Old Bakehouse Publications, 1998.

Jakubowski, Maxim, and Nathan Braund. *The Mammoth Book of Jack the Ripper.* Robinson Publishing, 1999.

PRO Files MEPO 3/140 (especially for the statement made by George Hutchinson). Available on microfilm at the Public Record Office, Kew.

Sugden, Philip. *The Complete History of Jack the Ripper.* Robinson Publishing, 1994.

Annie Farmer

Tuesday, 20 November 1888

On 20 November 1888 Annie Farmer picked up a client whom she took back to her usual lodging house, Satchell's, at 19 George Street. There the man paid for a bed for the two of them.

About two hours later Annie let out a terrible scream and appeared in the kitchen, bleeding from a wound in her throat. Other lodgers went to intercept the man whom Annie said had attacked her, but he ran from the house fully clothed, turned into Thrawl Street, and managed to escape in the crowds.

Annie was able to give a full description of the man. She said he was about 36 years old, 5 feet 6 inches tall, with a dark complexion and a black mustache but no whiskers. He had been wearing a shabby-genteel suit and a round black felt hat and looked like a respectable man.

Rumors began to circulate around Whitechapel that there had been another murder, but it soon became clear that

Annie's wound was superficial. It had been inflicted with a blunt blade and was quite shallow. When the police discovered that Annie had concealed some coins in her mouth, it soon became clear that this was more likely a case of a prostitute robbing her client than a Ripper attack. It seemed that Annie had decided to rob the man by injuring herself and then screaming that she had been attacked by the Ripper. Knowing full well that he would have to answer to an irate mob intent on lynching him and only later finding out what had really happened, the client chose self-preservation and ran for his life.

Suggestions for further reading:

Begg, Paul, Martin Fido, and Keith Skinner. *The Jack the Ripper A–Z*. Headline, 1996.

Rose Mylett

Thursday, 20 December 1888

Constable Robert Goulding was on his regular beat in Poplar at 4:15 A.M. on 20 December when he walked down Clarke's Yard and found the body of a woman. There were no obvious signs of injury, her clothing had not been disarranged, and a later search of her possessions would show that robbery was an unlikely motive for an attack upon her because she carried 1 shilling and twopence in her pocket.

The dead woman was soon identified as 26-year-old Rose Mylett, and the inquest to determine the cause of her death was held at Poplar Coroner's Court before Wynne Edwin Baxter over two days, 2 and 9 January 1889. Much of the medical evidence given was suspect, to say the least.

Before the doctors were heard, other witnesses were called who supplied information about Rose's movements on the night leading up to her death. Charles Ptolomay, an infirmary night attendant at the Poplar Union, told the court he had seen Rose talking to two sailors in Poplar High Street, not far from Clarke's Yard. Ptolomay had been walking up England Row on his way to work at 7:55 P.M. on 19 December, and the sailors had seemed to be behaving suspiciously. At one point Ptolomay heard Rose cry out, "No, no, no!" which caused him to pay special attention to the two men. According to Ptolomay, the shorter of the two men was the one speaking to Rose. He was about 5 feet 7 inches tall. The taller one, who was 5 feet 11 inches or so, walked up and down while the other spoke in a low tone. This taller sailor looked like "a Yankee," according to Ptolomay. Finally, Ptolomay said he believed Rose to be sober at the time.

Rose had been seen again at 2:30 A.M. on the 20th by Alice Graves, and this time Rose seemed to well under the influence of drink. She was outside the George public house in Commercial Road, in the company of two men, but Graves was unable to supply any reliable descriptions apart from saying that they were sailors.

The postmortem had been carried out by Dr. Matthew Brownfield, who concluded that Rose had been strangled. His report stated, in part, "On the neck there was a mark, which had evidently been caused by cord drawn tightly around the neck, from the spine to the left ear. . . . There were also impressions of the thumbs and middle index fingers of some person plainly visible on each side of the neck."

Dr. Robert Anderson, the assistant commissioner of the Metropolitan Police CID, was not convinced by Dr. Brownfield's report. For one thing, Brownfield had described how the killer must have positioned himself behind Rose in order to tighten the ligature around her neck, but the ground in the yard where she was found was soft and there were no other footprints or signs of a struggle. Furthermore, Brownfield's original report stated that Rose had never given birth to any children, but her mother, who lived in Pelham Street near Baker's Row, said Rose had been married to an upholsterer named Davis and that they had one child, a daughter, who was now aged seven. Finally, Dr. Brownfield stated that there was no sign of alcohol in Rose's stomach, which conflicted with the evidence given by Alice Graves, who had seen her drunk outside the George. For these reasons Dr. Thomas Bond, the police surgeon to A Division, was called in to give his opinion.

At first it was Bond's assistant, General Police Surgeon Alexander McKellar, who made the examination, but Bond later went to the mortuary himself. His report supported Brownfield's conclusions, but, sent back by the police to take a second look, Bond finally concluded that death was owing to natural causes and that Rose Mylett had choked to death while drunk. The supposed marks of strangulation upon her neck were very faint and had probably been caused by her stiff velvet collar.

Coroner Baxter dismissed Bond's evidence on the grounds that Bond had seen the body much later than the other medical gentlemen. As a result, with only Dr. Brownfield's evidence to rely on, the jury returned a verdict of "Murder by some person or persons unknown."

Suggestions for further reading:

Begg, Paul, Martin Fido, and Keith Skinner. *The Jack the Ripper A–Z*. Headline, 1996.

Jakubowski, Maxim, and Nathan Braund. *The Mammoth Book of Jack the Ripper*. Robinson Publishing, 1999.

PRO Files MEPO 3/140 and MEPO 3/143. Available on microfilm at the Public Record Office, Kew.

Elizabeth Jackson

Ca. Tuesday, 4 June 1889

Details of parts of a body found in the river Thames suggest that they were discovered between 31 May and 25 June 1889. However, the death certificates give the dates as running from 4 to 10 June that year.

The body parts were wrapped in clothing, and some of these items bore a name tape that read "L. E. Fisher." However, the body parts were identified by means of old scars as belonging to Elizabeth Jackson, a prostitute who lived in Sloan Square. The crime was never seriously considered to be a Ripper murder.

Suggestions for further reading:

Begg, Paul, Martin Fido, and Keith Skinner. *The Jack the Ripper A–Z*. Headline, 1996.

Alice McKenzie

Wednesday, 17 July 1889

Police Sergeant Edward Badham had already had firsthand experience of Jack the Ripper's handiwork, being the officer who had taken Annie Chapman's body to the mortuary in September 1888. Now, on the night of 16–17 July almost a year later, he was busily checking on the beat officers under his control.

At 12:48 A.M. on 17 July Sergeant Badham encountered Constable Walter Andrews in Castle Alley, on the corner of Old Castle Street, close to the Three Crowns public house. The two officers exchanged a few words, with Badham assuring himself that all was well, and then parted. Sergeant Badham then walked up Castle Alley toward Wentworth Street while Constable Andrews walked in the opposite direction, down Castle Alley toward Whitechapel High Street. The narrow alleyway was obstructed by a few tradesmen's carts and barrows, so it wasn't until Andrews was almost upon two of those carts that he saw the body of a woman lying between them. Her throat had been cut, and blood still flowed from the wound. Her skirts had been turned up, exposing her abdomen, which appeared to have been

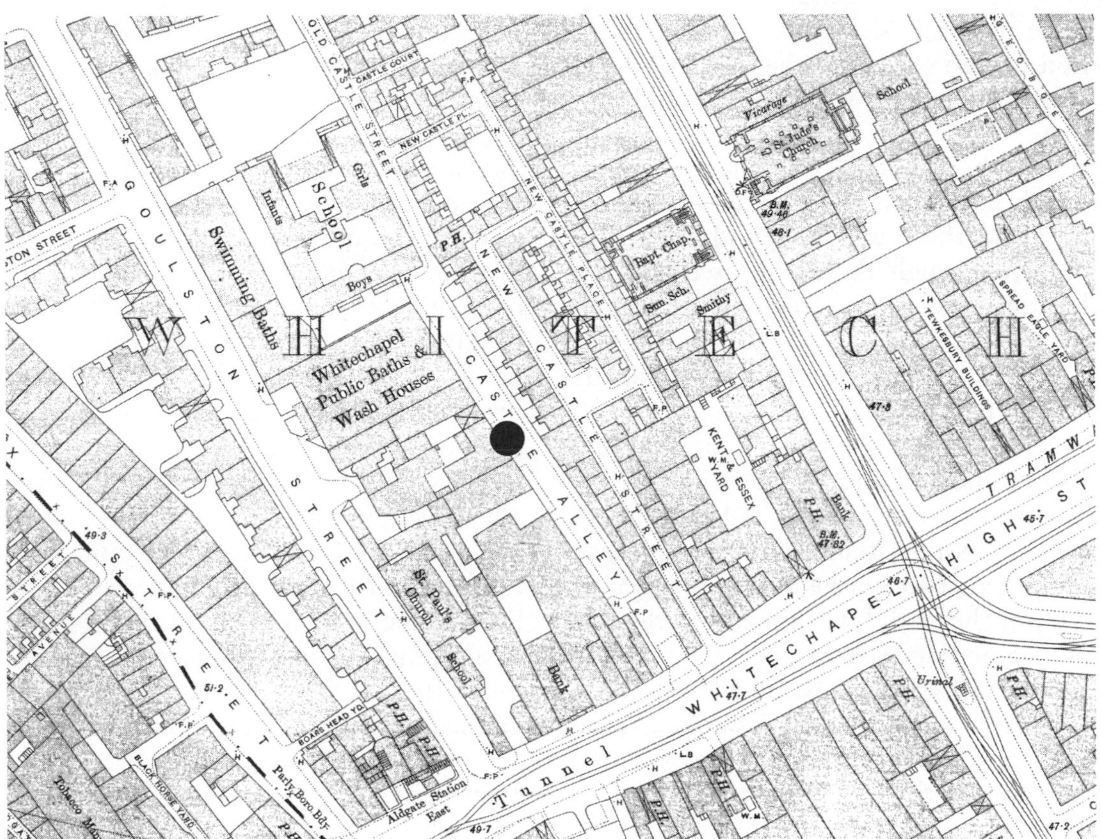

The spot where Alice McKenzie was murdered early on 17 July 1889

mutilated, and Andrews had no doubt that he had found yet another Ripper victim. He bent down and tentatively touched the woman's flesh. She was still quite warm, which indicated that the attack must have taken place very recently, possibly within the last minute or so. Perhaps the killer was still around.

At that moment Andrews heard footsteps farther up the alley in Old Castle Street. Ignoring standing orders that any officer finding a body should remain with it, Andrews gave chase, blowing his whistle to obtain assistance, and soon found a man carrying a dinner plate and heading toward Wentworth Street. Andrews stopped the man, who explained that he was Isaac Lewis Jacob of 12 New Castle Place and that he was on his way to McCarthy's chandler's shop to buy himself some supper. Quite correctly, Andrews insisted that Jacobs come back to the body with him until he could be questioned.

Andrews's whistle had been heard by Sergeant Badham, who now ran back down Old Castle Street to find Andrews in Castle Alley, shouting, "Come on quick!" Continuing down Castle Alley, Badham saw the woman lying on the pavement near the two carts. She was on her back, and there was a good deal of blood under her head in the footway. Giving instructions to Andrews not to leave the body, the sergeant went to find other constables and in due course despatched Constable George Neve to search the area while Constable Joseph Allen was sent to fetch the doctor and the duty inspector from Commercial Street Police Station.

Dr. George Bagster Phillips arrived at Castle Alley at 1:10 A.M., by which time it was raining "sharply," according to his notes. He noted that the woman's head was turned sharply to the right and that there was an incised wound in the left side of her neck. The woman's clothing had been turned up to expose her genitals, and there was a wound in the abdomen, though there appeared to have been no attempt at disemboweling, as in the previous cases.

Detective Inspector Edmund Reid arrived on the scene soon afterward and ordered men to make inquiries at the lodging houses and coffee houses in the district to see if anyone had been in recently, possibly stained with blood. Once the doctor had finished his initial examination, the body was lifted onto the police ambulance for removal to the Whitechapel mortuary, and it was then that Reid noticed a clay smoking pipe and a bronze farthing that had lain beneath the body.

No time was wasted in opening the inquest on the dead woman, who had rapidly been identified as Alice McKenzie. The proceedings began on 17 July, the same day the body had been found, before Wynne Edwin Baxter at the Working Lad's Institute on Whitechapel Road.

The first witness was John McCormack, also known as John Bryant, who had been living with Alice for the past six or seven years, most recently at a common lodging house at 52 Gun Street. He explained that he had come home from work at about 4 P.M. on 16 July and had given Alice 1 shilling and eightpence before going to bed to get some sleep. The eightpence had been to pay for their bed for the night, and the shilling was for Alice to buy some supplies.

Sometime between 10 and 11 P.M., McCormack had awakened and gone down to check whether Alice had paid for their bed. He was told that she had gone out without paying, but, fortunately, the lodging-house keeper had told him that he could be trusted for the money, so he had gone back to bed, finally rising at 5:45 A.M. on the 17th. McCormack admitted that he and Alice had argued on that last evening, which was perhaps why she had neglected to pay the eightpence to the lodging-house keeper. The only other information he could give was that he believed Alice had originally come from Peterborough, but he could not say whether she had ever been married or had any children.

The second witness was Elizabeth Ryder, who was also known as Betsy. She was the wife of the lodging-house keeper at 52 Gun Street and confirmed that John McCormack and Alice had lived at the house on and off for the past 12 months. She had last seen Alice when the other woman walked from the kitchen of the lodging house into the street at about 8:30 P.M. the night of the 16th. Later, around 11 P.M. or so, John McCormack had come down to ask whether Alice had paid the bed money, and Elizabeth had told him "No." Finally, Elizabeth confirmed that when they were not staying with her, McCormack and Alice usually stayed at Crossingham's lodging house.

Constable Neve was then called to prove that Alice McKenzie had occasionally sold herself as a prostitute. Though others had denied that Alice earned any money by this method, Neve indicated that the police believed that she had and said he had seen her talking to men several times in Gun Street, Brick Lane, and Dorset Street.

The final witness on this first day was Sarah Smith, the manager of the Whitechapel Baths and Washhouses. The bath house was on Goulston Street but backed on to Castle Alley, and Sarah's room was at the back, overlooking the spot where the body was found. She had gone to bed between 12:15 and 12:30 A.M. on the morning of 17 July and had then sat reading in bed for some time. Though her windows were closed, she was certain that she would have heard any cry for help from Alice. In the event, Sarah heard nothing until the policeman blew his whistle.

Before discussing the proceedings of the second day of the inquest, it is important to clear up the timetable and geography of this attack. Castle Alley ran from Whitechapel High Street to its junction with Old Castle Street. It was about 135 yards long, and there were three lamps in the alley itself. The first was on the left, about 23 yards from Whitechapel High Street. The second, which was close to where Alice McKenzie's body was found, was also on the left but another 50 yards along the alley. The final lamp was at the right-angled bend where the alley joined Old Castle Street, opposite the Three Crowns public house, which backed onto the alley but fronted onto New Castle Street. Finally, there was a fourth lamp in New Castle Street, another 58 yards toward Wentworth Street.

At 12:15 A.M. on the 17th, Constable Allen had briefly stopped under the lamp where Alice's body would later be found and enjoyed a brief bite of supper before continuing on his beat. Five minutes afterward, at 12:20 A.M., Constable Andrews entered Castle Alley from Whitechapel High Street on his regular beat. He was in the alley until about 12:23 A.M. and saw nothing suspicious. During his time there he saw Myer Jacobs, the landlord of the Three Crowns, shutting his establishment for the night.

Andrews's beat took him along Old Castle Street into Wentworth Street and then right toward Commercial Street. He then turned down Goulston Street, then Middlesex Street, then went back along Wentworth Street and back down Old Castle Street, so it was 12:48 A.M. when he next walked down Castle Alley and found the body. The killer, whoever he was, may have heard the constable's approach down Old Castle Street and made good his escape down Castle Alley and out into Whitechapel High Street.

The second day of the inquest was 19 July. After Inspector Reid had given details of finding the farthing and clay pipe and of the efforts his men had made to trace the miscreant, Dr. Phillips was called to give medical evidence. As with the hearing on Mary Kelly, few details were given beyond the statement that the immediate cause of death was blood loss due to the left carotid artery being severed. Phillips's written report, however, gives more detail. Two jagged cuts in the throat, each 4 inches long, began on the left side behind the sterno mastoid muscle and finished above the larynx. The deeper cut had divided the left carotid artery and penetrated the vertebrae, but the larynx and windpipe were undamaged, meaning Alice could still have called out. These wounds were not typical of the Ripper, consisting, apparently, of stabs into the throat with the knife then being pulled forward and out.

There was a single long cut on the abdomen that began 7 inches below the right nipple and was deepest where it began. It was 7 inches long and was not quite straight, inclining first inward and then outward. On the right side of the abdomen were seven scratches that merely divided the skin, and there were seven similar scratches below the large cut and between it and the genitals. One of those cuts, on the mons veneris, was distinctly deeper than the others.

Bruises high on the chest indicated that the killer had held Alice down with one hand while he inflicted wounds upon her with the other. Dr. Phillips did not believe that the murder was the handiwork of the Whitechapel killer, but although he was not called to give evidence at the inquest, Dr. Bond had also examined the body, and he disagreed, saying

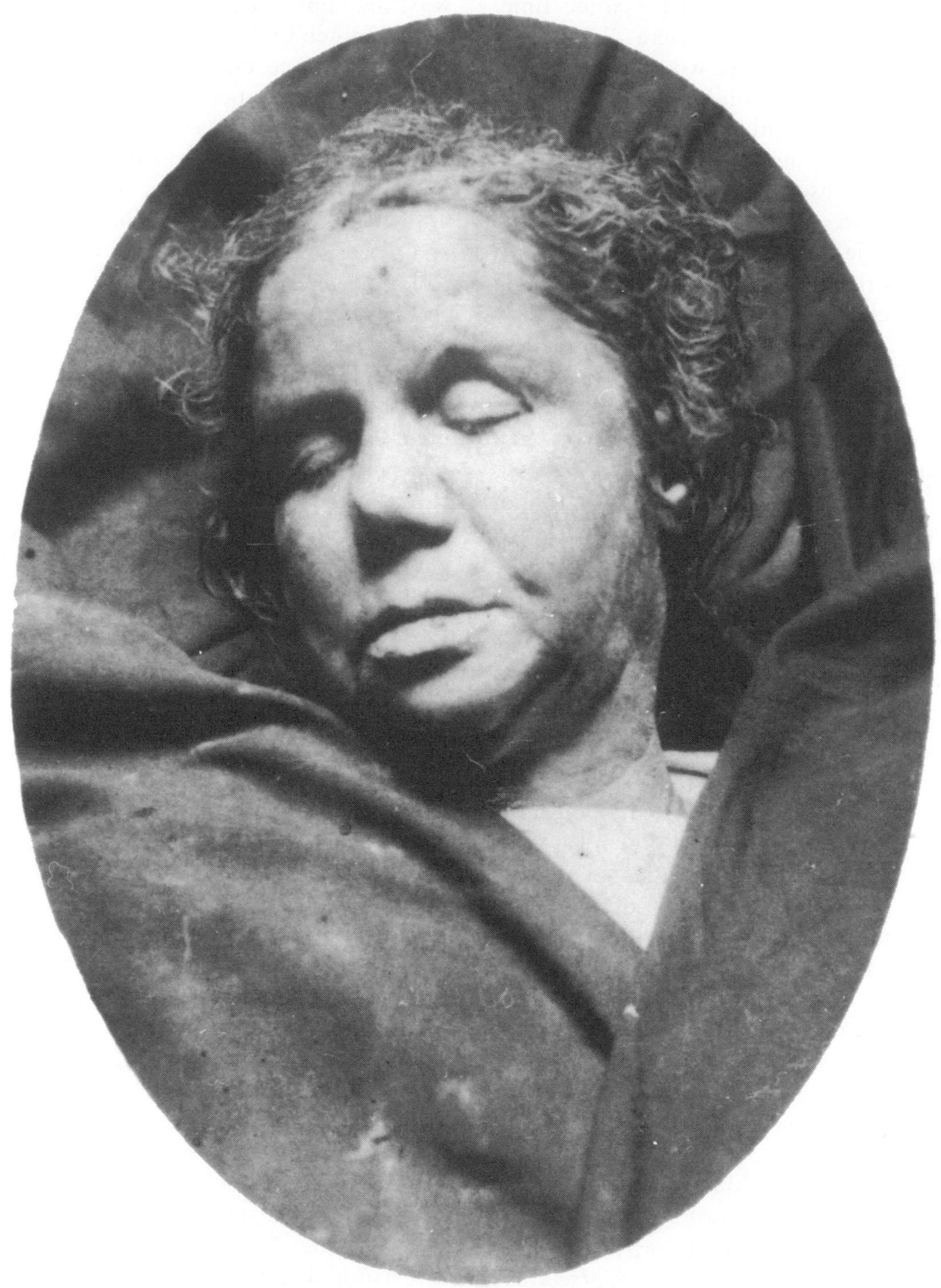

Alice McKenzie lying in the mortuary. Her body was found in Castle Alley on the morning of 17 July 1889. She had been stabbed in the throat, and there were minor mutilations upon her abdomen. She was most likely Jack the Ripper's seventh and final victim. (Public Record Office, London)

that he clearly saw the Ripper's hand in this crime.

After Phillips had given his testimony, a prostitute named Margaret Cheeks was called. She too lodged at 52 Gun Street and had been missing on the night Alice McKenzie was murdered. At first it was believed that Margaret too had been killed and that this night might prove to be another double event like the killings of Elizabeth Stride and Catherine Eddowes, but Margaret had been staying with her sister and was appearing simply to prove that she was still alive. She contributed nothing else to the inquest.

The final witness was Margaret Franklin, who had been a friend of Alice. She had known Alice for 14 or 15 years and had been sitting on the step of a barber's shop at the Brick Lane end of Flower and Dean Street, along with Catherine Hughes and Sarah Mahoney, at 11:40 P.M. on 16 July. Alice passed them, heading toward Whitechapel and Margaret asked her how she was getting on. Alice replied, "All right. I can't stop now," and then walked on. She did not appear to have been drinking.

The inquest was adjourned once more, until 14 August, when the usual verdict was returned. Little else could be discovered beyond the fact that Alice had gone drinking that night with a blind boy named George Dixon. They had gone to a pub near the Cambridge Music Hall at about 7:10 P.M., and during the evening George had heard Alice asking someone to buy her a drink. The man had replied, "Yes," and a few minutes afterward Alice had escorted George back to the lodging house at 52 Gun Street, left him there, and gone back out alone.

There was also an arrest that at first looked very promising. A man named William Wallace Brodie gave himself up to the police, admitted to being the Whitechapel killer, and said that his latest crime, the murder of Alice McKenzie, bothered him. It was soon shown that Brodie, who is discussed further in the "Suspects" section, could not have been the killer and was almost certainly insane.

Suggestions for further reading:

Begg, Paul, Martin Fido, and Keith Skinner. *The Jack the Ripper A–Z*. Headline, 1996.
Jakubowski, Maxim, and Nathan Braund. *The Mammoth Book of Jack the Ripper*. Robinson Publishing, 1999.
PRO Files MEPO 3/140. Available on microfilm at the Public Record Office, Kew.
Sugden, Philip. *The Complete History of Jack the Ripper*. Robinson Publishing, 1994.

The Pinchin Street Torso

Ca. Sunday, 8 September 1889

The man who walked into the London offices of the *New York Herald* had an all too familiar tale to tell—Jack the Ripper had struck again!

Giving his name as John Cleary and his address as 21 White Horse Yard, the man said a body had been found by a policeman at about 11:20 P.M. on Saturday, 7 September, in Back Church Lane, which wasn't far from the site of one of the previous atrocities, the murder of Elizabeth Stride in Berner Street. Cleary had received this information from the most impeccable of sources, a police inspector whom he knew very well and whom he had met by accident in Whitechapel High Street.

Almost immediately two reporters were detailed to go to the area and find out precisely what had happened. They tried, without success, to inveigle Mr. Cleary into going with them, but he declined. On the way down the staircase from the *Herald* offices, he changed his story slightly, saying his informant wasn't a serving policeman but an ex-officer.

In due course the two reporters arrived at Back Church Lane but found no signs of police activity. When they did finally find an inspector and a constable, they asked for further details of the latest terrible Ripper murder but were met with blank stares. There had been no murder in Back Church Lane or anywhere else. It seemed that they had been the victims of a hoax.

Nothing more would have been thought about this incident but for a find made by Constable William Pennett a couple of days later. Constable Pennett was on his beat, and at about 5 A.M. on Tuesday, 10 September, he checked the railway arches in Pinchin Street, which was just off Back Church Lane. All the arches were boarded off and used as storage areas except one, the first arch, closest to Back Church Lane. There was nothing suspicious to attract Pennett's attention, and he continued on his beat.

Half an hour later, at 5:30 A.M., something inside that first arch caught the light from Constable Pennett's lantern, and he decided to take a closer look. To his horror he found the almost naked body of a woman lying face downward, though that description was a misnomer because her head, along with her legs, had been removed. She was lying 18 feet from the main roadway and about 1 foot from the right wall of the arch. Her right arm was doubled beneath her body, and her left lay by her side. She wore only a torn chemise, which was positioned over her neck and right shoulder.

Senior officers were called and soon determined that the woman had not been murdered where she was found. There was almost no blood in the archway and the body had started to decompose, indicating that she had been dead for some time when she was dumped. In fact, the eventual medical opinion was that she had been dead for 36 hours or more, putting the most probable date of her death at sometime on Sunday, 8 September. It did not escape police officers such as James Monro, commissioner of the Metropolitan Police, that the date was the anniversary of Annie Chapman's death. Had Jack the Ripper killed again? The body was moved to the mortuary at St. George's-in-the-East so a postmortem could be performed.

In a report dated 11 September, Monro was already speculating that this killing was not another Ripper crime. He gave five reasons. First, there was nothing to indicate that death had been caused by the cutting of the throat, as in the previous crimes attributed to the Ripper. The torso had not been drained of blood, as would have been the case if the victim had bled to death from such a wound.

Second, there was no mutilation beyond the dismemberment itself. It was true that in at least two previous cases, those of Chapman and Kelly, the killer had made an attempt to remove the head, but this act had been combined with other bodily mutilations.

Third, there was no evisceration. In truth, this was only partly so. The torso did show a long gash on the front, extending downward to the genital region, but there had been no removal of the intestines.

Fourth, there had been no removal of any internal organs such as the heart, kidneys, or uterus; and finally, the murder had not been committed in the street, as had all the others except of course the murder of Mary Jane Kelly.

Once the story of the Pinchin Street Torso broke in the newspapers, the *New York Herald* gave the police information about its mysterious visitor, John Cleary. It seemed he had known about the murder at least a day before it took place and three full days before the body was found. Surely he was either the killer or knew who was, and it became a matter of urgency to trace him.

Chief Inspector Swanson visited the *Herald* offices and spoke to the night editor, Mr. Cowen, and one of the reporters, Mr. Fletcher, but they could

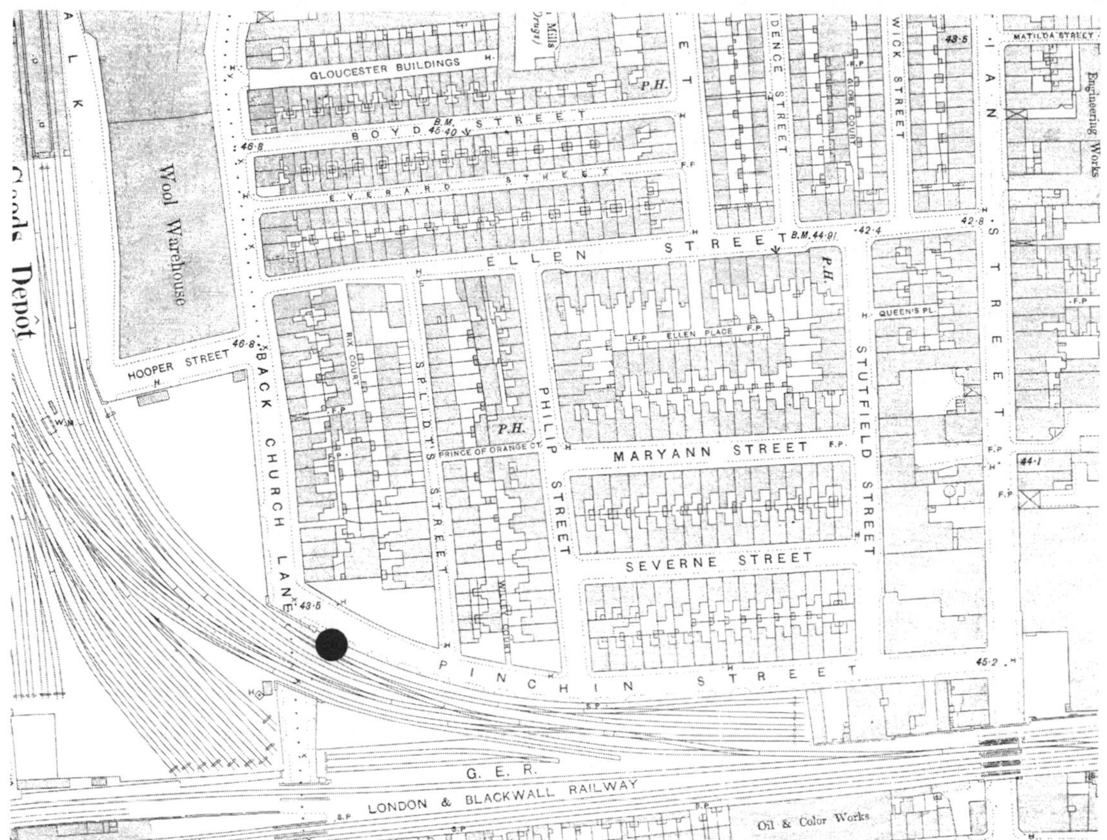

The railway arch where the Pinchin Street Torso was found. The body lay just inside the first arch and was clearly visible from the street.

throw no more light on Cleary. A visit to 21 White Horse Yard was then made, but Mr. Yates, the man in charge there, said he had never had a guest named Cleary. There had been a John Leary who had lived there until three weeks ago, when he was evicted for rent arrears. In due course John Leary was traced to his new address, but it became clear that he wasn't the man who had visited the offices of the *Herald*.

Reports on the attempts to find Cleary finally brought a news vendor, John Arnold, to surrender himself to the police. He explained that he had given the story to the *Herald* in good faith. He told the police that on the night of Saturday, 7 September, he had been in the King Lud public house and, after he left, was walking up Fleet Street when a man in uniform said, "Hurry up with your papers, another horrible murder." When he asked where the killing had taken place, the man replied, "In Back Church Lane."

According to Arnold, the man who had given him this information wore a black uniform with a black cord shoulder strap and lightish-colored buttons. He wore a cheese-cutter cap and was aged 35 or 36. His height was 5 feet 6 or 7 inches, and he had a fair complexion and a fair mustache. He was carrying a brown paper parcel 6 to 8 inches long. Attempts were made to trace this man, but they all led to nothing.

The postmortem on the torso was carried out on 11 September. The report included the information, among other factors, that the head had been cut off at the lower part of the neck, and the thighs had been separated at the hip joints. The trunk was plump and well formed, with full breasts, fair skin, and dark brown hair on the pubes and axilla. The arms were well shaped and the hands small with well-kept nails. There was a single incision in the front that had cut through the skin and muscles of the abdomen. There were also a number of small bruises on the forearms and arms, varying in size from a sixpenny to a shilling. The left wrist had two cuts, one of which just grazed the skin, the other having cut through it.

It had taken the killer two incisions to remove the head. The first began at the spinal column and had been carried around the neck from left to right, ending in front on the right side. The second incision began on the right side in front and carried around to the back, joining the first cut but leaving a small tongue of skin. The spinal column had been divided at the junction of the fifth and sixth cervical vertebrae.

The thighs had each been separated by two or three sweeping circular cuts beginning just below the hip bone and carried downward and inward around the buttocks. It was calculated that the woman would have been about 5 feet 3 inches tall, was certainly aged more than 25 but probably nearer to 35, and had borne no children, though she was not a virgin. The only other evidence of import was that a very sharp knife had been used to make all the cuts, which had been inflicted after death, and they had all been made from right to left except those separating the right thigh.

Identifying the body proved to be impossible. There were suggestions that it might be Lydia Hart, who lived in Ellen Street and had been missing for some days, but according to the *New York Herald,* Hart was found alive and well in the local infirmary. Other suggestions were made as to who the torso might be, but no firm identification was ever made.

Suggestions for further reading:

Begg, Paul, Martin Fido, and Keith Skinner. *The Jack the Ripper A–Z.* Headline, 1996.

PRO Files MEPO 3/140. Available on microfilm at the Public Record Office, Kew.

Frances Coles

Friday, 13 February 1891

Ernest Thompson had not been a police officer for very long, having just joined the force at the end of 1890. Now, on the night of 12 February 1891, he was on beat duty for the first time. As he began to trudge the streets he could have had no inkling that his was to be a hard baptism.

At 2:15 A.M. on the 13th Constable Thompson was patrolling along Chamber Street and was about to enter Swallow Gardens when he heard footsteps moving away from him, heading in the direction of Royal Mint Street. He thought nothing of this sound until he turned into Swallow Gardens and saw, lying on her back, a woman who had obviously been attacked. Shining his lantern on the prostrate form, Thompson saw to his horror that the woman's throat had been cut and blood was still issuing from the wound. Even worse perhaps was the fact that as he stared down at this terrible scene, drawing his whistle to summon assistance, one of the woman's eyes flickered open.

Thompson's whistle brought two brother officers Constable Hyde and Constable Hinton, to his aid. While Thompson stayed with the dying woman, Hyde ran to fetch Dr. Oxley and Hinton dashed to the police station in Leman Street to alert the inspector and get more assistance.

Dr. Oxley pronounced the woman dead, but Dr. George Bagster Phillips later examined her as well. He noted that the throat wound seemed to have been caused by a sawing action, the blade being drawn across from left to right,

The narrow thoroughfare where Frances Coles was attacked. Her attacker ran southward, underneath the railway arches, thus evading capture.

then from right to left, and once more from left to right. The woman's clothing had not been disturbed, and there were no other injuries or mutilations beyond an injury to the back of the head, indicating that the victim must have been thrown down forcibly.

The body was moved to the Whitechapel Mortuary, and a careful search of the immediate area was made, but nothing of interest was found except for a two-shilling piece, wrapped in two pieces of old newspaper and hidden in the space behind a water pipe and some brickwork. This coin was discovered about 18 yards from where the body had lain.

Almost immediately there was a false alarm. A man named William Friday, known to all his friends as Jumbo, came forward to explain that he worked at the Great Northern Railway Depot in Royal Mint Street and had passed down that thoroughfare at about 1:45 A.M. on the 13th. He had noticed a man and a woman standing in a doorway and noted that the woman wore a black hat. He was shown the hat worn by the dead woman and positively identified it as the one he had seen. This meant that the man seen with the woman was very probably her killer, as she must have been attacked within half an hour of Friday's sighting. Two brothers named Knapton, who also worked at the depot, said that they had passed down Royal Mint Street just before Jumbo and had also seen the couple. Between these three witnesses a description of the wanted man was drawn up.

Unfortunately, this evidence all led to nothing. Kate McCarthy lived at 42

Royal Mint Street, and her beau was Thomas Fowles, who lived not far away in Back Church Lane. Fowles worked as a doorman at a club on Commercial Street, and on the night of the 12th McCarthy had gone to see him there sometime between 7:30 and 8 P.M. The club closed at midnight, but it was perhaps 12:30 A.M. on the 13th by the time McCarthy and Fowles left and began to walk home together. They arrived at Kate's house at about 1:15 A.M. and stood on her doorstep talking for half an hour or so. They had seen the Knaptons and Jumbo, all of whom they knew quite well, pass by on their way to work and had exchanged "Good-nights" with them. The promising lead of the man seen with the dead woman turned out to be nothing of the kind. This incident also illustrates how easily witnesses could provide false and misleading information.

The woman found in Swallow Gardens had actually been in possession of two hats. The black one she was wearing appeared to be brand new, but she also had an older hat pinned to her dress. News of this detail brought forward witnesses who tentatively identified the body as that of Frances Coles, and this identification was confirmed by James William Coles of the Bermondsey Workhouse, who said the body was that of his daughter, and by Mary Ann Coles, who confirmed that Frances was her sister.

The inquest on Frances Coles opened on 15 February before Wynne Edwin Baxter at the Working Lad's Institute. It was adjourned several times, with further hearings taking place on 16, 20, 23, and 27 February, during which a total of 55 witnesses were heard. One of those was a man suspected not only of being the murderer of Frances Coles but of being Jack the Ripper himself.

James Thomas Sadler was a ship's fireman who had certainly spent most of the two days before Frances died in her company. They had argued and had both drunk heavily during the time they were together. However, in due course it was shown that Sadler's story of his movements was true and that it was highly unlikely that he was the man responsible for taking France Coles's life. He was able to prove that he had been at sea on the S.S. *Winestead* when four of the supposed Ripper victims, Nichols, Chapman, Stride, and Eddowes, had been killed. As a result, he was discharged on 3 March, to loud cheers from his supporters. His story is examined more carefully in the "Suspects" section of this book.

Though some believed that the Ripper had reappeared on the streets of London, the idea did not hold sway for long, and once again Dr. Phillips gave the opinion that this murder was not a Ripper crime. What is certain is that no further crimes in the area were ever attributed to Jack the Ripper.

Suggestions for further reading:

Begg, Paul, Martin Fido, and Keith Skinner. *The Jack the Ripper A–Z*. Headline, 1996.

Jakubowski, Maxim, and Nathan Braund. *The Mammoth Book of Jack the Ripper.* Robinson Publishing, 1999.

PRO Files MEPO 3/140. Available on microfilm at the Public Record Office, Kew.

Sugden, Philip. *The Complete History of Jack the Ripper.* Robinson Publishing, 1994.

Summary

Let me now consider the evidence for each of the names in this section being a victim of Jack the Ripper. We can begin by immediately discounting Fairy Fay, who never existed. This subtraction leaves the following:

Annie Millwood—Attacked Saturday, 25 February 1888

Perhaps the most significant factors in this case are that the attack took place on a weekend, close to the epicenter of the Ripper's territory, and involved an attack by a

Frances Coles (said by some to be the most attractive of the victims) was murdered in Swallow Gardens on 13 February 1891 and was the last woman ever considered to be a possible Ripper victim. She may have been killed by Thomas Sadler, though it is also possible that she met her death at someone else's hand. (Public Record Office, London)

single stranger and knife wounds to the lower torso and genital region. As a result, I contend that Annie Millwood was probably the first victim of the Ripper.

***Ada Wilson*—Attacked at 12:30 A.M. Wednesday, 28 March 1888**

Ada sustained throat wounds and the description of her assailant bore a resemblance to later sightings of a man believed to be the Ripper, but there are strong grounds for discounting Ada as a possible early victim.

To begin with, the location of the attack is far to the east of what appears to have been the Ripper's hunting ground. Burdett Road isn't that far from Buck's Row, but the inclusion of this location would put the epicenter of the attacks much farther to the east. Furthermore, the motive in this case appears to have been purely robbery, and the assailant knocked on the front door—hardly Jack's style.

There is a remote possibility that this was an early attack by the man who would later inspire terror in the East End, but the balance of probability is that this crime had nothing to do with Jack the Ripper.

***Emma Elizabeth Smith*—Attacked at ca. 1:30 A.M. Tuesday, 3 April 1888**

Once again the primary motive for this attack seems to have been robbery, but the strongest reason for discounting this event as a Ripper crime is the fact that, according to Emma herself, three men were involved. In addition, Emma was raped, and a blunt instrument, rather than a knife, was used. It is possible that the trauma of the attack caused some confusion in Emma's mind, but it is highly unlikely that this assault involved the Ripper.

***Martha Tabram*—Attacked at ca. 2:30 A.M. Tuesday, 7 August 1888**

I have referred to the frenzy of the attack upon Martha and the *Illustrated Police News* report that there were indications that she was throttled. I do not believe that the soldier she went with was her killer and think that the probability is that some other man whom Martha met later was to claim her life.

I do not believe that the fact that the throat was not cut and there were no mutilations indicates that Jack the Ripper was not involved. It is much more likely that such a maniacal attack so close to the epicenter of the murders is suggestive of an early attack by a killer who later perfected a more reliable technique for subduing his victims. I contend that Martha Tabram was the first fatality at the hands of the Ripper. This conclusion, if accepted, increases the likelihood that an even earlier attack, the one upon Annie Millwood, *may* also have been Jack's handiwork.

***Mary Ann Nichols*—Attacked at ca. 3:35 A.M. Friday, 31 August 1888**

No authors argue that Mary Ann was not a victim of the serial killer. Most refer to her as the canonical first victim, and there can be little doubt that she was murdered by the man later given the sobriquet Jack the Ripper by the author of a letter and postcard sent to the Central News Agency.

***Annie Chapman*—Attacked at ca. 5:30 A.M. Saturday, 8 September 1888**

There is little argument that Annie Chapman was one of the Ripper's victims.

***Susan Ward*—Attacked ca. Saturday, 15 September 1888**

Although reports on this particular attack are sketchy, the story does have three elements that might suggest it was a Ripper crime. First, a knife was used; second, the attack was in the Commercial Road area; and third, it took place on a weekend, which seems to fit the killer's pattern.

Countering this evidence is the fact that the victim had time to scream and frighten her assailant away, and the fact that a knife was used at the commencement of the attack, with no evidence of strangulation preceding it, seems to indicate that this assault was not a Ripper crime.

***Elizabeth Stride*—Attacked at ca. 12:58 A.M. Sunday, 30 September 1888**

What are we to make of all the various sightings in Berner Street on the night of 29–30 September? A timetable may be drawn up according to the statements made and the witnesses' own calculations. It reads as follows:

29 September

- 11:30 P.M.—William Marshall goes to stand at his front door, 64 Berner Street.
- 11:45 P.M.—Morris Eagle leaves the club with his young lady.
- William Marshall sees a man and a woman not far from his house. They later walk off toward the club.
- Matthew Packer sells grapes to a man and woman.
- 12 P.M.—Marshall goes back inside.

30 September

- 12:30 A.M.—Packer closes his shop.
- Constable Smith walks down Berner Street, sees a man and woman.
- William West leaves the club by the side entrance to put some literature in the printing office.
- Fanny Mortimer stands at her door, 36 Berner Street.
- West and two companions leave the club by the street door.
- Joseph Lave goes into Berner Street from the club to get some fresh air. He soon goes into Dutfield's Yard.
- 12:35 A.M.—Eagle returns to the club by the side entrance.
- 12:40 A.M.—Lave goes back into the club.
- 12:44 A.M.—Earliest possible time of the attack upon Elizabeth.
- 12:45 A.M.—Israel Schwartz encounters the man who calls him Lipski.
- 12:45 A.M.—James Brown sees a man and woman near the school.
- 12:54 A.M.—Latest possible time of the attack upon Elizabeth.
- 1 A.M.—Mortimer goes indoors.
- Constable Smith passes the end of Berner Street in Commercial Road.
- Louis Diemschutz finds the body.
- Constable Lamb in Commercial Road hears of the murder.
- Constable Smith arrives at the scene.
- 1:13 A.M.—Edward Johnston arrives in Dutfield's Yard.
- Constable Smith goes to get the police ambulance.
- 1:16 A.M.—Dr. Blackwell arrives.

This timetable is obviously inconsistent. For instance, Mortimer saw nothing of Schwartz's encounter with the quarreling couple at the entrance to the yard, and Smith's own timing puts him in two places at the same time. Only two people used timepieces to measure their arrival at the scene: Dr. Blackwell consulted his watch when he arrived in Dutfield's Yard, and Louis Diemschutz timed his arrival by a tobacconist's clock in Commercial Road. We must assume, therefore, that Blackwell's timing is exact and Diemschutz's out by not more than a minute. A more accurate timetable for the hours from 12:20 to 1:20 A.M. would thus be:

- 12:30 A.M.—Matthew Packer closes his shop.

William West leaves the club by the side entrance to put some literature in the printing office.
Joseph Lave leaves the club and goes into Berner Street.
12:32 A.M.—West and two companions leave the club by the street door.
12:34 A.M.—Morris Eagle returns to the club by the side entrance.
12:35 A.M.—Lave returns to the club.
Constable Smith walks down Berner Street and sees a man and a woman.
12:36 A.M.—Fanny Mortimer stands at her front door.
12:42 A.M.—Mortimer goes back inside.
12:43 A.M.—James Brown sees a man and a woman near the school.
12:44 A.M.—Earliest possible time of the attack upon Elizabeth, according to the medical evidence.
12:47 A.M.—Israel Schwartz encounters the man who calls him Lipski
12:54 A.M.—Latest possible time of the attack upon Elizabeth, according to the medical evidence.
12:56 A.M.—Constable Smith passes the end of Berner Street.
1 A.M.—Louis Diemschutz finds the body.
1:03 A.M.—Edward Spooner arrives at Dutfield's Yard.
1:05 A.M.—Constable Lamb in Commercial Road hears of the murder.
1:08 A.M.—Constable Smith arrives at the scene.
1:13 A.M.—Edward Johnston arrives in Dutfield's Yard.
Smith goes to get the police ambulance.
1:16 A.M.—Dr. Blackwell arrives.

Though many of these times are approximate, they do make sense of the various statements and explain why witnesses do not refer to seeing each other in their evidence.

An important point was made by Edward Spooner in his evidence. We know that he arrived at the murder scene before Constable Lamb, so he must have been in Dutfield's Yard by, say, 1:04 A.M. Spooner reported that blood still flowed from the wound in the throat, which indicated that Elizabeth Stride's heart was still pumping, albeit very weakly. The medical opinion was that it took her about a minute and a half to bleed to death, indicating that she had been attacked just a few minutes before.

This point shows that the doctors were slightly out in estimating the time of death and that Elizabeth had actually been attacked at about 12:58 or 12:59 A.M., probably at the very moment that Diemschutz turned his cart into Berner Street. This conclusion in turn leads us to an interesting dichotomy and raises further points of argument. First, if the man who called out "Lipski" to Israel Schwartz were the killer, then he stayed with Elizabeth for about 12 minutes before attacking her. This theory is of course possible, but improbable. The murders of Annie Chapman and Catherine Eddowes showed that the killer worked quickly, and a 12-minute wait was hardly his style. Second, many authors have used the fact that Schwartz's description is similar to that given by Lawende in the murder of Catherine Eddowes to show that the crimes were related. If we accept this argument, then we also have to accept that Jack the Ripper spent a minimum of 12 minutes in Berner Street with a woman he had already assaulted by throwing her to the ground.

The only other similarity between the murder of Elizabeth Stride and that of the other Ripper victims is that the throat was cut from left to right while the victim was lying on the ground. But let us return to the evidence of the timetable. We can argue that the killer was probably disturbed by Diemschutz, but even if he was, he would still have had about one full minute in which to inflict whatever injuries he wished. He would not have passed into the yard once Diemschutz's cart had actually turned into Berner Street. Surely it is not tenable to state that even if he and Elizabeth had passed into the yard just as Diemschutz's cart approached his turn, the killer would not have had time to inflict further injuries. At the very least, Elizabeth's clothing would have been disturbed as he prepared to mutilate her.

In about five minutes, or probably less, Jack the Ripper had time to throttle Catherine Eddowes, slash her throat, lift her clothing, mutilate her body, remove internal organs, and mutilate her face. Are we expected to believe that this killer, with admittedly only about a minute with his previous victim, succeeded only in dragging her to the floor by her scarf and then cutting her throat once?

It is possible that Elizabeth Stride was murdered by Jack the Ripper, but my opinion is that it is equally likely that she was not.

Catherine Eddowes—Attacked at ca. 1:38 A.M. Sunday, 30 September 1888

There can be little doubt that Catherine Eddowes was butchered by Jack the Ripper.

The Whitehall Mystery—Attacked ca. Wednesday, 3 October 1888

This limbless, headless torso was found in the Thames, far from Jack's usual hunting ground. The corpse bore none of the abdominal mutilations characteristic of the canonical murders and was only ever linked to the other murders by the gentlemen of the press. The conclusion is that the Whitehall Mystery had nothing to do with the Whitechapel Mystery.

Mary Jane Kelly—Attacked at ca. 4 A.M. Friday, 9 November 1888

Though Mary Jane Kelly is accepted by most authors as the final canonical victim, others suggest that she was the victim of a copycat killer. There are a several reasons for this disagreement, but the main ones are: that she was killed after a gap of a month, and therefore Eddowes should rightly be the final victim; that at about 25 she was much younger than the other victims; and that she was the only one killed indoors.

I find it difficult to believe that a copycat could have been responsible for Mary Kelly's death. The sheer savagery of the killer surely indicates that she died at the hand of someone who was growing in confidence and arrogance, and there is no significance in any of the factors that separate Mary from the other victims. The only true factor is that for the first time Jack had time to carry out his fantasies undisturbed by policemen on the beat or passing pedestrians and gave full vent to his impulses.

Annie Farmer—Attacked Tuesday, 20 November 1888

There can be little doubt that Annie Farmer inflicted wounds upon her own throat in an attempt to rob her client of a few coins. She was certainly not attacked by Jack the Ripper, as the weapon used was described as a blunt blade.

Rose Mylett—Attacked at ca. 4 A.M. Thursday, 20 December 1888

Though Rose's name was added to the list of Ripper victims at Scotland Yard, there were no mutilations and no knife wounds whatsoever. Jack the Ripper may well have used strangulation to subdue his victims, but after the carnage of Miller's Court it is unlikely that this alone would have satisfied him. We must also remember that Rose was in the company of two sailors for most of the evening and that Poplar is far to the east of Jack's usual territory. These factors lead to the conclusion that Rose Mylett was not killed at the hands of the Ripper.

***Elizabeth Jackson*—Attacked ca. Tuesday, 4 June 1889**

There is nothing to link Elizabeth's death with the Ripper, but there may be links with the Whitehall Mystery of 1888.

***Alice McKenzie*—Attacked at ca. 12:48 A.M. Wednesday, 17 July 1889**

Medical evidence differed when it came to Alice McKenzie. Dr. Phillips thought she wasn't a victim of Jack the Ripper; Dr. Bond thought she was. Though it is true that Dr. Phillips's opinion must carry more weight since he saw the body days before Bond did, it will be best if we consider the similarities and differences between this crime and the others.

First, the similarities. The left carotid artery was cut, the cuts were made from left to right while the victim was on the ground, abdominal injuries were inflicted after death, and Alice did not cry out. Next, the differences. The wounds in the neck were smaller, the air passages were undivided, there were no indications of strangulation, the abdominal wounds were not severe, and the abdominal cavity was not opened. However, as stated earlier, it may well be that the killer was disturbed by hearing the approach of Constable Andrews. I have largely discounted Elizabeth Stride as a possible victim because there was no attempt at mutilation. In this case there was. As for the absence of strangulation, it is well documented that some killers do change their methods, and if we are correct in assuming that Martha Tabram was a Ripper victim, then Jack had already changed his approach once before.

Of much more significance, perhaps, are the series of scratches on the stomach. If Alice were the victim of a killer who wished to make it appear that the Ripper had struck again, why did he inflict seven minor marks on her abdomen? Could it be that the killer was indicating his tally? If so, then it could not be a copycat killer because most press reports of the time placed the number of victims higher, and there would consequently have been more scratches.

This factor leads me to believe that it is more than likely that Alice McKenzie was indeed a Ripper victim.

***The Pinchin Street Torso*—Attacked ca. Sunday, 8 September 1889**

Though it is true that the most likely date of the attack upon this unidentified woman was the anniversary of Annie Chapman's death, it does not fit the pattern of Ripper attacks in any other way. James Monro gave his own creditable opinion as to why this crime should not be placed among the litany of Ripper crimes, and he argued the case persuasively. The case has more possible links with the Whitehall Mystery and the murder of Elizabeth Jackson.

***Frances Coles*—Attacked at 2:15 A.M. Friday, 13 February 1891**

Although I have suggested that the Ripper might well have altered the way he killed, I do not believe that Frances Coles was one of his victims because there are too many variations.

In the first place, she was apparently thrown down to the ground, which is a different method of initial attack. Her throat was cut by means of a sawing motion, and she was killed far to the south of the Ripper's usual hunting ground. Allied to this is the gap of more than 18 months since the last possible Ripper victim, Alice McKenzie.

Though we can discount the absence of abdominal mutilations as a factor because the approach of Constable Thompson might well have disturbed the killer, and the crime took place on a weekend, which appears to have been Jack's pattern, I still feel that the dissimilarities are such that Frances can be discounted as a Ripper victim.

To sum up, then, it is my opinion that only the following crimes can, arguably, be placed at Jack's door:

Attack upon Annie Millwood, White's Row, Saturday, 25 February 1888
Murder of Martha Tabram, George Yard, Tuesday, 7 August 1888
Murder of Mary Ann Nichols, Buck's Row, Friday, 31 August 1888
Murder of Annie Chapman, Hanbury Street, Saturday, 8 September 1888
Possibly murder of Elizabeth Stride, Berner Street, Sunday, 30 September 1888
Murder of Catherine Eddowes, Mitre Square, Sunday, 30 September 1888
Murder of Mary Jane Kelly, Miller's Court, Friday, 9 November 1888
Probably murder of Alice McKenzie, Castle Alley, Wednesday, 17 July 1889

Depending on which candidate one favors, other victims can be placed at Jack's door. Thus, those who favor an American connection may also include Carrie Brown, who was murdered in the United States. Those who claim that George Chapman or William Bury were the Ripper would include their other victims too. These other murders are not, however, part of the true Ripper series, so they have been covered in the "Miscellaneous" section of this book.

2

The Witnesses

All witnesses are referred to in this section. Those who described an individual seen near the scene of a murder are also mentioned in the "Descriptions" section. Most witnesses are also mentioned in the narrative of the case they were involved in. (See "The Victims" section.)

Albrook, Lizzie

Lizzie Albrook was a resident of Miller's Court and a friend of **Mary Jane Kelly** who was present in Kelly's room when Joseph Barnett called on the evening of 8 November 1888. In one interview with the press Lizzie said of Kelly, "About the last thing she said was, 'Whatever you do, don't you do wrong and turn out as I have.' She had often spoken to me in this way and warned me against going on the streets as she had done. She told me, too, that she was heartily sick of the life she was leading and wished she had money enough to go back to Ireland where her people lived. I do not believe she would have gone out as she did if she had not been obliged to do so to keep herself from starvation."

See also Barnett, Joseph

Arnold, John

A news vendor apparently also known as John Cleary or John Leary who visited the offices of the *New York Herald* to report a new Ripper murder two days before the **Pinchin Street Torso** was found. He surrendered to the police and said he had heard the story of the murder from a man in uniform in Fleet Street. Attempts were made to trace this man but without success.

Barnett, Joseph

A resident of Buller's lodging house in New Street, Bishopsgate, and **Mary Jane Kelly**'s lover. They had lived together at 13 Miller's Court until 30 October, when he moved out after a quarrel over Mary inviting another woman to share their home.

He visited Mary on the evening of 8 November, staying with her until around 8 P.M. He identified Mary's body by her hair and eyes, though some reports have incorrectly claimed that it was by her ears and eyes. He suffered from echolalia, meaning that he was in the habit of repeating the last few words of anything said to him. He gave evidence at the inquest.

See also Albrook, Lizzie; "The Suspects": Barnett, Joseph

Bates, Thomas

A witness at **Elizabeth Stride**'s inquest on 3 October 1888. He was the watchman at the lodging house at 32 Flower and Dean Street. He repeated the story Elizabeth had told about the *Princess Alice* disaster.

Benjamin, Corporal

A soldier stationed at the Tower who was absent on the night when **Martha**

Tabram met her death. He returned to his barracks on 9 August 1888 and was able to prove that he had spent the night of the murder with his father.

Best, J.

Resident of 82 Lower Chapman Street and a witness at **Elizabeth Stride**'s inquest. He testified that he and a friend, John Gardner, had seen Elizabeth with a man in the Bricklayer's Arms, Settles Street, at about 11 P.M. on 29 September 1888. He was able to give a description of the man.

See also Gardner, John; "Descriptions": Physical Descriptions—Elizabeth Stride

Bierman, Rose

Witness after the attack upon **Ada Wilson,** Bierman lived at the same address, 9 Maidman Street. Ada lived on the ground floor, and Rose and her mother lived in two rooms upstairs. According to press reports, at about 12:30 A.M. on 28 March 1888 Rose heard terrible screams coming from downstairs. Rushing to investigate, she found Ada bleeding from wounds in her throat and a young, fair man leaving through the front door. Rose summoned help from two constables, but the assailant had by then made his escape.

Birrell, Emily

A friend of **Catherine Eddowes** who had given Catherine a pawn ticket in her name. The ticket was found among Catherine's possessions in Mitre Square, and news of it caused John Kelly to come forward and identify the body.

See also Kelly, John

Blackwell, Dr. Frederick William

A medical practitioner of 100 Commercial Street who with his assistant, Edward Johnston, was awakened by Constable Collins sometime between 1:05 and 1:10 A.M. on Sunday, 30 September 1888, to be told that a woman had been found with her throat cut in Dutfield's Yard, Berner Street.

Johnston was despatched to the scene while Blackwell dressed and followed a few minutes later. He timed his arrival at Dutfield's Yard at 1:16 A.M. and stated that the woman, **Elizabeth Stride,** had been dead for 20 to 30 minutes. Blackwell gave evidence at the inquest on 2 October and was recalled on the 5th to confirm that Elizabeth had not eaten grapes before she died, thus refuting Matthew Packer's claim that he had sold some to her and a male companion around midnight.

Blackwell believed that Elizabeth had been standing when she was attacked, that her head had been pulled back by means of the scarf around her neck, and that there had been a struggle, as demonstrated by the smearing of blood on her right hand. He disagreed with the findings of Dr. George Bagster Phillips, who performed the postmortem.

See also Johnston, Edward; Packer, Matthew; Phillips, Dr. George Bagster; "The Police": Collins, Reserve Constable Albert

Blenkingsop, James

A night watchman who was on duty at some roadworks in St. James's Place on the morning of 30 September 1888. Although not called as a witness at the inquest upon **Catherine Eddowes,** he did tell police that at about 1:30 A.M. a respectably dressed man had stopped and asked him if he had seen a man and a woman pass by. He replied that some people had passed, but he had taken no particular notice of them.

It is possible that the man Blenkingsop saw was one of the detectives who set out in search of the killer after Eddowes's body was discovered. If that is the case, then Blenkingsop had the time of the encounter wrong.

Bond, Dr. Thomas

The police surgeon to A Division and heavily involved in the Ripper investigation. He submitted reports on **Mary Jane Kelly, Alice McKenzie,** and **Rose Mylett**. He also penned a general report on the entire series of crimes for Dr. Robert Anderson. He believed that Alice McKenzie was a Ripper victim.

See also "The Police": Anderson, Dr. Robert

Bousfield, Mary

Also known as Mary Luckhurst, she lived at 4 Star Place, Commercial Street and had been **Martha Tabram**'s landlady. She was a witness at Tabram's inquest on 23 August 1888, when she stated that she had known the dead woman as Martha Turner. She said Martha had been living with a man named William Turner, and the couple had left her house six weeks before Martha was killed, owing rent.

Bowyer, Thomas

Resident of 37 Dorset Street and John McCarthy's assistant. On the morning of 9 November 1888, McCarthy sent Bowyer to **Mary Jane Kelly**'s room at 13 Miller's Court to see if he could collect some of the back rent she owed. There was no answer to his knocking, so he glanced through the broken window and saw the body. He reported his find to his employer and then went to the Commercial Street Police Station for help. He was a witness at Kelly's inquest.

See also McCarthy, John

Brittain, Charles

Employed at Barber's Horse Slaughterer's of Winthrop Street. After being told of the discovery of **Mary Ann Nichols**'s body, allegedly by Constable John Thain, he followed his fellow workers, Henry Tomkins and James Mumford, to view the body.

See also Mumford, James; Tomkins, Henry

Brown, Dr. Frederick Gordon

The City police surgeon who submitted a report on **Catherine Eddowes.** He also inspected the body of **Alice McKenzie.** He believed that although the Mitre Square murderer showed no medical expertise he had shown some degree of anatomical knowledge that enabled him to identify and remove the kidney. This statement of course is based on the assumption that the killer was actually seeking the kidney.

See also "Miscellaneous": Lusk Kidney

Brown, James

Resident of 35 Fairclough Street. Appeared at **Elizabeth Stride**'s inquest on 5 October 1888 to say that on the way to buy his supper early in the morning of 30 September, he had seen a man and a woman standing by the wall of the school. He was sure the woman was Elizabeth and furnished a basic description of the man with her. Some time later, but before he had finished his supper, he heard cries of "Murder," apparently from Louis Diemschutz and Isaac Kozebrodsky, who were running to find a policeman.

See also Diemschutz, Louis; Kozebrodsky, Isaac M.; "Descriptions": Physical Descriptions—Elizabeth Stride

Brownfield, Dr. Matthew

The metropolitan police surgeon for K, or the West Ham, Division. He was the first doctor to examine the body of **Rose Mylett** and performed the postmortem upon her. He concluded she had been strangled with some kind of ligature. His conclusions were first supported by Dr. Thomas Bond, but later Bond decided that the death was more likely to have resulted from natural causes. The coroner, Wynne Edwin Baxter, agreed with Brownfield and dismissed Bond's evidence so that a verdict of murder was returned.

See also Bond, Dr. Thomas

Bryant, John

See McCormack, John

Cadoche, Albert

Resident of 27 Hanbury Street and a witness at **Annie Chapman**'s inquest on 19 September 1888. He reported that he had gone into his yard soon after 5:15 A.M. on 8 September 1888 and heard a voice say, "No." Shortly afterward he went back outside and heard a sound as if something were falling against the fence. His evidence put the time of this occurrence at very soon after 5:25 A.M.

Cheeks, Margaret

A prostitute who lodged at 52 Gun Street and was a friend of **Alice McKenzie**. On the night Alice was murdered, Margaret was found to be missing, and at first the police believed that she too might have fallen victim to the killer. Margaret appeared at Alice's inquest on 19 July 1889 to say that she had been staying with her sister. She added nothing to the sum of knowledge on Alice McKenzie's murder.

Clapp, George

Caretaker in a warehouse at 5 Mitre Square. He was on duty on the morning **Catherine Eddowes** was murdered and was called to the inquest to testify that he had heard nothing.

Coles, James William

Resident of the Bermondsey Workhouse and the father of **Frances Coles**. He identified her body.

Coles, Mary Ann

Sister of **Frances Coles**. Identified her body.

Connolly, Mary Ann

Prostitute, also known as Pearly Poll, who lived at Crossingham's lodging house, 35 Dorset Street. She went to the Commercial Street Police Station on 9 August 1888 and stated that she knew the dead woman (**Martha Tabram**) as Emma Turner. She said she had been out with "Emma" on the night of 6 August, and they had spent most of the evening with two soldiers.

A parade was arranged at the Tower on 10 August to see if Connolly could identify either or both of the soldiers. Unfortunately, Connolly did not appear, and a police search for her led to her being found on 12 August. A new parade was arranged for the 13th, when Connolly did attend but failed to pick anyone out, claiming now that her soldiers had worn white hatbands. The following day yet another parade was arranged at the Wellington Barracks, where Connolly did pick out two men, but both were able to prove they had been elsewhere on the night in question.

Mary Ann Connolly gave evidence at the inquest on 23 August 1888.

See also "Others Who Played a Part": Allen, Elizabeth

Cooper, Eliza

Resident of Crossingham's lodging house at 35 Dorset Street and an acquaintance of **Annie Chapman** and Ted Stanley. The two women appeared to share Stanley's favors, which may have led to some animosity between them. What is certain that Eliza appeared at Annie's inquest on 19 September 1888 to testify that she had argued with Annie on 4 September over a piece of soap that Annie had borrowed for Ted's use but never returned.

After the two women went drinking together in the Britannia public house, the argument flared up again. Some reports stated that the quarrel was over some money; Eliza had allegedly taken a florin from Harry the Hawker and replaced it with a halfpenny. Other reports stated that Annie threw a halfpenny at Eliza in return for the soap she had borrowed. Whatever the truth of the matter, the conflict ended with Eliza striking Annie and causing bruising to her chest. These bruises were still evident when the postmortem examination of Annie's body was made.

See also Stanley, Ted; "Others Who Played a Part": Harry the Hawker

Coram, Thomas

Appeared at the inquest on **Elizabeth Stride** on 3 October 1888, though his evidence did not add much to the store of knowledge for that murder.

On the night of 29–30 September he had been visiting friends near Brady Street and was walking home along Whitechapel Road when he found a bloodstained knife on the doorstep of number 253. He handed the weapon to Constable Joseph Drage, who took it to Leman Street Police Station. There was much discussion as to whether this knife could have inflicted the fatal wound upon Elizabeth. Dr. Phillips deduced that it could have, but that it was not the ideal weapon because it would have proved unwieldy. The main point, though, is that the knife was found at 12:30 A.M., at which time, according to the medical and other evidence, Elizabeth Stride was still alive.

See also Phillips, Dr. George Bagster; "The Police": Drage, Constable Joseph William

Cox, Mary Ann

Resident of 5 Miller's Court, a friend of **Mary Jane Kelly**'s, and a witness at her inquest. Cox was a prostitute who, returning to her room at 11:45 P.M. on 8 November 1888, saw Mary in the company of man with a carrotty moustache who was carrying a can of beer. Cox heard Mary singing, then and later, and testified that Mary's room was quiet at 3 A.M. She heard a man's footsteps as he left the court at 5:45 A.M. but could not say from which room he left.

Cross, Charles

A resident of Doveton Street, Cambridge Heath Road, who found **Mary Ann Nichols**'s body early on the morning of 31 August 1888 as he walked down Buck's Row on his way to his work at Pickford's in Broad Street. Moments later he was joined by Robert Paul and, after checking briefly to see whether the woman was alive, they carried on to work, finding Constable Jonas Mizen along the way and informing him about their find.

Cross appeared at the inquest on 3 September 1888. Many texts erroneously give his name as George Cross and state incorrectly that he and Paul were friends.

See also Paul, Robert

Crow, Alfred George

A carman of 35 George Yard Buildings who arrived home at 3 A.M. on 7 August 1888 and saw someone lying on the landing. This was almost certainly the body of **Martha Tabram**. He appeared at the inquest as a witness.

Darrell, Elizabeth

Sometimes referred to as Elizabeth Long, she was a resident of 32 Church Street.

Some reports give her surname as Durrell. She appeared at **Annie Chapman**'s inquest on 19 September 1888 to say she had been walking down Hanbury Street at 5:30 A.M. on the morning of the murder when she saw a woman she later identified as Annie, speaking to a man. She furnished a description of the man.

See also "Descriptions": Physical Descriptions—Annie Chapman

Davis, John

A carman who worked in Leadenhall Market and lived at 29 Hanbury Street, sharing the front room in the attic with his wife and three sons, he was a witness at **Annie Chapman**'s inquest on 10 September 1888.

On the morning of 8 September 1888, he rose at 5:45 A.M. At about 6 A.M., he started to go into the yard but found Annie's body lying there. He did not step down into the yard but rushed back down the passageway and out into Hanbury Street. Obtaining assistance from James Green, James Kent, and Henry John Holland, Davis went back to the yard, later running off to find a policeman.

See also Green, James; Holland, Henry John; Kent, James

Diemschutz, Louis

Steward of the International Workingmen's Educational Club of 40 Berner Street and also a seller of costume jewelry at street markets. He found the body of **Elizabeth Stride** in Dutfield's Yard when he returned to the club to deposit his stock after spending Saturday, 29 September 1888, at Westow Hill Market near Crystal Palace.

After turning into the yard, his horse shied to the left, and Diemschutz saw that there was something on the ground close to the club wall. He poked it with his whip and then climbed down from his cart and struck a match, whereupon he saw that he had found the body of a woman. Thinking that it might be his wife, he went into the club and, finding her safe in the building, went back outside with others.

A more careful inspection revealed that the woman's throat had been cut, and Diemschutz ran southward to search for a policeman, in company with Isaac Kozebrodsky. Upon reaching Fairclough Street, they turned left and in due course found Edward Spooner with his girlfriend outside the Bee Hive public house. Diemschutz and the others returned to Dutfield's Yard, and he was still there when the police arrived. He was a witness at Stride's inquest, appearing on 1 October.

See also Diemschutz, Mrs.; Kozebrodsky, Isaac M.; Spooner, Edward

Diemschutz, Mrs.

Wife of Louis Diemschutz, she was inside the club building when the body of **Elizabeth Stride** was discovered. At one stage she stood at the side entrance to the club, in Dutfield's Yard, and saw blood that had flowed from where Elizabeth lay back to the doorway. Upon seeing this she screamed, which brought more members from inside the club out into the yard. Though she did not appear as a witness at the inquest, she was interviewed by the *Times* and stated that she had been in the kitchen at the probable time of the murder and had heard no noise or screams from the yard.

See also Diemschutz, Louis

Dixon, George

A blind man who was a friend of **Alice McKenzie**'s. On the night of 16 July 1889 she took him to a public house near the Cambridge Music Hall, and he heard her asking some man to buy her a drink.

Soon afterward Alice took George back to the lodging house at 52 Gun Street and left him there while she went out again.

Donovan, Timothy

Deputy at Crossingham's lodging house at 35 Dorset Street. He gave evidence at **Annie Chapman**'s inquest on 10 September 1888, confirming that she had been a resident of the house for about four months. He had last seen her in the kitchen at 1:45 A.M. on the day she died, 8 September 1888.

Dukes, Dr. William P.

Police surgeon whose base was at 75 Brick Lane. He was the first doctor called to Miller's Court, the scene of the murder of **Mary Jane Kelly,** on the morning of 9 November 1888 but was not called to give evidence at the inquest. When Dr. George Bagster Phillips arrived on the scene, he took over from Dr. Dukes.

Durrell, Elizabeth

See Darrell, Elizabeth

Eagle, Morris

A member of the International Workingmen's Educational Club in Berner Street who resided at 4 New Road, Commercial Street. He appeared at **Elizabeth Stride**'s inquest on 1 October 1888 to say that he had chaired a discussion, titled "Why Jews Should Be Socialists," inside the club on the evening of Saturday, 29 September 1888.

After the discussion ended, Eagle left the club by the Berner Street door at 11:45 P.M. to escort his young lady home. He returned by the yard entrance at 12:35 A.M. on Sunday the 30th and did not notice anything on the ground by the gates, though he admitted that it was dark and he may have missed Elizabeth's body.

Back inside the club, he joined a friend who was singing in Russian and was still there about 20 minutes later when Louis Diemschutz reported that there was a woman lying in the yard. It was Eagle who struck a match outside so that those assembled saw that the woman's throat had been cut. He then ran for assistance, going north along Berner Street and turning into Commercial Road, where he found two constables, Lamb and Collins. He returned to the yard with the policemen and later, when instructed to do so, ran to the police station in Leman Street to report the matter to the inspector.

See also Diemschutz, Louis; "The Police": Collins, Reserve Constable Albert; Lamb, Constable Henry

Ede, Thomas

A railway signalman called to give evidence at **Annie Chapman**'s inquest on 17 September 1888. He reported that he had seen a man outside the Forester's Arms public house with a knife blade protruding from his pocket on 8 September, the day of the murder. This man was traced and shown to be Henry James, a lunatic who had nothing to do with the murders. Ede was recalled to the inquest on 22 September to confirm this identification.

See also "The Suspects": James, Henry

Evans, John

Night watchman at Crossingham's lodging house, 35 Dorset Street. Appeared at **Annie Chapman**'s inquest on 10 September 1888 to say that he had seen Annie leave the house early on the morning of 8 September and turn up Little Paternoster Row toward Brushfield Street. He believed she was a little the worse for drink at the time.

Fisher, Elizabeth

A sister of **Catherine Eddowes**, she lived at 33 Hatcliffe Street, Greenwich. Though Catherine's other sisters tended to ostracize her owing to her habit of constantly trying to borrow money, Elizabeth did meet Catherine from time to time and was on friendly terms with her. She said Catherine had left Thomas Conway because he got drunk occasionally and hit her.

See also Gold, Eliza; Jones, Emma

Foster, Elizabeth

A friend of **Mary Jane Kelly**. Though she was not called to give evidence at the inquest, she did tell the press that had been drinking with Kelly in the Ten Bells public house on the evening of 8 November 1888.

Foster, Frederick

The surveyor who drew up plans of Mitre Square and the routes to where the Goulston Street graffito was found for the inquest on **Catherine Eddowes**. He was also the man who made sketches of the injuries she had suffered.

Fowles, Thomas

A resident of Back Church Lane who was employed as a doorman at a club in Commercial Street. On the night of **Frances Coles**'s murder his girlfriend, Kate McCarthy, came to meet him at the club and he later walked her to her home at 42 Royal Mint Street. They spent some time talking on her doorstep, during which they were seen by three people who knew them both: William Friday and the Knapton brothers. Later all three men went to the police and said they believed they had seen the dead woman with a man on a doorstep in Royal Mint Street. Clearly all three were recalling the sighting of Kate and Thomas.

See also Friday, William

Franklin, Margaret

A friend of **Alice McKenzie**'s and a witness at her inquest on 19 July 1889. Margaret stated that she and two other women, Catherine Hughes and Sarah Mahoney, had been sitting on the step of a barber's shop in Flower and Dean Street at 11:40 P.M. on the night of 16 July. They had seen Alice pass, heading toward Whitechapel, and Margaret had exchanged a few words with her.

See also Hughes, Catherine; Mahoney, Sarah

Friday, William

Also known as Jumbo. After the murder of **Frances Coles** on 13 February 1891, he came forward to say that he had seen a woman he believed to be the victim talking to a man in Royal Mint Street. Although he gave a reasonable description, it transpired that he had seen Kate McCarthy and Thomas Fowles, both of whom Friday actually knew.

Gardner, John

Resident of 11 Chapman Street and a witness at **Elizabeth Stride**'s inquest. He and a friend, J. Best, had seen Elizabeth with a man in the Bricklayer's Arms, Settles Street, at about 11 P.M. on 29 September 1888. Gardner mentioned that he had noticed the flower pinned to Elizabeth's dress.

See also Best, J.; "Descriptions": Physical Descriptions—Elizabeth Stride

Gold, Eliza

Sister of **Catherine Eddowes** and a resident of 6 Thrawl Street. She was a witness at Catherine's inquest, where she described her as being of sober habits.

See also Fisher, Elizabeth; Jones, Emma

Goldstein, Leon

Fanny Mortimer of 36 Berner Street reported that she had spent some time at her front door in the early hours of 30 September 1888. During that time the only person she saw was a man carrying a shiny black bag. Some have claimed that this was a sighting of Jack the Ripper. In fact, the truth is much more mundane. When press reports of **Elizabeth Stride**'s murder mentioned this man with the bag, Leon Goldstein reported to the police at Leman Street Police Station on 1 October 1888 and said that he was the man Mortimer had seen. Goldstein, of 22 Christian Street, said he had visited a coffee house in Spectacle Alley and had passed down Berner Street on his way home. He had indeed been carrying a black shiny bag, but it held only empty cigarette boxes.

See also Mortimer, Fanny

Graves, Alice

A witness at **Rose Mylett**'s inquest who said she had seen Rose early on 20 December 1888, the night she died, outside a public house in Commercial Street with two men.

Green, Emma

A resident of New Cottage, 2 Buck's Row, the house next to where **Mary Ann Nichols** was murdered. Green appeared at the inquest on 17 September 1888 to confirm the time she and her family had retired for the night on 30 August. None of the family had heard anything until Green was awakened by the police knocking on her door at 4 A.M. on 31 August.

Green, James

A resident of 36 Acton Street, Burdett Road, who was employed at Bayley's packing-case manufacturers of Hanbury Street, he appeared at **Annie Chapman**'s inquest on 12 September 1888. Together with James Kent, a fellow employee of Bayley's, he had been standing outside their work premises when John Davis ran out of number 29 and cried for assistance because he had found a body in the yard. Green, Kent, and Henry John Holland went into number 29 with Davis and, after viewing the body, went to find a policeman.

See also Davis, John; Holland, Henry John; Kent, James; "Others Who Played a Part": Bayley, Joseph and Thomas

Hardiman, Harriett

A resident of 29 Hanbury Street, she ran the cat's-meat shop that fronted the street and slept in the shop with her 16-year-old son.

She appeared at the inquest on **Annie Chapman** on 12 September 1888 to say that she had retired for the night at 10:30 A.M. on 7 September. She had heard nothing during the night until, at about 6 A.M., she was awakened by footsteps and noise in the corridor outside. She sent her son to investigate, and he returned to say that a woman's body had been found in the yard.

Harris, Harry

A resident of Castle Street who, together with Joseph Lawende and Joseph Hyam Levy, spent the night of 29 September 1888 at the Imperial Club in Duke's Place and left at 1:35 A.M. on the 30th. The three saw a couple standing at the top of Church Passage, and the woman may have been **Catherine Eddowes**, but Harris did not take particular notice of them, was unable to supply any description, and was not called at the inquest.

See also Lawende, Joseph; Levy, Joseph Hyam

Harstein, Eva

A resident of 14 Berner Street. Though she was not called to give evidence at **Elizabeth Stride**'s inquest, she did inform the two private detectives, Grand and Batchelor, that she had found some white flower petals and a bloodstained grape stalk in the entry to Dutfield's Yard.

See also "Others Who Played a Part": Batchelor, J. H.; Grand, Mr.

Harvey, Maria

A witness at **Mary Jane Kelly**'s inquest and a resident of 3 New Court, Dorset Street, Harvey stated that she had stayed in Mary's room with her on the nights of Monday and Tuesday, 5 November and 6 November 1888. Confused press reports state that she was the women present at 13 Miller's Court when Joseph Barnett called on the night of 8 November, but in fact that woman was Lizzie Albrook. Maria had spent that afternoon drinking with Mary, but they had finally parted at about 7:30 P.M.

See also Albrook, Lizzie; Barnett, Joseph

Hatfield, James

A mortuary attendant who assisted Robert Mann in the laying out of **Mary Ann Nichols**'s body, he appeared at the inquest on 17 September 1888 to confirm Mann's story that the police had not given orders not to touch the body.

See also Mann, Robert

Hewitt, Francis

Superintendent of George Yard Buildings and a witness at **Martha Tabram**'s inquest. His home was just 12 feet away from the murder spot, but he had heard nothing during the night. His wife, however, had heard a single cry of "Murder!" but it had been much earlier in the evening than the probable time of the murder.

Holland, Ellen

Sometimes quoted in press reports as Jane Oram. Her evidence and the supposed testimony of Oram are identical, and I assume, therefore, that they are one and the same person.

Holland was a resident of 18 Thrawl Street and had there shared a room with **Mary Ann Nichols**. She assisted in identifying Nichols and gave evidence at her inquest on 3 September 1888 to say she had seen Mary Ann at the corner of Osborn Street and Whitechapel Road on the night of her murder. They discussed whether Mary Ann should come back to the lodging house at Thrawl Street, but Mary Ann said that she had no money. Holland last saw Mary Ann walking unsteadily eastward along Whitechapel Road.

Holland, Henry John

A resident of 4 Aden Road, Mile End, and a witness at **Annie Chapman**'s inquest on 12 September 1888, Holland had been on his way to work in Chiswell Street when John Davis ran out of 29 Hanbury Street and cried for help. Holland, James Green, and James Kent, who had been standing outside Bayley's at 23a, followed Davis back down the passageway and viewed the body.

Holland was the only one of the men who ventured down into the yard itself; the others remained at the top of the steps. He ran off to find a policeman, found one on fixed-point duty in Spitalfields Market, and told him of the discovery. The officer explained that he could not leave his post, which angered Holland so much that later the same day he went to Commercial Street Police Station and made a complaint.

Hughes, Catherine

One of the women sitting on the barber's-shop step in Flower and Dean Street with Margaret Franklin when **Alice McKenzie** passed on the night of 16 July 1889. She was not called to give evidence at the inquest.

See also Franklin, Margaret; Mahoney, Sarah

Hutchinson, George

A resident of the Victoria Home in Commercial Street. He did not appear as a witness at **Mary Jane Kelly**'s inquest but presented himself at the police station after it had closed on 12 November 1888 to make a statement.

He claimed that he had seen Kelly with a man on the morning she had been murdered. Hutchinson was able to furnish a detailed description of the man, which he elaborated on in subsequent interviews with the press.

See also "The Suspects": Hutchinson, George (Britain)

Jacob, Isaac Lewis

A resident of 12 New Castle Place who early on the morning of 17 July 1889 was on his way to purchase his supper from McCarthy's chandler's shop in Dorset Street when he was stopped by Constable Walter Andrews, who informed him that he had just found the body of a woman (**Alice McKenzie**). Jacob was detained until he could show that he had played no part in the crime.

See also "The Police": Andrews, Constable Walter

Jenny

A prostitute only ever identified by her Christian name. She was never called to give evidence at any inquest but was interviewed on 1 October 1888, the day after the so-called double event (the murders of **Elizabeth Stride** and **Catherine Eddowes**). Jenny said she was absolutely sure who the murderer was, but her description and the other details she gave seem to show that she was once again referring to the stories of the man known as Leather Apron.

Johnston, Edward

Assistant to Dr. Blackwell at the doctor's surgery at 100 Commercial Road. Early on the morning of 30 September 1888 he was awakened by Constable Collins, who told him a body had been found in Dutfield's Yard, Berner Street. Johnston informed Dr. Blackwell and, while the doctor dressed, accompanied Collins back to Berner Street.

Johnston noted that the wound in **Elizabeth Stride**'s throat had stopped bleeding but that her body still felt warm. He gave evidence at the inquest on 3 October, describing the position of the body.

See also Blackwell, Dr. Frederick William; "The Police": Collins, Reserve Constable Albert

Jones, Emma

Sister of **Catherine Eddowes** and a resident of 20 Bridgewater Place. She had not been friendly toward Catherine, possibly owing to the latter's habit of trying to borrow money from time to time.

See also Fisher, Elizabeth; Gold, Eliza

Jones, Joseph

Owner of a pawn shop at 31 Church Street, Spitalfields. Two tickets for items pledged at his shop were found among **Catherine Eddowes**'s possessions. One was in the name of Emily Birrell and the other Jane Kelly.

See also Birrell, Emily

Kelly, John

Catherine Eddowes's lover and a witness at her inquest. Reports that the initials "T. C." were tattooed on Catherine's arm led Kelly to come forward on 2 October 1888 and make a positive identification of the Mitre Square victim. He and Catherine had lodged together at Cooney's lodging house, 55 Flower and Dean Street.

See also Birrell, Emily

Kennedy, Mrs.

See Lewis, Sarah

Kent, James

Employed at Bayley's packing-case manufacturers of 23a Hanbury Street. He appeared at **Annie Chapman**'s inquest on 12 September 1888.

Together with James Green, he was outside Bayley's when John Davis ran out of number 29 and cried for assistance. Kent, Green, and Henry John Holland went into number 29 with Davis and saw the body. Kent was so distressed that he could not go with the others to find a policeman but had to fortify himself with some brandy. Afterward he obtained a piece of sacking from his employer's premises and threw it over Annie's body.

See also Davis, John; Green, James; Holland, Henry John; "Others Who Played a Part": Bayley, Joseph and Thomas

Kentorrich, Barnett

A resident of 38 Berner Street, next door to the International Workingmen's Educational Club, on the opposite side to Dutfield's Yard. He was not called as a witness at the inquest for **Elizabeth Stride** but when interviewed said he had heard nothing on the night of the murder.

Kidney, Michael

Paramour of **Elizabeth Stride** and a witness at her inquest on 3 October 1888. He had lived with Elizabeth for the past three years but had last seen her on Tuesday, 25 September, in Commercial Street. Elizabeth had apparently told people that she and Kidney had argued, which is why she had left him, but he denied this story and said he had expected her to be waiting for him when he got home from work that night.

There is evidence, however, that Kidney and Elizabeth did have problems. She reported him for assault on 6 April 1887, and in July of the following year he served three days in prison for being drunk and disorderly.

On 1 October, two days before he gave evidence at the inquest, Kidney appeared at Leman Street Police Station to complain about the efforts being made to track down the Whitechapel killer and to say that if he were the officer on duty where the murder of Elizabeth had taken place, he would kill himself.

Killeen, Dr. Timothy Robert

Killeen's surname is sometimes incorrectly given as Keeling. His surgery was situated at 68 Brick Lane. He was called to examine the body of **Martha Tabram** on the morning of 7 August 1888 and was a witness at the inquest on 9 August. His thoughts and words about Martha's injuries are often misquoted.

Kozebrodsky, Isaac M.

Member of the International Workingmen's Educational Club in Berner Street.

Kozebrodsky was inside the club when Louis Diemschutz came inside just after 1 A.M. on 30 September 1888 to say that a woman, later identified as **Elizabeth Stride**, was lying outside in the yard. Kozebrodsky went outside with Diemschutz and others and saw that the woman's throat had been cut. He and Diemschutz ran down Berner Street and into Fairclough Street, looking for a policeman. Though they did not find one, they did find Edward Spooner outside the Bee Hive public house, and all three then returned to the yard.

Kozebrodsky did not appear at the inquest.

See also Diemschutz, Louis; Spooner, Edward

Kranz, Philip

Editor of *Der Arbeter Fraint,* whose printing offices were accessible from Dutfield's Yard. He appeared as a witness at **Elizabeth Stride**'s inquest on 5 October 1888 to say that he had been in the offices but had heard no cries for assistance. He admitted that there was a good deal of singing coming from the club at the time the murder must have taken place, so he might have missed a cry.

Lane, Catherine

A lodger at 32 Flower and Dean Street with her husband, Patrick. She appeared at the inquest on **Elizabeth Stride** on 3 October 1888 to say that she had seen Elizabeth on Thursday, 27 September, and that Elizabeth had told her she had argued with Michael Kidney and left him. Kidney denied this story. Lane said she had last seen Elizabeth between 7 and 8 P.M. on Saturday the 29th in the kitchen of the lodging house. Before this she had seen Stride cleaning Elizabeth Tanner's private rooms.

See also Kidney, Michael; Tanner, Elizabeth

Lave, Joseph

A resident of the International Workingmen's Educational Club at 40 Berner Street and a witness at **Elizabeth Stride**'s inquest. He testified that he had walked through Dutfield's Yard about fifteen minutes before the murder. He had gone outside to get some fresh air and had walked about the yard, feeling his way along the wall because it was so dark. He remarked that everything was very quiet and said he was sure there was no body on the ground at the time.

Law, Private

A soldier at the Tower who confirmed Private John Leary's story that they had been out drinking together on the night **Martha Tabram** was murdered.

See also Leary, Private John

Lawende, Joseph

A resident of 45 Norfolk Road, Dalston, and a witness at **Catherine Eddowes**'s inquest. Together with two friends, Joseph Hyam Levy and Harry Harris, he had spent the night of 29 September 1888 at the Imperial Club, 16–17 Duke's Place. They left at about 1:35 A.M. on the 30th and saw a man and a woman talking at the top of Church Passage, which led into Mitre Square.

Lawende took particular notice of the couple and later identified Catherine Eddowes by her clothing as the woman he had seen. He furnished a description of the man but did not think he would recognize him if he saw him again.

See also Harris, Harry; Levy, Joseph Hyam; "The Police": Foster, Detective Superintendent Alfred Lawrence; "Others Who Played a Part": Crawford, Henry Homewood; "Descriptions": Physical Descriptions—Catherine Eddowes; "Miscellaneous": Anderson's Witness

Leary, Private John

A soldier picked out by Constable Thomas Barrett, who was trying to identify a soldier he had seen loitering in Wentworth Street on the night of **Martha Tabram**'s murder, at the parade held at the Tower on 8 August 1888. Leary was able to prove that he had been out drinking with Private Law.

See also Law, Private; "The Police": Barrett, Constable Thomas

Letchford, Charles

A resident of 39 Berner Street who was not called to give evidence at the inquest on **Elizabeth Stride**. When interviewed he reported that he had walked up the street at 12:30 A.M. on 30 September 1888 but had seen nothing out of the ordinary. His statement has caused some confusion because he also said that his sister stood in the street for 10 minutes or so from 12:50 A.M. on. This information has led to the assumption that Fanny Mortimer might have been the sister he referred to, but her maiden name was Skipp, not Letchford.

See also Mortimer, Fanny

Levy, Joseph Hyam

A resident of 1 Hutchinson Street, Aldgate, and a witness at **Catherine Eddowes**'s inquest. Together with Joseph Lawende and Harry Harris, he had spent the night of 29 September 1888 at the Imperial Club in Duke's Place and had left at 1:35 A.M. on the 30th.

The three men noticed a man and a woman standing at the top of Church Passage. For some reason the couple distressed Levy, and he commented "I don't like going home by myself when I see these sorts of characters about." Having said that, he did not take particular notice of the couple and was unable to supply any description.

See also Harris, Harry; Lawende, Joseph

Lewis, Maurice

A resident of Dorset Street and a friend of **Mary Jane Kelly**. Though he was not called to give evidence at the inquest, his statements appear to back up those made by Caroline Maxwell. Lewis said that he had seen Kelly drinking in the Britannia public house at about 10 A.M. on 9 November 1888. In other reports he is said to have claimed that he saw her drinking with "Julia and Danny" in the Horn of Plenty sometime during the evening she was killed.

See also Maxwell, Caroline

Lewis, Sarah

A resident of 24 Great Pearl Street, but early in the morning of 9 November 1888 she was staying with the Keylers at 2 Miller's Court after an argument with her husband. She was a witness at **Mary Jane Kelly**'s inquest and testified that she had seen a man standing in Dorset Street, looking up Miller's Court, at about 2:30 A.M. This man was almost certainly George Hutchinson. Lewis also said she heard a single cry of "Murder" just before 4 A.M.

In addition, Sarah told the police about an encounter with a man on Wednesday, 7 November, in Bethnal Green Road. She had been out with a friend when the man accosted them and asked them to go with him down a passageway. They did so, whereupon he put down the black bag he was carrying and reached inside his coat as if to fetch something out. At that point the women ran away. Sarah said she had seen this same man as she passed the Britannia public house on her way to Miller's Court on 9 November.

Press reports seem to confuse this witness with a Mrs. Kennedy, who tells the same story, indicating that Kennedy and Lewis are the same woman.

See also Hutchinson, George; "Others Who Played a Part": The Keylers

Llewellyn, Dr. Rees Ralph

Llewellyn's surgery was based at 152 Whitechapel Road, and he was called out by Constable John Thain on the morning of 31 August 1888. He examined the body of **Mary Ann Nichols** in Buck's Row and made a second examination later that morning at the mortuary after Inspector Spratling noticed the abdominal injuries. He performed the postmortem on 1 September and gave evidence at the inquest that same day. He was recalled on 17 September to confirm that none of Mary Ann's internal organs had been removed by her killer.

Long, Elizabeth

See Darrell, Elizabeth

Luckhurst, Mary

See Bousfield, Mary

Mahoney, Elizabeth

Wife of Joseph Mahoney and resident with him at 47 George Yard Buildings. After returning home in the early hours of 7 August 1888, she ventured out again to purchase some supper from a shop in Thrawl Street. She returned home again at about 1:50 A.M. and saw no one on the stairs where **Martha Tabram**'s body was later found. She was called as a witness at the inquest on 9 August 9th.

See also Mahoney, Joseph

Mahoney, Joseph

A resident of 47 George Yard Buildings and the husband of Elizabeth. They had spent the Bank Holiday enjoying themselves and returned home at 1:40 A.M. on 7 August 1888, after which Joseph stayed in for the rest of the night. He did not notice anyone lying on the stairs where **Martha Tabram**'s body was later found and was not called to give evidence at the inquest.

See also Mahoney, Elizabeth

Mahoney, Sarah

One of the women sitting on the barber's-shop step in Flower and Dean Street with Margaret Franklin when **Alice McKenzie** walked passed them on the night of 16 July 1889. She was not called to give evidence at the inquest.

See also Franklin, Margaret; Hughes, Catherine

Malcolm, Mary

Appeared at the inquest on **Elizabeth Stride** on 2 October 1888. She lived at 50 Eagle Street, Red Lion Square, and stated that she had viewed the body in the mortuary and identified it as her sister, Elizabeth Stokes. According to Malcolm, she knew the dead woman was her sister because of a mark on her leg caused by an adder bite when she was a child.

Malcolm claimed she had been awakened at the exact time of the murder by feeling her sister kiss her and said she had known immediately that something was wrong. She went on to blacken her sister's character terribly, saying that Stokes had been immoral and a drunkard, which was why her husband had left her, and had later turned to prostitution. Her entire testimony was rendered useless when Elizabeth Stokes appeared at the inquest herself, demonstrating that she was very much alive.

Mann, Robert

The mortuary keeper who, with James Hatfield, stripped and washed **Mary Ann**

Nichols's body. There was some dispute at the inquest, where he gave his evidence on 17 September 1888, as to whether the police had given instructions that the body was not to be touched. Mann and Hatfield both insisted that they had received no such orders. The coroner told the jury to ignore Mann's evidence because he was unreliable and subject to fits.

See also Hatfield, James

Marshall, William

A resident of 64 Berner Street and a witness at **Elizabeth Stride**'s inquest on 5 October 1888. He had viewed the body in the mortuary and stated that it was a woman he had seen, with a man, between his house and the club, but on the opposite side of the road. He gave a description of the man.

See also "Descriptions": Physical Descriptions—Elizabeth Stride

Maxwell, Caroline

A resident of Dorset Street and a witness at **Mary Jane Kelly**'s inquest. Caroline's evidence was contentious because she claimed to have seen Kelly long after the medical and other evidence indicated that the latter was dead.

Maxwell said that she had seen Kelly between 8 and 8:30 A.M. on 9 November 1888 and again an hour later. In the first meeting Kelly confessed she had the "horrors of drink" upon her, whereupon Caroline told her to have another drink in order to steady herself. Mary said she had already done so but had vomited it up. When Maxwell saw Mary an hour later, Mary was talking to a man outside the Britannia public house.

This testimony has been seized upon by some writers to suggest first that Kelly wasn't the woman whose body was found inside her room at Miller's Court and second that it proves that Kelly was pregnant because she was obviously suffering from morning sickness. Both are wild fantasies, and a much more likely explanation is that Caroline Maxwell got the date wrong and the two sightings took place earlier in the week, though Maxwell did say that she could fix the date accurately because when she met Kelly she was in the process of returning some china her husband had borrowed from another resident of Dorset Street.

McCarthy, John

Owner of a chandler's shop at 27 Dorset Street and the landlord of 26 Dorset Street and the houses in Miller's Court, which were known locally as "McCarthy's rents." He sent Thomas Bowyer to see if he could collect some back rent from **Mary Jane Kelly** on the morning of 9 November 1888.

After Bowyer returned and told of his discovery of Mary's body, McCarthy accompanied him back to Miller's Court to see for himself before sending Bowyer for the police. He followed Bowyer to the police station in Commercial Street and later broke down the door to let police into Mary's room. He was a witness at the inquest.

See also Bowyer, Thomas; "The Suspects": McCarthy, John

McCarthy, Kate

A resident of 42 Royal Mint Street. On the night of **Frances Coles**'s murder she met her beau, Thomas Fowles, and he walked her home. They spent some time talking on the doorstep of her house, during which they were seen by William (Jumbo) Friday and the Knapton brothers. All three men subsequently went to the police and said they believed they had seen the dead woman, possibly with her killer, just before she was murdered.

It is difficult to reconcile these statements with the fact that all three witnesses knew Kate and Thomas.

See also Friday, William

McCormack, John

Paramour of **Alice McKenzie,** also known as John Bryant, he was a porter who worked mostly for several Jewish tailors around Hanbury Street. He and Alice lived in various locations together but mainly at a common lodging house at 52 Gun Street.

McCormack appeared at the inquest on 17 July 1889. He testified that he and Alice had argued because Alice had not paid the price of their bed for the night, even though he had given her the money. Fortunately for him, the lodging-house keeper trusted him for the cash, and at the time of the murder he was back in bed at Gun Street.

McKellar, Alexander

General police surgeon and assistant to Dr. Thomas Bond, he carried out an examination of the body of **Rose Mylett** at the request of Dr. Robert Anderson after the latter had come to doubt the findings of Dr. Matthew Brownfield. McKellar and Bond both concluded that the death had been owing to natural causes, in opposition to Brownfield, who believed Rose had been strangled with a ligature. Brownfield's opinion prevailed.

See also Bond, Dr. Thomas; Brownfield, Dr. Matthew; "The Police": Anderson, Dr. Robert

Monk, Mary Ann

Had once been an inmate of the Lambeth Workhouse with **Mary Ann Nichols** and helped in the identification of her body. Monk gave evidence at the inquest on 3 September 1888.

Morris, Ann

Sister-in-law of **Martha Tabram** and a resident of 23 Fisher Street, Cambridge Heath Road. She appeared at the inquest on 23 August 1888 to say that she had seen Martha outside the White Swan public house on the evening of 6 August 1888.

Morris, George James

Night watchman at Kearley and Tongue's warehouse in Mitre Square and an ex-policeman with the Metropolitan.

At the time of the murder of **Catherine Eddowes** on 30 September 1888, Morris was sweeping the landings inside the warehouse, and the door that led into the square was ajar. However, he heard nothing until Constable Edward Watkins came to him for assistance. After viewing Catherine's body himself, he ran out into Aldgate, blew his whistle, and obtained help from Constables James Thomas Holland and James Harvey. He was a witness at the inquest.

See also "The Police": Harvey, Constable James; Holland, Constable James Thomas

Mortimer, Fanny

A resident of 36 Berner Street. Interviewed by the police investigating the murder of **Elizabeth Stride,** she said she had been standing at her front door for most of the time between 12:30 and 1 A.M. on Sunday, 30 September 1888. She said she had first gone just after she heard the beat policeman walk past her house. During her time at the door, she saw no one except a man carrying a shiny black bag who walked past. She was not called to give evidence at the inquest.

Fanny Mortimer cannot have been correct when she said she was at her door for most of that half hour, or she would have seen some of the scenes reported by other witnesses, including the assault upon the woman at Dutfield's Yard. The timetable means that at best, Mortimer was at her doorstep for perhaps six minutes, and her own initial reports put it at no more than 10 minutes. As for the man with the shiny black bag, he was later identified at Leon Goldstein.

See also Goldstein, Leon

Mulshaw, Patrick

Resident of 3 Rupert Street who was employed as a night watchman. On 31 August 1888 he was guarding some works in Winthrop Street. He heard nothing during the night and saw no one after midnight except two constables, one of whom was Constable John Neil. Soon after **Mary Ann Nichols**'s body was found a man passing by told him about the discovery. This man remained unidentified. Mulshaw gave this evidence at the inquest on 17 September.

Mumford, James

One of the men employed at Barber's Horse Slaughterer's in Winthrop Street who went to view **Mary Ann Nichols**'s body after being told about it by Constable John Thain.

See also Brittain, Charles; Tomkins, Henry

Nichols, William

Resident of 12 Coburg Road, Old Kent Road, and the estranged husband of **Mary Ann Nichols.** He identified her body on 1 September 1888, and it is said that he looked into the coffin and remarked, "Seeing you as you are now, I forgive you for what you have done to me." He gave evidence at her inquest on 3 September 1888 and told about the breakup of their marriage. He denied that their marital problems had been caused by an affair on his part and instead attributed them to his wife's drinking habits.

Olsson, Sven

Clerk to the Swedish Church in Princes Square and a witness at the inquest on **Elizabeth Stride** on 5 October 1888. Olsson said Elizabeth had registered with the church on 10 July 1868 and gave some details of her history. He contradicted a story Elizabeth herself had told of two of her children being privately educated by the Swedish Church. Olsson confirmed, however, that Elizabeth had occasionally been given financial assistance by the church and indeed had received 1 shilling on 20 September 1888, along with a Swedish hymn book.

Oram, Jane

See Holland, Ellen

Oxley, Dr.

The first doctor on the scene when **Frances Coles** was murdered, called out by Constable Hyde. Oxley officially pronounced Frances dead, though Dr. Phillips later examined her body as well.

See also Phillips, Dr. George Bagster; "The Police": Hyde, Constable

Packer, Matthew

A fruiterer and greengrocer trading from premises at 44 Berner Street, he was involved in the investigation into **Elizabeth Stride**'s death. When interviewed initially by Sergeant Stephen White on 30 September 1888, Packer said he had seen nothing the previous night and had closed his shop at 12:30 A.M.

On 2 October two private detectives, Grand and Batchelor, interviewed Packer, who then claimed to have sold grapes to a man in Elizabeth's company at about

11:45 P.M. on the 29th. As a result of this information, Sergeant White was sent to speak to Packer again on 4 October. Spoken to briefly, Packer confirmed the grapes story and was later taken by the two private detectives to see Sir Charles Warren.

Packer amended his story more than once to fit established facts, and his evidence was largely worthless, though it has been seized upon by some writers, especially those who would claim a Masonic or Royal conspiracy. Packer was not called to give evidence at the inquest.

See also "Others Who Played a Part": Batchelor, J. H.; Grand, Mr.; Richardson, Joseph Hall; "Letters and Correspondence": Threatening Letter of 6 October 1888; "Myths and Errors": Elizabeth Stride

PALMER, AMELIA

Resident of 30 Dorset Street, her surname is sometimes reported as Farmer. She was one of those who identified the body of **Annie Chapman**, who was a friend of hers, but she incorrectly named Annie's husband as Frederick. She stated that Annie had recently been living at Crossingham's lodging house at 35 Dorset Street. She gave evidence at the inquest on 10 September 1888 and gave details of when she had last seen the dead woman.

PAUL, ROBERT

A resident of 30 Foster Street, he is often erroneously referred to as John Paul. On the morning of 31 August 1888 he was on his way to work at Corbett's Court, which was situated on the corner of Hanbury Street and Commercial Street. He encountered Charles Cross in Buck's Row, and Cross pointed out a body (**Mary Ann Nichols**) to him. The two men checked to see whether the woman was alive before continuing on to their respective places of work. On the way they spotted Constable Jonas Mizen and reported the find to him. Paul appeared at the inquest on September 17th.

See also Cross, Charles

PAUMIER, MRS.

Though not called to give evidence at **Mary Jane Kelly**'s inquest, she believed she had seen the Ripper.

Paumier was a chestnut vendor working on the corner of Widegate Street and Sandys Row. On the morning of 9 November 1888 she saw a man carrying a black, shiny bag who approached from Artillery Row and commented, "I suppose you have heard about the murder in Dorset Street?" When she said she had, the man added, "I know more about it than you do," and then walked off down Sandys Row. She was able to supply a basic description.

PEARLY POLL

See Connolly, Mary Ann

PHILLIPS, ANNIE

A resident of Dilston Road, Southwark Park Road, and the daughter of **Catherine Eddowes,** Annie was a witness at the inquest and stated that she had last seen her mother 25 months before the murder. Since then she had changed addresses and had not told her mother where she was in case Catherine tried to borrow money from Annie and her family.

PHILLIPS, DR. GEORGE BAGSTER

The police surgeon for H Division, resident of 2 Spital Square, Spitalfields, and heavily involved in the Ripper investigations. His first case was the murder of **Annie Chapman** on 8 September 1888, when he was called out by Inspector

Joseph Chandler. Phillips conducted the postmortem on the afternoon of 8 September and testified at the inquest on 13 September, holding back some of the details of the injuries to spare the feelings of the jury and the public. He did opine that the killer had surgical skill. He was recalled to the inquest on 19 September to discuss the bruises he had found on Annie's chest. His estimate of the time of death was at odds with the evidence of other witnesses.

Phillips was also called out to the murder of **Elizabeth Stride** in Berner Street on 30 September. He was the second doctor on the scene, arriving after Dr. Blackwell had examined the body. Both doctors carried out the postmortem on 1 October, and Dr. Phillips appeared at the inquest on 3 October. He was recalled two days later, on 5 October, to refute the rumors that Elizabeth had eaten grapes before she died.

Phillips was also present at the inquest on **Catherine Eddowes**. He did not give evidence himself, but his opinion, stated clearly in a report from Chief Inspector Swanson, was that the killer had shown no anatomical knowledge. Neither did he believe that the man who had killed Eddowes was the same one who had claimed Stride's life.

His next case was that of **Mary Jane Kelly**. Phillips was present when the door to 13 Miller's Court was forced open. He was one of the doctors who performed the postmortem on 10 November 1888 and gave evidence at the inquest on 12 November, again keeping many of the details back.

Phillips was then consulted in the murder of **Alice McKenzie** on 17 July 1889. He was called to the scene and arrived in Castle Alley at 1:10 A.M. He performed the postmortem and gave his evidence to the inquest on 19 July, again giving very few details of the injuries he had found. He did not believe that this murder had been committed by the man who had been styled Jack the Ripper.

On 13 February 1891 Phillips attended the scene of **Frances Coles**'s murder, noting that the throat wound appeared to have been caused by a sawing action. Again, he did not think that this murder was a Ripper crime.

See also Blackwell, Dr. Frederick William; "The Police": Chandler, Inspector Joseph Luniss

Pickett, Catherine

A resident of Miller's Court, she was not called as a witness at **Mary Jane Kelly**'s inquest but had said she had heard Kelly singing on the night of the latter's death. Pickett wanted to go down to complain because the noise was disturbing her, but her husband, David, prevented her from doing so. In the morning, at about 7:30 A.M., Pickett knocked on Mary's door with the object of borrowing a shawl, but when there was no reply she assumed Mary was asleep.

Prater, Elizabeth

Resident of 20 Miller's Court, the room directly over number 13, the scene of **Mary Jane Kelly**'s murder, Prater was a witness at Kelly's inquest. She testified that she had been awakened by her kitten at a time she estimated to be about 4 A.M. and had then heard a single cry of "Murder."

Preston, Charles

A resident of the lodging house at 32 Flower and Dean Street and a witness at **Elizabeth Stride**'s inquest on 3 October 1888. He had last seen Elizabeth in the kitchen of the house between 6 and 7 P.M. on 29 September. He was able to give some background on the dead woman, including details of her husband having run a coffee stall in Poplar. He also mentioned that Elizabeth had once faced a drunk and disorderly charge for an occurrence in the Queen's Head, Commercial Street.

Ptolomay, Charles

Night attendant at the Poplar Union Infirmary and a witness at **Rose Mylett**'s inquest. He said he had seen Rose talking to two sailors, and possibly involved in an argument with one of them, on 19 December 1888, the night before she died. He supplied descriptions of both men.

Purkiss, Walter

Incorrectly referred to by some writers as Walter King, he was a resident of Essex Wharf, Buck's Row, almost opposite Brown's Stable Yard gate, where **Mary Ann Nichols** was murdered. He appeared at the inquest on 17 September 1888 to say that he and his family, most of whom had spent a restless night, had heard nothing until awakened by Constable John Neil.

Reeves, John Saunders

A resident of 37 George Yard Buildings who found the body of **Martha Tabram** on 7 August 1888. Reeves found Constable Thomas Barrett and returned to the scene with him. He gave evidence at Martha's inquest.

See also "The Police": Barrett, Constable Thomas

Richardson, Amelia

A resident of 29 Hanbury Street who occupied the front room on the first floor with her 14-year-old grandson, Thomas. She appeared at **Annie Chapman**'s inquest on 12 September 1888 and said she had retired on the night of 7 September at 9:30 P.M. She had slept fitfully and had been wide awake at 3 A.M. on the 8th. About half an hour later she heard her neighbor Mr. Thompson leave, and he called out "Good morning" to her. She had heard no one else in the passageway that led to the yard.

At 6 A.M. she heard noise in the corridor and sent her grandson to find out what was happening. He returned to say that a woman had been murdered in the yard, whereupon she went to take a look for herself, by which time the passageway was crowded with police and other men.

See also Richardson, John; Richardson, Thomas

Richardson, John

Amelia Richardson's son and a resident of 2 John Street. He appeared at **Annie Chapman**'s inquest on 12 September 1888. He reported that he occasionally checked the yard from which his mother ran her packing-case business and had done so at 4:45 A.M. on 8 September. At the time, one of his boots was causing him trouble, so he sat on the steps that led down into the yard and, using a knife, cut a piece of leather from the offending boot. Though it was just getting to be light, he did not see the body lying just a few feet in front of him.

According to the medical evidence, Annie should have been in the yard at this time, so it was believed that Richardson's view had been obstructed by the swing door that opened outward into the yard. However, it is much more likely, taking into account the testimony of other witnesses, that the medical testimony was in error and that Annie Chapman had died later than Dr. Phillips believed.

At the inquest, Richardson had to display the knife he habitually carried that he had used to mend his boot. It was shown that it could not have inflicted Annie's wounds.

See also Phillips, Dr. George Bagster; Richardson, Amelia

Richardson, Thomas

Resident of 29 Hanbury Street and the grandson of Amelia Richardson, with whom he lived. Though he did not give evidence at **Annie Chapman**'s inquest, he did go to investigate the noise in the passageway at 6 A.M. on 8 September 1888, at his grandmother's behest. He returned to tell her that a body had been found in the yard.

See also Richardson, Amelia

Ryder, Elizabeth

Also known as Betsy Ryder, she was the wife of the lodging-house keeper at 52 Gun Street and a witness at **Alice McKenzie**'s inquest on 17 July 1889. She gave evidence regarding Alice's movements on her last night and confirmed that Alice and her lover, John McCormack, had also been known to stay at Crossingham's lodging house at 35 Dorset Street.

See also McCormack, John

Saunders, Dr. William Sedgewick

Called in to examine the stomach contents of **Catherine Eddowes** for possible traces of any narcotic or drug. He appeared at the inquest to say that he had found none. Furthermore, it was his view that the murderer possessed no anatomical knowledge. Later he gave the view that the kidney sent to George Lusk was nothing more than a student prank.

See also "Letters and Correspondence": Newspaper Letter of 5 December 1888; "Miscellaneous": Lusk Kidney

Schwartz, Israel

Resident of 22 Ellen Street, Back Church Lane. Early on the morning of 30 September 1888 he had turned into Berner Street from Commercial Road. Approaching Dutfield's Yard, he saw a woman standing in the gateway. A man stopped to speak to her, but an argument seemed to break out, for the man tried to pull the woman into the yard. She resisted, whereupon he turned her around and threw her onto the pavement, causing her to scream out three times.

In order to avoid this confrontation, Schwartz, who spoke very little English, crossed to the other side of the street. As he was passing the couple he noticed another man in the shadows, lighting his pipe, though later press reports often amend this detail to say the man was drawing out a knife.

The first man called out, "Lipski," apparently to the man with the pipe, who then began to follow Schwartz. Schwartz quickened his pace and dashed as far as the railway arches. Turning to check if he was still being followed, he saw that the man with the pipe had vanished.

After the murder of **Elizabeth Stride**, Schwartz went voluntarily to the police to tell them what he had seen. Taken to view the body in the mortuary, he said he believed it was the woman he had seen. He gave descriptions of both men.

There is no record of Schwartz being called to give evidence at the inquest and no reports of his evidence being heard by the coroner in camera, but Dr. Robert Anderson, writing about the meaning of the term *Lipski,* does refer to "the evidence given by Schwartz at the inquest," so there is a possibility that his testimony was heard in secret. It is equally possible that Anderson was mistaken.

See also "The Police": Anderson, Dr. Robert; "Miscellaneous": Anderson's Witness; Lipski, Israel

Sequeira, Dr. George William

Summoned from his surgery at 34 Jewry Street by Constable Holland on 30 September 1888 to examine the body of **Catherine Eddowes** in Mitre Square, he did not make a detailed examination, preferring to leave it to the official police surgeon, Dr. Frederick Gordon Brown.

He gave evidence at the inquest, during which he said he did not believe the killer had shown any degree of particular anatomical skill or knowledge.

See also Brown, Dr. Frederick Gordon

Simonds, Mary Elizabeth

A nurse at the Whitechapel Infirmary, she appeared as a witness at **Annie Chapman**'s inquest on 13 September 1888 to testify that she and another woman named Frances Wright had undressed and washed Annie's body in the Whitechapel Mortuary.

See also Wright, Frances

Smith, Fountain

Brother of **Annie Chapman** and a witness at her inquest on 12 September 1888, he stated that he had seen her shortly before her death and had given her two shillings.

Smith, Sarah

Manager of the Whitechapel Baths and Washhouses on Goulston Street, she was a witness at **Alice McKenzie**'s inquest on 17 July 1889. She testified that at the time of the murder she had been reading in bed. Her room overlooked the murder site, but she had heard nothing. She did hear Constable Walter Andrews blow his whistle in order to summon assistance.

See also "The Police": Andrews, Constable Walter

Spooner, Edward

Sometime just after 1 A.M. on Sunday, 30 September 1888, Spooner was outside the Bee Hive public house, on the corner of Fairclough and Christian Streets, with his young lady. They saw two men run past and go as far as Grove Street, where they turned back. As they passed Spooner again, he asked them what the problem was, and they told him a woman had been found with her throat cut in Dutfield's Yard, Berner Street.

Spooner returned with the two men, Isaac Kozebrodsky and Louis Diemschutz. When they reached the yard he bent down to lift the woman's head and found her chin slightly warm and blood still flowing from the wound in her throat.

Spooner, who resided at 26 Fairclough Street, appeared at the inquest on **Elizabeth Stride** on 2 October and, in addition to describing what he had seen in the yard, confirmed that he had helped Constable Henry Lamb shut the yard gates. Spooner also confirmed that Elizabeth had been wearing a flower on her jacket and had grasped a packet of cachous in her hand.

See also Diemschutz, Louis; Kozebrodsky, Isaac M.; "The Police": Lamb, Constable Henry

Stanley, Ted

Also known as "the Pensioner," he was a resident of 1 Osborn Place, Brick Lane. His nickname came about because his friends and acquaintances believed he had served in the Essex Regiment and was in receipt of an army pension. When he appeared before the police, he confirmed that he had never served in the Essex but had served in the Hampshire Militia and was not in fact receiving any military pension. He was a friend or client of **Annie Chapman**'s and had sometimes paid for her bed at Crossingham's lodging house at 35 Dorset Street. He appeared at Commercial Street Police Station on 14 September 1888 to outline his movements on the night of Annie's murder.

There was a suggestion that the argument between Annie and Eliza Cooper had been over a piece of soap Annie had borrowed for Stanley's use.

See also Cooper, Eliza

Stevens, William

A painter and resident of Crossingham's lodging house at 35 Dorset Street, he knew **Annie Chapman** and had seen her in the house on 7 September 1888, when she told him she had been to the hospital. Later he was present when the box containing the pills she had been given broke, and he saw Annie pick up the piece of envelope subsequently found in the yard of 29 Hanbury Street and use it to wrap the pills. This testimony effectively laid to rest the "clue" of the envelope bearing the crest of the Sussex Regiment.

Stokes, Elizabeth

The sister of Mary Malcolm, who appeared at **Elizabeth Stride**'s inquest in the early stages to identify the dead woman as Stokes. After that fiasco, Elizabeth Stokes herself appeared as a witness in order to prove that she was not the dead woman. By this time her character had been well and truly demolished by Malcolm.

See also Malcolm, Mary

Sutton, Dr. Henry Gowan

Called in by Major Henry Smith, the acting commissioner of the City of London Police, to report on the kidney sent to George Lusk, he stated that it was his firm opinion that the kidney had been placed in spirits within a few hours of its removal from the body. This meant that it could not have come from a dissecting room because such organs would not be preserved so quickly.

See also "Miscellaneous": Lusk Kidney

Tabram, Henry Samuel

A foreman furniture packer and resident of 6 River Terrace, East Greenwich, he was the estranged husband of **Martha Tabram**. Having read reports of the crime in the newspapers, he came forward and made a formal identification of the dead woman on 14 August 1888. He appeared at the inquest on 23 August.

Tanner, Elizabeth

Deputy keeper of the lodging house at 32 Flower and Dean Street where **Elizabeth Stride** had lodged on and off, she appeared at the inquest on 3 October 1888 to give identification evidence. She told of Elizabeth's history, saying she believed Elizabeth to have been Swedish and that her husband and two children had died in the *Princess Alice* disaster.

Tanner also stated that she had seen the dead woman at 6:30 P.M. on 29 September in the Queen's Head public house on Commercial Street and again, in the kitchen of the lodging house, at about 7 P.M. Before that Elizabeth Stride had cleaned her private rooms at the lodging house, for which Tanner paid her sixpence.

Tomkins, Henry

A resident of Coventry Street, Bethnal Green, and employed at Barber's Horse Slaughterer's Yard in Winthrop Street, he gave evidence at **Mary Ann Nichols**'s inquest on 3 September 1888 to say that he and his fellow workers, James Mumford and Charles Brittain, had been told about the finding of the body by Constable John Thain when Thain called to collect his cape on his way to fetch Dr. Llewellyn.

Tomkins and Mumford had gone to look at the body at 4:15 A.M. They were followed a few minutes later by Brittain. Tomkins stayed at the spot until the body was taken away on the police ambulance.

See also Brittain, Charles; Llewellyn, Dr. Reese Ralph; Mumford, James

Turner, William

Resident of the Victoria Working Men's Home in Commercial Street and a witness at **Martha Tabram**'s inquest, he stated that he had lived with Martha, on and off, for 10 years, leaving her occasionally because of her drinking habits. They had last parted some three weeks before her death, and he had last seen her in Leadenhall on 4 August 1888.

Van Turney, Julia

Resident of 1 Miller's Court, was opposite **Mary Jane Kelly**'s room, and a witness at Kelly's inquest. She testified that Kelly and Joe Barnett had lived peacefully together and that Barnett was kind to Kelly. Van Turney referred to the broken window of Mary's room and said it had been smashed a few weeks before the murder by Mary herself when she was drunk. She also told of another of Kelly's admirers, a costermonger named Joe, who had ill-treated Mary because she lived with Barnett.

See also Barnett, Joseph

Walker, Edward

Resident of 16 Maidswood Road, Camberwell, and the father of **Mary Ann Nichols**. He identified his daughter's body on 1 September 1888 and gave evidence at her inquest later that same day.

West, William

Resident of 2 William Street and a witness at **Elizabeth Stride**'s inquest. He was in Dutfield's Yard at 12:30 A.M., taking some literature to the printing office of *Der Arbeter Fraint*. He left the club by the main door with his brother and Louis Stanley and later returned through the yard. At no time did he notice a body lying on the ground.

Wilkinson, Frederick William

The deputy at Cooney's lodging house at 55 Flower and Dean Street and a witness at **Catherine Eddowes**'s inquest. He confirmed that Catherine and John Kelly had stayed at the lodging house.

Wright, Frances

Together with Mary Simonds, she stripped and washed the body of **Annie Chapman**. She was not called to give evidence at the inquest.

See also Simonds, Mary Elizabeth

Young, Captain

Of the 1st Battalion of the Sussex Regiment, stationed at Farnborough. Interviewed by the police in relation to the portion of envelope found in the yard where **Annie Chapman** was murdered, he said anyone could have bought the envelope in the canteen.

3

The Police

Every police officer who played any part in the investigations of the various murders is included in this section. Some played very minor roles; others had a much greater involvement. Obviously, the officers are also mentioned in the cases they worked on. (See "The Victims" section.)

Let me begin with a little historical background. The Metropolitan Police area was defined by the Act of 1829 as an area of about a 7-mile radius from Charing Cross. To begin with, there were 17 divisions based around the following areas:

A: Westminster
B: Chelsea
C: Mayfair and Soho
D: Marylebone
E: Holborn
F: Kensington
G: Kings Cross
H: Stepney
K: West Ham
L: Lambeth
M: Southwark
N: Islington
P: Peckham
R: Greenwich
T: Hammersmith
V: Wandsworth

In 1865 three more divisions were added:

W: Clapham
X: Willesden
Y: Holloway.

In 1886 another division was created, which is germane to the Ripper story because it was J: Bethnal Green. There were no more changes until 1921.

Abberline, Inspector Frederick George

One of the most experienced officers involved in the Whitechapel murders, he is believed by some, erroneously, to have been in overall charge of the case.

Before the murders, in 1873, Abberline was promoted to inspector and then transferred to the H Division, where he remained until 1887, when he was transferred first to A Division and then to Scotland Yard.

After the murder of **Mary Ann Nichols** he was seconded (temporarily assigned) back to the Whitechapel area because of his unprecedented local knowledge; once the series of deaths had been established, he was placed in charge of the detectives investigating the murders.

In later years Abberline came to accept that Severin Klosowski, alias George Chapman, was Jack the Ripper.

See also "Miscellaneous": Abberline Diaries; Lipski, Israel; "The Suspects": Chapman, George

Allen, Constable Joseph

Allen was Constable 423H. Early on 17 July 1889, the morning that **Alice McKenzie** met her death, Allen spoke briefly to his fellow officer, Constable

Walter Andrews, who would later find the body. About 30 minutes before Alice was found, Allen had paused to eat a snack under a lamp in Castle Alley, very close to where the body would later be discovered.

Sergeant Badham later sent Allen to fetch the doctor and to inform the duty inspector at Commercial Street Police Station of the murder.

See also Andrews, Constable Walter; Badham, Sergeant Edward

Anderson, Dr. Robert [later Sir]

Appointed assistant commissioner for crime on 31 August 1888, the day of **Mary Ann Nichols**'s murder, he placed Chief Inspector Donald Sutherland Swanson in charge of the case.

On 8 September 1888, the day of **Annie Chapman**'s murder, Anderson went on holiday to Switzerland, at his doctor's orders, to recover from the stresses of overwork. He was recalled after the so-called double event of 30 September, the murders of **Elizabeth Stride** and **Catherine Eddowes,** and soon afterward, on 6 October, was placed in overall command of the investigation and appointed assistant commissioner of the CID. He remained in charge until the case files were finally closed in 1892.

Anderson believed **Martha Tabram** was the first victim of the Whitechapel killer, and in two books, *Criminals and Crime* (1907) and *The Lighter Side of My Official Life* (1910) he stated categorically that the identity of the Ripper had been known. Anderson's unnamed suspect was later named by Swanson, in his handwritten comments in the margins of his copy of *The Lighter Side,* as Kosminski.

See also Swanson, Chief Inspector Donald Sutherland; "Miscellaneous": Anderson's Suspect; Anderson's Witness; *Criminals and Crime: Some Facts and Suggestions;* Goulston Street Graffito; *The Lighter Side of My Official Life;* Swanson Marginalia; "The Suspects": Kosminski, Aaron

Andrews, Constable Walter

Andrews, Constable 272H, was the officer who found the body of **Alice McKenzie** on 17 July 1889. After speaking to Sergeant Badham he was walking on down Castle Alley, heading toward Whitechapel High Street, when he found Alice between two carts. He blew his whistle, which summoned Badham back to the scene, and detained a passerby, Isaac Lewis Jacob, who proved to have no involvement in the crime.

See also Badham, Sergeant Edward; "The Witnesses": Jacob, Isaac Lewis

Andrews, Inspector Walter

Andrews became involved in the latter part of 1888 after he escorted two prisoners, Roland Gideon and Israel Barnet, from London to Montreal to answer charges of blowing up the Central Bank of Toronto. From there he was directed to New York on the Ripper investigation, and it is probable that he was asked to look especially into Dr. Francis Tumblety. However, this investigation is not proof that Tumblety was a major suspect. It is just as likely that Andrews was simply asked to check out Tumblety because the latter had jumped bail in London.

This American investigation has been misrepresented by some authors who have read more into it than was actually the case. In an interview with the *St. Louis Republican* Andrews remarked that Scotland Yard at that time (December 1888) had 23 detectives, 2 clerks, and 1 inspector engaged on the investigation. This comment was picked up by the *Daily Telegraph* and *Pall Mall Gazette* and exaggerated into claims that 6 detectives, the 2 clerks, and the inspector were actively searching in the United States.

See also "The Suspects": Tumblety, "Dr." Francis

Arnold, Superintendent Thomas

Arnold was the head of H Division at the time of the murders, but he was on leave before the events of 30 September 1888. He was one of the officers anxious to have the Goulston Street graffito erased in the **Catherine Eddowes** case, and he sent an inspector with a wet sponge to wipe it off.

An idea of Arnold's reliability may be gathered from a quotation in an interview with the *Eastern Post* in February 1893, in which he stated, "I still hold the opinion that not more than four of these murders were committed by the same hand. They were the murders of Annie Chapman in Hanbury Street, Mrs Nicholls in Buck's Row, Elizabeth Stride in Berner Street and Mary Kelly in Mitre Square." In that one short passage Arnold got the chronology wrong, along with the names of two of the victims or possibly the location of the last murder.

See also "Miscellaneous": Goulston Street Graffito

Badham, Sergeant Edward

Badham played a role in three of the Ripper investigations. On 8 September 1888 he was sent to assist Inspector Chandler and took the body of **Annie Chapman** to the mortuary on the police ambulance.

On 12 November, it was Badham who took George Hutchinson's statement after the inquest on **Mary Jane Kelly** had closed.

Finally, he was involved in the **Alice McKenzie** case on 17 July 1889 when he went to the assistance of Constable Walter Andrews, the officer who found the body.

See also Andrews, Constable Walter; Chandler, Inspector Joseph Luniss

Barrett, Constable Thomas

Barrett was Constable 226H. He was called to the scene of **Martha Tabram**'s murder on 7 August 1888 by John Saunders Reeves. Barrett was a witness at the inquest on 9 August; in addition to telling of the finding of the body and his actions thereafter, he also referred to a soldier he had seen in Wentworth Street early on the morning of the 7th. Barrett attended a parade at the Tower on two occasions and on the second picked out two men as possibly the man he had seen. Both identifications were erroneous, but only one, that of Private John Leary, was named in records of the case.

See also "The Witnesses": Leary, Private John; Reeves, John Saunders

Beck, Inspector Walter

The first police officer at the scene of **Mary Jane Kelly**'s murder. He was the duty inspector at Commercial Street Police Station when Thomas Bowyer and then John McCarthy told him what they had found in Miller's Court. He went to the scene with Detective Dew.

See also Dew, Detective Walter; "The Witnesses": Bowyer, Thomas; McCarthy, John

Bradford, Colonel Sir Edward Riley Colborne

Became the Metropolitan police commissioner after Monro, in 1890, and therefore played little part in the investigations.

See also Monro, James

Bruce, Alexander Carmichael

The assistant commissioner of the Metropolitan Police, he played little part in the investigations but did visit the sites of the murders of **Mary Ann Nichols** in Buck's Row and **Annie Chapman** in Hanbury Street.

Byfield, Sergeant James George

The duty sergeant at Bishopsgate Police Station on the evening of 29 September and the morning of 30 September 1888, he was present when **Catherine Eddowes** was taken into custody for drunkenness; it was he who later discharged her.

Cartwright, Constable

Received instructions from Inspector Spratling, after the murder of **Mary Ann Nichols**, to search the neighborhood. He found nothing.

See also Spratling, Inspector John

Caunter, Sergeant Eli

The officer who traced Mary Ann Connolly after she failed to appear at the Tower to attend a parade of soldiers on 10 August 1888 in order to identify the men she said she and **Martha Tabram** had been with on the night of the latter's death. Caunter traced Connolly to her cousin's house in Fuller's Court, Drury Lane, two days later on 12 August.

See also "The Witnesses": Connolly, Mary Ann

Causby, Inspector William

Causby played a small part in the investigation. Together with Sergeant Thick he organized an identification parade in which John Pizer, also known as Leather Apron, was picked out by Emmanuel Violenia as the man he had seen with **Annie Chapman** not long before her murder.

See also Thick, Sergeant William; "Others Who Played a Part": Violenia, Emmanuel Delbast; "The Suspects": Pizer, John

Chandler, Inspector Joseph Luniss

The first police officer at the scene of **Annie Chapman**'s murder in Hanbury Street, he sent for the doctor and for other officers from the police station. Later, after the body was moved, he conducted a search of the yard and found a portion of envelope containing two pills.

A witness at the inquest on 13 September 1888, he confirmed the finding of the leather apron close to the tap and described the layout of the yard and the fact that the door opened outward on the left-hand side.

See also "Others Who Played a Part": Sickings, Laura

Collard, Inspector Edward

Duty inspector at Bishopsgate Police Station on the morning of 30 September 1888, he was alerted to the murder of **Catherine Eddowes** in Mitre Square and went there, timing his arrival at 2:03 A.M. He ordered an immediate search of the area and house-to-house inquiries on 1 October. He appeared at the inquest.

Collins, Reserve Constable Albert

Collins, Constable 12HR, was on duty with Constable Lamb on the morning of Sunday, 30 September 1888, in Commercial Road when Morris Eagle told them of the discovery of **Elizabeth Stride**'s body. He was instructed by Lamb to fetch the doctor, which he did, returning soon afterward with Dr. Blackwell's assistant, Edward Johnston. Later still, at 5:30 A.M., Collins washed the blood away from Dutfield's Yard.

See also Lamb, Constable Henry; "The Witnesses": Blackwell, Dr. Frederick William; Eagle, Morris; Johnston, Edward

Cunningham, Inspector James Henry

Working in C Division, Mayfair and Soho, he was drafted into Whitechapel during the Ripper scare.

Dew, Detective Walter

Dew accompanied Inspector Beck to the scene of **Mary Jane Kelly**'s murder on 9 November 1888. He is more famous as the man who captured Hawley Harvey Crippen in 1910. He published a memoir titled *I Caught Crippen* in 1938. This book referred to the Whitechapel murders but was filled with inaccuracies.

See also Beck, Inspector Walter

Drage, Constable Joseph William

Drage, Constable 282H, was on duty in Whitechapel Road on the morning of 30 September 1888. He noticed a man bend down close to the front step of number 253 and walked toward him to see what he was doing. The man, Thomas Coram, pointed out a bloodstained knife lying on the step. Drage took possession of the knife and took it, along with Coram, to Leman Street Police Station.

See also "The Witnesses": Coram, Thomas

Dudman, Sergeant

An officer of the City Police, he helped Inspector Izzard and Sergeant Phelps keep public order after the murder of **Catherine Eddowes** in Mitre Square on 30 September 1888.

See also Izzard, Inspector; Phelps, Sergeant

Elliott, Detective Constable George

One of the first officers to come to the aid of Constable Thompson after the latter discovered the body of **Frances Coles** on 13 February 1891.

See also Thompson, Constable Ernest

Enright, Detective Sergeant Patrick

The officer detailed to take charge of **Mary Ann Nichols**'s body at the mortuary. He was called to answer a question at the inquest on 3 September 1888 and confirmed that he had given express instructions to Robert Mann and James Hatfield, the mortuary attendants, not to touch the body.

See also "The Witnesses": Hatfield, James; Mann, Robert

Foster, Detective Superintendent Alfred Lawrence

A City policeman who was present in Mitre Square soon after the body of **Catherine Eddowes** was discovered. He was later given the care of Joseph Lawende, which demonstrates that Lawende was believed to be a most important witness.

See also "The Witnesses": Lawende, Joseph

Gallagher, Constable John

Constable 221H and the officer who arrested Charles Ludwig in Whitechapel High Street on the morning of 18 September 1888.

See also "The Suspects": Ludwig, Charles

Godley, Detective Sergeant George

Assisted Inspector Spratling in a search of the railway yards and embankments after the murder of **Mary Ann Nichols** in Buck's Row. Godley would achieve fame in 1903 as the officer who arrested Severin Klosowski, a.k.a. George Chapman.

See also Spratling, Inspector John; "The Suspects": Chapman, George

Goulding, Constable Robert

The officer who found the body of **Rose Mylett** on the morning of 20 December 1888. The undisturbed state of her clothing, the absence of any apparent injury, and the fact that she had not been robbed led Goulding to assume that she had died of natural causes.

Halse, Detective Constable Daniel

Plainclothes officer on duty the morning of 30 September 1888 along with Sergeant Outram and Constable Marriott. They were near St. Botolph's Church, on the corner of Aldgate and Houndsditch, when they heard the news of the murder of **Catherine Eddowes** in Mitre Square. After going to the square, Halse set out on a search of the area but, finding nothing, returned to Mitre Square. There he received news of the discovery of the apron and graffito in Goulston Street, so he went to Leman Street Police Station, along with Detective Hunt. From there they went to Goulston Street and spoke to the officer who had found the items, Constable Long.

Halse was present when the graffito was rubbed out and was the only officer at the scene to make an objection. He gave evidence at the subsequent inquest on Catherine Eddowes.

See also Hunt, Detective Baxter; Long, Constable Alfred; Marriott, Detective Constable Edward; Outram, Detective Sergeant Robert; "Miscellaneous": Goulston Street Graffito

Hart, Constable

Hart, Constable 161H, was the first officer to answer Constable Thompson's whistle after the discovery of **Frances Coles**'s body on 13 February 1891. It was Hart who ran for the doctor.

See also Thompson, Constable Ernest

Harvey, Constable James

Harvey, Constable 964, was a witness at **Catherine Eddowes**'s inquest. On the morning of 30 September 1888 his beat included Church Passage. He stated that he entered the passage and walked as far as the entrance to Mitre Square at approximately 1:40 A.M. but saw nothing. He was dismissed from the police force in July 1889.

Hayes, Superintendent

A Windsor police officer who, during the investigation into **Annie Chapman**'s death, reported that she had been arrested for drunkenness at Windsor but had not been prosecuted for the offense.

Helson, Inspector Joseph Henry

Based in the Bethnal Green, or J, Division, he was the senior officer in the investigation into **Mary Ann Nichols**'s murder. Helson discovered the abdominal injuries at the mortuary and summoned Dr. Llewellyn back to make a second examination.

See also "The Witnesses": Llewellyn, Dr. Rees Ralph

Hemingway, Chief Constable

Chief constable of the Cardiff police. When **Mary Jane Kelly**'s antecedents were being investigated, he informed a reporter that he knew of no one fitting her description who had come to the attention of the police in that area.

Hinton, Constable

Hinton came to the aid of Constable Ernest Thompson after the latter had discovered the body of **Frances Coles** on 13 February 1891. Hinton dashed to the police station at Leman Street to get further police assistance.

See also Thompson, Constable Ernest

Holland, Constable James Thomas

Holland, Constable 814, was summoned to assist Constable Watkins by George Morris after the murder of **Catherine Eddowes** on 30 September 1888. He dashed to the surgery of Dr. Sequeira in Jewry Street to get medical aid.

See also Watkins, Constable Edward; "The Witnesses": Morris, George James; Sequeira, Dr. George William

Hunt, Detective Baxter

Went with Constable Halse to Leman Street Police Station to receive news of Constable Long's discovery of the apron and graffito in Goulston Street on the morning of 30 September 1888 after **Catherine Eddowes**'s body was discovered. Hunt later left Halse to guard the graffito while he returned to Mitre Square to report the find to Inspector McWilliam.

He also made a search, with Detective Sergeant John Mitchell, for Thomas Conway, Catherine's husband, but they found only another man of the same name serving in the 18th Royal Irish Regiment.

See also Halse, Detective Constable Daniel; Long, Constable Alfred; McWilliam, Inspector James; Mitchell, Detective Sergeant John; "Miscellaneous": Goulston Street Graffito

Hutt, Constable George

Hutt, Constable 968, was the officer in charge of the cells at Bishopsgate Police Station on the night of 29–30 September 1888. He checked on **Catherine Eddowes,** who had been detained for drunkenness, from time to time. When he judged her to be sober and capable of looking after herself, Hutt took her to Sergeant Byfield, who discharged her. He saw her turn left outside the station door and estimated later that it would have taken her no more than eight minutes to reach Mitre Square.

See also Byfield, Sergeant James George

Hyde, Constable

Assisted Constable Ernest Thompson after the discovery of **Frances Coles**'s body on 13 February 1891. Hyde ran to the surgery of Dr. Oxley and returned with him to the scene.

See also Thompson, Constable Ernest; "The Witnesses": Oxley, Dr.

Imhoff, Constable Henry

Imhoff, Constable 211H, was the officer who arrested Nikaner Benelius on 27 November 1888 after the latter walked into Harriett Rowe's home in Buxton Street and frightened her. Benelius was cleared of any involvement in the murders.

See also "The Suspects": Benelius, Nikaner

Izzard, Inspector

An officer of the City Police who helped Sergeant Dudman and Sergeant Phelps to keep order after the murder of **Catherine Eddowes** in Mitre Square on 30 September 1888.

See also Dudman, Sergeant; Phelps, Sergeant

Johnson, Constable John

Johnson, Constable 866, was on duty in The Minories early on the morning of 18 September 1888 when he heard a woman cry, "Murder." Going to where the sound had emanated from, Three Kings Court, he found Elizabeth Burns in the company of Charles Ludwig. Burns appealed for assistance, and Johnson saw Ludwig off. Only then did Burns mention that her assailant had had a knife. Johnson went in search of Ludwig but failed to find him.

See also "The Suspects": Ludwig, Charles

Jones, Sergeant

Another City police officer present in Mitre Square after the body of **Catherine Eddowes** was discovered on 30 September 1888. Jones searched the area around the body and discovered a thimble, three boot buttons, and a mustard tin, which held the two pawn tickets that would soon lead to identification of the body.

Kerby, Sergeant

One of the officers who attended the scene of **Mary Ann Nichols**'s murder in Bucks Row and assisted in the removal of the body to the mortuary.

Lamb, Constable Henry

Lamb, Constable 252H, was with Reserve Constable Collins between Batty Street and Christian Street on Commercial Road early on the morning of 30 September 1888. The two officers were walking toward Berner Street when Morris Eagle ran up to them and said a woman had been attacked in Dutfield's Yard.

The two officers returned with Eagle, and Lamb instructed Collins to run for the doctor. He also told Eagle to report what had happened to the inspector at the Leman Street Police Station.

Lamb touched the woman's face and found it slightly warm. He also tried to find a pulse, but without success. Soon afterward he closed the gates to the yard, finding that he could do so without disturbing the position of the body.

On 2 October he appeared at **Elizabeth Stride**'s inquest, where he also stated that he had warned the men in the yard to stay back in case they got blood on themselves and were suspected as a result. He also examined the houses and water closets in the yard but found nothing.

See also Collins, Reserve Constable Albert; "The Witnesses": Eagle, Morris

Littlechild, Chief Inspector John George

At the time of the Whitechapel murders Littlechild was head of the Secret Department, which later became the Special Branch. He is not known to have played a major part in the investigations but is important for his writing of the Littlechild letter in 1913, which named Tumblety as a likely suspect.

See also "Others Who Played a Part": Moore, Charles; "Miscellaneous": Littlechild Letter; "The Suspects": Tumblety, "Dr." Francis

Long, Constable Alfred

Long, Constable 254A, was on duty in the Goulston Street area on the morning of 30 September 1888. At 2:55 A.M. he found the piece of apron and the graffito on the wall of the staircase of 108–119 Wentworth Model Dwellings, close to the Wentworth Street end of Goulston Street.

He left a brother officer to guard the writing while he took the stained apron to Commercial Street Police Station. He gave evidence at the inquest for **Catherine Eddowes**, and he was criticized by a juror for not searching the rooms in the building where the discovery was made.

Long was dismissed from the force in July 1889 for being drunk on duty.

See also "Miscellaneous": Goulston Street Graffito

Macnaghten, Sir Melville Leslie

Macnaghten became assistant chief constable of the Metropolitan Police in June 1889, after the five canonical murders. He claimed to possess secret information that enabled him to know with certainty who the killer was but said he had destroyed all the documents. Whether or not this claim should be taken with a pinch of salt, he did pen the Macnaghten Memoranda in 1894, which named three suspects and finally claimed that Montague John Druitt was the most likely suspect. Macnaghten published his memoirs, *Days of My Years,* in 1914.

See also "Miscellaneous": Aberconway, Lady; Goulston Street Graffito; Macnaghten Memoranda; "The Suspects": Druitt, Montague John

Marriott, Detective Constable Edward

Plainclothes officer on duty on the morning of 30 September 1888, along with Constable Halse and Sergeant Outram.

Marriott was on the corner of Aldgate and Houndsditch when he received news of the murder of **Catherine Eddowes** in Mitre Square. He went to the square and then set out to search the immediate area. He found nothing and was not called to give evidence at the inquest.

See also Halse, Detective Constable Daniel; Outram, Detective Sergeant Robert

McCarthy, Constable John

McCarthy is known to have been involved in the investigation only through some press reports and through the Macnaghten Memoranda, which state that he was employed on the Cutbush case in 1891.

See also "Miscellaneous": Macnaghten Memoranda; "The Suspects": Cutbush, Thomas Hayne

McWilliam, Inspector James

Attended the scene of **Catherine Eddowes**'s murder in Mitre Square on the morning of 30 September 1888. Detective Hunt told him of the discovery of the graffito and piece of apron in Goulston Street, and McWilliam ordered that the writing be photographed. He was present when Dr. Brown matched the piece of apron with that still worn by Catherine Eddowes.

See also Hunt, Detective Baxter; "The Witnesses": Brown, Dr. Frederick Gordon; "Miscellaneous": Goulston Street Graffito

Mitchell, Detective Sergeant John

Slightly involved in the **Catherine Eddowes** investigation. Together with another detective, Baxter Hunt, he tried to trace Thomas Conway, the dead woman's husband. The two officers did find a Thomas Conway serving in the 18th Royal Irish regiment, but he proved to be the wrong man.

See also Hunt, Detective Baxter

Mizen, Constable Jonas

Mizen, Constable 55H, was the officer to whom Charles Cross and Robert Paul reported the finding of **Mary Ann Nichols**'s body early on 31 August 1888. Mizen went to the scene in Buck's Row, only to find Constable Neil already there. Neil sent Mizen to fetch the police ambulance and further help from Bethnal Green Police Station. Mizen gave evidence at the inquest on 3 September.

Monro, James

Before the murder of **Mary Ann Nichols,** Monro was the assistant commissioner of the Metropolitan Police. During the period of the five canonical murders he served briefly as head of the Detective Service and was then appointed commissioner, replacing Sir Charles Warren, whose resignation was accepted on 9 November 1888, the date of **Mary Jane Kelly**'s murder.

See also Warren, Sir Charles

Monsell, Colonel Bolton

Monsell was chief constable of the Metropolitan Police, in which capacity he visited the sites of two of the murders, those of **Mary Ann Nichols** and **Annie Chapman.** Later, in July 1891, he shared the direction of the investigation into **Alice McKenzie**'s murder, along with Monro.

See also Monro, James

Moore, Chief Inspector Henry

Described by newspaper sources of the time as the officer in charge of the murder investigations. He was interviewed by the *Pall Mall Gazette* in November 1889, and the resulting report claimed that Moore had stated that he had visited the scene of **Mary Jane Kelly**'s murder and that parts of her body had been placed around the room on nails. This detail was clearly disproved by the medical reports, which showed that all of Kelly's body parts were either on the bed or on one of the two wooden tables.

Moulson, Constable George

Moulson, Constable 216T, was the first officer at the scene when Montague John Druitt's body was pulled from the river Thames on 31 December 1888.

See also "The Suspects": Druitt, Montague John

Neil, Constable John

Neil, Constable 97J, found the body of **Mary Ann Nichols** in Buck's Row after Charles Cross and Robert Paul had left the scene. Neil signaled for help to Constable Thain, whom he sent for Dr. Llewellyn. He was soon joined by Constable Mizen, who had been alerted by Cross and Paul, and whom Neil sent for the ambulance and further police assistance.

Neil also woke Walter Purkiss at Essex Wharf, helped to lift the body onto the ambulance, and then accompanied it to the mortuary, along with Mizen and Sergeant Kerby. He was present when Inspector Spratling noticed the abdominal mutilations. He appeared at the inquest on 1 September 1888.

See also Kerby, Sergeant; Mizen, Constable Jonas; Spratling, Inspector John; Thain, Constable John; "The Witnesses": Cross, Charles; Llewellyn, Dr. Rees Ralph; Paul, Robert

Neve, Constable George

Neve, Constable 101H, was one of the officers who came to the aid of Sergeant Badham after the body of **Alice McKenzie** was found on 17 July 1889. Neve was detailed to search the immediate area but found nothing. He appeared at Alice's inquest, also on 17 July, to testify that the police believed the dead woman had been a prostitute and that he had seen her talking to men, and apparently soliciting, in the streets around the area.

Outram, Detective Sergeant Robert

Plainclothes officer on duty on the morning of 30 September 1888, along with Constable Halse and Constable Marriott. These three were on the corner of Aldgate High Street and Houndsditch when they heard the news of the murder of **Catherine Eddowes** in Mitre Square. After going to the scene, Outram set out on a search of the area but found nothing. He did not give evidence at the inquest.

See also Halse, Detective Constable Daniel; Marriott, Detective Constable Edward

Patrick, Constable John

Patrick, Constable 91H, was the arresting officer in the Aaron Davis Cohen case and charged Cohen with being a wandering lunatic at the Thames Magistrate's Court on 7 December 1888. Later that same day, Patrick escorted Cohen to the Whitechapel Workhouse Infirmary.

See also "The Suspects": Cohen, Aaron Davis

Pearse, Constable Richard

Pearse, Constable 922, is not named as playing an active part in any of the investigations, but he was the officer who lived at 3 Mitre Square. The spot where **Catherine Eddowes** was murdered could be clearly seen from his bedroom window, but he heard and saw nothing on the morning that she met her death. Pearse had retired for the night at 12:20 A.M. on 30 September 1888 and did not wake until a fellow officer knocked on his door at about 2:20 A.M.

Pennett, Constable William

Pennett, Constable 239H, found the **Pinchin Street Torso** in a railway arch on 10 September 1889. After obtaining assistance, he searched the remaining arches and arrested two sailors and a bootblack who were sleeping rough.

Phelps, Sergeant

An officer of the City Police who helped Inspector Izzard and Sergeant Dudman in keeping good public order after the murder of **Catherine Eddowes** in Mitre Square on 30 September 1888.

See also Izzard, Inspector; Dudman, Sergeant

Pinhorn, Inspector Charles

Played a part in two of the murder investigations. He assisted Chief Inspector West at the site of the murder of **Elizabeth Stride** on 30 September 1888 and also investigated the **Pinchin Street Torso** murder of September 1889.

See also West, Chief Inspector

Race, Inspector William Nixon

The officer who arrested Thomas Cutbush on 9 March 1891.

See also "The Suspects": Cutbush, Thomas Hayne

Reid, Inspector Edmund John James

After Abberline had been transferred to A Division, Reid replaced him as head of the CID in H Division.

Reid attended the scene of **Elizabeth Stride**'s murder in Dutfield's Yard and later went to the mortuary to take down her description. But perhaps the most important part Reid placed in the investigation occurred at the inquest into the death of **Alice McKenzie,** when he reported that he had held a watching brief, or observational role, when coins similar to those in the **Annie Chapman** case had been found at the murder scene. This statement has been held by some writers to be proof that coins were placed at the scene of Chapman's murder in Hanbury Street. It must be remembered, however, that at the time of that murder Reid was on leave and played no part in the investigation.

More evidence of Reid's reliability, or lack thereof, may be gathered from the fact that he believed there were nine Ripper murders, that no part of any of the bodies was ever taken away, and that the Ripper's knife was a blunt one.

See also Abberline, Inspector Frederick George

Robinson, Constable Louis Frederick

Robinson, Constable 931, was the City policeman who arrested **Catherine Eddowes** for being drunk and disorderly in Aldgate High Street on the evening of 29 September 1888. He was assisted by Constable Simmons.

See also Simmons, Constable George

Roots, Inspector Thomas

Roots is not known to have played any active part in the murder investigations, but he did write a report on Robert Donston Stephenson, dated 26 December 1888 and intended for Inspector Abberline.

See also Abberline, Inspector Frederick George; "The Suspects": Stephenson, Robert Donston

Sagar, Detective Constable Robert

Sagar is mentioned in a 15 September 1946 article in *Reynolds News* as having kept a special watch on a suspect. The report read, in part, "Inspector Robert Sagar, who died in 1924, played a leading part in the Ripper investigations. In his memoirs he said 'We had good reason to suspect a man who worked in Butchers Row, Aldgate. We watched him carefully. There was no doubt that this man was insane, and after a time his friends thought it advisable to have him removed to a private asylum. After he was removed, there were no more Ripper atrocities.'" It is not known to whom Sagar was referring; it seems probable that he invented this story.

Simmons, Constable George

The officer who helped Constable Robinson to take **Catherine Eddowes** to the police station after she was arrested for being drunk and disorderly in Aldgate High Street.

See also Robinson, Constable Louis Frederick

Smith, Constable William

Smith was Constable 452H. His beat, which included Berner Street on the night of the so-called double event, the murders of **Elizabeth Stride** and **Catherine Eddowes**, 30 September 1888, took him about half an hour to patrol. At 12:30 A.M. on the 30th he walked down Berner Street and saw a woman he later identified as Elizabeth Stride standing opposite Dutfield's Yard with a man. Smith described the man as 5 feet 7 inches tall, clean shaven, and aged about 28. He was respectable looking, wore a dark felt deerstalker hat and dark clothing, and had a newspaper parcel in his hand about 18 inches long and 6 or 8 inches broad.

Half an hour later Smith again turned into Berner Street and saw a small crowd outside Dutfield's Yard. Upon going to investigate he found other police officers already there and saw Stride's body. Smith went to fetch the police ambulance at the same time that Edward Johnston arrived to make a medical examination of the body.

See also "The Witnesses": Johnston, Edward; "Descriptions": Physical Descriptions—Elizabeth Stride

Smith, Major Henry

At the time of the murders Major Smith was acting commissioner of the City of London police, and because Sir James Fraser, the commissioner, was on leave at the time of the murder of **Catherine Eddowes**, Smith took charge of the investigation.

He wrote his memoirs, titled *From Constable to Commissioner,* in 1910. In the book he made several false or erroneous claims, including a statement that he was once within five minutes of the murderer and had found a public sink where the Ripper had just washed his bloodstained hands. His documented movements of the night of 29–30 September 1888 clearly show this to have been impossible.

See also "Miscellaneous": Lusk Kidney

Spicer, Constable Robert

Spicer, Constable 101H, believed that he had captured Jack the Ripper and been admonished for doing so!

In 1931 Spicer, who had been dismissed from the force in April 1889 for being drunk on duty, wrote to the *Daily Express* to report that at the height of the investigations he had found a doctor with a prostitute named Rosy. Noting that the doctor had bloodstained cuffs and the ubiquitous medical bag, though it was brown, not black, Spicer took him into custody but was castigated by his superiors for detaining a respectable man.

See also "Others Who Played a Part": Rosy

Spratling, Inspector John

Visited the scene of **Mary Ann Nichols**'s murder on 31 August 1888 and later attended the mortuary to write down a description. While there he noticed the abdominal mutilations and called out Dr. Llewellyn to examine the body a second time. Spratling and Sergeant Godley also carried out a search of the railway yards and embankments close to the murder scene but found nothing. Spratling gave evidence at the inquest on 3 September.

See also Godley, Detective Sergeant George; "The Witnesses": Llewellyn, Dr. Rees Ralph

Stockley, Chief Inspector James

Not known to have played a part in the Ripper investigations beyond his own claim that he often disguised himself in order to patrol the area.

Stride, Constable Walter Frederick

A serving officer and the nephew of John Thomas Stride, who was the dead husband of **Elizabeth Stride,** he attended his aunt's inquest and assisted in proving her identity from mortuary photographs of the body.

Swanson, Chief Inspector Donald Sutherland

In overall charge of the investigation from 1 September until 6 October 1888. After 6 October he remained the desk officer in charge, reporting to Dr. Robert Anderson.

He and Anderson worked well together, and it was Swanson who wrote the penciled notes in his personal copy of Anderson's *The Lighter Side of My Official Life* that named Kosminski as the primary suspect, though Swanson erroneously stated that Kosminski had died soon after his incarceration in Colney Hatch.

See also Anderson, Dr. Robert; "Miscellaneous": Goulston Street Graffito; Lusk Kidney; Swanson Marginalia; "The Suspects": Kosminski, Aaron

Thain, Constable John

Thain, Constable 96J, answered the signal of Constable Neil after the latter had discovered the body of **Mary Ann Nichols** on 31 August 1888. Thain went to fetch Dr. Llewellyn, apparently calling at a horse-slaughterer's yard in Winthrop Street first in order to collect his cape, which he had left there earlier, though he later insisted he had sent it there with a fellow officer.

Thain was one of the officers who helped lift the body onto the police ambulance, but he then stayed at the crime scene until Inspector Spratling arrived. He gave evidence at the inquest.

See also Neil, Constable John; Spratling, Inspector John; "The Witnesses": Llewellyn, Dr. Rees Ralph

Thick, Sergeant William

Involved in the investigation throughout the entire series of murders but mainly remembered for the arrest of John Pizer after the murder of **Annie Chapman** and Pizer's subsequent identification as "Leather Apron."

See also "The Suspects": Pizer, John; Thick, Sergeant William

Thompson, Constable Ernest

Thompson, Constable 240H, found the body of **Frances Coles** on 13 February 1891 when he was on beat duty for the very first time. He heard footsteps of someone apparently leaving the scene but did not give chase, obeying standing orders to stay with the body until assistance arrived. His whistle summoned Constables Hyde and Hinton, who ran for the doctor and further police aid.

Tragically, Thompson was killed in the line of duty nine years later, in 1900, when he was stabbed as he tried to arrest a man named Barnett Abrahams for causing a disturbance at a coffee stall.

See also Hinton, Constable; Hyde, Constable

Vellensworth, Sergeant

The officer sent to the Pope's Head public house at Gravesend to investigate the suspect William Henry Pigott.

See also "The Suspects": Pigott, William Henry

Warren, Sir Charles

Appointed the commissioner of the Metropolitan Police in 1886, Warren soon became unpopular. This state of affairs was not helped by his actions on 13 November 1887, when he sent troops into Trafalgar Square to clear a demonstration by the unemployed. One man was killed and many others were injured.

As the murders progressed, Warren became even more unpopular, and the press began to demand his resignation. Whatever he did appeared to invite ridicule, and events culminated in a public relations fiasco when Warren allowed himself, as a test, to be tracked by bloodhounds in Regent's Park.

Warren's resignation was finally accepted on 9 November 1888, the day of **Mary Jane Kelly**'s murder, and some authors have seen significance in this juxtaposition of events. In fact, it was pure coincidence. Warren had written an article for *Murray's Magazine* defending police actions and had been castigated by Home Secretary Henry Matthews for not clearing the article with the Home Office before its publication. This rebuke led directly to Warren leaving his office.

See also "Others Who Played a Part": Brough, Edwin; Matthews, Right Honourable Henry, M.P.; "Miscellaneous": Bloodhounds; Goulston Street Graffito

Watkins, Constable Edward

Watkins discovered **Catherine Eddowes**'s body on the morning of 30 September 1888. He sought assistance from George Morris, a watchman at Kearley and Tongue's warehouse, and stayed with the body while Morris ran for help.

See also "The Witnesses": Morris, George James

Webb, Inspector Richard

Though he is not noted for having played a part in any of the murder investigations, it was reported in the *Police Review* that Webb was involved in the attempt to trace the killer, so he is mentioned here for the sake of completeness.

West, Chief Inspector

The officer involved in coordinating the inquiries under Abberline, West was an acting superintendent at the time of the **Mary Ann Nichols** and **Annie Chapman** murders and suggested, at the time of the latter, that Abberline, who was already involved in the Nichols investigation, should be placed in overall charge of the detectives on the ground.

See also Abberline, Inspector Frederick George

White, Sergeant Stephen

Sent to interview the residents of Berner Street on 30 September 1888 after the murder of **Elizabeth Stride**. That day he spoke to, among others, Matthew Packer, who ran his shop from number 44. Packer said he had seen and heard nothing. But on 4 October the *Evening News* carried a story in which Packer now claimed that he had sold grapes to Elizabeth and a male companion at about 11:45 P.M. on 29 September. As a result, White was sent back to interview Packer again, only to find him in the company of two private detectives, Grand and Batchelor. He finally did speak to Packer again, at the mortuary, where Packer confirmed the story of the grapes.

Though he played no other major part in the investigation at the time, Sergeant White reappeared in a story in the *People's Journal* after his death in 1919. The article claimed that White was one of the officers sent out in disguise in an attempt to catch the killer. Although this may have been true, the article then made claims that cannot be substantiated.

According to the story, White submitted a report that claimed that two officers had been watching a certain alley behind the Whitechapel Road that could be entered only where the police were watching. The article continued, "It was a bitter cold night when I arrived at the scene to take the reports of the two men in hiding. I was turning away when I saw a man coming out of the alley. He was walking quickly but noiselessly, apparently wearing rubber shoes which were rather rare in those days. I stood aside to let the man pass, and as he came under the wall lamp I got a good look at him."

The man was then described as 5 feet 10 inches tall and about 33 years old; shabbily dressed; and with a long, thin face, delicate nostrils, jet-black hair, brilliant eyes, and long, snow-white hands and fingers.

The report of White's remarks continued by saying that White had an uneasy feeling that the man was sinister and wanted to detain him but had no reason to do so. The man then stumbled, and White took that opportunity to briefly engage him in conversation. The man, who had a soft, musical voice, bade White good-night and went on his way. The narrative continued, "As he turned away, one of the police officers came out of the house he had been in, and walked a few paces into the darkness of the alley. 'Hello, what is this?' he cried, and then he called in startled tones for me to come.

"In the East End we are used to some shocking sights but the sight I saw made the blood in my veins turn to ice. At the end of the cul-de-sac huddled against the wall, there was the body of a woman, and a pool of blood was streaming along the gutter from her body. It was clearly another of those terrible murders." The story went on to say that White gave chase, searching for the man he had seen just moments before, but failed to find any trace of him.

It is clear that this story had no basis in fact. The only occasion when any Ripper-related crime might be said to have taken place in a cul-de-sac, or alleyway, as described in this narrative, was the murder of Elizabeth Stride in Dutfield's Yard. Although White did play a part in that investigation, there was certainly no police presence in the yard at the time of the murder.

Other writers seeking to favor a particular candidate for the Ripper have claimed that this description in fact referred to either the Mitre Square murder of **Catherine Eddowes** or the Castle Alley murder of **Alice McKenzie.** In each of these cases there was more than one way in and out of the location, and again there is no evidence that the police were in hiding, watching those particular locations.

See also "The Witnesses": Packer, Matthew; "Others Who Played a Part": Batchelor, J. H.; Grand, Mr.

Williamson, Chief Constable A. F.

The chief constable of the Metropolitan Police. He is not known to have played an active part in the investigations.

4

Others Who Played a Part

This section includes all those who were in some way involved in the Whitechapel investigations but were not victims, witnesses, police officers working on the cases, or doctors examining the evidence.

Aarons, Joseph

Treasurer of the Whitechapel Vigilance Committee, which was chaired by George Lusk.

See also Lusk, George Akin; "Miscellaneous": Lusk Kidney; Vigilance Committees

Allen, Elizabeth

A resident of Crossingham's Lodging House at 35 Dorset Street. Though she did not appear at any of the inquests, *The Echo* of 20 September 1888 reported that Allen, together with Eliza Cooper, had given the police information that pointed to a particular suspect who apparently lived close to Bucks Row. According to the report, this suspect's name had originally been mentioned by Pearly Poll (Mary Ann Connolly). No further information is known.

See also "The Witnesses": Connolly, Mary Ann

Bachert, William Albert

A member of the Whitechapel Vigilance Committee and by 1890 its chairman, Bachert sought to play an active role in the investigations. He was called as a reserve juror at the inquest into the death of **Frances Coles** in February 1891, but Coroner Wynne Edwin Baxter refused to have him considered for inclusion on the jury. Bachert protested loudly, shouting that the authorities knew he would inquire too closely into the death.

See also Baxter, Wynne Edwin; "Miscellaneous": Vigilance Committees

Barnett, Daniel

Brother of Joseph Barnett, **Mary Jane Kelly**'s lover. It may be that when Maurice Lewis reported seeing Mary Kelly drinking with "Danny and Julia" in the Horn of Plenty the night before she was murdered, he was erroneously referring to Joseph, though he may have actually meant Daniel. Some press reports gave "Danny" as Joseph Barnett's nickname, though it is clear that this was an error caused by confusion between the two brothers. Many writers assume that "Julia" was Julia Van Turney.

Batchelor, J. H.

One of two private detectives of 283 The Strand who were hired by the Whitechapel Vigilance Committee and the *Evening News* to investigate the circumstances surrounding the murder of **Elizabeth Stride**. They were the two officers who found Matthew Packer and Eva Harstein.

See also Grand, Mr.; "The Witnesses": Harstein, Eva; Packer, Matthew; "Miscellaneous": Vigilance Committees

Baxter, Wynne Edwin

Coroner for the South Eastern District of Middlesex, he presided over the inquests of no fewer than seven of the possible Ripper victims: **Annie Millwood, Mary Ann Nichols, Annie Chapman, Elizabeth Stride, Rose Mylett, Alice McKenzie,** and **Frances Coles.**

A rather flamboyant individual, he criticized the police and claimed that the motive behind some of the murders was the obtaining of certain bodily organs for financial gain. Baxter had a tendency to allow inquests to drag on interminably.

Bayley, Joseph and Thomas

Brothers who ran a packing-case manufacturing operation at 23a Hanbury Street. James Green and James Kent were waiting outside Bayley's premises when John Davis ran to them, seeking assistance, on 8 September 1888 after finding the body of **Annie Chapman.**

On 11 September a piece of crumpled paper, heavily bloodstained, was found in Bayley's yard, and it was surmised that the killer had made his escape by climbing over the fences that separated 29 and 23a. The police countered this suggestion by stating that the paper had not been in the yard on the morning of the murder.

See also "The Witnesses": Davis, John; Green, James; Kent, James

Best

A journalist (whose full name is unknown) who claimed that he penned some of the Jack the Ripper letters. If true, it is likely that he wrote only the "Dear Boss" letter and the "Saucy Jack" postcard.

See also "Letters and Correspondence": The "Dear Boss" Letter of 27 September 1888; The "Saucy Jack" Postcard of 1 October 1888

Brough, Edwin

A man who provided two bloodhounds, Burgho and Barnaby, for use in hunting down the Ripper. He was based in Scarborough and supplied the two dogs for trials held in Regent's Park, but he demanded their return after he found that they had been taken to the scene of a burglary in an attempt to track down the criminal. Brough was concerned that someone might try to injure his animals, which were not insured.

See also "The Police": Warren, Sir Charles; "Miscellaneous": Bloodhounds

Buki, Mrs.

A name mooted as that of a previous landlady of **Mary Jane Kelly.** When Mrs. Carthy was interviewed by the press, she stated that Mary had stayed with Mrs. Buki when she first arrived in London.

See also Carthy, Mrs.

Bulling, Thomas J.

A journalist who worked for the Central News Agency; it was suggested in the Littlechild letter that he may have written the "Dear Boss" letter and the "Saucy Jack" postcard.

See also Moore, Charles; "Letters and Correspondence": The "Dear Boss" Letter of 27 September 1888; The "Saucy Jack" Postcard of 1 October 1888; "Miscellaneous": Littlechild Letter

Burns, Elizabeth

The prostitute who was attacked by Charles Ludwig in September 1888. Some press reports refer to her as having only one arm, so she may well be the One-Armed Liz referred to in a later entry.

See also One-Armed Liz; "The Suspects": Ludwig, Charles

Carthy, Mrs.

Resident of Breezer's Hill, off the Ratcliff Highway. She informed the press that she had been **Mary Jane Kelly**'s landlady after Mary had moved out of Mrs. Buki's house. Mary stayed with Mrs. Carthy until the end of 1886, when she went to live with a man who worked in the building trade.

Interestingly, Mrs. Carthy is the only corroborative source for the stories that Mary had worked in a high-class brothel in the West End. Her story included the comment that at one stage Mrs. Buki had accompanied Mary to a fashionable house in Knightsbridge to recover some of her possessions.

See also Buki, Mrs.

Chapman, John

Annie Chapman's husband. He was a coachman by trade and died on Christmas Day, 1886. It was his death, and the resulting end of the 10-shilling weekly allowance he paid to Annie, that led to her final decline into drunkenness and prostitution.

Chappell, Mary

Chappell, a close friend of Mrs. Fiddymont, who was the landlady of the Prince Albert, was with Fiddymont when they saw a bloodstained man in the public bar a couple of hours after **Annie Chapman** had been murdered on 8 September 1888.

See also Fiddymont, Mrs.

Clarke, George

The man for whom Clarke's Yard, where **Rose Mylett**'s body was discovered, was named. He was a builder's merchant who stored materials in the yard.

Cohen, Jacob

One of the witnesses whose testimony helped to have Aaron Kosminski committed. Cohen reported, among other things, that Kosminski ate bread from the gutters, refused to wash or work, and had once threatened his own sister with a knife.

See also "The Suspects": Kosminski, Aaron

Collier, George

The deputy coroner for the South Eastern District of Middlesex, who, in Wynne Edwin Baxter's absence, conducted the inquest on **Martha Tabram**.

See also Baxter, Wynne Edwin

Colwell, Sarah

A witness who came forward after the murder of **Mary Ann Nichols**, Sarah Colwell lived in Brady Street and claimed that in the early hours of 31 August 1888 she had been awakened by the sound of a woman screaming. Colwell also heard running footsteps, as if the woman were being chased, and the next morning she and others believed they had found some spots of blood in Brady Street. This information led to the suggestion that Mary Ann Nichols had been attacked in Brady Street and that her body had then been dragged to Buck's Row, where it was finally discovered. The medical testimony, however, showed quite clearly that Mary Ann had been killed where she was found.

Conway, Thomas

Catherine Eddowes's husband and the man whose initials she had tattooed on her forearm. Their relationship had broken down years before she was murdered.

The Copseys

A married couple who were among the residents of 29 Hanbury Street at the time of **Annie Chapman**'s murder. They were cigar makers.

Cowdry, Samuel and Sarah

Samuel and Sarah Cowdry lived at Ingleside, Rose Hill Road, Wandsworth, and employed **Mary Ann Nichols** from April to July 1888, until she absconded from their service with clothing valued at 3 pounds 10 shillings.

Cox, Sarah

A widow who was one of the residents of 29 Hanbury Street at the time of **Annie Chapman**'s murder on 8 September 1888.

Crawford, Henry Homewood

A solicitor who appeared at **Catherine Eddowes**'s inquest, acting on behalf of the police, to request that Joseph Lawende's description of the man he had seen with Eddowes be withheld. This underlines the importance the police were placing on that description.

See also "The Witnesses": Lawende, Joseph

Cusins, Mary

A lodging-house keeper in Little Paternoster Row, which ran off Dorset Street, she informed the police that one of her residents, Joseph Isaacs, had been behaving strangely just before **Mary Jane Kelly** was murdered.

See also "The Suspects": Isaacs, Joseph

Danny

See Barnett, Daniel

Diplock, Dr. Thomas Bramah

The coroner who conducted the inquest into the death of Montague John Druitt.

See also "The Suspects": Druitt, Montague John

Drew, Thomas Stuart

A resident of York Road, Walworth, and a blacksmith by trade, he was the man who is said to have lived with **Mary Ann Nichols** between June 1883 and October 1887.

Fiddymont, Mrs.

Landlady of the Prince Albert public house, she saw a man enter her establishment at approximately 7 A.M. on 8 September 1888, just a short time after **Annie Chapman** had been brutally murdered. The man had blood on his hands and below his left ear. He drank a single half-pint of beer very quickly and then left. A friend of Mrs. Fiddymont, Mary Chappell, followed the man out and pointed him out to Joseph Taylor, a bystander.

Mrs. Fiddymont attended at least two identification parades, and possibly a third, in an attempt to trace this man. She failed to identify anyone at the first two, those for William Henry Pigott and John Pizer, but she may also have attended a parade involving Jacob Isenschmid. If so, it is possible that she picked Isenschmid out, as she then played no further part in the inquiry.

See also Chappell, Mary; "The Suspects": Isenschmid, Jacob; Pigott, William Henry; Pizer, John

Finlay, Alexander

See Freinberg, Alexander

Fisher, Elizabeth [Lizzie]

Catherine Eddowes's sister and a resident of 33 Hatcliffe Street, Greenwich. She did not appear at her sister's inquest but did inform the press that Catherine had

had a good character and had split from her husband, Thomas Conway, only because he got drunk and beat her.

See also Conway, Thomas

Fitzgerald, Annie

Believed to be an alias used by **Elizabeth Stride** when she appeared before the Thames Magistrate's Court on charges of being drunk and disorderly.

Freinberg, Alexander

The real name of Alexander Finlay, a resident of 51 Leman Street, who ran a coffee stall on Whitechapel High Street and was attacked by Charles Ludwig on the morning of 18 September 1888.

See also "The Suspects": Ludwig, Charles

Grand, Mr.

One of two private detectives based at 283 The Strand who were hired by the Whitechapel Vigilance Committee and the *Evening News* to investigate after the murder of **Elizabeth Stride**. They found Matthew Packer and Eva Harstein.

See also Batchelor, J. H.; "The Witnesses": Harstein, Eva; Packer, Matthew; "Miscellaneous": Vigilance Committees

Harris, B.

Secretary of the Whitechapel Vigilance Committee, which was chaired by George Lusk and met at the Crown public house on Mile End Road.

See also Lusk, George Akin; "Miscellaneous": Lusk Kidney; Vigilance Committees

Harry the Hawker

A friend of **Annie Chapman,** he did not appear at her inquest but was mentioned as the possible source of the argument between Annie and Eliza Cooper. This story was denied by Eliza herself.

See also "The Witnesses": Cooper, Eliza

Hart, Lydia

Named as possibly being the **Pinchin Street Torso** victim at the time of the investigation. However, according to the *New York Herald,* Hart was found alive and well in the local infirmary.

Hawes, Harry

The undertaker who arranged for the burial of **Annie Chapman**'s body. His business operated from premises at 19 Hunt Street.

Hawkes, G. C.

The undertaker who arranged for the burial of **Catherine Eddowes**'s body. He operated from 41a Banner Street.

Hickey, Ellen

Involved in the Cohen/Kaminsky case, she was alleged to have assaulted a Mr. N. Cohen and was bailed to appear at the Thames Magistrate's Court on 7 December 1888. When Cohen did not appear to give evidence, the case against Ellen was dropped. It has been mooted that because this case was on the same sheet as that of Mary Jones and Gertrude Smith, who were accused of keeping a brothel, it is likely that the assault took place at that same brothel. Also on the same sheet was Aaron Davis Cohen, which implies that his presence at the same brothel raid led to his arrest.

See also Jones, Mary; Smith, Gertrude; "The Suspects": Cohen, Aaron Davis; Kaminsky, Nathan

Houchin, Dr. Edmund King

The doctor who certified Aaron Kosminski as being insane.

See also "The Suspects": Kosminski, Aaron

Humphreys, Mrs.

The woman who was frightened by Dr. Holt, the White-Eyed Man. She was in

George Yard on 11 November 1888 when Holt stepped out of the fog, his face blackened, and frightened her. When she demanded to know what he was doing, Holt laughed and ran off, causing Humphreys to scream, "Murder!" Holt had to be rescued from the mob that came to her aid and was later able to prove his innocence.

See also "The Suspects": Holt, Dr. William

Johannes

Charles Ludwig's landlord (whose full name is unknown).

See also "The Suspects": Ludwig, Charles

Jones, Mary

Charged along with Gertrude Smith with keeping a brothel. The same charge sheet mentions Ellen Hickey, for assault upon N. Cohen, and Aaron Davis Cohen as charged with being a wandering lunatic.

See also Hickey, Ellen; Smith, Gertrude; "The Suspects": Cohen, Aaron Davis; Kaminsky, Nathan

The Keylers

Residents of Miller's Court at the time of **Mary Jane Kelly**'s murder. Sarah Lewis was on her way to the Keylers' home on 9 November 1888 when she saw a man standing opposite the court as if waiting for someone to come out. Subsequent information showed that man was almost certainly George Hutchinson.

See also "The Witnesses": Hutchinson, George; Lewis, Sarah

Langham, Samuel Frederick

The coroner who presided over **Catherine Eddowes**'s inquest.

Lees, Robert James

A clairvoyant who claimed to have identified Jack the Ripper and whose story was seized upon by those advocating the Royal/Masonic Conspiracy theory. It is alleged that Lees followed a psychic track that ended at the house of a senior surgeon. This surgeon is supposed to be Dr. William Gull. The story has no basis in fact.

Levisohn, Wolf

A witness at the trial of George Chapman, a.k.a. Severin Klosowski, who, it is alleged, swore that Chapman was not the Ripper. He added that a more plausible suspect was a barber's assistant from Walworth Road who had been seen in Commercial Street on the night of 30 September 1888, the so-called double event of the murders of **Elizabeth Stride** and **Catherine Eddowes**.

See also "The Suspects": Chapman, George; Pedachenko, Dr. Alexander

Lusk, George Akin

President of the Whitechapel Vigilance Committee and the recipient on 16 October 1888 of the so-called Lusk kidney, sent to him after the murder of **Catherine Eddowes**.

See also "Letters and Correspondence": Lusk "From Hell" Letter of 15 October 1888; "Miscellaneous": Lusk Kidney; Vigilance Committees

Macdonald, Dr. Roderick

The coroner at **Mary Jane Kelly**'s inquest. The speed with which he conducted the proceedings has led some authors to suggest that there was a police or high-level cover-up. More likely he simply did not wish the lurid details of the murder to be published, as had been the case for the previous crimes.

Margaret

Supposedly a friend of **Mary Jane Kelly**. Newspaper reports after Kelly's murder claimed that Margaret had seen Kelly on the day before the murder and that the latter claimed she was thinking of killing herself because she didn't have any money. Other reports, however, erroneously named the victim of the Miller's Court murder as Lizzie Fisher, and it is likely that Margaret's story referred to Fisher in the mistaken belief that Lizzie had been the women killed.

Matthews, Right Honourable Henry, M.P.

Home secretary at the time of the murders, he accepted the resignation of both Sir Charles Warren and James Monro and was heavily criticized for that and the fact that the Home Office refused to sanction a reward for the apprehension of the killer.

See also "The Police": Monro, James; Warren, Sir Charles

Mickeldy, Joe

A supposed friend of Leather Apron, Mickeldy was never called to give evidence at any inquest but was interviewed by a *Star* reporter. He was almost certainly the only man who could have correctly identified Leather Apron and would have been able to state with certainty whether John Pizer was known by that name. Unfortunately, his thoughts on the subject were not recorded.

See also "The Suspects": Pizer, John

Mill, Ann

A resident of 32 Flower and Dean Street and the bedmaker there, she was not called as a witness at **Elizabeth Stride**'s inquest, but when interviewed by the press she described the dead woman in glowing terms, saying, "a better hearted, more good natured, cleaner woman never lived."

Montagu, Samuel

The member of Parliament for the Whitechapel area at the time of the murders. He was in favor of a reward being offered for information leading to the arrest of the killer and added his weight to pleas for the same from the various vigilance committees. In due course Montagu put up 100 pounds of his own money.

See also "Miscellaneous": Vigilance Committees

Moore, Charles

A senior journalist working for the Central News Agency at the time of the murders, he was suggested by Chief Inspector Littlechild as the probable author of the "Dear Boss" and "Saucy Jack" communications. Others, however, believed that the writer was his subordinate, Thomas Bulling.

See also Bulling, Thomas J.; "The Police": Littlechild, Chief Inspector John George; "Letters and Correspondence": The "Dear Boss" Letter of 27 September 1888; The "Saucy Jack" Postcard of 1 October 1888; "Miscellaneous": Littlechild Letter

Morris, Annie

Said to be an alias used by **Elizabeth Stride**. Press reports stated that a prostitute named One-Armed Liz had been to view Stride's body at the mortuary and had identified her as Annie Morris.

See also One-Armed Liz

One-Armed Liz

A friend of **Elizabeth Stride** and who allegedly identified Stride's body as that of Annie Morris, suggesting, therefore, that Morris was an alias used by Stride.

See also Burns, Elizabeth; Morris, Annie

Openshaw, Dr. Thomas Horrocks

Interviewed on the subject of the kidney sent to George Lusk (this story is given in the "Miscellaneous" section), he gave the opinion that it was human and had been preserved in spirits of wine. His findings were misquoted in the press where the kidney was described as "ginny" and as having been taken from a 45-year-old woman who had Bright's disease. Openshaw wrote to the *Times* to complain that the phrases used were nothing more than journalistic embellishments.

See also "Letters and Correspondence": Dr. Openshaw Letter of 19 October 1888; "Miscellaneous": Lusk Kidney

Pash, Florence

Named by those who support the Masonic Conspiracy theory as a friend of **Mary Jane Kelly** who subsequently give information that Walter Sickert had painted clues to the crimes into some of his works.

See also "The Suspects": Masonic Conspiracy

Phoenix, Elizabeth

Sister-in-law of Mrs. Carthy who visited Leman Street Police Station after **Mary Jane Kelly**'s murder to say that the description of the dead woman fitted that of someone who had lodged with Mrs. Carthy some years before. This information led to the police interviewing Mrs. Carthy and obtaining more background on Kelly.

See also Carthy, Mrs.

Reed, F. S.

Assistant to Dr. Frederick Wiles at 56 Mile End Road. On 18 October 1888 he was consulted by members of the Whitechapel Vigilance Committee about the Lusk Kidney. After pronouncing it to be human and having been preserved in spirits of wine, he took it to Dr. Thomas Horrocks Openshaw at the London Hospital.

See also Openshaw, Dr. Thomas Horrocks; Wiles, Dr. Frederick; "Miscellaneous": Lusk Kidney

Richardson, Joseph Hall

A journalist who, at the time of the murders, worked for the *Daily Telegraph*. He interviewed Matthew Packer and helped publicize the story of the grapes being sold to **Elizabeth Stride** and her male companion.

See also "The Witnesses": Packer, Matthew

Ringer, Matilda

Landlady of the Britannia public house.

See also Ringer, Walter

Ringer, Walter

The landlord of the Britannia public house, which was on the corner of Dorset and Commercial Streets and at which **Mary Jane Kelly** was a regular customer. From the surname of the landlord and his wife, the locals often referred to the Britannia as "Ringers'."

Rosy

A prostitute found talking to a potential client, in Henage Street, by Constable Spicer, who subsequently identified the "client" as a doctor whose clothing was bloodstained and who carried a brown bag. Spicer arrested the doctor but was later castigated for detaining a respectable man.

See also "The Police": Spicer, Constable Robert

Sickings, Laura

A young child who supposedly found bloodstains in the yard of 25 Hanbury Street after the murder of **Annie Chapman** in September 1888. This alleged discovery led to suggestions that the Ripper had made his escape by crossing over the fences that separated number 29 from number 27 and then over another fence into the yard of number 25. However, Inspector Chandler was able to state that the stain was in fact urine.

See also "The Police": Chandler, Inspector Joseph Luniss

Sims, George Robert

A journalist who, at the time of the murders, worked for the *Referee* and published his articles under the name *Dagonet.* He appeared to have excellent contacts with the police and wrote many stories on the Ripper murders. He came to believe rumors that the killer had drowned in the Thames just after the murder of **Mary Jane Kelly** and so accepted that Montague John Druitt was the Ripper. This belief led to the penning of the Littlechild letter, sent to Sims in 1913, which named Dr. Tumblety as a more likely suspect.

See also "Miscellaneous": Littlechild Letter; "The Suspects": Druitt, Montague John; Tumblety, "Dr." Francis

Smith, Gertrude

Charged with Mary Jones with keeping a brothel. The same charge sheet mentioned Ellen Hickey, for assault upon N. Cohen, and Aaron Davis Cohen as charged with being a wandering lunatic.

See also Hickey, Ellen; Jones, Mary; "The Suspects": Cohen, Aaron Davis; Kaminsky, Nathan

Smith, H.

The Hanbury Street undertaker who supplied the hearse that took **Annie Chapman**'s coffin to its final resting place.

Squibby

Squibby was a professional thief who was known to be violent and always resisted arrest. Soon after the murder of **Annie Chapman** in September 1888, Squibby was being chased by the police, and passersby, believing that he must be the Ripper, joined in to help. Squibby took refuge in a lodging house in Flower and Dean Street and soon gave himself up to the police, asking for protection from the mob.

Stead, William Thomas

A journalist who, at the time of the murders, was the editor of the *Pall Mall Gazette,* he published many articles on the Ripper murders that were critical of the police investigation. One of the contributors from whom Stead accepted articles was Robert Donston Stephenson, and Stead came to believe that Stephenson might well have been the killer.

See also "The Suspects": Stephenson, Robert Donston

Stevens, Frederick

A resident of Crossingham's lodging house at 35 Dorset Street. Though he didn't appear at **Annie Chapman**'s inquest, he told the press that he had enjoyed a pint of beer with her early on the morning of 8 September 1888.

Thompson, Mr.

One of the residents of 29 Hanbury Street at the time of **Annie Chapman**'s murder. On the morning of the murder he left the house at 3:30 A.M. but saw nothing out of the ordinary.

Violenia, Emmanuel Delbast

A publicity-seeking witness who apparently gave false testimony to boost his own importance. After the murder of **Annie Chapman** Violenia came forward to tell the police that he had seen two men arguing with Annie early on the morning of 8 September in Hanbury Street. He added that one of the men had told Annie he would knife her.

After the arrest of John Pizer, Violenia attended an identity parade and picked out Pizer, whom he said he knew as Leather Apron. Pizer denied knowing Violenia except by sight and swore that the latter could not possibly know any nickname he might have. In due course the police dismissed Violenia as a credible witness and reprimanded him for wasting their time.

See also "The Suspects": Pizer, John

Walker, Mr.

One of the residents of 29 Hanbury Street at the time of **Annie Chapman**'s murder. He was a maker of tennis boots who shared a room with his retarded adult son, Alfred.

Walter, Emily

A woman interviewed by the *Star* newspaper who stated that a man had asked her to go with him into the yard of 29 Hanbury Street early on the morning that **Annie Chapman** was murdered.

Warden, Wally

Another supposed alias used by **Elizabeth Stride**.

West, Mr.

A resident of Crossingham's lodging house in Dorset Street. He said he knew who Leather Apron was and that he had seen him hanging about outside the lodging house in the weeks before **Annie Chapman** was murdered.

Wiles, Dr. Frederick

Had a surgery at 56 Mile End Road where the Whitechapel Vigilance Committee first took the Lusk kidney for a medical opinion. Dr. Wiles was not available, and the kidney was examined by his assistant, F. S. Reed.

See also Reed, F. S.; "Miscellaneous": Lusk Kidney

Winslade, Henry

A resident of 4 Shore Street, Paxton Road, Chelsea, the Thames waterman retrieved Montague John Druitt's body from the river at Chiswick on 31 December 1888.

See also "The Suspects": Druitt, Montague John

5

Chronology

1887	
28 June	Israel Lipski poisons Miriam Angel at 16 Batty Street. **See** "The Victims": Elizabeth Stride; "Miscellaneous": Lipski, Israel
22 August	Israel Lipski is hanged at Newgate prison.
30 September	Michael Ostrog is transferred from Wandsworth prison to the Surrey Pauper Lunatic Asylum. **See** "The Suspects": Ostrog, Michael
13 November	Bloody Sunday rally.
26 December	Date of the supposed murder of Fairy Fay. See "The Victims": Fairy Fay
1888	
6 January	Oswald Puckridge is admitted to Hoxton House Asylum. **See** "The Suspects": Puckridge, Oswald
23 January	James Kelly escapes from Broadmoor. **See** "The Suspects": Kelly, James
25 February	Annie Millwood is stabbed. **See** "The Victims": Annie Millwood
10 March	Michael Ostrog is discharged from the Surrey Pauper Lunatic Asylum.
21 March	Annie Millwood is discharged to the South Grove Workhouse.
28 March	Ada Wilson is attacked. **See** "The Victims": Ada Wilson
31 March	Annie Millwood dies.
3 April	Emma Elizabeth Smith is attacked and raped. See "The Victims": Emma Elizabeth Smith
4 April	Emma Smith dies
5 April	Inquest on Annie Millwood. The verdict is death from natural causes.
27 April	Ada Wilson is released from the hospital.
26 July	Robert Donston Stephenson books himself into the London Hospital. **See** "The Suspects": Stephenson, Robert Donston
4 August	Oswald Puckridge is released from Hoxton House Asylum.
6 August	Bank Holiday.
7 August	Martha Tabram is murdered. **See** "The Victims": Martha Tabram
9 August	Martha Tabram inquest opens.
13 August	Mary Ann Connolly attends parade of

	soldiers at the Tower. **See** "The Victims": Martha Tabram; "The Witnesses": Connolly, Mary Ann
14 August	Mary Ann Connolly attends a second parade, this time at the Wellington Barracks. She picks out two men. Henry Samuel Tabram identifies Martha Tabram's body.
23 August	Second and final day of Tabram inquest.
31 August	Mary Ann Nichols is murdered. **See** "The Victims": Mary Ann Nichols
1 September	William Nichols and Edward Walker both make positive identifications of Mary Ann Nichols's body. Inquest on Mary Ann Nichols opens.
3 September	Second day of Nichols inquest.
6 September	Mary Ann Nichols is buried.
8 September	Annie Chapman is murdered. **See** "The Victims": Annie Chapman
9 September	William Henry Pigott is arrested. **See** "The Suspects": Pigott, William Henry
10 September	The Whitechapel Vigilance Committee is formed in the Crown public house on the Mile End Road. George Lusk is elected chairman. See "Others Who Played a Part": Lusk, George Akin; "Miscellaneous": Vigilance Committees Chapman inquest opens. John Pizer, a.k.a. Leather Apron, is arrested. **See** "The Suspects": Pizer, John
11 September	Jacob Isenschmid is named as a suspect. **See** "The Suspects": Isenschmid, Jacob John Pizer is released.
12 September	Second day of Chapman inquest.
13 September	Third day of Chapman inquest. Isenschmid is arrested and finally certified as a lunatic.
14 September	Annie Chapman is buried. Edward McKenna is arrested. **See** "The Suspects": McKenna, Edward Ted Stanley, also known as the Pensioner, attends Commercial Street Police Station to explain his whereabouts and movements at the time of Annie Chapman's murder. **See** "The Victims": Annie Chapman; "The Witnesses": Stanley, Ted
15 September	The probable date of the attack on **Susan Ward**. See "The Victims": Susan Ward
17 September	Third day of Nichols inquest and date of the first Jack the Ripper letter. **See** "Letters and Correspondence": 17 September 1888 Letter
18 September	Charles Ludwig is arrested. **See** "The Suspects": Ludwig, Charles

19 September	Fourth day of Chapman inquest.
22 September	Fourth and final day of Nichols inquest.
26 September	Fifth and final day of Chapman inquest.
	John Fitzgerald confesses to being the murderer of Annie Chapman. **See** "The Suspects": Fitzgerald, John
27 September	A Jack the Ripper letter arrives at the Central News Agency. **See** "Letters and Correspondence": The "Dear Boss" Letter of 27 September 1888
29 September	John Fitzgerald is released.
30 September	Elizabeth Stride is murdered. **See** "The Victims": Elizabeth Stride
	Catherine Eddowes is murdered. **See** "The Victims": Catherine Eddowes
	The Goulston Street graffito is found. **See** "The Victims": Catherine Eddowes; "Miscellaneous": Goulston Street Graffito
1 October	The "Saucy Jack" postcard is received at the Central News Agency. **See** "Letters and Correspondence": The "Saucy Jack" Postcard of 1 October 1888
	Inquest on Elizabeth Stride opens.
2 October	Second day of Stride inquest.
	John Kelly makes a positive identification of Catherine Eddowes. **See** "The Witnesses": Kelly, John
	Matthew Packer tells the story of the man he sold grapes to. **See** "The Victims": Elizabeth Stride; "The Witnesses": Packer, Matthew; "Myths and Errors": Elizabeth Stride Had Eaten or Held Grapes Just before Her Death
3 October	Copies of the letter and postcard received by the Central News Agency are published by the police.
	Third day of Stride inquest
	The trunk of a female is found in the New Scotland Yard building on the Embankment. **See** "The Victims": The Whitehall Mystery
4 October	The newspapers publish facsimile copies of the 27 September letter and "Saucy Jack" postcard.
	Inquest on Catherine Eddowes opens.
5 October	Fourth day of Stride inquest.
6 October	Elizabeth Stride is buried.
8 October	Catherine Eddowes is buried.
11 October	Second and final day of Eddowes inquest.
16 October	George Lusk receives a parcel containing the "From Hell" letter and half a kidney, which later proves to be human. **See** "Letters and Correspondence": Lusk "From Hell" Letter of

	15 October 1888; "Miscellaneous": Lusk Kidney
	Robert Donston Stephenson writes to the police to give his interpretation of the Goulston Street graffito.
21 October	Maria Coroner of Bradford is charged with causing a breach of the peace by sending letters purporting to come from the killer. **See** "Miscellaneous": Coroner, Maria
23 October	Fifth and final day of Stride inquest.
30 October	Joseph Barnett moves out of 13 Miller's Court. **See** "The Victims": Mary Jane Kelly; "The Suspects": Barnett, Joseph
7 November	"Dr." Francis Tumblety is arrested. **See** "Miscellaneous": Littlechild Letter; "The Suspects": Tumblety, "Dr." Francis
8 November	Sir Charles Warren resigns. **See** "The Police": Warren, Sir Charles
9 November	The Lord Mayor's Show. Mary Jane Kelly is murdered. **See** "The Victims": Mary Jane Kelly
11 November	Dr. William Holt, the White-Eyed Man, is arrested. **See** "The Suspects": Holt, Dr. William
12 November	The inquest on Mary Jane Kelly opens and closes.
	George Hutchinson walks into Commercial Street Police Station and makes a statement about a man he saw with Kelly before her murder. **See** "The Witnesses": Hutchinson, George; "The Suspects": Hutchinson, George (Britain)
	Dr. Holt is released by the police.
	John Avery confesses to the murders. He is drunk and receives 14 days' imprisonment with hard labor. **See** "The Suspects": Avery, John
16 November	Tumblety is charged with gross indecency and is then bailed.
17 November	Nikaner Benelius is arrested. **See** "The Suspects": Benelius, Nikaner
18 November	Michael Ostrog is sentenced in Paris to two years for theft.
19 November	Mary Jane Kelly is buried.
20 November	Annie Farmer is attacked. **See** "The Victims": Annie Farmer
	Tumblety's case appears in the calendar but is postponed to 10 December.
24 November	Tumblety flees to France.
30 November	Montague John Druitt is dismissed from his school. **See** "The Suspects": Druitt, Montague John
1 December	Most likely date of Druitt's suicide.

6 December	Aaron Davis Cohen is arrested. **See** "The Suspects": Cohen, Aaron Davis
7 December	Robert Donston Stephenson leaves the London Hospital.
20 December	Rose Mylett is murdered. **See** "The Victims": Rose Mylett
24 December	George Marsh visits the police to state his belief that the killer is Robert Donston Stephenson. **See** "The Suspects": Stephenson, Robert Donston
26 December	Stephenson writes to the police, naming Dr. Morgan Davies as the killer. **See** "The Suspects": Davies, Dr. Morgan
31 December	Montague John Druitt's body is found in the river Thames.

1889

2 January	Inquest on Druitt returns a verdict of suicide.
3 February	William Henry Bury murders his wife in Scotland and then gives himself up to the police, claiming that he is Jack the Ripper. **See** "The Suspects": Bury, William Henry
24 April	William Henry Bury is hanged at Dundee.
3 May	Date of last entry in the Maybrick diary. **See** "Miscellaneous": Maybrick Diary; "The Suspects": Maybrick, James
11 May	James Maybrick dies.
4 June	Probable date of Elizabeth Jackson's murder. See "The Victims": Elizabeth Jackson
17 July	Alice McKenzie is murdered. See "The Victims": Alice McKenzie Inquest on McKenzie opens.
19 July	Second day of McKenzie inquest.
14 August	Third and final day of McKenzie inquest.
8 September	Probable date of the murder of the Pinchin Street Torso victim. See "The Victims": The Pinchin Street Torso
10 September	The Pinchin Street Torso is found.
20 October	Aaron Davis Cohen, a.k.a. David Cohen, dies in Colney Hatch.

1891

4 February	Aaron Kosminski is incarcerated. **See** "The Suspects": Kosminski, Aaron
13 February	Frances Coles is murdered. See "The Victims": Frances Coles
15 February	Inquest on Frances Coles opens.
16 February	James Thomas Sadler is charged with Coles's murder. **See** "The Suspects": Sadler, James Thomas Second day of Coles inquest.
20 February	Third day of Coles inquest.
23 February	Fourth day of Coles inquest.

27 February	Fifth and final day of Coles inquest.
3 March	Sadler is discharged.
5 March	Thomas Hayne Cutbush is detained as a lunatic. He escapes the same day and attacks two women with a knife. **See** "The Suspects": Cutbush, Thomas Hayne
9 March	Cutbush is arrested, charged with wounding, and later sent to Broadmoor.
23 April	Carrie Brown, a.k.a. Old Shakespeare, is murdered in New York. **See** "Miscellaneous": Brown, Carrie.

1894

23 February	The Macnaghten Memoranda are written. **See** "Miscellaneous": Macnaghten Memoranda

1897

25 December	George Chapman claims his first known victim when Isabella Mary Spink dies. **See** "The Suspects": Chapman, George

1901

13 February	Elizabeth Taylor becomes the second victim of George Chapman.

1902

22 October	Maud Eliza Marsh becomes George Chapman's third victim.

1903

7 April	George Chapman, a.k.a. Severin Klosowski, is hanged for murder.
28 May	Dr. Francis Tumblety dies in New York.

1913

23 September	The Littlechild letter, about Tumblety, is written. **See** "Miscellaneous": Littlechild Letter.

6

Descriptions

This section includes any description that we may reasonably assume to be that of a man responsible for one of the murders. This selection is not based on the assumption that all the murders were by the same hand. Rather, I have taken each case individually to determine who, if anyone, was most likely to have seen the murderer. Also included are comments on the reliability of witnesses and the likelihood that the man seen was indeed the killer.

The section also includes psychological profiles constructed many years after the crimes.

Physical Descriptions

The best way to tackle this subject is to first give every description that any witness gave and then to discuss whether the man described may have been the Ripper. Let us take this crime by crime, concentrating on the crimes that might with some degree of likelihood be placed at Jack's door. The murders for which no witness saw anyone who might have been the killer have been omitted.

Annie Chapman

Only one witness saw anyone in the vicinity of Annie Chapman's murder: Elizabeth Darrell saw a man with a woman she believed was Chapman on the pavement outside 29 Hanbury Street. If Darrell was correct in identifying Chapman as the woman she saw, then the man was almost certainly Annie's killer. The description, as it appeared in police records and newspaper reports, read: "Dark complexioned, wearing a brown deerstalker hat, believed to be wearing a dark coat though she could not be sure on that point. He appeared to be a little taller than Annie and seemed to be a foreigner over 40 years of age. In summation, he was shabby-genteel."

Darrell admitted that she did not see the man's face, so her impression of his age and coloring may be regarded as uncertain. However, from this description we can accept the following as fact: height a little over 5 feet—say a maximum of 5 feet 4 inches—and wearing a brown deerstalker.

See also "The Witnesses": Darrell, Elizabeth

Elizabeth Stride

In the case of Elizabeth Stride there were a plethora of sightings. The witnesses were J. Best and John Gardner, William Marshall, Matthew Packer, Constable Smith, James Brown, and Israel Schwartz.

Best and Gardner may be taken together. They saw Elizabeth Stride with a man in the Bricklayer's Arms, Settles Street, at about 11 P.M. on 29 September 1888. They described Elizabeth's companion as "five feet five inches tall, had a black moustache, sandy eyelashes, and wore a morning suit and a billycock hat." Although the woman was almost certainly Elizabeth, there is no evidence that her companion was her killer. If he was, then he stayed in her company for a further two hours, which is hardly typical of Jack.

William Marshall described a man of "clerky appearance, some five feet six inches tall, stout, wearing a small black coat, dark trousers and a peaked sailor's cap." Marshall saw the couple about 11:45 P.M., so still more than an hour before Elizabeth met her death.

Matthew Packer's evidence has to be taken with a large grain of salt, but he described Stride's companion as "aged 25–30, about five feet seven, wearing a long black coat and a soft felt hat. He had broad shoulders and was stout." Packer's sighting was at about 11:45 P.M.

Constable Smith saw a man with Elizabeth whom he described as "five feet seven inches tall, clean shaven, aged around 28, wearing dark clothes and a dark hard felt deerstalker hat." This sighting was at about 12:30 A.M., just half an hour before the body was found.

James Brown saw a woman he believed to be Elizabeth with a man on the street at about 12:45 A.M. He described the man as stout, about 5 feet 7 inches tall, and wearing a long coat that reached almost to his heels.

Finally we have Israel Schwartz, who was frightened by a man he saw throw Elizabeth to the ground. This man, who appeared to have a companion, though this detail is highly debatable, was described as "aged about 30, five feet five inches tall, fair complexion, dark hair, small brown moustache, full face, broad shouldered, wearing a dark jacket and trousers, and a black cap with a peak."

There are many discussions over whether Elizabeth Stride was in fact a victim of Jack the Ripper, but when it comes to the descriptions we may work back from the next murder. Although it is true that there are a number of "ifs" here—if Joseph Lawende did see Catherine Eddowes, if his description is in any way accurate, and so forth—we may say that if we accept those assumptions as true, then Lawende saw the Ripper, and if he did, and if Stride was a Ripper victim, then the descriptions we can accept as most reliable are those of later sightings, which bear some resemblance to Lawende's. However, to be on the safe side, we will accept the sightings of Schwartz and Constable Smith.

See also Catherine Eddowes; "The Witnesses": Best, J.; Brown, James; Gardner, John; Marshall, William; Packer, Matthew; Schwartz, Israel; "The Police": Smith, Constable William

Catherine Eddowes

The only realistic witness was Joseph Lawende, who saw a man with a woman he claimed was Catherine at the top of Church Passage. If he was correct, then the man was almost certainly the Ripper. Lawende described him as "young, middle-height, had a small fair moustache, wearing what looked like navy serge and a deerstalker's cap." According to later reports he was about 30 years old, 5 feet 7 or 8 inches tall and of medium build, with a fair complexion and mustache. He wore a pepper-and-salt loose jacket, a gray cloth cap with a peak, and a reddish neckerchief tied in a knot. Lawende thought he looked like a sailor.

See also "The Witnesses": Lawende, Joseph

Mary Jane Kelly

In Mary Jane Kelly's case, there are two possible witnesses. The most detailed description was given by George Hutchinson, and another was given by Sarah Lewis. For completeness, I also include the description provided by Mary Ann Cox.

Hutchinson's statement was as follows:

> About 2:00 A.M., 9th, I was coming by Thrawl Street, Commercial Street, and just before I got to Flower and Dean Street I met the murdered woman Kelly and she said to me "Hutchinson, will you lend me sixpence." I said "I can't, I have spent all my money going down to

> Romford." She said "Good morning, I must go and find some money." She went away towards Thrawl Street. A man coming in the opposite direction to Kelly tapped her on the shoulder and said something to her. They both burst out laughing. I heard her say "Alright" to him and the man said "You will be alright for what I have told you." He then placed his right hand around her shoulders. He also had a kind of a small parcel in his left hand, with a kind of a strap round it. I stood against the lamp of the Queens Head Public House and watched him. They both then came past me and the man hung down his head with his hat over his eyes. I stooped down and looked him in the face. He looked at me stern. They both went into Dorset Street. I followed them. They both stood at the corner of the court for about 3 minutes. He said something to her. She said "Alright my dear, come along, you will be comfortable." He then placed his arm on her shoulder and gave her a kiss. She said she had lost her handkerchief. He then pulled his handkerchief, a red one, out and gave it to her. They both then went up the court together. I then went to the court to see if I could see them but could not. I stood there for about three quarters of an hour to see if they came out. They did not so I went away.

Though I find this statement difficult to accept at face value and have explained in the "Summary" section what I feel was Hutchinson's motivation for making it, I have included the general points in the summary table.

Sarah Lewis may well have seen Hutchinson standing in Dorset Street, but her description of the man was "not tall but stout, wearing a black wideawake hat."

Finally, Mary Ann Cox's description of a blotchy-face man with a carrotty mustache, about 36 years old and 5 feet 5 inches tall, dressed in shabby dark clothes with a dark overcoat and a black billycock hat and carrying a quart can of beer, is discounted because the time she saw him, about 11:45 P.M., would have been several hours before Mary was murdered.

See also "The Witnesses": Cox, Mary Ann; Hutchinson, George; Lewis, Sarah; "The Suspects": Hutchinson, George (Britain)

Summary Table

In summation, then, taking the witnesses most likely to have seen the Ripper we have only the list given in the summary table.

Of these, if we discount Hutchinson as being just too unbelievable and Lewis because she almost certainly saw Hutchinson himself, we are left with the following physical summary:

Jack the Ripper was relatively short, probably no more than 5 feet 6 inches tall. He had a pale, probably brown mustache and a fairly stout build and was somewhere between 25 and 35 years old. He habitually wore dark clothing and probably possessed a deerstalker hat.

Psychological Descriptions

Most profiles include information on the possible childhood history of the killer, such as the probability that he had a domineering mother and an absent father, but what we are looking for in the psychological profiles is information to narrow down our search. Only then can we look into a particular candidate's history and find out what else fits.

There have been several psychological profiles of the Whitechapel killer. One of the first was created by Supervisory Special Agent John E. Douglas of the U.S. Federal Bureau of Investigation (FBI) Behavioral Science Unit at Quantico in Virginia. His profile, created in 1988, the hundredth anniversary of the crimes, included the following personal properties of the Ripper:

Summary Table

	Height	*Mustache*	*Age*	*Headgear*	*Clothing*	*Build*
Darrell	5ft 4in	Not seen	Unreliable	Deerstalker	Dark	NA
Smith	5ft 7in	None	28	Deerstalker	Dark	NA
Schwartz	5ft 5in	Brown	30	Black cap	Dark	Broad
Lawende	Middle?	Fair	30	Deerstalker	Dark	Medium
Lewis	Not tall	NA	NA	Wideawake	NA	Stout
Hutchinson	5ft 6in	Slight	34–35	Dark felt	Dark	NA

> An asocial loner. Dress neat and orderly. Employment in positions where he could work alone and experience vicariously his destructive fantasies, perhaps as a butcher or hospital or mortuary attendant. Sexual relationships mostly with prostitutes. May have contracted venereal disease. Aged in his late twenties. Employed since the murders were mostly at the weekends. Free from family accountability and so unlikely to have been married. Not surgically skilled. Probably in some form of trouble with the police before the first murder. Lived or worked in the Whitechapel area and his first homicide would have been close to his home or place of work. Undoubtedly the police would have interviewed him.

Another discussion of the murders was written by Professor David Canter of Liverpool University. In summarizing the Ripper's characteristics, he stated that the killer was probably very familiar with the area. Canter formed what he called the circle hypothesis, which, much simplified, stated that if all the crimes are plotted onto a map, then the center of the area of activity would be close to where the killer lived. This theory of course has limited use if one cannot decide precisely which crimes were by Jack's hand.

One other factor, largely overlooked by previous writers, is that no matter when the series of murders started and finished, only two victims were ever subjected to facial mutilations, and it has been suggested that such injuries are indicative of the victim being known to the killer. If true, this detail would imply that the Ripper knew Catherine Eddowes and Mary Jane Kelly.

After all this, about all I can add is that Jack almost certainly lived close to the epicenter of the murders and close to the site of his first attack. This theory leads to its own problem because I cannot state with certainty which incident was the first. It is almost certainly true that Mary Ann Nichols was not the first victim, in which case the epicenter would shift toward an area bounded by Brick Lane to the east, Goulston Street to the west, Whitechapel High Street to the south, and Brushfield Street to the north.

Finally, we may be able to add to the scant physical description and the general area of the Ripper's abode the possibility that he knew both Eddowes and Kelly. That, however, is the sum total of the knowledge of our unknown killer, all of it based on speculation and incomplete information.

7

Letters and Correspondence

Many hundreds of letters were sent to the police, left nailed to trees, and found in London streets. One, which read, "S.S. *Northumbria Castle*. Left ships. Am on trail again. Jack the Ripper," was found in a bottle that washed ashore between Sandwich and Deal in December 1888.

Most of these letters deserve little consideration and are quite obviously from cranks. There are, however, a small number that deserve closer scrutiny either because they may well be genuine or they have been claimed as such by other writers pushing pet theories. These letters are considered in this section. Where reference numbers are given, they are from the Public Record Office.

17 September 1888 Letter [Ref: HO144/221/A49301C]

It has long been held that the name *Jack the Ripper* given to the killer was taken from a letter sent to the Central News Agency on 27 September 1888. In fact, there is an earlier letter that uses the epithet. It reads:

> 17th September 1888
>
> Dear Boss
> So now thay say I am a Yid when will thay lern Dear old Boss? You an me know the truth dont we. Lusk can look forever hell never find me but I am rite under his nose all the time. I watch them looking for me and it gives me fits ha ha I love my work an I shant stop until I get buckled and even then watch out for your old pal Jacky.
>
> Catch me if you Can
> Jack the Ripper

The letter carried a postscript:

> Sorry about the blood still messy from the last one. What a pretty necklace I gave her.

At first glance, it appears simply to demolish the argument that the Ripper's name came from the "Dear Boss" letter of 27 September, but it has much wider implications than this. The postscript referred to leaving the last victim "a pretty necklace." That victim was of course **Annie Chapman**, who was murdered in the yard of 29 Hanbury Street on 8 September. Although it may be argued that the "pretty necklace" was nothing more than the victim's gashed throat, the phrase might also refer to something new, something the killer hadn't done before, which was to remove the intestines from Annie's abdomen and throw them over her shoulder. Purists may say that this is a far-fetched assumption, but the phraseology suggests that the writer is talking about something more than a cut throat, no matter how severe that particular wound might have been.

This notion leads to an astounding conclusion. The medical evidence was given at the inquest on 14 September 1888 by Dr. George Bagster Phillips, but beyond saying that the body was terribly mutilated and the throat was deeply dissevered, Phillips gave no details of the mutilations. Dr. Phillips was recalled to

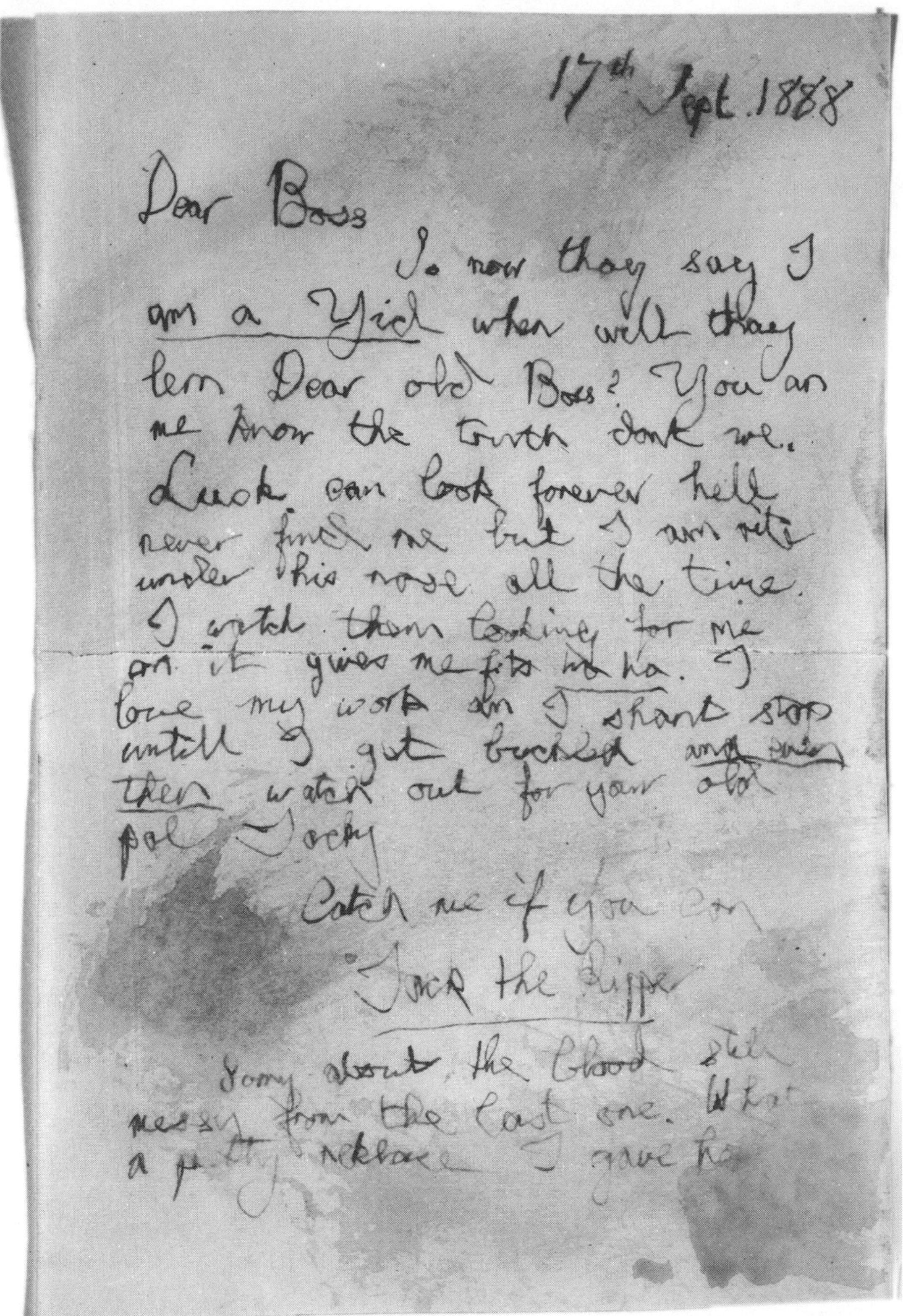

17th Sept. 1888

Dear Boss

So now they say I am a Yid when will they lern Dear old Boss? You an me know the truth dont we. Lusk can look forever hell never find me but I am rite under his nose all the time. I watch them looking for me an it gives me fits ha ha. I love my work an I shant stop untill I get buckled and even then watch out for your old pal Jacky

Catch me if you Can

Jack the Ripper

Sorry about the blood still messy from the last one. What a pretty necklace I gave her

The letter that may have really *coined the name "Jack the Ripper." It was sent on 17 September 1888, and the postscript implies that the writer had knowledge of the murder of Annie Chapman that only the killer would have known. If so, then this was a genuine letter from Jack.* (Public Record Office, London)

the inquest on 19 September, when all the gory details were given, but that testimony is largely irrelevant. The details were not reported in the press because they were held to be indecent, but even if they had been, the letter had already been written by then.

In short, if we believe that the letter writer is referring to the throwing of the intestines around the shoulder when he writes of the "pretty necklace," then the letter must have been written by the killer. Furthermore, the letter uses phrases that reappear later in both the Lusk letter and the "Dear Boss" letter, implying either that all three were written by the same person or that the later two were forgeries by someone who had seen the 17 September letter. If the later letters were *not* forgeries, then the Lusk kidney must have been genuine.

See also "The Witnesses": Phillips, Dr. George Bagster

The "Dear Boss" Letter of 27 September 1888 [Ref: MEPO 3/142/2]

This letter was posted to the Central News Agency on 27 September 1888 (though dated 25 September) and forwarded to Scotland Yard on 29 September. Written in red ink, it read:

> 25 Sept. 1888
>
> Dear Boss,
>
> I keep on hearing the police have caught me but they won't fix me just yet. I have laughed when they look so clever and talk about being on the right track. That joke about Leather Apron gave me real fits. I am down on whores and I shan't quit ripping them till I do get buckled. Grand work the last job was. I gave the lady no time to squeal. How can they catch me now. I love my work and want to start again. You will soon hear of me with my funny little games. I saved some of the proper red stuff in a ginger beer bottle over the last job to write with but it went thick like glue and I can't use it. Red ink is fit enough I hope ha ha. The next job I shall clip the ladys ears off and send to the police officers just for jolly wouldn't you. Keep this letter back till I do a bit more work, then give it out straight. My knife's so nice and sharp I want to get to work right away if I get a chance.
>
> Good luck.
> Yours truly,
> Jack the Ripper.
> Don't mind me giving the trade name

Then, written down the side of the letter was another postscript:

> Wasn't good enough to post this before I got all the red ink off my hands curse it. No luck yet. They say I'm a doctor now ha ha.

The text of this letter was first published in the *Daily News* on the morning of 1 October 1888. A facsimile was published in the *Evening News* of 4 October.

Now, it must be remembered that the text of the earlier, 17 September letter was never published. This letter uses the same name for the sender and also begins "Dear Boss." In addition, it uses the words *fits* and *buckled* and the phrases *I love my work* and *ha ha,* which also appeared in the earlier letter. There can be two only possibilities. Either the letter was written by someone who had seen the earlier missive, or it was by the same author. I do not think it matters that the second was grammatically correct whereas the first contained spelling mistakes, or that the handwriting appeared to be different. It is easy enough to disguise one's script, write with the other hand, hold the pen awkwardly, and so on. However, I think it more likely that this second letter was a press invention and that the writer had knowledge of the earlier letter. Indeed, the earlier letter

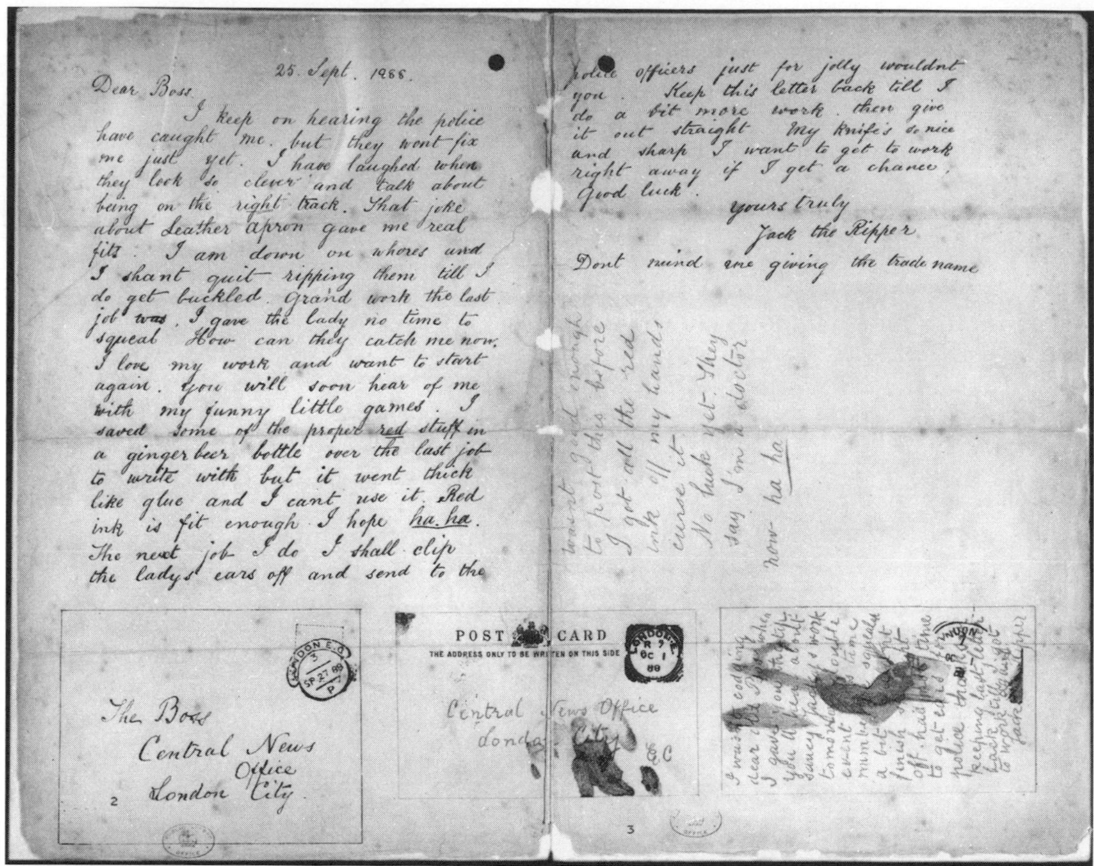

25. Sept. 1888.

Dear Boss

I keep on hearing the police have caught me but they wont fix me just yet. I have laughed when they look so clever and talk about being on the right track. That joke about Leather apron gave me real fits. I am down on whores and I shant quit ripping them till I do get buckled. Grand work the last job was. I gave the lady no time to squeal. How can they catch me now. I love my work and want to start again. You will soon hear of me with my funny little games. I saved some of the proper red stuff in a ginger beer bottle over the last job to write with but it went thick like glue and I cant use it. Red ink is fit enough I hope ha. ha. The next job I do I shall clip the ladys ears off and send to the police officers just for jolly wouldnt you. Keep this letter back till I do a bit more work, then give it out straight. My knife's so nice and sharp I want to get to work right away if I get a chance. Good luck.

yours truly

Jack the Ripper

Dont mind me giving the trade name

wasnt good enough to post this before I got all the red ink off my hands curse it. No luck yet. They say I'm a doctor now ha ha

The Boss
Central News
Office
London City.

POST CARD
THE ADDRESS ONLY TO BE WRITTEN ON THIS SIDE

Central News Office
London City
E C

An illustration showing the "Dear Boss" letter and the "Saucy Jack" postcard. Many authors have argued that the letter was the first to give the "Jack the Ripper" name, though it clearly first appeared in the 17 September. Others have claimed that the postcard contained details of the double event that only the killer could have known and that this in turn underlines Elizabeth Stride's status as a Ripper victim. It is likely that both communications were written by the same person, but the writer was most likely a hoaxer. Note that the general language was also used in letters purported to come from the Yorkshire Ripper in the late twentieth century. Those letters too proved to be hoaxes. (Public Record Office, London)

might have given the author the idea of writing to the police.

The "Saucy Jack" Postcard of 1 October 1888 [Ref: MEPO 3/142/2]

This postcard, posted to the Central News Agency on 1 October, was apparently in the same hand as the "Dear Boss" letter. It read:

> I was not codding dear old Boss when I gave you the tip, you'll hear about Saucy Jacky's work tomorrow double event this time number one squealed a bit couldn't finish straight off. Had not got time to get ears for police thanks for keeping last letter back till I got to work again.
> Jack the Ripper.

The text of this postcard was reproduced in the afternoon edition of the *Star* on 1 October 1888. A facsimile of it was published in the *Evening News* of 4 October.

Once again we can see links with the earlier letters. At the time the postcard was received, the facsimile of the "Dear Boss" letter had still to be released, and the 17 September letter never would be published, yet we see the following similarities.

The "Dear Boss" beginning has already been mentioned, and this postcard uses the phrase *dear old Boss,* which was used in the 17 September letter. This time there are three possibilities. Either the postcard was by a third person altogether, or it was by the same forger who had written the "Dear Boss" letter, or all three were written by the same person.

It has long been suggested that the sender of the postcard was a hoaxer because the card was postmarked 1 October and could have been placed in a postbox early that morning, after the news of the murders of **Elizabeth Stride** and **Catherine Eddowes** had become widespread and the text of the 27 September letter had been published. Although this explanation may be true, it does not explain why the handwriting was the same as the "Dear Boss" letter, or why the writer would use a phrase from the 17 September letter. The likelihood of a third hand may be discounted. Either all three letters were written by the same person or this postcard was written by the same hoaxer who penned the 27 September letter and had seen, or knew about, the 17 September missive.

Threatening Letter of 6 October 1888 [Ref: MEPO 3/142/139]

The letter appears to be in the same hand as the "Dear Boss" letter and "Saucy Jack" postcard. It is dated 6 October 1888.

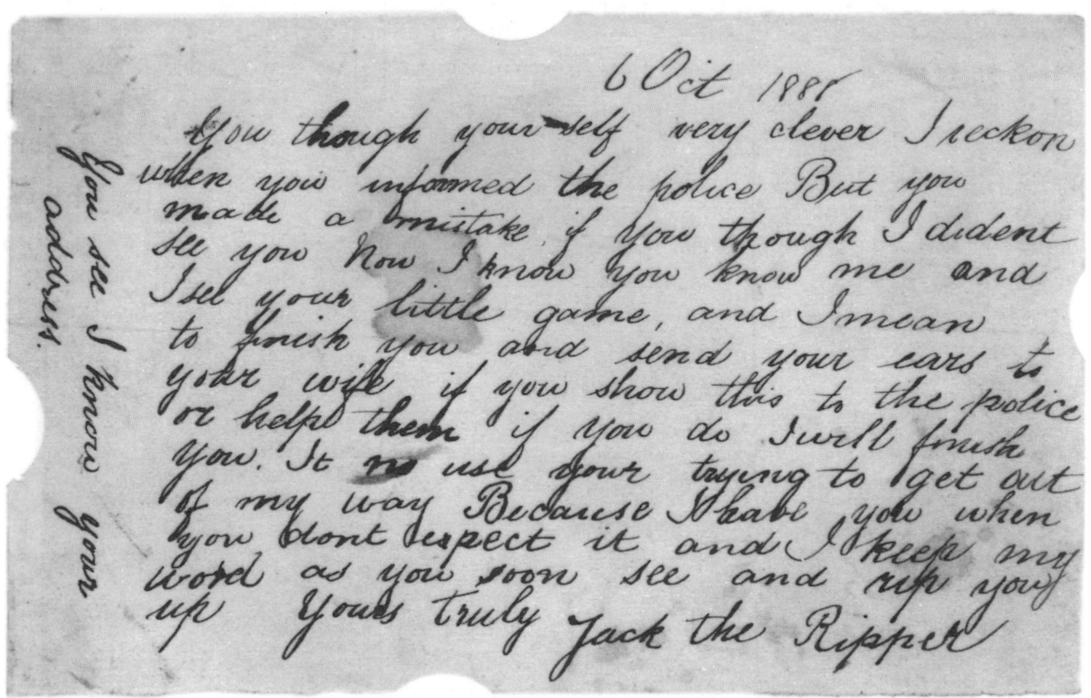

6 Oct 1888

You though your-self very clever I reckon when you informed the police But you made a mistake if you though I dident see you Now I know you know me and I see your little game, and I mean to finish you and send your ears to your wife if you show this to the police or help them if you do I will finish you. It no use your trying to get out of my way Because I have you when you dont expect it and I keep my word as you soon see and rip you up Yours truly Jack the Ripper

You see I know your address.

The threatening letter judged by some to have been been sent to a witness in the Ripper case, possibly Joseph Lawende. Though the writing is similar to that in the "Dear Boss" letter and "Saucy Jack" postcard, it was probably written be by a different person. It is also most likely a hoax. (Public Record Office, London)

> You though your-self very clever I reckon when you informed the police. But you made a mistake if you though I dident see you. Now I know you know me and I see your little game, and I mean to finish you and send your ears to your wife if you show this to the police or help them if you do I will finish you. It no use your trying to get out of my way. Because I have you when you dont expect it and I keep my word as you soon see and rip you up. Yours truly Jack the Ripper.

Down the left-hand side of the letter is a postscript:

> You see I know your address

It has been suggested that this letter was posted in northwest London on 6 October and was apparently intended for one of the witnesses in either the **Elizabeth Stride** or **Catherine Eddowes** murders, probably Israel Schwartz or Joseph Lawende. The Stride inquest had its fourth day on 5 October, but also in the news at the time was Matthew Packer's story about selling grapes to a man who was with Elizabeth Stride shortly before her death. That story had broken in the *Evening News* of 4 October, so one possible explanation is that the author of the "Dear Boss" and "Saucy Jack" communications was now adding to the tension by seeking to intimidate a possible witness. It would also, if made public, add veracity to Packer's statements.

There is, however, a problem with this theory. The file held at the Public Record Office clearly shows that this letter was found in the street between Princess Road and Selhurst Railway Station, so it was obviously never posted at all.

See also "The Witnesses": Lawende, Joseph; Packer, Matthew; Schwartz, Israel

8 October 1888 Letter

This letter, used by the theorists who believe James Maybrick was the Ripper to back up their claims that the Liverpool merchant was the killer, is headed "Galashiels" in Scotland and reads:

> Dear Boss,
>
> I have to thank you and my Brother in trade, Jack the Ripper for your kindness in letting me away out of Whitechapel.
>
> I am now on my road to the tweed Factories. I will let the Innerleithen Constable or Police men know when I am about to start my nice Little game. I have got my knife replenished so it will answer both for Ladies and Gents. Other 5 Tweed ones and I have won my wager.
>
> I am Yours
> Truly
> The Ripper

In the first place, the usual reprint of this letter substitutes the word *brothers* for *brother* at the beginning of the letter. The document is reproduced in this volume and it will be seen that there is no "s" on the end of this word. What might be mistaken for a letter "s" is nothing more than a flourish such as also appears on the next line down at the end of the word *Ripper.*

Although the handwriting may possibly bear a resemblance to that in other notes and letters, this communication is plainly a hoax. It refers to killing both men and women and talks of the genuine Ripper as the author's "brother in trade," and it is plain that no letter was received by the Scottish police, as the writer promised.

See also "The Suspects": Maybrick, James

Lusk "From Hell" Letter of 15 October 1888

This letter was sent to George Lusk with part of a human kidney. It was posted on 15 October 1888 and received on the 16th. It read:

> From hell
> Mr Lusk

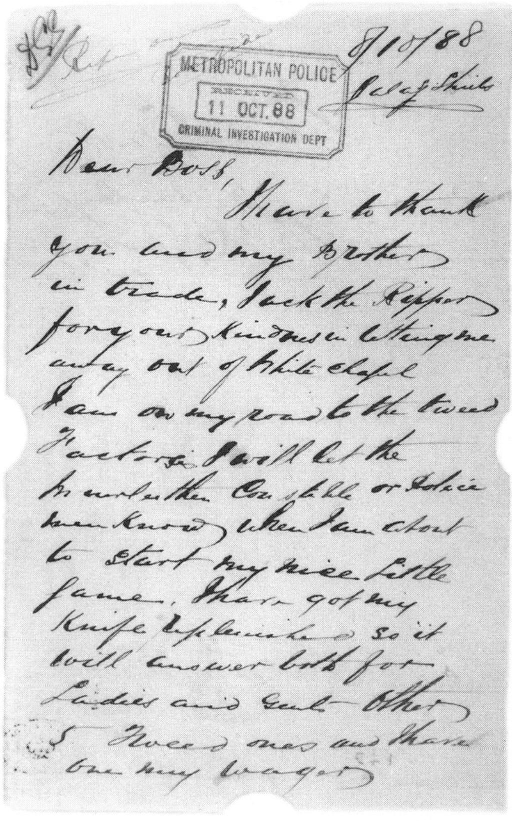

METROPOLITAN POLICE
RECEIVED
11 OCT. 88
CRIMINAL INVESTIGATION DEPT

8/10/88
Galashiels

Dear Boss,
I have to thank
you and my brother
in trade, Jack the Ripper
for your kindness in letting me
away out of Whitechapel
I am on my road to the Tweed
Factory. I will let the
[illegible] Constable or Police
men know when I am about
to start my nice little
game. I have got my
Knife replenished so it
will answer both for
Ladies and Gents other
5 Tweed ones and have
one my wager

I am Yours
Truly
The Ripper

PUBLIC RECORD OFFICE

149

The Galashiels letter held to have been written by James Maybrick by those who accept him as the killer and the Maybrick Diary as genuine. As discussed in the text, there is nothing in this letter that offers any degree of proof that it was written by Jack the Ripper. (Public Record Office, London)

> Sor,
> I send you half the Kidne I took from one women prasarved it for you tother piece I fried and ate it was very nise I may send you the bloody knif that took it out if you only wate a whil longer
>
> signed Catch me when
> you can
> Mishter Lusk.

This communication has been the subject of much debate. The provenance of the kidney itself is considered elsewhere (see "Miscellaneous" section), so here let us just look at the letter.

Perhaps the most important observations are that it was addressed to Lusk and contained the phrase *Catch me when you can.* The writer of the 17 September letter had also apparently been obsessed by Lusk, the chairman of the Whitechapel Vigilance Committee, because that earlier letter mentioned him by name and the writer had used an almost identical phrase to sign off. Once again, it appears that the "From Hell" letter was written either by the same hand or by a hoaxer who had seen the earlier letter.

If the letter of 17 September is genuine and this letter was from the same source, then the "From Hell" letter too must be genuine and the enclosed kidney must indeed have been taken from the body of **Catherine Eddowes.**

Other authors have commented on the probability that the author of this missive was actually intelligent and literate and deliberately disguised both his handwriting and the fact that he really could

From hell

Mr Lusk

Sor

I send you half the
Kidne I took from one women
prasarved it for you tother piece
I fried and ate it was very nise. I
may send you the bloody knif that
took it out if you only wate a whil
longer

signed Catch me when
you Can
Mishter Lusk

The letter that accompanied the portion of human kidney sent to George Lusk of the Whitechapel Vigilance Committee. It has been the subject of much debate, with some writers believing it to be genuine and others stating it is a hoax. On the balance of probabilities, it is likely genuine, and it is probable that the accompanying kidney came from Catherine Eddowes. (London Hospital, Whitechapel)

spell. Thus, for instance, though he manages to misspell the word *knife,* he does not render it as the usual *nife* but shows his awareness of the initial "k" by spelling it *knif.* It is my opinion that the writer was literate and knew full well how to spell but was attempting to throw the police off.

It may interest the reader to know that there may have been another communication addressed to Lusk. An article in the *Star* of 19 October 1888, referring to the note sent with the kidney, read in part, "A few days before he received the parcel Mr Lusk received a postcard supposed to come from the same source."

See also "Miscellaneous": Lusk Kidney; Vigilance Committees

Dr. Openshaw Letter of 19 October 1888

News of Dr. Openshaw's findings on the Lusk kidney had been reported in the newspapers by this time, and he had been personally interviewed by the press on 19 October. It may have been these reports that led to this letter being sent to him at the London Hospital. The letter read:

> Old boss you was rite it was the left kidny i was goin to hopperate agin close to your ospitle just as i was goin to dror me nife along of er bloomin throte them cusses of coppers spoilt the game but i guess i wil be on the job soon and will send you another bit of innerds
> Jack the Ripper

The letter carried a poem as a postscript, which read:

> O have you seen the devle
> with his mikerscope and scalpul
> a lookin at a kidney
> with a slide cocked up

Two factors lead me to conclude that the writer of this letter may be the same man who penned the note sent with the human kidney to George Lusk.

First, the writing is very similar, and second—and in my opinion more importantly—there is again the obvious attempt to disguise an element of literacy. For instance, in the second line the writer spelled *kidney* as *kidny,* he but spelled it correctly in his postscript. Also, in the body of the letter he spelled *hospital* as *ospital,* but he spelled the word correctly on the envelope itself. On that same envelope he managed to spell *pathological* correctly but apparently could not manage *right, operate, knife,* or *will* in the body of the letter.

However, I must stress that I am only slightly inclined to believe that the author was the same as the writer of the "From Hell" letter, and this letter may well be a hoax.

See also "Others Who Played a Part": Openshaw, Dr. Thomas Horrocks; "Miscellaneous": Lusk Kidney

Newspaper Letter of 5 December 1888

This letter is also considered significant by the Maybrick theorists because it is written on a piece of newspaper on which the first full article is headed with the word *Liverpool.* The letter was sent to Dr. William Sedgwick Saunders. It was headed "England" and read:

> Dear Boss,
> Look out for 7th inst.
> Am trying my hand at disjointing and if can manage it will send you a finger.

It is signed "Yours Jack the Ripper" and appears to have been written slightly over another address: "Saunders Esq Police Magistrate."

Although it is true that the Liverpool article appears on this page, there is another article at the bottom of the left-hand column that begins with the words

Dr. Openshaw
Pathological curator
London Hospital
White chapel

Old boss you was rite it was
the left kidny i was goin to
hopperate agin close to your
ospitle just as i was goin
to dror mi nife along of
er bloomin throte them
cusses of coppers spoilt
the game but i guess i wil
be on the job soon and will
send you another bit of
innerds jack the ripper

O have you seen the devle
with his mikerscope and scalpul
a lookin at a kidney
with a slide cocked up

The envelope and letter sent to Dr. Openshaw at the London Hospital after his views about the Lusk kidney had been made public. Note that the word pathological *is spelled correctly on the envelope, as is the word* Dr. *This indicates a deliberate attempt by the writer to disguise his real level of literacy, a trait also shown in earlier communications such as the 17 September letter and the "From Hell" letter.* (London Hospital, Whitechapel)

Brick Lane. Could not the author have held that to be significant, or is this yet another case of theorists seeing only what they wish to see?

The fact is that there is no evidence that the Ripper tried "disjointing" apart from a possible attempt to decapitate **Annie Chapman,** and there was no Ripper crime on or around 7 December, the nearest being the death of **Rose Mylett,** which is highly unlikely to have been Jack's work, on 19 December. This letter is yet another hoax and should be viewed as such.

See also "The Witnesses": Saunders, Dr. William Sedgwick; "The Suspects": Maybrick, James

Conclusions

It is a truism that few serial killers actually write to the police, but such correspondence has been known. In the case of the Yorkshire Ripper a hoaxer, using much the same language demonstrated in these pages, caused an entire police investigation to take completely the wrong track when letters and a tape were sent to police by someone who claimed to be the killer. In the United States, murderers such as the Zodiac Killer have sent letters to the authorities, so it is possible, if not likely, that Jack the Ripper may have communicated with the police.

Of all the Ripper letters, I believe circumstances dictate that the following are most likely to be genuine:

- The letter of 17 September because it referred to giving his last victim "a pretty necklace," and I hold that this comment referred to the

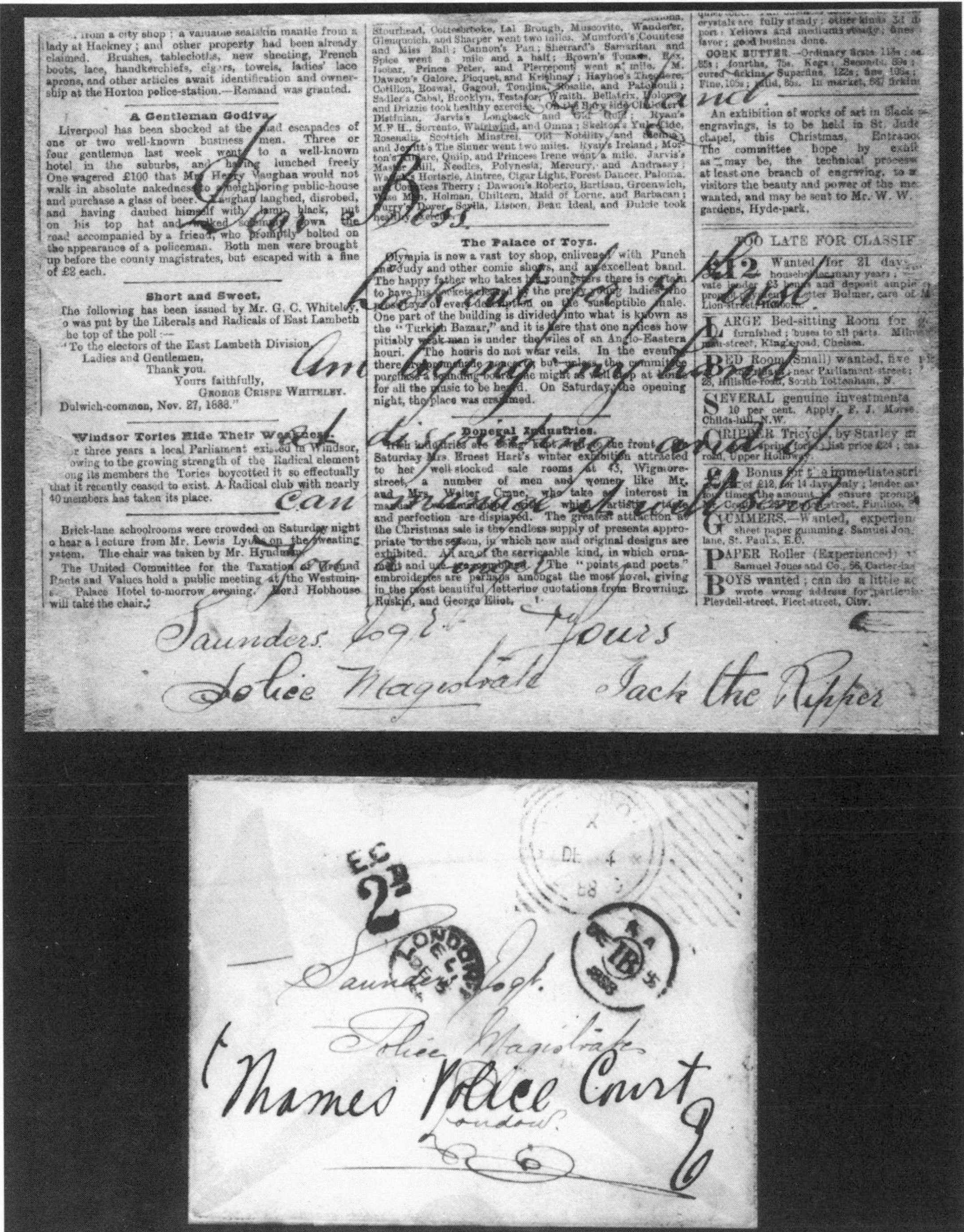

... from a city shop; a valuable sealskin mantle from a lady at Hackney; and other property had been already claimed. Brushes, tablecloths, new sheeting, French boots, lace, handkerchiefs, cigars, towels, ladies' lace aprons, and other articles await identification and ownership at the Hoxton police-station.—Remand was granted.

A Gentleman Godiva.

Liverpool has been shocked at the mad escapades of one or two well-known business men. Three or four gentlemen last week went to a well-known hotel in the suburbs, and having lunched freely One wagered £100 that Mr. Henry Vaughan would not walk in absolute nakedness to a neighboring public-house and purchase a glass of beer. Vaughan laughed, disrobed, and having daubed himself with lamp black, put on his top hat and walked solemnly down the road accompanied by a friend, who promptly bolted on the appearance of a policeman. Both men were brought up before the county magistrates, but escaped with a fine of £2 each.

Short and Sweet.

The following has been issued by Mr. G. C. Whiteley, who was put by the Liberals and Radicals of East Lambeth at the top of the poll:—

"To the electors of the East Lambeth Division,
Ladies and Gentlemen,
Thank you.
Yours faithfully,
GEORGE CRISPE WHITELEY.
Dulwich-common, Nov. 27, 1888."

Windsor Tories Hide Their Weakness.

For three years a local Parliament existed in Windsor, but owing to the growing strength of the Radical element among its members the Tories boycotted it so effectually that it recently ceased to exist. A Radical club with nearly 40 members has taken its place.

Brick-lane schoolrooms were crowded on Saturday night to hear a lecture from Mr. Lewis Lyons on the sweating system. The chair was taken by Mr. Hyndman.

The United Committee for the Taxation of Ground Rents and Values hold a public meeting at the Westminster Palace Hotel to-morrow evening. Lord Hobhouse will take the chair.

The Palace of Toys.

Olympia is now a vast toy shop, enlivened with Punch and Judy and other comic shows, and an excellent band. The happy father who takes his youngsters there is certain to have his pockets cleared by the pretty young ladies who ... of every description on the susceptible male. One part of the building is divided into what is known as the "Turkish Bazaar," and it is here that one notices how pitiably weak man is under the wiles of an Anglo-Eastern houri. The houris do not wear veils. In the evening there ... but unless the committee purchase a sounding board he might as well ... for all the music to be heard. On Saturday, the opening night, the place was crammed.

Donegal Industries.

Irish industries are being kept ... On Saturday Mrs. Ernest Hart's winter exhibition attracted to her well-stocked sale rooms at 43, Wigmore-street, a number of men and women like Mr. and Mrs. Walter Crane, who take an interest in ... which artistic ... and perfection are displayed. The greatest attraction at the Christmas sale is the endless supply of presents appropriate to the season, in which new and original designs are exhibited. All are of the serviceable kind, in which ornament and use are combined. The "points and poets" embroideries are perhaps amongst the most novel, giving in the most beautiful lettering quotations from Browning, Ruskin, and George Eliot.

An exhibition of works of art in black ... engravings, is to be held in St. Jude's ... chapel, this Christmas. Entrance ... The committee hope by exhib... as ... may be, the technical process ... at least one branch of engraving, to ... visitors the beauty and power of the me... wanted, and may be sent to Mr. W. W. ... gardens, Hyde-park.

TOO LATE FOR CLASSIF...

LARGE Bed-sitting Room for ... furnished; 'buses to all parts. ... King's-road, Chelsea.

BED Room (Small) wanted, five ... near Parliament-street; ... South Tottenham, N.

SEVERAL genuine investments ... 10 per cent. Apply, F. J. Morse ... Childs-hill, N.W.

GUMMERS.—Wanted, experienced ... sheet paper gumming. Samuel Jones ... lane, St. Paul's, E.C.

PAPER Roller (Experienced) ... Samuel Jones and Co., 56, Carter-lane ...

BOYS wanted; can do a little ... wrote wrong address for particular... Pleydell-street, Fleet-street, City.

Dear Boss

Saunders Esqr. Yours
Police Magistrate Jack the Ripper

Saunders Esqr.
Police Magistrate
Thames Police Court
London
E

Another letter held by theorists who believe James Maybrick was the killer to have been written by James, supposedly proving that he was the killer. The reason given is the so-called significance of the word Liverpool *in the first full paragraph. Note, however, that the final paragraph in that same column begins with the words* Brick Lane *and so has a much more direct link to the Whitechapel crimes.* (Public Record Office, London)

fact that the killer had thrown **Annie Chapman**'s intestines over her shoulder. That detail had not been made public at the time the letter was written.

- The "From Hell" letter sent to George Lusk with the kidney on 15 October because the writer of the earlier letter seemed in some way obsessed with Lusk and his Vigilance Committee and because of the phraseology in common with the earlier letter.
- Possibly the Openshaw letter of 19 October because of the attempt to disguise the writer's literacy and the similar handwriting to the "From Hell" letter.

8

Miscellaneous

Listed in this section are all those who are recognized as part of the Whitechapel murders history but who cannot be described as witnesses, investigating officers, or others involved in the cases at the time.

This section also includes comments on letters, diaries, and other documents that are important to the case (other than those purportedly written by the killer, which appear in the "Letters and Correspondence" section).

Abberline Diaries

Three volumes supposedly written by Inspector Abberline and belonging now to Joseph Sickert. They form part of the foundation of the Royal/Masonic Conspiracy theory but are almost certainly forgeries because, among other errors, the author reverses the detective's initials and hence claims to be G. F Abberline.

See also Sickert, Joseph Gorman; "The Police": Abberline, Inspector Frederick George; "The Suspects": Masonic Conspiracy

Aberconway, Lady

Christabel Mary MacLaren, second Baroness Aberconway and the youngest daughter of Sir Melville Leslie Macnaghten, transcribed the Lady Aberconway version of the Macnaghten Memoranda from her father's notes and showed the document to Daniel Farson in 1959 when he was researching the murders for his book.

See also Macnaghten Memoranda

Anderson's Suspect

As stated in the next entry, Robert Anderson referred to the Ripper as a low-class Jew who could not be charged because the only possible witness refused to give evidence against him. This suspect was never named, but writers have suggested two possibilities: Aaron Kosminski and Aaron Davis Cohen.

See also "The Suspects": Cohen, Aaron Davis; Kosminski, Aaron

Anderson's Witness

Dr. Robert Anderson wrote, in magazine articles and in his memoirs, *The Lighter Side of My Official Life,* that the killer's identity was known as an established fact. Anderson referred to this suspect, whom he never named, as a low-class Jew who was identified by a witness who refused to give evidence against him because the witness too was a Jew.

The only possible Jewish witnesses are Joseph Lawende or Israel Schwartz, and when other factors are taken into account, as discussed elsewhere in this book, the likelihood is that the witness was almost certainly Lawende.

See also *The Lighter Side of My Official Life;* "The Witnesses": Lawende, Joseph; Schwartz, Israel; "The Police": Anderson, Dr. Robert

Belloselski, Prince Serge

A Russian exile who showed writer Donald McCormick an issue of the *Ochrana*

Gazette from 1909 that discussed the files held on Vassily Konovalov and supposedly stated that Konovalov used the alias Alexei or Alexander Pedachenko.

See also *Ochrana Gazette;* "The Suspects": Pedachenko, Dr. Alexander

Bloodhounds

Two dogs, Burgho and Barnaby, were supplied by Edwin Brough, a professional breeder from Scarborough, for trials. The idea was that the hounds would be taken to the scene of the next atrocity and track the killer to his lair. In a well-publicized trial, Sir Charles Warren allowed himself to be tracked through Regent's Park, much to the amusement of the press.

Further tests showed that there would be much difficulty involved in having the dogs track a man through the crowded East End streets, and the idea of using them was abandoned. This fact had not been made known to the police at the time of **Mary Jane Kelly**'s murder; hence the delay in breaking into her room because the officers at the scene believed the bloodhounds were on their way.

See also "The Police": Warren, Sir Charles; "Others Who Played a Part": Brough, Edwin

Brown, Carrie

A prostitute in New York, also known as Old Shakespeare from her habit of quoting the bard whenever she was drunk.

On 23 April 1891 Carrie and a male friend arrived at the East River Hotel, Manhattan, where she lived. The assistant housekeeper, Mary Miniter, noted that the man appeared cagey and hid his features as if he wished to avoid being seen. The two went up to Carrie's room.

The next morning the night clerk found Carrie's strangled, stabbed, and mutilated body in her room. There were wounds all over her body, reminiscent of the Ripper's method of attack. On the floor lay a black-handled table knife that had been used to inflict the injuries. A description of the man seen with Carrie was drawn up, but all Mary Miniter could say was that he was aged about 32, 5 feet 8 inches tall, of slim build, and had a sharp nose and a heavy moustache, which was light in color. However, this suspect was soon forgotten when it was noticed that bloodstains led from Carrie's room to the one across the hallway.

This room was occupied by an Algerian, Ameer Ben Ali, and the police came to believe that he had waited until Carrie's mysterious customer had left before going across to her room and murdering her. He was duly charged, found guilty, and sentenced to life imprisonment.

For 11 years that was the way things remained until a new investigation showed that the blood trail from Carrie's room to Ameer's had been tracked there by clumsy police boots. Ameer was pardoned and returned to Algeria. The real killer was never found.

This crime has been suggested as an indication that Jack the Ripper left London some time after he had killed **Mary Jane Kelly** and that he murdered Carrie Brown in America. There is nothing to really link the crimes, and this sequence suggests that Jack remained dormant for some time between the murders of Kelly and Brown. Others claim that Jack was not dormant all that time but escaped after killing **Frances Coles** in London in February 1891. However, it is highly unlikely that Carrie Brown's murder was a Ripper crime.

Bury, Ellen

The wife of William Bury, who was murdered by her husband in Dundee in 1891 and who would, if her husband were the

Ripper, have been the final victim to die at his hands.

See also "The Suspects": Bury, William Henry

Convalescent Police Seaside Home

Situated at 51 Clarendon Villas, Brighton, in East Sussex, the home was opened in March 1890. It is supposedly where Anderson's witness made his identification of the Ripper after the alleged killer was incarcerated there.

See also Anderson's Witness

Cook, Elizabeth

Cook had nothing to do with the Ripper case, but she lived at 6 Cleveland Street and was confused by writer Stephen Knight with Annie Elizabeth Crook. Thus, she has become part of the so-called Masonic Conspiracy theory.

See also Crook, Annie Elizabeth; "The Suspects": Masonic Conspiracy

Coroner, Maria

A resident of Bradford who gained her degree of notoriety by being the only person charged, on 21 October 1888, with sending a false communication, purporting to be from Jack the Ripper, to the police. As such she is the only writer of such a letter who can be identified with certainty. Her letters stated that the Ripper would commit a murder in Bradford.

Criminals and Crime: Some Facts and Suggestions

A book by Sir Robert Anderson published in 1907. There is a section on the Ripper murders within the book in which Anderson claimed that the killer was finally incarcerated in an asylum. Two names have been suggested for this suspect—Aaron Kosminski and Aaron Davis Cohen.

See also "The Police": Anderson, Dr. Robert; "The Suspects": Cohen, Aaron Davis; Kosminski, Aaron

Crook, Alice Margaret

The supposed daughter of Annie Crook and Prince Albert Victor, Duke of Clarence, and the only child of their secret marriage, she forms an important part of the Masonic Conspiracy theory and, according to that story, was brought up by the painter Walter Sickert.

See also Crook, Annie Elizabeth; Madewell, Lizzie; "The Suspects": Albert Victor, Duke of Clarence; Masonic Conspiracy

Crook, Annie Elizabeth

According to the Masonic Conspiracy theory, Annie Crook secretly married Prince Albert Victor, Duke of Clarence. It is true that she gave birth to a daughter, Alice, in 1885. On Alice's birth certificate are no details of her father, leading conspiracy theorists to the conclusion that he was in fact the prince.

The subsequent story is full of errors. For example, Annie was not living at 6 Cleveland Street in 1888, as believed by conspiracy theorists, though she had lived there earlier. She was not a Roman Catholic and was not arrested and incarcerated for the rest of her life. She died in 1920 in the Lunacy Ward of the Fulham Road Workhouse.

See also Crook, Alice Margaret; "The Suspects": Albert Victor, Duke of Clarence; Masonic Conspiracy

Cutbush, Superintendent Charles Henry

Uncle of suspect Thomas Cutbush. In 1896 he committed suicide by shooting himself, leading some authors to suspect that he knew his nephew was in fact the killer. However, Charles Cutbush had suffered from depression for many years after sustaining a blow to the head.

See also "The Suspects": Cutbush, Thomas Hayne

Dearden, Dr. Harold

Told a story about the Great War (World War I, 1914–1918) that involved Jack the Ripper. Apparently Dearden was in the trenches on 9 November 1918 when a fellow officer mentioned that this was the second time he had had a birthday ruined. The previous occasion had been on 9 November 1888, when his party had been disrupted by the arrival of a dangerous lunatic at his father's private mental asylum. Since this was the same day as the murder of **Mary Jane Kelly**, the suggestion is that this lunatic was none other than Jack the Ripper, which would explain why the murders stopped.

Druitt, Ann

Montague John Druitt's mother was mentioned in Druitt's suicide note, in which he stated that he felt he was going to "be like mother."

After an attempted suicide Ann Druitt was taken to the Brooke Mental Asylum in Clapton in July 1888. Certified as insane, she was later transferred to another asylum in Brighton. She died in a third asylum in Chiswick, in 1890.

See also "The Suspects": Druitt, Montague John

Druitt, Dr. Lionel

Montague John Druitt's cousin and the supposed author of a pamphlet titled "The East End Murderer—I Knew Him," which has never been traced. Lionel Druitt emigrated to Australia in 1886.

See also "The East End Murderer—I Knew Him"; "The Suspects": Druitt, Montague John

Druitt, William Harvey

Elder brother of Montague John Druitt and a resident of Bournemouth. Upon hearing that Montague had not been seen in his chambers for some time, William visited London and found the farewell note that was produced and read at Montague's inquest in January 1889.

See also "The Suspects": Druitt, Montague John

Dutton, Dr. Thomas

Ran a surgery at 130 Aldgate at the time of the murders and later wrote a book titled *The Chronicle of Crime,* which consisted of three volumes covering all the important crimes committed during his tenure at Aldgate and of course included the Ripper murders. Dutton believed that the killer was a doctor (unnamed in Dutton's book) who blamed the whores of the East End for his son's death.

Dutton showed the book to writer Donald McCormick in 1932, and Dutton's theory is the foundation of the idea that the killer was Dr. Pedachenko. All copies of the three volumes have apparently been lost, and the book has not been seen since 1935.

See also "The Suspects": Pedachenko, Dr. Alexander

"The East End Murderer—I Knew Him"

A document or pamphlet supposedly written by Lionel Druitt and published by him in Australia. A witness described having seen and read the pamphlet in Australia, where it was said to have been published, but no trace of the pamphlet's existence could be found.

See also Druitt, Dr. Lionel; "The Suspects": Druitt, Montague John

Goulston Street Graffito

Writing on the wall of a stairwell supposedly left by Jack the Ripper on the morning of the so-called double event, the murders of **Elizabeth Stride** and **Catherine Eddowes.**

The writing was discovered, along with a piece of Catherine Eddowes's apron, stained with blood and fecal matter, in the doorway of 108–119 Wentworth Model Dwellings, Goulston Street, by Constable Alfred Long. The only reason for linking the writing with the apron is that neither had been noticed by Long when he had last patrolled the area.

The writing was rubbed out before it could be photographed, at the express order of Sir Charles Warren, an act which many previous writers have viewed as evidence of a cover-up of some kind. However, Warren's comment that he was afraid of anti-Jewish demonstrations if the writing were seen and linked with the murders was entirely reasonable, and there need have been nothing sinister in his actions.

There is no firm agreement on what the graffito actually said. Warren himself said that the message was "The Juwes are The men That Will not be Blamed for nothing." This wording was confirmed by Constable Long, but Long claimed that the second word was actually spelled "Juews." Superintendent Arnold, who also saw the message, gave the second word as "Juews" as well. Another variant was that of Dr. Hermann Adler, acting chief rabbi of Great Britain, who in letters to Warren referred to the spelling as "Juewes."

A slightly different wording was noted by Chief Inspector Swanson, who had the graffito as "The Juwes are the men who will not be blamed for nothing." Yet another version was quoted by Dr. Anderson, who had it that the message was "The Jewes are not the men to be blamed for nothing," whereas Sir Melville Macnaghten had it as "The Jews are the men who will not be blamed for nothing."

Further versions came from the City police officers on the scene. Halse had "The Juwes are not the men that will be blamed for nothing"; Inspector McWilliam had "The Jewes are the men that will not be blamed for nothing"; and Major Henry Smith recorded "The Jews are the men that won't be blamed for nothing."

We can discount the versions of Smith, Macnaghten, and Anderson, none of whom actually saw the writing. Of the rest we can arrive only at an assumption of the truth by agreeing that the consensus was that the message most likely read, "The Juwes are the men that will not be blamed for nothing."

After all this, there is of course no proof that the writing was the handiwork of the killer. Some observers noted that the letters appeared to be blurred as if they had been there for some time. Others claimed that the graffito was new and crisp.

It may be that the writing had nothing to do with Jack and that he accidentally deposited the apron close to it. An alternative is that he noticed the writing and left the apron there to lead the authorities to believe he had written the message.

One factor the reader should be wary of: Several authors have sought to decipher their particular versions of the graffito to create anagrams or other cryptic messages. Such far-fetched efforts should be treated with the utmost skepticism.

See also "The Police": Anderson, Dr. Robert; Arnold, Superintendent Thomas; Halse, Detective Constable Daniel; Long,

Constable Alfred; Macnaghten, Sir Melville Leslie; McWilliam, Inspector James; Swanson, Chief Inspector Donald Sutherland; Warren, Sir Charles

Kosminski, Wolf

The brother of Aaron Kosminski and a resident of Sion Square. The records show that on 15 July 1890 Aaron Kosminski was discharged from the Mile End Old Town Infirmary into the care of his brother, presumably Wolf because Aaron had been admitted from Sion Square on 12 July.

See also "The Suspects": Kosminski, Aaron

Lipski, Israel

A convicted killer who murdered a woman in Batty Street, which runs parallel to Berner Street.

Lipski was a Polish Jew who lived in the attic room of 16 Batty Street. The room below his was home to a young married couple, Isaac and Miriam Angel, and on 28 June 1887 Miriam Angel and Israel Lipski were found in the house, both having been poisoned with nitric acid. Lipski was apparently infatuated with Miriam Angel, though there is no evidence that she encouraged him or returned his feelings. She died, but Lipski recovered and was subsequently charged with murder. He was tried at the Old Bailey, convicted, and hanged at Newgate Prison on 22 August 1887.

After his conviction the word *Lipski* came to be used as an insult toward Jewish people in the East End of London. Inspector Abberline gave this explanation for the mysterious stranger seen by Israel Schwartz on the night of **Elizabeth Stride**'s murder using the word; Abberline believed it was directed not at the man's supposed accomplice but at Schwartz himself as a derogatory epithet.

See also "The Police": Abberline, Inspector Frederick George; "The Witnesses": Schwartz, Israel

The Lighter Side of My Official Life

Memoirs of Sir Robert Anderson, first published in 1910 in *Blackwood's Magazine* and also in book form. In this book Anderson claimed that the identity of the Ripper was known and that the murderer had been identified by the only witness who ever got a good look at him.

See also Anderson's Suspect; Anderson's Witness; "The Suspects": Kosminski, Aaron

Littlechild Letter

A letter from Chief Inspector John Littlechild to George Robert Sims, a journalist, dated 23 September 1913. Sims had apparently questioned Littlechild about the possibility that "Dr D." (probably Montague John Druitt) was the Ripper. However, the germane portion of the letter referred instead to Dr. Tumblety; it was the first document to suggest that this quack American "doctor" might have been the Ripper.

In some respects the letter was self-contradictory, describing Tumblety as a very likely suspect but then discounting the notion that he was a sadist. It was also in error when it claimed that the suspect had committed suicide. Tumblety died of natural causes in 1903.

See also "The Suspects": Druitt, Montague John; Tumblety, "Dr." Francis

Lusk Kidney

On the evening of Tuesday, 16 October 1888, George Lusk, the chairman of the Whitechapel Vigilance Committee, received a small parcel at his home. Upon opening it he found half of a kidney and a note that came to be known as the

"From Hell" letter. Though he was greatly disturbed, he took no further action that night.

The following morning Lusk attended a meeting of the committee at the Crown public house on Mile End Road and mentioned the parcel to Joseph Aarons, the treasurer. Aarons; B. Harris, the committee secretary; and two other members, Mr. Reeves and Mr. Lawton, arranged to visit Lusk at his home the next day so they could see the item. On the morning of 18 October the kidney was accordingly viewed by the assembly. The consensus was that the letter was either an appalling hoax from some sick individual or the genuine article, a note from Jack the Ripper. Joseph Aarons suggested taking the package to Dr. Frederick Wiles at his surgery at 56 Mile End Road to obtain a medical opinion.

Dr. Wiles was not in when the party called, but his assistant, F. S. Reed, was, and Reed gave the opinion that the kidney was human and had been preserved in spirits of wine. However, a more detailed examination was necessary, and Reed offered to take the kidney to Dr. Thomas Horrocks Openshaw, the curator of the Pathological Museum at the London Hospital. The committee members stayed behind and awaited Reed's return.

In due course Reed returned to number 56 and said Dr. Openshaw had expressed the opinion that the kidney belonged to a female who had been in the habit of drinking, that it was part of a left kidney, and that the woman had died at about the same time as the Mitre Square victim, **Catherine Eddowes.**

This news soon became public, and the next day, 19 October, a Press Association

The London Hospital, as it is today. This is where the parcel containing the Lusk kidney and the accompanying "From Hell" letter were taken for examination. It is also where the later letter to Dr. Openshaw was sent. See the "Letters and Correspondence" section for a full discussion of these items and illustrations of both. (Yvonne Berger)

report appeared that expanded on Dr. Openshaw's comments. Now it was plain that the kidney was a "ginny" kidney, or one that had belonged to a person who had been a heavy drinker. Furthermore, the report said the woman from whom it had been taken was aged about 45, and the kidney had been removed sometime in the past three weeks. The obvious conclusion was that the kidney was the one taken from Catherine Eddowes and that the letter had been sent by the killer.

Things, however, were not that simple. On the same day that the report appeared, Dr. Openshaw was interviewed by the *Star* newspaper and denied almost all of the details given in the earlier article. He said it was impossible to say that the kidney was female or how long ago it had been removed. About all that could be said was that the item was half of a left human kidney that had been divided longitudinally.

Further investigation was needed, so the kidney was taken to Leman Street Police Station. The police there passed it on to their City colleagues because Eddowes had been murdered in the City. The City police handed the kidney on to Dr. Frederick Gordon Brown, who examined it and wrote a report. Unfortunately, that report has been lost, and we have to base our knowledge of Brown's opinion on the writings of Chief Inspector Swanson and Major Smith.

Swanson gave some details on 6 November in a report for the Home Office in which he said, "The result of the combined medical opinion they have taken upon it, is that it is the kidney of a human adult, not charged with a fluid, as it would have been in the case of a body handed over for purposes of dissection to an hospital, but rather as it would be in a case where it was taken from the body not so destined."

In short, Swanson was saying that the kidney had not been obtained from a corpse belonging to a medical school because such bodies were immediately preserved in formalin. This kidney bore no traces of formalin but instead had been preserved in spirits. Much would be made later of the suggestion that the delivery of the kidney was a rather sick prank perpetrated by medical students, but this statement from Swanson largely negates that notion. If a medical student had sent the kidney, it should have borne signs that it had been preserved in formalin.

Major Smith's comments on the kidney appeared in his book, *From Constable to Commissioner,* in 1910. Though we cannot be sure of Smith's reliability, he confirmed that the idea of a medical prank was untenable. He also made two other interesting points. First, he referred to the renal artery. This artery is some 3 inches long, and, according to Smith, 2 inches of the left renal artery remained in Catherine Eddowes's body and 1 inch was attached to the kidney sent to Lusk. Second, Smith stated that the kidney remaining in Catherine's body was in an advanced state of Bright's disease and that the kidney sent to Lusk was in precisely the same state. If both of these comments could be proved, they would go a long way toward showing that the kidney did indeed come from Catherine Eddowes. However, there are arguments both for and against Major Smith's two important points.

To begin with, an article by Dr. Brown claimed that there was no renal artery remaining on the Lusk kidney because it had been trimmed by whoever sent it. Another article, by Dr. Sedgwick Saunders in the *Evening News,* claimed that Catherine Eddowes's right kidney was perfectly healthy. However, we may turn to Dr. Brown for vindication of at least one of Smith's points. Brown's inquest deposition clearly stated that the kidney remaining in Catherine Eddowes's body was "pale, bloodless with slight congestion of the base of the pyramids." Those symptoms are indications of Bright's disease.

What can be stated as fact after all this time? It appears that the medical opinion confirmed that the kidney was a left human kidney that bore signs of Bright's disease and had been preserved in spirits, not formalin. It had therefore not been taken from a dissecting room and hence is unlikely to have been a medical prank. It is also a fact, according to Dr. Brown, that Catherine Eddowes's remaining kidney bore signs of Bright's disease. I do not think we can rely on Major Smith's comments on the renal artery because Dr. Brown clearly stated that the organ had been trimmed.

In order for this package to have been a hoax, the prankster would have had to obtain a human kidney without recourse to a dissecting room. Furthermore, he would have to have found one with Bright's disease. These factors, though unlikely, are of course possible, and a hoax cannot be discounted, but the balance of probabilities lead us to the conclusion that the kidney was in fact the one taken from Catherine Eddowes in Mitre Square, which meant that the person who sent it was her killer and the "From Hell" letter was genuine.

See also "The Witnesses": Brown, Dr. Frederick Gordon; Saunders, Dr. William Sedgwick; "The Police": Smith, Major Henry; Swanson, Chief Inspector Donald Sutherland; "Others Who Played a Part": Aarons, Joseph; Harris, B.; Lusk, George Akin; Openshaw, Dr. Thomas Horrocks; Reed, F. S.; Wiles, Dr. Frederick; "Letters and Correspondence": Lusk "From Hell" Letter of 15 October 1888; Dr. Openshaw Letter of 19 October 1888

Macnaghten Memoranda

Document written by Sir Melville Leslie Macnaghten naming three suspects. There are three versions of the memoranda (which is why it is generally referred to in plural form): the Lady Aberconway version found by Daniel Farson in 1959; the Scotland Yard version, which was first detailed by Donald Rumbelow in 1975; and the Gerald Melville Donner (Macnaghten's grandson) version. This third version was described by Philip Loftus, a friend of Gerald Donner, who said he saw it in the early 1950s, but it has not resurfaced since this reported sighting. The other two versions are important and will now be quoted in detail.

The Lady Aberconway version began by referring to the case of Thomas Cutbush. This reference was followed by a summary of the five canonical murders and then Macnaghten's views on the identity of the killer. It read:

> A much more rational and workable theory, to my way of thinking, is that the "rippers" brain gave way altogether after his awful glut in Miller's Court and that he then committed suicide, or, as a less likely alternative, was found to be so helplessly insane by his relatives, that they, suspecting the worst, had him confined to some Lunatic Asylum.
>
> No one ever saw the Whitechapel murderer (unless possibly it was the City P.C., who was a beat near Mitre Square) and no proof could in any way ever be brought against anyone, although very many homicidal maniacs were at one time, or another, suspected. I enumerate the cases of 3 men against whom Police held a very reasonable suspicion. Personally, after much careful and deliberate consideration, I am inclined to exonerate the last 2, but I have always held strong opinions regarding no 1, and the more I think the matter over, the stronger do these opinions become. The truth, however, will never be known, and did indeed, at one time lie at the bottom of the Thames, if my conjections [sic] be correct.
>
> No 1. Mr M. J. Druitt a doctor of about 41 years of age & of fairly good family, who disappeared at the time of the

Miller's Court murder, and whose body was found floating in the Thames on 31st Dec: i.e., 7 weeks after the said murder. The body was said to have been in the water for a month, or more—on it was found a season ticket between Blackheath and London. From private information I have little doubt that his own family suspected this man of being the Whitechapel murderer; it was alleged that he was sexually insane.

No. 2. Kosminski, a Polish Jew who lived in the very heart of the district where the murders were committed. He had become insane owing to many years indulgence in solitary vices. He had a great hatred of women, with strong homicidal tendencies. He was (and I believe still is) detailed in a lunatic asylum about March 1889. This man in appearance strongly resembled the individual seen by the City P.C., near Mitre Square.

No. 3. Michael Ostrog, a mad Russian doctor & a convict & unquestionably a homicidal maniac. This man was said to have been habitually cruel to women, & for a long time was known to have carried about with him surgical knives & other instruments; his antecedents were of the very worst & his whereabouts at the time of the Whitechapel murders, could never be satisfactorily accounted for. He is still alive.

The Scotland Yard version also referred to Thomas Cutbush and then went on to discuss the victims. I quote from that point:

Now the Whitechapel Murderer had 5 victims—& 5 victims only,—his murders were

(i) 31st Aug '88. Mary Ann Nichols, at Buck's Row, who was found with her throat cut, & with (slight) stomach mutilation.

(ii) 8th Sept '88. Annie Chapman—Hanbury Street: throat cut—stomach & private parts badly mutilated & some of the entrails placed around the neck.

(iii) 30th Sept '88. Elizabeth Stride—Berner's Street. throat cut, but nothing in the shape of mutilation attempted, & on same date

Catherine Eddowes, Mitre Square, throat cut, & very bad mutilation, both of face and stomach.

9th November. Mary Jane Kelly—Miller's Court, throat cut, and the whole of the body mutilated in the most ghastly manner.

The last murder is the only one that took place in a room, and the murderer must have been at least 2 hours engaged. A photo has been taken of the woman, as she was found lying on the bed, without seeing which it is impossible to imagine the awful mutilation.

With regard to the double murder which took place on 30th Sept., there is no doubt that the man was disturbed by some Jews who drove up to a Club, (close to which the body of Elizabeth Stride was found) and that he then, "nondum satiatus," went in search of a further victim who he found at Mitre Square.

It will be noticed that the fury of the mutilations increased in each case, and, seemingly, the appetite only became sharpened by indulgence. It seems, then, highly improbable that the murderer would have suddenly stopped in November '88, and been content to recommence operations by merely prodding a girl behind some 2 years & 4 months afterwards. A much more rational theory is that the murder's brain gave way altogether after his awful glut in Miller's Court, and that he immediately committed suicide, or, as a possible alternative, was found to be so hopelessly mad by his relations, that he was by them confined is some asylum.

No one ever saw the Whitechapel Murderer: many homicidal maniacs were suspected, but no shadow of proof could be thrown on any one. I may mention the cases of 3 men, any one of whom would have been more likely than Cutbush to have committed this series of murders:

(1) A Mr M. J. Druitt, said to be a doctor & of good family, who disappeared at the time of the Miller's Court murder, whose body (which was

said to have been upwards of a month in the water) was found in the Thames on 31st Dec.—or about 7 weeks after that murder. He was sexually insane and from private info I have little doubt but that his own family believed him to have been the murderer.

(2) Kosminski, a Polish Jew, & resident in Whitechapel. This man became insane owing to many years indulgence in solitary vices. He had a great hatred of women, specially of the prostitute class, & had strong homicidal tendencies; he was removed to a lunatic asylum about March 1889. There were many circs connected with this man which made him a strong "suspect."

(3) Michael Ostrog, a Russian doctor, and a convict, who was subsequently detained in a lunatic asylum as a homicidal maniac. This man's antecedents were of the worst possible type, and his whereabouts at the time of the murders could never be ascertained.

This version went on to discuss inaccuracies in a newspaper article about Cutbush and then referred briefly to the murders of Martha Tabram, Alice McKenzie, Frances Coles, and the Pinchin Street torso, discounting them as possible Ripper victims.

See also Aberconway, Lady; "The Police": Macnaghten, Sir Melville Leslie; "The Suspects": Cutbush, Thomas Hayne; Druitt, Montague John; Kosminski, Aaron; Ostrog, Michael

Madewell, Lizzie

Masonic Conspiracy theorists erroneously claim that Lizzie Madewell was Alice Margaret Crook. On 1 October 1888 Madewell was run down by a cab near 1 New Bridge Street and was rushed to St. Bartholomew's Hospital. She stayed there until 20 October, and news of the accident was published in the *Illustrated Police News* without giving Lizzie's name (which researchers later discovered in medical records). This report was seized upon by the conspiracy theorists as proof that John Netley had attempted to run over Alice Crook.

See also Crook, Alice Margaret; "The Suspects": Masonic Conspiracy; Netley, John Charles

Mansfield, Richard

An actor who became indirectly involved in the hysteria surrounding the Ripper crimes.

Mansfield, an American, was appearing at the Lyceum in a production of *Dr Jekyll and Mr Hyde*. His too-convincing performance led to verbal attacks from people who felt that his on-stage transformation from a meek, kind doctor to a mad serial killer encouraged murder. In an attempt to stave off such criticism, Mansfield offered to present a special performance for the Suffragan Bishop of London's fund, which was attempting to open a laundry that would employ reformed prostitutes. Unfortunately, this project did not succeed, and Mansfield had to cancel the show, thus incurring financial loss.

Maybrick Diary

A 63-page diary fragment supposedly written by James Maybrick at the time of the murders as a record of the murders he committed in Whitechapel. The first suspicions about its authenticity should be raised by the fact that the early pages were torn out. Why should Maybrick have used an old book when he could easily have afforded a new diary to record his thoughts? Be that as it may, the diary contained few checkable points and is undated throughout except the final entry, which purported to have been made on 3 May 1889.

Forensic tests on both paper and ink have led to conflicting results, but the consensus is that the diary is old, and the possibility that it was written in the late

1880s has not been ruled out. However, even if the diary is contemporary with the crimes, it does not prove Maybrick to be the killer.

See also "The Suspects": Maybrick, James

Maybrick Watch

A gold watch found soon after the Maybrick diary and bought from Stewarts of Wallasey by Mr. Albert Johnson. It contains scratches that read, "J. Maybrick" and "I am Jack," along with the initials of the five canonical victims.

The scratches have been tested and seem to date back many years, but a couple of points immediately come to mind. First, the watch remained undiscovered for more than 100 years and was conveniently found only after the diary had come to light. More importantly, perhaps, the author of the diary stated that his first victim was killed in Manchester. If the watch were genuine, then surely it should bear some reference to this unknown sixth victim as well as the other five.

See also Maybrick Diary; "The Suspects": Maybrick, James

Ochrana Gazette

Issued by the Ochrana, the tsar's secret police, as a news bulletin to its European agents. One edition, January 1909, supposedly stated that the Ripper crimes had been committed by a Russian agent named Pedachenko who was employed to kill prostitutes to show the London police in a bad light.

See also "The Suspects": Pedachenko, Dr. Alexander

Old Shakespeare

See Brown, Carrie

Robertson, Terence

The author of an article in *Reynolds News* on 29 October 1950 that identified the first victim of the Ripper as **Fairy Fay**. Since that victim was fictitious, the result of earlier press errors, the rest of the article should be viewed with suspicion.

Sickert, Joseph Gorman

Sickert, who claimed to be the son of Walter Sickert, was responsible for the original story behind the Masonic Conspiracy theory. However, in 1978 he retracted his claims and told the *Sunday Times* that he had made up the entire story.

See also "The Suspects": Masonic Conspiracy

Stride, John Thomas

Elizabeth Stride's husband, who died in 1884.

Swanson Marginalia

Notes written in a copy of Sir Robert Anderson's memoirs, *The Lighter Side of My Official Life,* by Chief Inspector Donald Swanson.

In that book Anderson said only that his favored suspect was a poor Polish Jew from Whitechapel. Anderson wrote that a witness unhesitatingly identified the incarcerated suspect, but he went on to say that the witness refused to give evidence. Underneath this text, Swanson wrote, "Because the suspect was also a Jew and also because his evidence would convict the suspect, and witness would be the means of murderer being hanged, which he did not wish to be left on his mind." In the margin next to this paragraph Swanson wrote, "And after this identification which suspect knew, no other murder of this kind took place in London."

On the endpaper of the same volume, Swanson penciled, "After the suspect had been identified at the Seaside Home where he had been sent by us with difficulty in order to subject him to identification and he knew he was identified. On suspect's return to his brother's house in Whitechapel he was watched by police (City C.I.D.) by day and night. In a very short time the suspect with his hands tied behind his back he was sent to Stepney Workhouse and then to Colney Hatch and died shortly afterwards—Kosminski was the suspect."

There is obviously some confusion here. It is true that Aaron Kosminski lived with his brother, Wolf, in Whitechapel and that he was transferred from a workhouse infirmary to Colney Hatch, but he did not die shortly afterward, nor did he exhibit any sign of violence. There was, however, another prisoner, Aaron Davis Cohen, who was violent after he was incarcerated and who died shortly after being sent to Colney Hatch. It has been mooted that his description is identical with that of Nathan Kaminsky, who had changed his name to Cohen to avoid detection, and that Swanson was likely mixing up Kosminski and Kaminsky.

See also Anderson's Suspect; Anderson's Witness; "The Police": Anderson, Dr. Robert; Swanson, Chief Inspector Donald Sutherland; "The Suspects": Cohen, Aaron Davis; Kosminski, Aaron; Kaminsky, Nathan

Victoria, Queen

Though no writer has yet had the temerity to actually name Victoria as a suspect, Stephen Knight did draw some confirmation for his conspiracy theory from a note that the queen wrote, dated 9 November 1888. This of course was the date of **Mary Jane Kelly**'s murder, and the note commented on the queen's urgings at the time of the "first murder." This remark led Knight to conclude that the queen had taken an interest before it was known that there would be a series of such murders. However, a careful reading of the actual document shows that the monarch was concerned with lighting in the East End and other measures that might improve public safety in general and reduce any opportunity for further crimes. An entry in her personal journal makes it clear that the "first murder" that concerned Victoria was that of **Emma Elizabeth Smith**, which was certainly not a Ripper crime.

Vigilance Committees

Several committees were set up by residents and tradesmen at the time of the murders to patrol the streets, collect information, and apply pressure to the authorities, especially in regard to the offering of a reward for information leading to the capture of the killers. The most significant such committee was of course the Whitechapel Vigilance Committee chaired by George Lusk, who received the kidney purporting to come from the body of **Catherine Eddowes**.

See also Lusk Kidney

Winslow, Lyttleton Stewart Forbes

A man with both medical and legal qualifications who believed he had identified the Ripper as G. Wentworth Bell Smith. The police investigated Winslow's claims and found them groundless, but he continued to press his story, which he then backed up by forged evidence. His theories are valueless.

See also "The Suspects": Smith, G. Wentworth Bell

9

Myths and Errors

No subject in the field of true crime contains more inaccuracies than Jack the Ripper narratives. Sloppy research has led to many errors being perpetuated, and some of these mistakes are unforgivable. Unfortunately, there are so many inaccuracies in print that it is well-nigh impossible to list every one of them. I have therefore approached this section in two ways. First, errors will be described and the truth stated. Second, only errors for the five canonical murders of Mary Ann Nichols, Annie Chapman, Elizabeth Stride, Catherine Eddowes, and Mary Jane Kelly will be discussed. I leave it to the reader to look for less serious mistakes in writings about related crimes.

Mary Ann Nichols

Mary Ann was born in 1851. In fact, she was born on 26 August 1845.

Mary Ann married at the age of 12. This error is usually made by authors who get the year of her birth wrong. Because Mary Ann actually married on 16 January 1864, those who state that she was born in 1851 have to assume that she was only 12 on her wedding day!

Mary Ann had two children. In fact, she had five.

Mary Ann was seen at 2:30 A.M. by Ellen Holland, on the corner of Osborn Street and Brick Lane. A simple reading of the maps shows that Brick Lane turns into Osborn Street, so the two do not form a "corner." In fact, Mary Ann was seen on the corner of Osborn Street and Whitechapel Road.

Mary Ann was last seen at 3:45 A.M., staggering down Whitechapel Road. Her body was found by Constable Neil at this time. The last time she was seen alive was 2:30 A.M.

Mary Ann's body was discovered by George Cross. Erroneous name for Charles Cross.

Cross found Mary Ann's body when he reached a spot opposite to Barber's slaughterhouse. This statement implies that the slaughterhouse was in Buck's Row. It was in fact in Winthrop Street.

John Paul. Erroneous name for Robert Paul.

Paul placed his hand upon the woman's breast in order to feel for a heartbeat. In fact, Paul accidentally brushed his hand against Mary Ann's breast when pulling her skirts down to preserve her modesty.

Paul and Cross were friends. They had never met before the date of the murder.

Paul and Cross ran off toward the nearest police station. In fact, they decided to carry on to work, intending to tell the first policeman they found of the murder.

Constable John Neil was the officer Cross and Paul found. In fact, it was Constable Jonas Mizen. Neil found the body himself after Cross and Paul had gone to find a policeman.

Constable Neil heard his colleague Constable Haine in Brady Street. The officer patrolling Brady Street was Constable John Thain.

Constable Neil hailed a colleague. This implies that he shouted. In fact, he flashed his lamp toward Thain, who saw the signal and came to Neil's aid.

Neil's call for assistance was heard by Constable Mizen. Actually, Mizen had been told by Cross and Paul that a woman was lying dead or drunk in Buck's Row and came to the scene to investigate.

Paul and Cross returned to the scene with Constable Mizen. Paul and Cross continued on to their respective workplaces in Corbett's Court and Broad Street.

Walter King. Erroneous name for Walter Purkiss, who lived with his family at Essex Wharf.

Mr. King slept on the second floor of Essex Wharf. As stated above, the correct name was Walter Purkiss, and he and his wife slept on the third floor.

Dr. Llewellyn sent for the ambulance. Constable Neil sent Constable Mizen to fetch the ambulance.

Dr. Llewellyn deduced that the killer was left-handed. He did originally think so, but he later changed his opinion and thought it doubtful.

Dr. Llewellyn deduced that the killer stood in front of his victim. Again, this was his original conjecture, amended later.

Dr. Llewellyn said that the killer used a very sharp knife. He actually said the knife was strong-bladed and moderately sharp.

The mutilations were discovered at the mortuary by Inspector Helson. They were found by Inspector Spratling, though Helson did see them soon afterward.

The whereabouts of Mary Ann's father were not known. At the time of Mary Ann's death he was living at 16 Maidswood Road, Camberwell, and he attended his daughter's funeral.

Mary Ann absconded from the home of her employers, the Cowdrys, with clothing worth in excess of 3 pounds, 10 shillings. Its stated worth was precisely 3 pounds, 10 shillings—not more, not less.

Mary Ann absconded with 3 pounds of her employers' money. She stole clothing, not cash.

Annie Chapman

Hanbury Street was just a few yards from Crossingham's lodging house. Crossingham's was at 35 Dorset Street, and a glance at any map will show that the two locations were much more than "a few yards" apart.

Number 29 was the home of 15 or 16 people. There were 17 people living there.

The victim's name was Annie May Chapman. Her full name was Eliza Anne Chapman.

Annie's husband was Frederick Chapman. His name was John Chapman.

Annie had two children. In fact, she had given birth to three.

John Davis's mother ran the packing-case business from 29 Hanbury Street. The packing-case business was run by Amelia Richardson, and her son was John Richardson. John Davis was the resident of the front attic room at 29 Hanbury Street and worked as a carman.

Albert Cadoche heard people talking in the yard of number 29. He heard only one word, "No," not a conversation.

Cadoche heard the sounds of a struggle. He heard a noise that sounded like something falling against the fence.

Cadoche lived at number 31. He actually lived on the other side, at number 27.

The fence between the houses was 4 feet high. It was 5.5 feet high.

Both of the workmen from Bayley's ran to the Commercial Street Police Station. The two men, James Green and James Kent, did not both go for the police. Kent was too affected and had to go for a brandy to steady himself. Green and Henry John Holland, a boxmaker who had been passing, ran to fetch the police and found Inspector Chandler on the corner of Hanbury Street and Commercial Street.

Bayley's premises were on the opposite side of Hanbury Street from the scene of the crime. The workshop was at 23a, on the same side as 29, where the crime took place.

Inspector Chandler was walking into Hanbury Street when the alarm was raised. Chandler was on Commercial Street, close to the corner of Hanbury Street.

Inspector Chandler cleared people out of the yard. When he arrived, there was no one in the yard. He later had people cleared out of the passageway.

Inspector Chandler's first thought was that the woman was drunk. This is total nonsense. We are expected to believe that an experienced police officer finds a woman with her entrails over one shoulder and believes she may be intoxicated!

Various items were placed at Annie's feet, including some or all of the following: two bright farthings, a penny, and two brass rings. The only items found were a small piece of coarse muslin, a small-tooth comb, a pocket comb in a paper case, and a portion of envelope containing two pills.

Annie's intestines were placed on her left shoulder. It was her right shoulder.

The apron found in the yard was partially submerged in a dish of water. There was a dish of water underneath the tap, but the apron was found nearby.

The envelope found in the yard was postmarked 20 August. It was postmarked "London, Aug 23, 1888."

Sergeant John Thick. Erroneous name for Sergeant William Thick.

Elizabeth Stride

Elizabeth was known as "Long Liz" because of her height. Elizabeth was only 5 feet 5 inches tall. "Long" was an East End nickname given to people named "Stride."

Elizabeth had three children. There is no evidence that this is the case. The only child we know about with certainty is a girl born on 21 April 1865 in Gothenburg. The child was stillborn.

Elizabeth had nine children. It is true that Elizabeth said she had had nine children, but there is no documentary evidence to support this statement.

Arthur Dutfield carried on business from the yard that bore his name. He had at one time but was operating from Pinchin Street at the time of the murder.

There was only one house in Dutfield's Yard. There was actually a row of cottages.

Constable Lamb was found by Louis Diemschutz and Isaac Kozebrodsky. Diemschutz and Kozebrodsky couldn't find any policemen. Morris Eagle found Constable Lamb and Constable Collins.

The doctor who attended the murder scene was Dr. William Blackfield. In fact it was Dr. Frederick William Blackwell.

Dr. Blackwell could not say whether Elizabeth was standing up or lying down when her throat was cut. At the inquest he stated quite clearly that Elizabeth's throat had not been cut while she was standing up. He added, "The throat might have been cut as she was falling, or when she was on the ground."

Dr. Blackwell said Elizabeth's throat had been cut from right to left. At the inquest he stated, "The incision in the neck commenced on the left side."

Dr. Phillips pronounced Elizabeth dead. Actually, Dr. Blackwell was the first medical man on the scene, and he determined that Elizabeth was beyond all human aid.

Elizabeth had some grapes clutched in her left hand. This statement is a mere invention to give greater credence to the evidence of Matthew Packer. All Elizabeth held were some cachous, in her left hand.

Elizabeth had some grapes, or grape stalks, in her right hand. It doesn't matter which hand the grapes are placed in, as they did not exist. As referred to above, Elizabeth held some cachous in her left hand.

Elizabeth had a corsage of fresh flowers pinned to her breast. She had a single red rose, backed by maidenhair fern.

Edward Spooner noticed that Elizabeth wore a red-and-white flower pinned to her breast. Spooner mentioned the single flower, and the cachous.

Elizabeth's hands were folded underneath her. The reports at the time clearly stated that Elizabeth's left arm was extended from the elbow, which meant that her left hand was most certainly not underneath her body. Furthermore, her right arm was lying across her body, and the right hand bore clotted blood.

William Marshall saw a couple outside number 63. Marshall lived at 64 Berner Street and claimed to have seen a couple talking on the pavement opposite number 58.

Elizabeth lived with Michael Kidney in Fashion Street, or at 33, 35, or 38 Dorset Street. Poor research led to much confusion over where Elizabeth lived. In fact, she lived for some time at 32 Flower and Dean Street and later with Michael Kidney at both 35 and 36 Devonshire Street.

Elizabeth met Kidney in early 1888. She actually met him for the first time three years before her death, or in 1885.

Catherine Eddowes

Catherine was 43 years old. She was born on 14 April 1842, so she was 46 years old when she died.

Catherine was one of 12 children. There were 11 children.

Catherine was also known as Emily Birrell. This error is the result of sloppy research. It is true that among Catherine's possessions was a pawn ticket in the name of Emily Birrell, but the ticket had been given to her by Emily, a friend with whom she had been picking hops.

Catherine had been arrested for being drunk in Bishopsgate. It was actually Aldgate High Street. She was taken to the Bishopsgate Police Station.

Catherine did not have a regular doss house to go to. Catherine usually stayed at Cooney's lodging house at 55 Flower and Dean Street, though she had recently had to stay at the Casual Ward in Mile End when her funds were too low for Cooney's. This error may have been made because she had no money for a bed on the afternoon of her death.

Catherine had been lodging in Church Street, Spitalfields, or with John Kelly in Thrawl Street. Again, Catherine usually stayed at Cooney's lodging house at 55 Flower and Dean Street.

Joseph Lawende, Joseph Hyam Levy, and Harry Harris left the Imperial Club at 1 A.M. Lawende checked his watch as they were leaving, and it was then 1:30 A.M.

Two other men saw Catherine with a man after Lawende saw her. This error is owing to press reports of the time. No one saw Catherine alive after the supposed sighting by Lawende and his friends.

Catherine was released from police custody just after midnight. She was released at 1 A.M.

Mitre Square was well lit by five lamps. An excellent map of Mitre Square was drawn at the time of the investigation. It shows two lamps, one on the edge of the pavement near a passage that led to St. James's Place and the other on the wall at the junction of Mitre Square and Church Passage. The square was not well lit, and the corner where the murder took place was the darkest part.

The watchman at Kearley and Tongue's warehouse was Herbert Morris. He was George James Morris.

Church Passage is 50 yards from Mitre Square. Church Passage leads into Mitre Square.

The body was found at 1:30 A.M. It was discovered at approximately 1:44 A.M.

Catherine's ovaries were removed. The killer removed her left kidney and part of her uterus.

Inspector Collard arrived with Dr. Brown. Collard arrived at the scene at 2:03 A.M. By then he had sent a constable to fetch Dr. Frederick Gordon Brown, who arrived at 2:18 A.M.

There was a sink close to the Goulston Street graffito, and it was wet with blood. There was no sink close to where the graffito and apron were found.

The apron was not there five minutes before it was found. The apron was found at 2:55 A.M. by Constable Alfred Long. He stated that he had last passed through the area at 2:20 A.M. and was sure the apron hadn't been there at that time. If he was correct, the killer had 35 minutes to dispose of the apron, not just five.

A sink off Dorset Street was found to contain bloody water. This detail comes from the memoirs of Major Smith and cannot be corroborated from any reports of the time.

The graffito was written in red chalk. The chalk was white.

Part of Catherine's right ear was missing. The killer did detach one of the lobes, but this piece fell out of Catherine's clothing as her body was being undressed.

After the earlier murders, Catherine had said she knew the identity of the killer. This story did circulate in the press, but there is no proof that she ever said any such thing.

Mary Jane Kelly

Thomas Boyer. Erroneous name for Thomas Bowyer.

Bowyer noticed the broken window as he turned to leave. He would have to have had x-ray vision, as the windows were around the corner.

The crime took place in Miller Court. The actual name was Miller's Court.

Mary's room was 12 feet by 15 feet square. I always believed that a square had to have equal sides. In this case, the room was described as being either 12 or 15 feet square. It can't have been both!

Mary met Joseph Barnett only the night before they moved to Miller's Court. The couple had previously lived in George Street, Little Paternoster Row, Dorset Street, and Brick Lane.

There were two windows, or a single window, to the left of the door. Not so; there were two windows on a different wall, around the corner from the door.

There was no lighting in Miller's Court. There was a lamp almost directly opposite Mary's door.

John McCarthy, who owned the Miller's Court properties, used them to control the prostitutes who lived there and was therefore their pimp. Pure speculation. There is no evidence whatsoever to support this notion.

Mary owed 35 shillings for rent. She owed 29 shillings.

The window was removed to get a better view of the room. No such event took place.

Entry to the room was forced within an hour of the body being discovered. The police stood around for hours waiting for the bloodhounds to arrive. Bowyer found the body at 10:45 A.M., and the door was finally forced at 1:30 P.M.

Mary was three months pregnant. She wasn't pregnant.

Mary's left arm was almost severed from her body. The arm was injured, but it was not almost severed.

Mary's breasts were on the table by the window, or on the table by the bed. One breast was under Mary's head; the other was by her right foot.

Mary's heart was on the table by the window. Mary's heart was missing.

Mary's nose was on the bedside table, or her ears were on the bedside table. The bedside table contained flesh removed from Mary's abdomen and thighs.

Mary's kidneys were on the table by the window. Mary's kidneys were also under her head.

Mary's liver lay on her right thigh, or on the table by the bed. Mary's liver lay between her feet.

Her head was attached only by skin. An attempt had been made to decapitate Mary, but her spinal column was still intact.

Parts of the body were hung on picture nails about the room. This statement is a total fabrication.

No part of the body was removed. Mary's heart was missing.

This crime followed the only murder (that of Catherine Eddowes) in which the killer throttled his victim. There was abundant evidence that Jack's usual method of killing was to first throttle his victim. Such signs had been found in both Nichols's and Chapman's murders.

Inspector Abberline and Superintendent Arnold had to leave the room to be physically sick. Simply not true.

Mary Ann Cox heard someone leave the court at 6:15 A.M., or 6:30 A.M. Her statement showed that she heard someone at 5:45 A.M.

Mary was buried on 18 November. The funeral actually took place on 19 November.

The above list is not exhaustive, and other errors have been found, some totally ludicrous. It seems that some "Ripperologists" do not like to have the facts get in the way of either a good story or a pet theory. I will now examine four of the most persistent legends in more detail.

Rings and Coins Were Found at Annie Chapman's Feet

Many, if not most, authors refer to brass rings and some coins placed deliberately at Annie Chapman's feet. The first time this detail ever appeared in print was in 1928 in Leonard Matters's book *The Mystery of Jack the Ripper.* In the chapter covering Annie's death, he stated, "Another interesting fact in this case was that two brass rings which the woman wore were taken from her fingers, and the trumpery contents of her dress pocket—two or three coppers and odds and ends—were carefully laid out at her feet."

This is a very clever invention because it hides an untruth among genuine fact. It is true that the "odds and ends" from Annie Chapman's pocket were found at her feet, and at the time it was said that they appeared to have been placed there by design. How easy then to add an item or two and have most writers swallow them as fact. Where did Leonard Matters get his idea of the rings and coins? Was it something he invented himself? Actually, the invention appears to have come from a senior police officer.

In July 1889 **Alice McKenzie** was murdered in Castle Alley. On the second day of the inquest, 18 July 1889, Inspector Edmund Reid gave his evidence. He explained that he had been present at the scene when the body was moved, and that beneath it were a broken clay pipe and a farthing, similar to those found in the Chapman case. That a farthing was found underneath Alice McKenzie's body is not in dispute, but what evidence is there that Inspector Reid was correct in stating that coins had also been found in the Chapman killing?

To begin with, Reid played no part in the Chapman investigation, so whatever he said about it would be hearsay and conjecture. There were no fewer than three people who did make statements as to what they had actually seen in the yard of 29 Hanbury Street: Inspector Chandler, who first made a confidential written report and then appeared at the inquest on 13 September 1888; James Kent, who was a witness at the scene and also appeared at the inquest; and finally Dr. Phillips, who made the medical examination and was also a witness at the inquest on the same day as Chandler.

These men gave details as to what they had actually found in the yard, and not one of them mentioned rings or coins being found at Annie Chapman's feet. There can be no doubt that had those rings and coins been there, they would have been recorded at least by Chandler and Phillips.

Let us now examine the reliability of Inspector Reid, the man who first mentioned the items. In later years Reid gave press interviews and wrote to the *Morning Advertiser* to state that there had been nine Ripper murders, that in no case was any part of the bodies taken away, and that the killer had used a blunt knife. Is this someone we can depend on? I think not.

The truth is that Inspector Reid played a very minor role in the Ripper investigations and in the course of giving evidence at the inquest on the one case he was involved in, he made an error in referring to a murder that had taken place almost a year before.

This error or invention was repeated by Major Henry Smith in his memoirs published in 1910. Smith, it will be recalled, made erroneous claims of his own, such as the statement that he was once within five minutes of the murderer. These errors were also publicized by Leonard Matters and then assumed the status of gospel that future writers have churned out without question.

One should, wherever possible, rely only on primary sources and firsthand witnesses. None of the people who stood in the yard in Hanbury Street and gazed at the brutalized body of Annie Chapman mentioned rings and coins beyond saying that rings appeared to have been torn from her fingers. These objects were not found at Annie's feet. They were an error of memory on the part of two police officers who played no part in the Chapman investigation and should, finally, be dismissed as such.

The Victims All Knew Each Other

This myth usually refers to the five canonical victims. Those who expound this particular theory give Dorset Street as the common address and claim that because the women all lived so close to each other at one time or another, they must have known one another.

Annie Chapman was indeed a resident of Crossingham's Lodging House at 35 Dorset Street, and Mary Jane Kelly lived in Miller's Court, which ran off Dorset Street, and the entrance to the court was opposite Crossingham's. This is not enough, however, to indicate that Kelly and Chapman would have known each other. When we look at the other three victims, we find that the entire argument is gossamer.

Mary Ann Nichols's movements are exceedingly well documented. We know which workhouses she stayed at, and on what dates. The detailed history of her movements showed that she only ever stayed at two lodging houses. One was situated at 18 Thrawl Street, and the other, known as the White House, was at 56 Flower and Dean Street.

Writers are determined to place Elizabeth Stride in Dorset Street, either at number 35 or, more usually, number 33, giving that as the address she shared with Michael Kidney. In fact, Elizabeth is known to have stayed at various lodging houses, including 32 Flower and Dean

Street as the most recent. When we come to the Dorset Street address we encounter problems because this error was made in the reports of the day and has been eagerly seized upon by those looking for evidence of a conspiracy or some other design to what were actually random killings. Those who bother to check the facts will find that Kidney told the Central News Agency that he had lived with Elizabeth at 35 Devonshire Street and that they had later moved to number 36 in the same street. Elizabeth herself gave Devonshire Street as her address when applying for relief from the Swedish Church in May 1886. Finally, Catherine Lane, a witness at Elizabeth's inquest, said she had heard Elizabeth say that she had once lived in Devonshire Street.

Catherine Eddowes was another resident of Flower and Dean Street and usually stayed at number 55. On 27 September 1888, her companion, John Kelly, stayed at 52 Flower and Dean Street. Once again, there is no evidence that she ever stayed in Dorset Street.

If we put this all together, the usual addresses of the five victims demonstrate that in fact there was a greater link to Flower and Dean Street than to Dorset Street. However, given the vast number of people living and working in the teeming streets of Whitechapel and Spitalfields, there is no reason to assume that any of the five knew each other.

Fine, say the theorists, but they all drank in the same public houses, so even if they didn't live close to each other they probably knew each other as fellow drinkers in their usual hostelries. We do not know every public house where the five victims drank every night, but we can name the ones referred to by witnesses. An examination of this evidence gives us the following list:

Mary Ann Nichols—the Frying Pan
Annie Chapman—the Britannia
Elizabeth Stride—the Queen's Head, the Bricklayer's Arms
Catherine Eddowes—not known
Mary Jane Kelly—the Britannia, the Horn of Plenty, the Ten Bells

So the only public house the women definitely had in common was the Britannia, at which Chapman and Kelly had been seen drinking. Again, this coincidence is not proof that they knew each other. Does every person who goes into a public house in Britain know every other drinker there? It isn't true today, and it wasn't true in 1888.

Elizabeth Stride Had Eaten or Held Grapes Just before Her Death

Matthew Packer certainly had a lot to answer for. His lack of credibility has been discussed in "The Witnesses" section. Here I will say only that he changed his story—the times of his supposed sale of the grapes to Elizabeth Stride's companion—and was in effect nothing more than a publicity seeker. What other evidence is there for the existence of the grapes?

In addition to Packer, six people confirmed the existence of the grapes. First we have reports from three people, Louis Diemschutz, Isaac Kozebrodsky, and Fanny Mortimer, published in the *Daily News* on 1 October, that the dead woman had been clutching a packet of sweetmeats in one hand and a bunch of grapes in the other. How credible are these statements?

Diemschutz, the only one of the three to be later called as a witness at the inquest, stated quite clearly in his testimony that he had not noticed Stride's hands. In response to a question from the coroner, he replied, "I did not notice what position her hands were in." He made no mention of the grapes or, for that matter, the cachous that actually were found in Elizabeth Stride's hand. If he had not even noticed what position her hands were in, how could he have noticed what those hands might contain?

Fanny Mortimer was the woman who began the persistent rumors, perpetuated down the years by dozens of writers on the subject, that the killer carried a shiny black bag. We know that she actually saw an innocent man, Leon Goldstein, who later came forward to explain his presence in Berner Street. Could it possibly be that Mortimer was simply enjoying her 15 minutes of fame?

Kozebrodsky had come down to view the body briefly before running off to find a policeman, and though we cannot simply dismiss his statement that there were grapes in Elizabeth's hand, we may view it as dubious given the statements of other witnesses.

Eva Harstein lived at 14 Berner Street, and she told the two private detectives, Grand and Batchelor, that she had seen a blood-stained grape stalk and some white flower petals in the yard after the body had been moved. Grand and Batchelor searched a drain in the yard and found a grape stalk. These then are our final three witnesses.

Harstein's statement must be treated with some caution. We know Elizabeth Stride was wearing a flower on her dress on the night she died, but it was a single red rose backed by maidenhair fern. How could a red rose shed white petals? It is plain that some other person must have been in or through the yard at some stage. We know of several members of the club who passed through the yard before the murder. The petals prove only that the yard wasn't the deserted place that some writers claim and that there must have been a fair amount of traffic through it in the course of a normal day.

If we accept that there was a grape stalk, as Eva Harstein and the two detectives say there was, how can we prove that it came from Elizabeth Stride? If someone else had deposited that stalk at any time during the day or night, then it would have become blood-stained when it was washed down the drain, along with any other debris from the yard. After all, Packer's shop was but a few doors away, and he had presumably been selling fruit from the time he opened for business until he finally put the shutters up for the night. He may well have sold grapes to a couple at some time that night, but we have only his word that the woman was Elizabeth Stride. Anyone could have deposited the grape stalk in or near Dutfield's Yard. Its existence does not prove Packer's veracity or that the other witnesses were accurate in saying they had seen grapes in Elizabeth's hand.

On the other side, we have the medical evidence. Two doctors were involved: Dr. Blackwell and Dr. Phillips. Both examined the body at the scene of the crime, and both appeared as witnesses at the inquest. Let us first consider their initial reports on the position of the body and what, if anything, Elizabeth held in her hands.

Dr. Blackwell reported, "The hands were cold. The right hand was open and on the chest, and was smeared with blood. The left hand, lying on the ground, was partially closed, and contained a small packet of cachous wrapped in tissue paper."

Dr. Phillips's testimony included the statement: "The left arm extended from elbow, which held a packet of cachous in her hand. Similar ones were in the gutter. I took them from her hand, and handed them to Dr. Blackwell."

There is a discrepancy here because, continuing his own evidence, Dr. Blackwell had said, "I removed the cachous from the left hand of the deceased, which was nearly open. The packet was lodged between the thumb and the first finger, and was partially hidden from view. It was I who split them in removing them from the hand."

The doctors agreed that Elizabeth held a packet of cachous in her left hand. Though they disagreed over who actually removed them, neither man made any mention of anything being held in the right hand.

Are we expected to believe that Elizabeth Stride's companion bought her some grapes at, say, midnight, and she then kept them in her hand, without eating any, for more than an hour? I think it reasonable to assume that if the grapes had been given to Elizabeth, she would have eaten some of them. Recalled to the inquest after Packer's story broke, both doctors gave evidence on the specific possibility of Elizabeth having eaten grapes.

Dr. Phillips reported, "Neither in the hands nor about the body of the deceased did I find any grapes, or connection with them. I am convinced that the deceased had not swallowed either the skin or seed of a grape within many hours of her death."

Dr. Blackwell was asked, "Did you perceive any grapes near the body in the yard?" He replied, "No," and when the coroner then asked, "Did you hear any person say that they had seen grapes there?" he responded, "I did not."

Having considered all these various witnesses, we must place most credibility on the experts. Neither doctor made any report of grapes, and although a stalk may have been found among the refuse in the yard, there is no proof that it had at any time belonged to Elizabeth Stride. The medical evidence showed that she had not eaten grapes, and that, I hope, is enough to finally lay this particular myth to rest.

The Killer Took the Key of 13 Miller's Court with Him

I fail to see why some authors have buried themselves in the "mystery" of the missing key to 13 Miller's Court. The suggestion is that either the killer took the key away with him after being let into Mary Jane Kelly's room by the woman herself or that the killer had to have a key to gain entrance, which implies that he must have been Joseph Barnett.

We know that access to the room had to be gained, finally, by John McCarthy smashing down the door with a pickaxe. Some writers ask why the photographer didn't simply open the door after he got inside. However, in actuality there was no removal of the window to gain access, and the photographer didn't get inside until after the door had been smashed in. We also know that, according to Barnett's later evidence, the key had been missing for some time, and he and Kelly were in the habit of getting inside by slipping their hands through a broken windowpane and pulling back the bolt. Barnett also testified that the lock was a spring type that locked automatically when the door closed.

Let us first examine the truth of this statement. We know from reports of the time that Mary's room was either 12 or 15 feet square. Let us assume the former, and that the room was a simple square, and that the only walls we need to consider are those with the door and windows.

Contemporary sketches and photographs show that the door was one brick away from the edge of the wall. Allowing one brick to be about 8 inches and allowing about 4 inches for the bolt to be positioned in from the edge of the door, we can assume that the distance from the corner of the room to the bolt was about 1 foot.

Turning now to the other wall, the one with the two windows, we need concern ourselves only with the window nearest the corner of the room. It too was one brick from the corner, but, allowing for the width of the window frame, we can say that the position where one would place one's arm through the broken pane was about 1 foot 6 inches from the corner of the building.

Using a little fundamental mathematics and Pythagoras's theorem, we can show that if one side of our triangle was 1 foot and the second was 1 foot 6 inches, then the third side, the distance one's arm needed to travel to open the bolt, was about 1 foot 9 inches. Even a person of Kelly's stature would have a reach of that length, so she could well have operated the latch as Barnett indicated.

We know that there were two broken panes in the window nearest to the door. In his testimony at the inquest Dr. Phillips stated, "There are two windows in the court. Two of the panes in the window nearest the passage were broken and finding the door locked, I looked through the lower pane." This tells us that there was one pane broken at the top and one at the bottom.

Further testimony came from Bowyer, who looked at the plans of the room and stated that he had looked through the farthest pane of the first window. Bowyer's testimony shows that, looking at the window from outside the room, *either* the top left *or* bottom left pane was broken. When added to the evidence of Dr. Phillips, this evidence shows that the two broken panes were either top left and bottom right or top right and bottom left. In other words, diagonally opposed panes were smashed. This conclusion does not alter our suggestion that Kelly could have reached in and opened the latch, because she could have reached up or down as appropriate. The time has now come to consider the evidence of another witness at the inquest.

Mary Ann Cox stated that at 11:45 P.M. on the night of 8 November, she decided to return home to her room at 2 Miller's Court, the last house on the left at the top of the court. As she turned into Dorset Street she saw Kelly with a man who had a carrotty mustache. They turned into the court just ahead of Cox, and as she entered the court they were just going into Mary's room.

This testimony indicated that Mary Jane Kelly, who, by Cox's evidence, was drunk, had no more than a few seconds to open the door to her room. Bearing in mind that the operation of walking around the corner, unlocking the bolt, and then opening the door in a state of inebriation might well take 10 seconds or more, we are led to the rather obvious conclusion that the door wasn't even locked. The suggestion, therefore, is that though Barnett and Kelly may well have used the broken-window trick when they were going out for any appreciable length of time, on a normal evening, when Kelly was soliciting or out drinking, the chances are that she left her door unlocked.

So far we have indicated that there is nothing sinister about the key being missing. The usual two occupants of the room, Barnett and Kelly, could easily have gained access in the way Barnett described, and Kelly may well have left the door unbolted most of the time. Once she was inside the room, the bolt would be sprung and the door would then be secure. The killer, then, had no need of a key. He was most likely taken into the room by Kelly and then simply closed the door after he had murdered her, locking it behind him. Barnett was probably telling the truth when he said that the key was already missing and the murderer did not take it away with him.

10

The Locations

Many of the streets mentioned in the stories are shown on the maps in the main body of the book and in this section. Other locations, such as public houses, lodging houses, and the like, are described here.

Lodging Houses

Cooley's—In Thrawl Street. **Mary Jane Kelly** lived here in April 1887.

Cooney's—At 55 Flower and Dean Street. **Catherine Eddowes**'s usual address. She had breakfast there with John Kelly on the morning of Saturday, 29 September 1888.

Crossingham's—Situated at 35 Dorset Street. **Annie Chapman** and **Alice McKenzie** both sometimes stayed there, and it was opposite the entrance to Miller's Court, where **Mary Jane Kelly** lived and was killed.

Crossman's—Also known as the Round House. Situated in Holloway Road, it was the house where John Pizer was staying when **Mary Ann Nichols** was murdered. **See** "The Suspects": Pizer, John

The Round House—**See** Crossman's

Victoria Workingmen's Home—Residence of George Hutchinson and located at 39–41 Commercial Street. **See** "The Suspects": Hutchinson, George (Britain)

The White House—Situated at 56 Flower and Dean Street, it was a common lodging house. **Mary Ann Nichols** stayed there briefly.

Public Houses and Clubs

The Bee Hive—On the corner of Fairclough Street and Christian Street. Edward Spooner was standing outside this pub when Louis Diemschutz and Isaac Kozebrodsky ran past looking for police assistance on the morning of 30 September 1888 after discovering **Elizabeth Stride**'s body.

The Britannia—Situated at the corner of Commercial Street and Dorset Street and also known as Ringer's from Walter and Matilda Ringer, who ran it. One of the public houses **Mary Jane Kelly** was known to frequent, and **Annie Chapman** had also been known to drink there.

The Crown—Located at 74 Mile End Road. It was here, on 10 September 1888, that a meeting of local ratepayers led to the formation of the Whitechapel Vigilance Committee under the chairmanship of George Lusk. Members of the committee made themselves available in the Crown each morning in order to receive information from members of the public.

The Frying Pan —Situated on the corner of Brick Lane and Thrawl Street, it was the house where **Mary Ann Nichols** was drinking during the hours before her death.

The George—On Commercial Road, Poplar. The establishment where Alice Graves saw **Rose Mylett** in the company of two sailors on the morning of 20 December 1888.

The Horn of Plenty—At the corner of Crispin Street and Dorset Street. This public house is sometimes mistaken for the Britannia by some writers. It was at the opposite end of the street.

International Workingmen's Educational Club—Situated at 40 Berner Street. Immediately to the south was Dutfield's Yard, where **Elizabeth Stride** was murdered. At the back of the club were the offices of *Der Arbeter Fraint* (The worker's friend). The building was first purchased in 1885 by a group of socialist Jews, and *Der Arbeter Fraint* was established there the following year. It was a favorite haunt of intellectual immigrants and anarchists. In March 1889 the club was the scene of a disturbance when it was attacked by a mob after the members had organized a demonstration in support of the unemployed. When police arrived to quell the mob, some of the club members took them for reinforcements for their opponents and promptly attacked them. As a result some, including Isaac Kozebrodsky and Louis Diemschutz, were prosecuted.

The Jack the Ripper—**See** The Ten Bells

The Prince Albert—Located in Brushfield Street. The licensee was Mrs. Fiddymont. Witnesses saw a bloodstained man in the public bar a couple of hours after **Annie Chapman** was murdered on 8 September 1888.

The Princess Alice—Still in existence but renamed the City Darts. Situated on the corner of Wentworth Street and Commercial Street, it is used as a landmark in the walking tour described in the "Resources" section and is mentioned in my discussion of George Hutchinson in the "Summary" section.

The Queen's Head—On the corner of Commercial Street and Fashion Street, it was the house where **Elizabeth Stride** drank on 29 September 1888 and outside which George Hutchinson saw a man with **Mary Jane Kelly** early on the morning of 9 November.

Ringer's—**See** The Britannia

The Ten Bells—On the corner of Fournier Street and Commercial Street. During the period 1976 to 1988 it was renamed the Jack the Ripper. It is still open to the public and has displays of Ripper ephemera.

The Three Crowns—Situated in Castle Alley, close to where **Alice McKenzie** was murdered in July 1889.

The Two Brewers—Situated in Brick Lane, this was where **Martha Tabram** and Mary Ann Connolly met the two soldiers on 6 August 1888.

White Swan—On Whitechapel High Street, it was another of the public houses where **Martha Tabram** and Mary Ann Connolly entertained the two soldiers.

Streets

Two of the most important streets mentioned in the stories of the murders have endured name changes since 1888. These are:

Berner Street—Now renamed Henriques Street, it was the scene of the murder of **Elizabeth Stride**.

Buck's Row—Now renamed Durward Street, it was the site of the murder of **Mary Ann Nichols**.

II

The Suspects

The "identification" of Jack the Ripper has attracted a great deal of nonsense over the years. Although some excellent research has named some prime suspects, some of whom deserve closer scrutiny, others have been put forward only because they fit, in however minor a way, one or more of the attributes that Jack is supposed to possess. Other candidates are simply ludicrous and beyond belief. See "The Literature" section for more information on authors and books whose theories are described in this section.

Below is a list of all those who have been suggested, however tentatively, each with a score giving the relative strength of the likelihood that he was the Ripper. The scoring system used is:

0—no credibility
1—very little credibility
2—a remote possibility
3—a reasonable possibility
4—a very good possibility.
5—a strong possibility

Albericci, Frederico

Also known as Fingers Freddy, Albericci is part of the Masonic Conspiracy theory. He was supposedly a footman employed by Sir William Gull at his home, 74 Brook Street, who aided the doctor and Lord Randolph Churchill in their search for the five canonical victims. Though Albericci is not said to have been the actual killer, he appears here because he was alleged to have been involved in the killings.

Chance of being the Ripper—0

Chance of being involved—0

See also Masonic Conspiracy

Albert Edward, Prince of Wales

Usually the Prince of Wales does not form part of the so-called Masonic or Royal Conspiracy theory. Those who have claimed involvement for him are confusing him with his son, Albert Victor, Duke of Clarence. However, John Wilding, author of *Jack the Ripper Revealed,* suggested that there might be evidence that the prince was indirectly involved by getting **Mary Jane Kelly** pregnant.

It is true that the prince and some of his companions kept a room in Watling Street where they would change their clothing in order to go out fire-watching inconspicuously, but the link with Mary Kelly and supposed orgies in which she was involved is pure supposition. The Masonic Conspiracy is discussed elsewhere in this section, and in dismissing that, I also dismiss any links with royal suspects.

Chance of being the Ripper—0

Chance of being involved—0

See also Albert Victor, Duke of Clarence; Masonic Conspiracy

Albert Victor, Duke of Clarence

Though the Masonic Conspiracy is covered later in this section, it has also been suggested that the Duke of Clarence was personally responsible for the murders. This notion is plainly nonsense because Prince Albert Victor's movements are well documented, and it can be shown that he was elsewhere at some of the critical times. For example, when **Mary Ann Nichols** was murdered he was at Danby Lodge, Grosmont, Yorkshire. When **Annie Chapman** was killed he was in York at the Cavalry Barracks. On the night of the so-called double event, the murders of **Elizabeth Stride** and **Catherine Eddowes,** he was with his grandmother, the queen, at Abergeldie, Scotland, and when **Mary Jane Kelly** died he was at Sandringham.

Unless these records were forged and a large number of people, including Queen Victoria, lied to hide the fact, Albert Victor could not have been involved. Anyone seriously suggesting the duke as a suspect would have to expand the Masonic Conspiracy theory to include a few hundred other names.

Chance of being the Ripper—0

See also Masonic Conspiracy

Arnold, John

A news vendor who walked into the offices of the *New York Herald* in London to announce that there had been a new Ripper atrocity two days before the **Pinchin Street Torso** was found. The name allegedly given by Arnold was either John Cleary or John Leary. Because this man appeared to have known about the crime before the body had been found, he was believed to be the killer. Once the crime had been linked to the Ripper murders, then, by definition, he was also believed to be Jack the Ripper.

In fact, Arnold denied having used any name other than his own and said he had been told the story by a uniformed man in Fleet Street. Though this man was never traced, Arnold was investigated and eliminated from the inquiry.

It should also be noted that most authorities deny that the Pinchin Street murder was in any way linked to the Ripper crimes.

Chance of being the Ripper—0

See also "The Witnesses": Arnold, John

Arthur, Sir George

A 28-year-old captain in the Royal Horse Guards who was a suspect at the time of the killings. It was his habit to spend a good deal of time in the Whitechapel area, and, attracting suspicion, he was arrested by the police. He was soon able to prove his innocence.

Chance of being the Ripper—0

Austin, Dick

Mentioned in Scotland Yard files that are now missing. On 5 October 1888, the chief constable of Rotherham contacted his colleagues in London to report that a discharged soldier named James Oliver had stated that he believed Austin to be the Ripper. Apparently Austin hated women and had said that if he had his way, he would kill every whore and rip her insides out.

Abberline appealed to all the divisions for any information on Austin, but without success. A second interview with Oliver was requested, but a report dated 19 October stated that he could add nothing new. Requests were made, however, or copies of the Jack the Ripper letters to be sent up to Yorkshire.

The last report, dated 24 October, refers to Oliver having seen the copies. He believed the writing "Dear Boss" letter to be very like Austin's and the "Saucy Jack" postcard slightly less so.

Chance of being the Ripper—2

See also "Letters and Correspondence": The "Dear Boss" Letter of 27 September 1888; The "Saucy Jack" Postcard of 1 October 1888

Avery, John

On 12 November 1888 Avery confessed to the police at King's Cross that he was the killer. He claimed that he would have committed even more murders except that he had lost the black bag he carried his knives in. He was soon proved to be innocent and ended up being sentenced to 14 days' hard labor for being drunk and disorderly.

Chances of being the Ripper—0

Barnardo, Dr. Thomas

His efforts to relieve poverty and suffering in the East End are well known. It is true that while the murders were taking place he visited 32 Flower and Dean Street, and after the murder of **Catherine Eddowes** he viewed her body and said he believed he had spoken to her in the kitchen there.

At the time of the murders the debate over the Ripper's supposed medical expertise led to a search for doctors who might have been involved, and because of his presence in the area, Barnardo has been named as a possible suspect, especially because he allegedly kept a diary in which the dates of the murders were left blank.

The theory has been expanded by the theorist Gary Rowlands, who suggested that Barnardo's lonely childhood and religious zeal led him to slaughter prostitutes in order to get them off the streets. He also claimed that Barnardo stopped killing only because an accident in a swimming pool soon after **Mary Jane Kelly**'s murder left him totally deaf.

Barnardo was born on 4 July 1845, so he was 43 at the time of the murders. This is far older than the composite figure experts have determined most likely to be the Ripper. Barnardo was instantly recognizable in the area, and his presence at or close to any of the murder locations would surely have been noted and remarked upon. Finally, photographs of Barnardo show a heavy mustache, turned up at the ends, which again does not fit the known descriptions of the Ripper.

Chance of being the Ripper—0

Barnett, Joseph

Put forward as a candidate most notably by writers Bruce Paley and Paul Harrison. The story is that Barnett was upset that his lover, **Mary Jane Kelly,** was prostituting herself, and after reading about the murder of **Martha Tabram,** he used the story to scare her off the streets. Unfortunately, this ploy worked only for a short time, so Barnett hit upon the idea of murdering friends of Mary in an effort to control her. When this too failed, he finally cracked and murdered the object of his desires.

The story is full of holes. To begin with, it is given as supposed fact that all five of the canonical victims knew each other. Harrison goes so far as to say that they all lived in the same street and drank in the same public houses. There is no evidence to support this statement. Errors of address have placed them all in Dorset Street at one time or another, but the known addresses of **Mary Ann Nichols, Annie Chapman, Elizabeth Stride, Catherine Eddowes,** and Mary Jane Kelly show plainly that they never lived in the same street.

Much is made of the missing key to 13 Miller's Court, and the stories express disbelief that the police couldn't simply use the method of entry Barnett referred to at the inquest: pulling the latch back by reaching through the broken window. After all, Barnett was there at Miller's Court, waiting with the police for someone to gain entry to the room. This is yet another error. The police arrived at Miller's Court at around 11 A.M., and the door was finally forced open at 1:30 P.M.. At no stage during those intervening hours was Barnett present in Miller's Court. So the prosaic truth is that the police did not open the door through the window because they did not know of this method, and Barnett was not there to tell them.

There are dozens of other errors that pepper the stories of Barnett being the Ripper. For instance, Harrison stated that it was not reasonable to assume that the killer had taken parts of Mary away with him. Why not? Hadn't he taken body parts from Chapman and Eddowes? Why should Kelly's murder be any different?

When we come to the discussion of why the Ripper killed, the exponents of the Barnett theory are on the thinnest of ice. Lust murder is dismissed because, according to the theorists, the murders would have gone on longer. They stopped with Mary Jane Kelly, so she must have been the target; hence, the motive must have been something else, such as jealousy; hence, the killer must have been someone close to her.

Such astounding leaps of logic defy belief. We are asked to accept that the Ripper killed by approaching his victims from behind, clasping a hand over the mouth, pulling the head back, and then slashing the throat. Never mind that this notion is in direct opposition to all the medical evidence that stated quite clearly that in most cases the victim's throat was cut while she lay on the ground.

Amazing suppositions are made about Barnett. First he is a staunch, right-thinking teetotaller and then, a chapter or two later, he is drunk when his landlord calls. Well, that discrepancy is easily explained: Mary must have driven him to drink. Then there is the not inconsiderable fact that Barnett had an alibi for the night Mary met her death. He was at his lodgings playing whist until 12:30 A.M. and then went to bed. Well, then, the writers tell us that he must have gotten up later and sneaked out to do the deed.

Finally, there is the coup de grâce in Harrison's book. He speaks at the end of a meeting with a descendant of Barnett's who provided him with an envelope of newspaper clippings relating to the Ripper murders. He was told that these were collected by Barnett himself, and, since the collection started in August 1888, it proved that Barnett knew a series of murders was starting before anyone else did. Well, yes, except for one startling fact: We are told that after Mary Kelly's death the Ripper murders stopped because Barnett had killed the person he wanted to. Why then does the series of articles continue to April 1891 and, presumably, the murder of **Frances Coles**?

As if this were not enough, we are also told that Barnett fitted the general description of the killer. The supposed sightings have been examined at length, and the best description of the killer, as far as his physical attributes go, tell us that he was about 5 feet 6 and sported a small brown mustache. Barnett was 5 feet 10 inches tall and had jet-black hair.

This entire theory depends on the idea that the motive for the murders was jealousy, which it plainly wasn't; that all the victims were known to each other, or at least to Mary Kelly, which they weren't; and that Barnett came up with the idea of a series of murders to persuade a woman not to sleep with other men. This is an idea worthy of an Agatha Christie novel, not the real world. It is totally illogical and based upon fallacies.

Chance of being the Ripper—1

See also "The Witnesses": Barnett, Joseph

Benelius, Nikaner

Benelius was arrested on 17 November 1888 after he walked into a house in Buxton Street occupied by Harriett Rowe. When Rowe asked him what he wanted he simply grinned at her, whereupon she rushed out of the house, found assistance, and had him arrested. He proved to be a Swedish traveler who was seeking directions and did not have a good grasp of English.

According to Detective Walter Dew, however, Benelius had already been questioned about **Elizabeth Stride**'s murder, possibly because of the Swedish connection. He had been thoroughly examined and his innocence proved.

Chance of being the Ripper—0

Blanchard, Alfred Napier

Blanchard was arrested in a Birmingham public house soon after the double event, the murders of **Elizabeth Stride** and **Catherine Eddowes,** when he was heard describing how he had committed the murders. He was charged, and when he appeared in court a few days later the magistrates were informed that he had been drunk and, after reading about the murders, had become excited and decided to claim them as his own. He was carefully checked out, and it was shown that he was in Birmingham when the crimes were committed.

Chance of being the Ripper—0

Brodie, William Wallace

The day after **Alice McKenzie** was murdered, Brodie walked into Leman Street Police Station and gave himself up, claiming to be the Whitechapel murderer and saying that only this latest crime had bothered him. He then made a full statement, which was clearly nonsense because it contained admissions such as the claim that he had walked from London to Land's End in Cornwall and back in half an hour, or possibly forty-five minutes. Nevertheless, his claim to be the killer was carefully checked, and he even appeared in the police court on 20 July, charged with Alice's murder, for which he was remanded until 27 July.

A careful check into Brodie's background proved that he had sailed for South Africa on 6 September 1888 and had not returned to England until 15 July 1889. It was clear that Brodie had severe mental problems. When he made his second appearance at the police court on 27 July, he was discharged but then rearrested for fraud.

Chance of being the Ripper—0

Chance of being the killer of Alice McKenzie—2

Brown, General

Mentioned in the Home Office files on 15 October 1888. A letter to "Jane Bromley" had not been addressed properly and could not be delivered. It was opened by the Post Office and found to contain a letter from an unnamed man in Eaton Place to his son, which had been placed in the wrong envelope by mistake. The writer stated that he believed General Brown to be the killer.

The intercepted letter was passed on to Sir Charles Warren, and on 17 October he replied that the general had been interviewed and cleared of any involvement.

Chance of being the Ripper—0

See also "The Police": Warren, Sir Charles

Buchan, Edward

Modern writers cannot understand why Jack the Ripper stopped killing. They believe, depending on who their particular favorite suspect is, that he was arrested for some other offense, caged in an asylum after the police caught him but kept it quiet, or committed suicide (though it is established fact that very few serial killers take their own lives). A favorite candidate for the suicide theory is of course Montague John Druitt, but others have been searched for, and this quest is what led to the suggestion that Buchan was the Ripper.

Buchan lived in Robin Hood Lane, Poplar, and killed himself on 19 November 1888. Beyond that one fact, there is nothing to link him with the crimes.

Chance of being the Ripper—1

See also Druitt, Montague John

Bull, William

Bull was charged on 5 October 1888 with the murder of **Catherine Eddowes** in Mitre Square after he walked into Bishopsgate Police Station and confessed to the crime. This arrest was another case of alcohol leading to false suspicion, for in due course Bull was able to prove that he had been home in bed at the time of the killing.

Chance of being the Ripper—0

Burrows, Edwin

Burrows was arrested on 8 December 1888 solely because he was wearing a peaked cap! Israel Schwartz had described a man wearing a peaked cap, which made such a garment grounds for suspicion. Detective Bradshaw of H Division and Detective Godley of J Division took Burrows, who lived at a common lodging house, to the King Street Police Station, where he proved that he was a vagrant who lived on a meager allowance of 1 pound per week from his kindly brother.

Chance of being the Ripper—0

Bury, William Henry

Along with suspects such as George Chapman and Dr. Cream, Bury is one of the few we know to be a murderer. In fact, like Chapman and Cream, he was hanged for the crime and has been suggested as a suspect by writer William Beadle.

Bury was born at Stourbridge on 25 May 1859 and was 29 years old at the time of the Whitechapel murders. His early life was uneventful, but Beadle does tell us that at one stage he was a horsemeat butcher, which would perhaps explain any anatomical knowledge that the Ripper may have exhibited.

We know that Bury moved to London in October 1887 and began working for James Martin, a general dealer. Bury lived with the Martins at their home in Quickett Street, Bow, but it appears that the house was more than a simple residence or place of work. Beadle's research indicates that it was actually a brothel. Be that as it may, what is known with certainty is that Bury became enamored of Ellen Elliott, a woman who lived and worked in the house. A relationship developed between them, and they eventually married on 2 April 1888 at Bromley Parish Church.

Unfortunately for the new Mr. and Mrs. Bury, things were already beginning to go wrong. Just before the wedding, toward the end of March, Bury had been dismissed by Martin for theft. His dismissal meant, of course, that Bury lost the security of his home as well as his employment.

The couple had several addresses over the next few weeks, all in Bow, and eventually settled at 3 Spanby Road. It is significant that at an earlier address their landlady had heard a terrible argument between the newlyweds and had found Bury kneeling on his wife and apparently attempting to cut her throat.

Although Bury was out of work, the couple did have something to fall back on. Before her marriage Ellen had inherited some shares worth the not inconsiderable amount of 300 pounds. Some of these were sold in late April 1888, and another block was sold on 7 June. By this time over 200 pounds' worth of the shares had been turned into cash, and Bury used part of the money to buy a horse and cart that he said he would use to sell sawdust.

The argument is that Bury actually used his horse and cart as a front so that he could travel to Whitechapel to go drinking and whoring. It is also suggested that although he did not live in the area where the murders took place, he would stable his horse there, giving him legitimate access to Whitechapel.

What is known is that in January 1889 Bury told Ellen's sister that he had found himself a job in Dundee paying 2 pounds a week and had also found work for Ellen at 1 pound a week. He lied to his landlord, saying they were moving to Australia, when actually he and Ellen took a ship from London to Dundee on 19 January 1889. Ten days later, on the 29th, they moved into a basement flat at 113 Princes Street.

The 10th of February was a crucial day for William Henry Bury. Early that morning he visited a friend, David Walker, who seemed interested in reading reports of the Ripper crimes in his newspaper. Bury threw the paper down and stormed out. Later he walked into the police station and announced that his wife was dead. He said he had awakened on 5 February to find her lying dead with a rope around her neck, obviously having committed suicide. He had stabbed the body once before stuffing it into a trunk.

The police went to the flat in Princes Street, but before they found Ellen's body they noted that behind a door someone had written in chalk, "Jack Ripper is at the back of this door," and on the stairway wall, "Jack Ripper is in this seller [sic]."

Ellen's body was in the trunk, but in addition to being strangled she had been terribly mutilated, and, in a scene reminiscent of some of the Whitechapel murders, her intestines protruded through one of the slashes in her stomach. Bury's story was naturally not believed, and he was arrested and charged with Ellen's murder. He faced his trial on 28 March and on 24 April 1889 was hanged at Dundee.

The case against Bury is that the murders started after he moved to London and stopped after he left; he was a known thief, and we believe Jack stole from his victims; he killed his wife in a manner similar to the Ripper murders; he fitted the psychological profile; he fitted the general physical description; and the writing in the tenement showed that someone, possibly Ellen, believed him to be the Ripper. Those who discount him as a suspect state that he couldn't have been the Ripper because the behavior he demonstrated after the murder of his wife was not consistent with the cool, calculated approach of Jack the Ripper.

Although many of these factors are true, there are other, more sensible arguments that need to be addressed before Bury can be said to be the Ripper. To begin with, he moved to London in late 1887 and always lived at Bow. Though he may well have had a stable in the Whitechapel area, there is nothing to show that he had the firsthand knowledge of Whitechapel and its environs that the Ripper clearly had. We can only even attempt to place the Whitechapel crimes at Bury's door if we agree that **Mary Jane Kelly** was his last victim because of his move to Scotland in January 1889. If we agree that the Ripper did commit more murders after that date (as I believe he did), then Bury cannot have been the killer. Finally, it is known that Bury took his wife to Wolverhampton, of all places, for a holiday in August 1888. We do not know what dates he was absent from London, but, as Beadle rightly points out, if it was at the beginning of that month we would have to state that either Bury was not the Ripper or **Martha Tabram** wasn't a Ripper victim. Also, if that holiday was at the end of the month, then it would completely exonerate Bury because **Mary Ann Nichols** was certainly a Ripper victim.

William Henry Bury may have failed to demonstrate the coolness of the man we seek for Jack the Ripper, but that alone is not enough to discount him as a possibility for the Whitechapel fiend. He certainly deserves a closer look.

Chance of being the Ripper—3

See also Chapman, George; Cream, Dr. Thomas Neil

Carroll, Lewis

The writer was seriously suggested as a candidate by Richard Wallace in his book *Jack the Ripper: "Light-Hearted Friend"* after research based on deleted passages from Carroll's diaries, held at the British Library. Wallace claimed that the deleted sections contained comments on the murders.

Charles Lutwidge Dodgson, whose pen name was Lewis Carroll, was 56 years old at the time of the murders and spent much of the autumn of 1888 at a summer cottage in Eastbourne. We are expected to believe that he regularly caught night trains back to London so he could commit his nefarious deeds. The suggestion is without foundation.

Chance of being the Ripper—0

Chapman, Dr. Frederick Richard

Chapman was given the pseudonym of Dr. Merchant by the theorist B. G. Reilly and was put forward as the Ripper because it has been suggested first that the Ripper must have been a doctor and second that the murders must have stopped because the killer died. Dr. Chapman was the only medical practitioner in the area who died after the murder of **Mary Jane Kelly.** There is nothing else to connect him with the murders.

Chance of being the Ripper—1

Chapman, George

At 12:30 A.M. on Wednesday, 22 October 1902, Maud Marsh died at the Crown public house, High Street, Islington. Dr. Stoker, who had been called to attend Maud, refused to issue a death certificate. He had attended another of George Chapman's girlfriends who had died after displaying identical symptoms. The doctor was convinced that he had witnessed a case of poisoning. He decided to do a postmortem.

Dr. Stoker was looking for arsenic but managed to find only minute traces of that substance. He sent tissue samples to two of his colleagues, who found that the arsenic present had probably been nothing more than impurities in another poison. That other substance was shown to be tartar emetic, an antimony-based irritant poison. A total of 20.12 grains of tartar emetic was found in Maud's remains.

Three days after Maud's death the doctors' findings were passed on to the police, and George Chapman was arrested for murder under his real name of Severiano (which all writers give as Severin) Antoniovitch Klosowski. Klosowski had led a checkered life until the moment of his arrest. Born in Poland, he arrived in England in June 1887 and took employment as a hairdresser's assistant in a shop at 70 West India Dock Road. Later he opened his own premises at 126 Cable Street, St. George's-in-the-East.

Shortly afterward, in October 1889, he married Lucy Baderski of Walthamstow, and the couple soon had a son. Lucy was dismayed when, within a few weeks of the wedding, a woman turned up who had traveled to England from Poland. She had two young children in tow and claimed to be legally married to Klosowski, who, however, soon sent her packing. On 3 March 1891 tragedy struck the couple when their young child died, and soon afterward, in April

1891, Klosowski and Lucy emigrated to America.

Lucy, again pregnant, returned to England in February 1892 after an argument but was joined by her husband two weeks later. On 12 May she gave birth to a daughter, Cecilia. The following year she decided she had finally had enough of her husband's womanizing ways and left, taking her daughter with her.

At the end of 1893, Klosowski met up with a woman named Annie Chapman, which should not be considered significant because the events at Hanbury Street had taken place years before, in September 1888. They lived together until December 1894, during which time Klosowski took to using her name and thereafter became known as George Chapman, a name he would use for the rest of his life.

Once the relationship with Annie had ended, Chapman needed to find new lodgings. He took a room with John Ward, one of the customers in the barbershop George ran. One of Ward's other lodgers was Isabella Spink, who had recently been deserted by her husband, Shadrach. George and Isabella became close, and at one stage John Ward's wife complained to her husband that she had seen Chapman and Isabella kissing on the stairs. When this incident was mentioned to Chapman, he pointed out that there was no impropriety because he would soon be marrying Mrs. Spink. In March 1896 Chapman and Isabella moved to Hastings, where he opened another barbershop in George Street. By all accounts it was a great success. Chapman provided shaves while Isabella played the piano for the customers' enjoyment.

Although Chapman found it fairly easy to start a relationship with a woman, he appeared to find it well-nigh impossible to end one. He may have already grown tired of Isabella during their stay in Hastings because on 3 April 1897 he bought an ounce of tartar emetic from William Davidson's chemist's shop on High Street, Hastings. It was estimated that a fatal dose of the substance was about 15 grains. The single ounce was equivalent to over 400 grains.

In September 1897 Chapman and Isabella returned to London, where he took the lease on the Prince of Wales public house in Bartholemew Square, off Old Street. It was there, on Christmas Day, that Isabella died after a period of illness. The cause of death was given as phthisis, a kind of consumptive disease.

Around Easter 1898 Chapman decided he needed a new barmaid. The woman who successfully applied for the position was Elizabeth Taylor, known to her friends as Bessie. It was not long before the two became lovers and Bessie took to calling herself Chapman. There may well have been some local gossip about how fast they had taken up with each other after Isabella's death, for the new lovers spent a year running the Grapes public house in Bishop's Stortford before returning to London in 1899.

On 23 March 1899 Chapman and Bessie moved to the Monument public house in Union Street. Bessie died there on 13 February 1901, like Isabella after a period of illness. Bessie was attended by Dr. Stoker, who gave the cause of her death as intestinal obstruction. In August that same year, Maud Marsh advertised for employment and, after being interviewed by Chapman, became the next barmaid at his pub.

George wasted little time with Maud. In September they visited her mother and announced that they wished to marry. Then, on 13 October, Maud began wearing a wedding ring and claimed that she and George had tied the knot.

In June 1902 Chapman moved to the Crown pub at 213 Borough High Street.

The lease on the Monument was just about up when a fire broke out on the premises. Chapman and Marsh were not there at the time, and the cause of the fire was difficult to determine. The insurance company suspected arson and refused to pay Chapman any compensation. He simply moved down the road and took over the Crown.

No sooner had Chapman moved into his new pub than his weakness for an attractive barmaid manifested itself again. Florence Rayner worked behind the bar, and Chapman fell for her in a big way, asking her to go to America with him. She refused, reminding him that he already had a wife living with him. The following month, Florence left his employment. Chapman had now tired of Maud. It was time for her to go.

The scenario was familiar. Maud fell ill and was fussed over by her ever-attentive lover, who brought her brandy and food. She did not improve, though, and by the time her sister, Mrs. Morris, paid her a visit Maud's condition was very poor indeed.

At Mrs. Morris's insistence, Maud was taken to Guy's Hospital, where she stayed from 28 July until 20 August. During that period Maud slowly recovered her strength, but on her return to the Crown, she fell ill again, finally dying on 22 October.

Once Chapman had been arrested for murder, the police began to look into the deaths of Isabella and Bessie. Both bodies were exhumed; Bessie's on 22 November and Isabella's on 9 December. Both were found to be remarkably well preserved, a sign of antimony poisoning, and the subsequent postmortems showed 3.83 grains of tartar emetic in Isabella and 29.12 grains in Bessie. On 31 December, Chapman was charged with two more murders.

The trial lasted for four days, from 16 to 19 March 1903. No witnesses were called for the defense, Chapman's counsel instead relying on the facts that Chapman had no apparent motive for killing the three women and that there was no direct evidence to show it was he who had administered the poison. The jury, however, took just 10 minutes to return a guilty verdict. Chapman took his sentence badly and had to be supported by two prison officers as he was taken down to the cells. On 7 April 1903 he had to be supported again while he stood over the trap at Wandsworth.

It has been suggested that George Chapman was also Jack the Ripper. The only evidence for this claim is the fact that Chapman was in Whitechapel at the time of the murders, operating a barbershop in Cable Street, and that he had once been a barber-surgeon in Poland. It has also been said that when Chapman was arrested by George Godley, Inspector Abberline remarked, "I see you've got the Ripper at last." This is certainly untrue because Abberline later reported that he became suspicious of Chapman only during the trial.

It should be remembered that whoever Jack the Ripper really was, he knew the dark alleyways of Whitechapel very well, something that could not be said for the then 22-year-old stranger from Poland. It is also highly unlikely that someone who butchered prostitutes with such ferocity would later turn to poisoning his victims. In addition, Chapman lived far to the east of the center of the murders, quite a distance even from the **Elizabeth Stride** murder in Berner Street. His coloring did not match any of the reasonable descriptions of a man seen with any of the victims and it is believed that throughout his adult life he sported a bushy black mustache. In short, the evidence is tenuous or nonexistent.

Chance of being the Ripper—2

See also "The Police": Abberline, Inspector Frederick George

Charrington, Frederick Nicholas

The heir to the Charrington brewing fortune, Frederick turned his back on his family business and instead took up religious zeal as his calling. Like Dr. Barnardo, he lectured against drink and prostitution and got hundreds of men and women to sign a temperance pledge.

He has been suggested as the Ripper because he was roughly the right age at 38, having been born on 4 February 1850. He lived alone and knew the East End well, though he did not live in the area. He was also the right sort of build and coloring. Proponents of this theory point out that he was well known in the area and would have been instantly recognized by his victims and thus able to lull them into a false sense of security.

Charrington was suggested as a suspect by M. J. Trow in his essay "The Way to Hell" in *The Mammoth Book of Jack the Ripper,* and Trow ended by admitting that there is no evidence whatsoever against Charrington. Trow merely used his name to demonstrate how easy it is to build a case against any named individual and did not seriously suggest Charrington as a candidate. (For another example, see the Peter Harpick entry in this section.)

However, for those who fail to see Trow's excellent point, I should perhaps add that because Charrington was so recognizable, his presence at the murder locations would have been commented upon, and the fact that he lived about a mile and a half from the farthest murder would also tend to rule him out.

Chance of being the Ripper—0

Chance of someone else "proving" that Charrington was the Ripper—4

See also Barnardo, Dr. Thomas; Harpick, Peter J.

Churchill, Lord Randolph Henry Spencer

See Masonic Conspiracy

Cleary, John

See Arnold, John

Cohen, Aaron Davis

On 6 December 1888, 23-year-old Aaron Davis Cohen was arrested. The fact that his case was minuted to be heard with that of a madam, Gertrude Smith, and two of her prostitutes, Mary Jones and Ellen Hickey, who had been arrested in a raid on a brothel, indicates that he was arrested at the same time.

Cohen was brought before the magistrates by Constable Patrick on 7 December as a lunatic who had been found wandering at large. His address was given as 86 Leman Street, which must have been an error because that was the address of a Protestant Boys' Club at the time. Cohen was taken from the court to the Whitechapel Workhouse Infirmary and subsequently, on 21 December, to the Colney Hatch Asylum, where he was admitted under the name David Cohen.

At Colney Hatch he proved to be violent, attacking other patients who came near him. He also refused food and tried to damage the ward. He died on 20 October 1889. One theory suggests that Cohen and Nathan Kaminsky were the same person and that he may have been the Ripper.

Chance of being the Ripper—4

See also Kaminsky, Nathan; "The Police": Patrick, Constable John; "Others Who Played a Part": Hickey, Ellen; Jones, Mary; Smith, Gertrude

Cohen, David

See Cohen, Aaron Davis

Cohn, Dr.

A suspect suggested by Inspector Lewis Henry Keaton, whose grasp of the facts of the Ripper case was tenuous, to say the least. In the first place, Keaton joined the police force in August 1891, after the Ripper crimes were over, so he had no firsthand knowledge. He stated that he believed the killer to be a doctor who was collecting specimens of infected wombs, thus missing the point that not all the victims were mutilated in that way and perpetuating the story of the American doctor seeking specimens that was first suggested by Wynne Edwin Baxter at **Annie Chapman**'s inquest. Finally, Keaton stated that he believed the killer used strychnine, an obvious allusion to Dr. Cream.

Chance of being the Ripper—0

See also Cream, Dr. Thomas Neil

Cornell, James

An Irishman who walked in Hyde Park with Martha Spencer and spoke to her about the Ripper murders. She made a complaint to the police, but Cornell was able to prove that he was not the murderer.

Chance of being the Ripper—0

Cow, Douglas

Cow was interviewed by the police at Rochester Row on 21 December 1888 after Fanny Drake of Clerkenwell Green made a complaint that he fitted the description of the wanted man and had grinned at her in a frightening manner. Cow was able to show that he was a respectable businessman of Cow and Company, India Rubber Merchants, and was subsequently released.

Chance of being the Ripper—0

Cream, Dr. Thomas Neil

Hanged at Newgate prison on 15 November 1892, Cream had first been found guilty of murder in Chicago in 1881 after poisoning his mistress's husband. He served 10 years for that offense and after his release came to England and settled in Lambeth.

In the latter part of 1891 he poisoned Ellen Donworth, Matilda Clover, Emma Shrivell, and Alice March by giving them strychnine. He began to incriminate himself and was arrested in June 1892.

The only factor that brings Cream into line as a suspect is the fact that his last words on the scaffold were, "I am Jack the . . ." before the rope tightened and snapped his neck. The truth is that at the time of the Whitechapel atrocities he was safely under lock and key in Chicago. There are of course those who say that this information is an error and that Cream was actually back in England at the time of the murders, having escaped from prison. I would reply that Cream did not live in the immediate area of the murders, did not have any demonstrable knowledge of the Whitechapel area, and was 38 years old at the time, which is right at the edge of the likely range for our composite character.

Chance of being the Ripper—0

Cutbush, Thomas Hayne

The nephew of Superintendent Charles Henry Cutbush, Thomas was detained as a lunatic on 5 March 1891 but escaped from the Lambeth Infirmary within hours. He was free for four days, during which he stabbed Florence Grace Johnson in the buttocks and tried to do the same to Isabelle Frazer Anderson. Arrested on 9 March, he was charged with malicious wounding and committed to Broadmoor, where he died in 1903.

Cutbush was first mooted to be the Ripper by the *Sun* newspaper on 13 February 1894. The claim was thoroughly investigated by the police and led directly to the penning of the Macnaghten Memoranda in an effort to refute the claims. It is surely impossible to reconcile the sadistic murders committed by Jack the Ripper with two relatively minor stabbings two years later. In addition, Cutbush was only 23 at the time of the murders and lived in Albert Street, Kennington, some distance from the Whitechapel area.

Chance of being the Ripper—0

See also "Miscellaneous": Cutbush, Superintendent Charles Henry; Macnaghten Memoranda

Davidson, John

Davidson's real name was John George Donkin. He was born at Morpeth in 1853 and by the end of 1881 had served two terms of imprisonment for assaults upon women. He served both of these terms in Newcastle prison: one month's hard labor was awarded on 6 January 1881, and a two months was given for his second offense on 22 December of the same year.

On the afternoon of 1 October 1888 he walked into the cabman's reading room at 43 Pickering Place, Westbourne Grove, West London, and spoke to Thomas Ryan, the man in charge of the premises. Davidson complained of the cold and asked for a chop to be cooked for him. While his meal was being prepared, the conversation turned to the news of the so-called double event (the murders of **Elizabeth Stride** and **Catherine Eddowes**), and eventually Davidson admitted that he was the killer. Ryan believed him to be drunk but nevertheless made arrangements to meet Davidson that same evening to find out more. Davidson did not turn up, but details of the encounter appeared in the London evening papers that day and were picked up by the *Newcastle Daily Chronicle* in an article dated 2 October. This story led the governor of Newcastle prison to contact the Metropolitan police and supply details of Davidson's history.

At first the police believed that Davidson was a very likely candidate. He had trained as a doctor and had considerable anatomical knowledge, dressed and spoke like a gentleman but had led a dissolute life, and had been married but later divorced. However, once Davidson's movements were examined more carefully, it became clear that he could not be the murderer because he was able to prove he had been elsewhere at the times of the crimes.

Chance of being the Ripper—0

Davies, Dr. Morgan

Davies was accused of being the Ripper by another suspect, Robert Donston Stephenson. During the time that Stephenson was being treated for neurasthenia at the London Hospital, he shared a room with a man named Dr. Evans who received frequent visits from Davies, a house surgeon at the hospital. During one of these visits the murders were discussed, and Davies demonstrated graphically how he believed the crimes had been committed. His description included anal penetration of the victims, and when Stephenson later heard the erroneous claim from the journalist William Thomas Stead that **Mary Jane Kelly** had been anally raped by her killer, he came to the conclusion that Davies was the murderer.

There is nothing else to link Davies with the crimes and no record of his even being interviewed by the police.

Chance of being the Ripper—2

See also Stephenson, Robert Donston

Deeming, Frederick Bailey

Deeming, who was certainly a mass murderer, was hanged in Australia on 23 May 1892 after being found guilty of the murder of his second wife. Before emigrating to that country he had murdered his first wife and four children in the district of Merseyside and cemented their bodies under the hearth of Dinham Villa in Rainhill. Press reports indicated that before he was executed he confessed to the last two canonical Ripper murders. This claim was strenuously denied by Deeming's solicitor, but it matters little because at the time of the Whitechapel crimes Deeming was in South Africa.

When he first arrived in Australia Deeming used the alias Druin or Drewen, which may have led to confusion between him and Montague John Druitt in the stories of the killer that supposedly emanated from Dandenong, Australia.

Chance of being the Ripper—0

See also Druitt, Montague John

Denny, Joseph

On 28 December 1888 Denny was seen accosting women in the King's Cross police section. He was wearing a long, astrakhan-trimmed coat at the time and came under suspicion because of George Hutchinson's description of the man he had supposedly seen with **Mary Jane Kelly**. Inquiries were made, and Denny was released after demonstrating that he was elsewhere at the time of the murder.

Chances of being the Ripper—0

See also Hutchinson, George (Britain); "The Witnesses": Hutchinson, George

Dodgson, Charles Lutwidge

See Carroll, Lewis

Donkin, John George

See Davidson, John

D'Onston, Dr. Roslyn

See Stephenson, Robert Donston

Druitt, Montague John

Druitt was the first suspect named in the Macnaghten Memoranda and was Macnaghten's personal choice as the man most likely to have been Jack the Ripper.

Montague John Druitt was born on 15 August 1857, which means that he was 31 at the time of the murders. His age is about right, but little else about Druitt fits profiles of the cold-blooded murderer who stalked the East End streets.

In 1880 Druitt graduated from New College, Oxford, and soon afterward he began teaching at a boy's boarding school at 9 Eliot Place, Blackheath. He was a keen cricketer and sportsman, accomplished at Fives, and he joined the Morden Cricket Club at Blackheath in 1881. By 1884 he had also been elected to the famous Marylebone Cricket Club (MCC).

In 1882 Druitt began a second career. Still teaching, he embarked on a career in law, was admitted to the Inner Temple on 17 May, and was called to the bar on 29 April 1885. For the next three years he appeared to enjoy success in both his professions, but tragedy struck him in 1888. In July of that year his mother, Ann Druitt, was admitted to the Brooke Asylum in Clapton, and four months later, on 30 November, Druitt was dismissed from his position at the school after getting into what press reports referred to as "serious trouble."

Nothing more was heard of Druitt until the afternoon of Monday, 31 December 1888. On that day, at approximately 1 P.M., Henry Winslade, a waterman, was on the Thames in his boat, close by Thorneycroft's Wharf, Chiswick. He spotted a body floating in the river and pulled it to the shore before going to fetch a policeman.

The first constable on the scene was George Moulson, who searched the body and found 2 pounds, 17 shillings, and twopence in cash; two checks, both drawn on the London and Provincial

Bank, one for 50 pounds and the other for 16 pounds; a first-class railway season ticket from Blackheath to London; the second half of a return ticket from Hammersmith to Charing Cross dated 1 December; a pair of kid gloves; a white handkerchief; and a gold watch on a silver chain with a spade guinea attached. In each pocket of the man's coat Moulson also found four large stones.

There was no formal identification on the body, which had been in the water for some time, but the checks must have still been legible and gave the authorities the name Druitt. The body was finally identified as Montague John Druitt by his brother William, who practiced as a solicitor in Bournemouth.

The inquest on the dead man took place on 2 January 1889 before Dr. Thomas Diplock at the Lamb Tap public house in Chiswick. William Druitt testified that he had first heard of his brother being absent from his chambers on 11 December, when a friend had contacted him and said that Montague had not been seen for more than a week. William began to investigate and found that Montague had been dismissed from his school. A search of Montague's chambers revealed a note, addressed to William, that read, "Since Friday I felt I was going to be like mother, and the best thing for me was to die." Not surprisingly, the jury returned a verdict that Montague had taken his own life while of unsound mind.

Just when did Montague John Druitt die? There has been some confusion because the reports of the inquest proceedings state clearly that William said his brother had been dismissed on 30 December. This is impossible because Druitt's body was found on 31 December and had been in the water for some time. It appears, then, that this press report was a misprint and that the correct date for Druitt's dismissal from the school was probably 30 November. It has been suggested by many authors that the reason for this dismissal was homosexual activity between Druitt and one or more of the pupils in his charge. There is no proof to support this allegation, although it is a possibility, especially because Druitt was not married and there is no evidence that he ever had a girlfriend.

We know that 30 November 1888 was a Friday. Because it was almost certainly on that date that Druitt was dismissed, it seems likely that it is the Friday referred to in Druitt's farewell note to his brother. If the note was written soon after his dismissal, then that time frame, together with the unused half of the railway ticket found on Druitt's body, leads most authors to suggest that Druitt threw himself into the Thames on Saturday, 1 December 1888. Why then was this troubled schoolmaster the strongest suspect of Sir Melville Macnaghten?

We must remember that the Ripper crimes were something totally new for the police of the day. They couldn't understand the motives for the murders and believed very strongly that at least the five canonical murders were evidence of a steadily failing mental state. Though modern experience tells us that serial killers rarely commit suicide, the belief at the time was that the Ripper's mind must have finally snapped sometime after the Miller's Court murder and that the killer would undoubtedly have taken his own life. One factor in police suspicion of Druitt, therefore, was that he took his own life at the right time. The killer must have killed himself soon after taking **Mary Jane Kelly**'s life; Druitt had done so; hence, Druitt must have been the killer.

Is this all the evidence Sir Melville Macnaghten had to go on? According to him it wasn't. He wrote, "From private information I have little doubt but that his own family believed him to have been the murderer." This sentence has led many writers to suggest that the source of this private information must actually have been a member of Druitt's family, an idea that was reinforced by the experience of Dan Farson.

In 1959 Farson was preparing a series of television programs, and for one program he needed information on Jack the Ripper. He made a public appeal for anyone who knew anything about the crimes to come forward. This request led to a large number of replies, two of which were significant.

The first was from a man named A. Knowles, who stated that he had been in Australia and had seen a document titled "The East End Murderer—I Knew Him." He said the document had been produced privately by a man named Lionel Druitt, Drewett, or Drewery and had been printed by a Mr. Fell of Dandenong about 1890.

The second reply was from Maurice Gold, who had been in Australia from 1925 to 1932 and had there met two men who claimed to know the identity of Jack the Ripper. These men both claimed that the killer was Montague John Druitt, and one, Edward MacNamara, told Gold that Lionel Druitt had once lodged with Mr. W. G. Fell of Dandenong and had left behind a paper proving that M. J. Druitt was the killer.

At first glance these stories appeared to be strong proof against Druitt, for Farson knew that Lionel Druitt was Montague Druitt's cousin and had emigrated to Australia in 1886. If a copy of the document could be found, then the case against Druitt would be that much stronger. Unfortunately, no such document could be traced in any library, archive, or file in Australia—or anywhere else, for that matter. A little more digging showed that a W. G. Fell was a storekeeper who had actually employed Maurice Gold in 1930. It was clear that the stories of the pamphlet were invention and error, possibly based upon the story of Frederick Deeming. The Australian "evidence" against Druitt simply did not exist.

Let us now return to Sir Melville Macnaghten's comments about Druitt. It is a simple matter to demonstrate that the "private information" could not have come from Druitt's family members. They would have been very unlikely to have supplied any evidence that proved their deceased relative to be Jack the Ripper. Furthermore, if such evidence had come from Druitt's family, one would expect them to have gotten their facts right. When we examine Macnaghten's statements about his strongest suspect, we see that very little of his information is correct.

Macnaghten claimed that Druitt resided with his own people and absented himself from time to time. In fact, researchers who have checked his known movements have concluded that all the evidence points to Druitt living at the school at 9 Eliot Place until his dismissal. Macnaghten stated confidently that the killer must have committed suicide soon after the Miller's Court murder, "on or about the 10th." In fact, the most likely date of Druitt's death was 1 December, three weeks after the murder of Mary Jane Kelly. Macnaghten wrote that his suspect was 41, when Druitt was 31; finally, he said the killer was a doctor, whereas Druitt was a teacher and barrister.

Macnaghten also erred when he wrote that the murders increased in severity. This notion is true only if we count only the five canonical murders as Ripper crimes and then further discount **Elizabeth Stride** as an example of that increasing severity because the killer was disturbed. The tenet collapses entirely if we place the death of **Martha Tabram** at Jack's door because she was attacked much more savagely than **Mary Ann Nichols**. Furthermore, if we believe that other victims, such as **Alice McKenzie**, followed Mary Jane Kelly, then the pattern of increased severity is again lost.

Is there any other evidence against Druitt? After all, his age was correct, he did die soon after the Miller's Court murder, and he obviously had mental problems. Might he still be a likely candidate?

Attempts have been made to show that Druitt had another base, closer to the epicenter of the murders. Writer Tom Cullen, for instance, has suggested that Druitt had chambers at 9 King's Bench Walk near the Victoria Embankment, but the Law Lists of 1886–1887 show that this is not the case. Other writers have stated that because Lionel Druitt assisted Dr. Thomas Thynne at 140 The Minories in 1879, Montague may have visited him there and gotten to know the East End well. However, the Medical Register and Medical Directory both record Lionel as working at 8 Strathmore Gardens, Kensington, in 1878 and 1880, showing that his stay at The Minories was a brief one.

There is circumstantial evidence showing that it is unlikely that Druitt even had the opportunity to commit some of the murders. We know that on 3 and 4 August he played cricket at Bournemouth. He did so again on the 10th and 11th, implying that he stayed in Bournemouth the whole time, which, if true, means that he wasn't in London when Martha Tabram died. On 1 September Druitt played cricket at Canford in Dorset, which suggests that he could not have killed Mary Ann Nichols, and finally, on 8 September at 11:30 A.M., he was playing at Blackheath, meaning that if he was the killer he was changed, cleaned, and enjoying his cricket game just six hours after butchering **Annie Chapman**.

As if all this were not enough, we must remember that Druitt was a very slender man, whereas our most reliable witnesses state that the killer was stout. There is nothing to link Druitt to the Whitechapel area or the murders, and if he had not taken his own life at the end of 1888 his name would never have been mentioned.

Perhaps the last word should be left to Inspector Abberline, who in 1903, in an interview with the *Pall Mall Gazette*, referred to the story that the Ripper had drowned himself in the Thames: "Yes, I know all about that story. But what does it amount to? Simply this. Soon after the last murder in Whitechapel the body of a young doctor was found in the Thames, but there is absolutely nothing beyond the fact that he was found at the time to incriminate him."

Chance of being the Ripper—1

See also Deeming, Frederick Bailey; Masonic Conspiracy; "The Police": Abberline, Inspector Frederick George; Macnaghten, Sir Melville Leslie; Moulson, Constable George; "Others Who Played a Part": Winslade, Henry; "Miscellaneous": Druitt, Ann; Druitt, Dr. Lionel; Druitt, William Harvey; "The East End Murderer—I Knew Him"; Macnaghten Memoranda

Duke of Clarence

See Albert Victor, Duke of Clarence

Edwards, Frank

Edwards is a suspect who came to light fairly recently. In 1959 George Reynolds was interviewed by the *Worthing Gazette* and *Reynolds News* and stated that in 1888, not long after the double event of 30 September, his cousin, 35-year-old Frank Edwards, had visited him at his home in Chichester, West Sussex. Edwards was wearing gold pince-nez and carried a razor and bloodstained shirt collar in an attaché case. There is nothing else to link Edwards to the crime.

Chance of being the Ripper—1

Father of G. W. B.

This suspect originated in a letter addressed to Daniel Farson from a correspondent in Australia who signed himself only "G. W. B."

According to this missive, when G. W. B. was a child he used to play in the London streets, and his mother had used the threat, "Come in, Georgie, or Jack the Ripper will get you." Such commonly used warnings were akin to the phrase "The bogeyman'll get you."

One day in 1889, Georgie's father overheard this remark, turned to his son, and announced, "Don't worry, Georgie. You would be the last person Jack the Ripper would touch." This phrase may have engendered some doubt in Georgie's mind, but his suspicions was not confirmed until some time later.

G. W. B.'s father was supposedly a drunken bully who married in 1876. For some reason he had set his mind on a daughter, but the only female child he had was born an imbecile. This tragedy led to more drinking, more violence, and finally severe mental problems until G. W. B.'s father commenced butchering whores on the streets of Whitechapel.

As he grew older, Georgie and his father argued, and in due course Georgie announced to his family that he was emigrating to Australia. His mother urged him to make his peace with his father, and Georgie followed her advice. In the ensuing reconciliation, his father told Georgie that he was indeed the Whitechapel murderer. He explained that on his murder sprees he habitually wore two pairs of trousers, removing the outer ones after he had claimed a victim and consigning them to the manure that he sold from a cart to support his family.

There are so many holes in this story that it is difficult to know where to begin. Why, if the story were true, would G. W. B. write anonymously to broadcast the event? Why did his father wear two pairs of trousers when there is ample evidence that Jack would not have been heavily bloodstained? Indeed, his method of attack almost certainly would have directed any spray of blood away from him when he struck. Finally, the real Ripper almost certainly lived alone, and it is highly unlikely that he was a married man with a family.

If G. W. B.'s father did exist, and did earn his living by peddling manure, then he continued to trade in the stuff long after he had officially retired.

Chance of being the Ripper—0

Fingers Freddy

See Albericci, Frederico

Fitzgerald, John

On 26 September 1888, Fitzgerald gave himself up to the police and confessed that he was the murderer of **Annie Chapman**. He was taken into custody, and his story was thoroughly checked out by the police, who found that it had no basis in fact because he had a provable alibi. As a result, Fitzgerald was released on 29 September.

Chance of being the Ripper—0

Fleming, Joseph

Fleming, a tentative suspect, was the man whom **Mary Jane Kelly** lived with before she met Joseph Barnett. The researcher Mark King found that a man of the same name died in Claybury Mental Hospital in 1920. There is no established link between that Fleming and the man Kelly knew, and it is pure speculation to suggest that even if they were one and the same, Fleming's mental problems meant that he was the Ripper.

Chance of being the Ripper—1

See also Barnett, Joseph; "The Witnesses": Barnett, Joseph

Fogelma

Fogelma was a Norwegian sailor who died in a U.S. lunatic asylum in 1902. After his death it was discovered that he had a large collection of newspaper cuttings relating to the Ripper crimes. There is nothing else to connect him with the murders.

Chance of being the Ripper—1

Foster, John

Foster is mentioned in the Scotland Yard files held at the Public Record Office as being arrested on suspicion in Belfast. Nothing else is known.

Chance of being the Ripper—1

Gibson, Pastor John George [Jack]

Gibson was suggested as a suspect by Robert Graysmith in *The Bell Tower.* His theory was based on a notorious American case, the murders of Blanche Lamont and Minnie Williams in a San Francisco church in 1895. Theo Durrant was arrested for those crimes, charged, found guilty, and finally executed on 7 January 1898. Graysmith's book attempted to show that Durrant was innocent and that the real culprit was the church pastor, John George Gibson. However, the book fails to make the case, and it is clear that Durrant was almost certainly guilty. Nonetheless, based on the premise that Gibson was the real killer, Graysmith also claimed that the pastor was in London at the time of the Ripper murders and was the Ripper.

Apart from the fact that Gibson was the right sort of age in 1888 (29) and fitted the general description of the killer, no proof can be found that he was ever in Whitechapel. In fact, it is almost certain that at the time of the murders, Gibson was serving at a church in Scotland. Graysmith also fancifully claimed that Gibson traveled down to London via Liverpool and posted letters from there to the police. But there is not one shred of evidence that Gibson had anything to do with the American murders, let alone the Whitechapel ones, and he cannot be considered a serious candidate. Furthermore, this book purporting to identify Jack contains some fundamental errors of fact.

Chance of being the Ripper—0

Gissing, George Robert

Gissing was a promising student who left college in Manchester ignominiously after marrying a prostitute. This fact is supposed to give him a motive for seeking out revenge on all his wife's kind in Whitechapel. There is nothing else to link him to the crimes apart from the fact that, at 31, he was the right sort of age in 1888. More telling is the fact that Gissing did not die until 1903, and there is no explanation of why he would have stopped killing years before his death.

Chance of being the Ripper—0

Gladstone, William Ewart

At the time of the murders Gladstone was the leader of Her Majesty's Opposition in Parliament, and his attitude toward prostitution was well known. He became the object of humor because of his habit of going so far as to take prostitutes home for tea and conversation so he could try to persuade them to change their ways. Some writers have suggested that his reforming zeal might have taken other avenues, including murder. The theory is plain nonsense and deserves no further comment.

Chance of being the Ripper—0

Grainger, William Grant

In March 1895 Grainger was seen running away from the area around Butler

Street in Spitalfields. He was stopped by police, and it was found that he had just attacked a woman named Alice Graham with a knife and inflicted a 1.5-inch wound in her abdomen. His excuse was that she had demanded too much money from him, presumably for her services.

The attack fueled speculation that Grainger was the Ripper. For the wounding he was sentenced to ten years' imprisonment and was finally released in 1902, though his own solicitor, Mr. Kebbel, said Grainger had admitted that he was indeed the Ripper and had subsequently died in prison.

The case was taken up by Dr. Lyttleton Forbes Winslow, who had already convinced himself that the Ripper was G. Wentworth Bell Smith. Therefore, Grainger (who for some reason Winslow called William Grant) must by definition have been innocent. More telling is that there is no proof that Grainger was even in London at the time of the canonical murders, and he may well have been in Cork. In addition, the wound he inflicted on Alice Graham was hardly typical of any Ripper attack; the Ripper was likely to attack the throat before inflicting any abdominal wounds.

Chance of being the Ripper—2

See also Smith, G. Wentworth Bell; "Miscellaneous": Winslow, Lyttleton Stewart Forbes

Grant, William

See Grainger, William Grant

Gray, Alfred

The arrest of Alfred Gray perhaps shows the depth of the hysteria at the time of the killings. He was a vagrant who was picked up in Tunis, Africa, in January 1889. In subsequent interviews the police discovered that he had recently come from Spitalfields, where he had lived with an Italian woman. Furthermore, he had a tattoo of a naked woman on his arm. There was nothing more to link him to the murders.

Chance of being the Ripper—1

Gull, Dr. William Withey

See Masonic Conspiracy

Harpick, Peter J.

In 1984 the book *Who He* was published. Its author, Jonathan Goodman, advanced Harpick as the killer and provided a history of the character. In due course he received a number of letters asking for more information, whereupon he had to gently point out that he had invented the character and that the name Peter J. Harpick was in fact an anagram of Jack the Ripper. This incident says a great deal about the attention to detail of many so-called serious students of the subject.

Chance of being the Ripper—0

Hewitt, Dr. John

Hewitt, suggested as a suspect by the researcher Steward Hicks, was mentally ill and confined to an asylum during 1888. However, the asylum records show that although Hewitt was in and out of the institution at various times, he was incarcerated at the time of the murders.

Chance of being the Ripper—0

Holt, Dr. William

Holt, who was attached to St. George's Hospital, was an amateur detective who sought to capture the Ripper by assuming disguises and patrolling the East End. On 11 November 1888, when hysteria was at its height after the brutal slaying of **Mary Jane Kelly**, Holt, his face blackened, stepped out of the fog in George Yard and frightened a woman named Humphreys. When she asked what he wanted and what he was doing, Holt just laughed and ran off. This behavior frightened Mrs. Humphreys even more and she screamed, "Murder!" at the top of her voice. A crowd came to her assistance, and Holt was attacked. Rescued by the police, he was able to prove his innocence and was released from custody on 12 November. Holt was the original White-Eyed Man because the glasses he wore were transformed, in press reports, into white rings painted around his eyes.

Chance of being the Ripper—0

See also White-Eyed Man; "Others Who Played a Part": Humphreys, Mrs.

Hutchinson, George [Britain]

Hutchinson was a witness who came forward after the inquest on **Mary Jane Kelly** had ended to give a detailed statement of a man he claimed he had seen with Kelly early on the morning of her death. The statement is far too detailed to be considered reliable; one has to ask why Hutchinson made it. Some writers have argued that his testimony may have been nothing more than publicity-seeking, but an equally strong argument is that he came forward because he had to after he learned that he had been seen standing opposite Miller's Court by Sarah Lewis.

Hutchinson lived close to the epicenter of the murders, was the right age and height, and, given what little we know of his physical description, may have matched the composite picture of Jack. Further investigation is needed, but Hutchinson is a very strong candidate who is discussed further in the "Summary" section.

Chance of being the Ripper—5

See also "The Witnesses": Hutchinson, George; Lewis, Sarah

Hutchinson, George [United States]

Hutchinson, suggested as a possible suspect by the *Pall Mall Gazette* of 12 January 1889, had been a resident of a lunatic asylum in Elgin, Illinois. He escaped and killed a woman in Chicago, apparently mutilating her body in a manner reminiscent of the Whitechapel crimes. He was recaptured but escaped again in 1884 or 1885. There is no evidence that he was in England at the time of the murders.

Chance of being the Ripper—2

Irwin, Jack

Irwin's name is mentioned in the Home Office files of 12 March 1889. A letter was received from A. H. Skirving of the Canadian police, based in Ontario, stating that there was a prisoner in Chatham, Ontario, who Skirving believed to be the Ripper. This man was Jack Irwin, but it was easily shown that he was not in England at the time of the murders.

Chance of being the Ripper—0

Isaacs, Joseph

Isaacs lived at Little Paternoster Row, off Dorset Street, at the time of the crimes. He lodged with Mary Cusins, who became suspicious of him when she heard him pacing his room and when he didn't venture out at all for a few days prior to **Mary Jane Kelly**'s death on 8 November 1888. After Kelly's murder, Isaacs vanished and Cusins took her suspicions to the police. Upon investigating, they found that Isaacs had left a violin bow behind and, believing he might return for it, asked Cusins to let them know if he did.

On 7 December Isaacs did return for the bow, and Cusins followed him to a pawnbroker's run by Julius Levenson. Inside the shop, Isaacs showed Levenson the bow, then stole a watch and ran off. Cusins informed the police of the episode and gave a description of the missing man. The following day, 8 December, Isaacs was arrested in Drury Lane. He was interviewed by Inspector Abberline, who must have been satisfied with the man's explanation because he was charged only with the theft of Levenson's watch.

Chance of being the Ripper—1

See also "The Police": Abberline, Inspector Frederick George

Isenschmid, Jacob

On 11 September 1888, three days after the murder of **Annie Chapman**, Dr. Cowan of Landseer Road and Dr. Crabb of Holloway Road walked into the police station at Holloway and said that a Mr. Tyler had spoken to them about his suspicions about one of his tenants, Jacob Isenschmid (whose name is sometimes given as Joseph Issenschmid or Issenschmidt). Detective Inspector Styles was told to investigate.

Styles began by visiting 60 Mitford Road, the residence of George Tyler, who informed him that Isenschmid had lived there since 5 September but had often stayed out late at night and was absent at the time of Annie Chapman's murder. Since that time Isenschmid had been missing, but Tyler did have the address of the man's wife, 97 Duncombe Road.

A visit to Duncombe Road revealed that Mrs. Isenschmid had not seen her husband since he had left her after an argument some two months before. She added that he was in the habit of carrying large knives around with him.

All the likely addresses were watched for this promising suspect, who was arrested on 12 September and taken to the police station at Holloway. He was judged to be insane and was sent first to the Islington Workhouse and then to the Grove Hall Lunatic Asylum. Because Isenschmid was still in custody during the later murders, he clearly could not have been Jack the Ripper.

Chance of being the Ripper—0

Issenschmidt, Joseph

See Isenschmid, Jacob

Jacobs

Sergeant Benjamin Leeson, who claimed to have been at the scene of **Frances Coles**'s murder, said that after that killing a rumor began that the Ripper wore a blue overall or a leather apron. His story went that a Jewish butcher named Jacobs who wore such an apron became the object of mob harassment and had to be rescued several times by police. There is no evidence that Leeson's story was based on fact.

Chance of being the Ripper—0

James, Henry

Thomas Ede made an appearance at **Mary Ann Nichols**'s inquest on 17 September 1888 to say that he had seen a man close to the Forester's Arms public house on Cambridge Heath Road on the day **Annie Chapman** met her death. This man wore a two-peaked cap and moved in a strange way, one of his arms appearing to be wooden. More importantly, he appeared to be carrying a knife because four inches of a blade protruded from his pocket.

The man was soon traced and turned out to be Henry James, who was well known in the district as a "harmless lunatic," according to press reports. Ede was allowed to see James and confirmed that he was the man he had seen on 8 September. As a result, Ede was called back to Nichols's inquest on 22 September to confirm the identification so James could be officially cleared.

Chance of being the Ripper—0

See also "The Witnesses": Ede, Thomas

Jill the Ripper

This generic term covers the suggestion that the killer was a woman. The usual suggestion (as in William Stewart's *Jack the Ripper: A New Theory*) is that she was a midwife or abortionist who could pass through the streets wearing blood-stained clothing without attracting much attention.

The strongest argument against this theory is that all the witnesses who saw anyone with one of the victims described a man. Though there is a slight possibility that the killer was a woman disguised as a man, none of the victims would have been at ease in the company of such a person, so the proposition is highly improbable.

Chance of being the Ripper—1

Kaminsky, Nathan

Kaminsky, a bootmaker of 15 Black Lion Yard, was diagnosed as suffering from syphilis on 24 March 1888 and was treated at the Whitechapel Workhouse Infirmary, from which he was discharged after six weeks.

Martin Fido suggested in *The Crimes, Detection and Death of Jack the Ripper* that Kaminsky was the real Leather Apron and that John Pizer was identified as such in error. This idea is based on the fact that Kaminsky's race, occupation, and age are identical with those of David Cohen, so the two must be one and the same. This notion in turn suggests that Kaminsky is the real second suspect named in the Macnaghten Memoranda and that the name *Kosminsky* was used in error. The theory assumes, of course, that Macnaghten's boast that he knew the killer's identity was the truth. If Fido is correct in naming Kaminsky as Cohen, then his age, 23, makes him a little young for the killer. Nevertheless, he is a more likely suspect than many others in this list.

Chance of being the Ripper—4

See also Cohen, Aaron Davis; Pizer, John; "Miscellaneous": Macnaghten Memoranda

Kelly, James

Kelly was born in 1860, which puts him in the right age range for the Ripper. An upholsterer by trade, he moved to London about 1878 and is believed to have taken lodgings with the Lamb family at 37 Collingwood Street in Bethnal Green. In 1881 he met 20-year-old Sarah Brider and moved in with her and her family at 21 Cottage Lane. He and Sarah married on 4 June 1883, and almost from the first there were violent arguments between them.

On 21 June 1883, during one of those arguments, Kelly stabbed his wife below her left ear. He was arrested while she received medical treatment at St. Bartholomew's Hospital. She died on 24 June, and on 1 August Kelly underwent trial for murder at the Old Bailey, where he was sentenced to death. His execution was fixed for 20 August 1883, but on the 17th he was reprieved and was later sent to Broadmoor, from which he escaped on 23 January 1888.

The problem with suggesting that Kelly was the Ripper is that he remained free until 11 February 1927, when he gave himself up at the gates of Broadmoor. He was readmitted and died there on 17 September 1929. So if Kelly was the murderer, why did he stop killing?

The theory is that the original argument with Sarah was over an affair Kelly had with **Mary Jane Kelly**. After his escape from Broadmoor, he supposedly returned to London to be with Mary but found that she had become a prostitute, so he killed her and all the women whom he had asked to help him find her. Once she was dead, of course, there was no further need to kill.

I find it hard to give credence to any theory that postulates a killer seeking one particular victim and killing all others who get in his way. This is the realm of fiction. More telling is that we have no idea where Kelly was living at the time of the murders, and his description, provided by his cousin, refers to dark hair and a heavy mustache, details that do not fit the likely descriptions of the killer.

Chance of being the Ripper—3

Kidney, Michael

Author A. P. Wolf suggested that the Ripper crimes were committed by Thomas Hayne Cutbush but that **Elizabeth Stride** was murdered by Kidney. The only reason behind this theory is that most victims are killed by someone they know, and Kidney did have a history of assault, having been charged on 6 April 1887 with assault upon Stride. On that occasion she didn't even appear in court to give evidence, and the charge was dropped. There is no other evidence against Kidney.

Chance of being the Ripper—0

Chance of being the killer of Elizabeth Stride—1

See also Cutbush, Thomas Hayne

Klosowski, Severin

See Chapman, George

Koch, Dr.

See Cohn, Dr.

Konovalov, Vassily

Konovalov is yet one more manifestation of the obfuscation based on the theory of a supposed Russian secret agent. He is supposed to have been a surgeon who murdered a woman in Paris in 1887, killed five prostitutes in Whitechapel in 1888, and murdered a woman in Russia in 1889, for which final crime he was confined to an asylum. There are obvious similarities with the Dr. Pedachenko story, and indeed Konovalov is alleged to be an alias of that person, as is Andrey Luiskovo.

The references to Konovalov are from author Donald McCormick, who said he was shown a copy of the *Ochrana Gazette* by Prince Serge Belloselski. Unfortunately, no other researcher has managed to trace that paper. In fact, there is no proof that Konovalov even existed or, if he did, that he and Pedachenko were one and the same.

Chance of being the Ripper—0

See also Pedachenko, Dr. Alexander

Kosminski, Aaron

At first glance, Aaron Kosminski must be considered to be a very strong suspect because he was named by two senior police officers as Jack the Ripper.

Initially, only hints were given as to who this suspect was, beginning with Sir Robert Anderson writing, in *Criminals and Crime* in 1907, that not only did he know the identity of the author of the letters to the Central News Agency but he also knew the identity of the killer, who, he said, had been "caged in an asylum."

This tantalizing snippet was expanded on in Anderson's memoirs, *The Lighter Side of My Official Life,* first serialized in *Blackwood's Magazine* and later published in book form. In one section Anderson wrote of the Whitechapel murders:

> Having regard to the interest attaching to this case, I am almost tempted to disclose the identity of the murderer and of the pressman who wrote the letter above referred to. But no public benefit would

> result from such a course, and the traditions of my old department would suffer. I will merely add that the only person who had ever had a good view of the murderer unhesitatingly identified the suspect the instant he was confronted with him; but he refused to give evidence against him.
>
> In saying that he was a Polish Jew I am merely stating a definitely ascertained fact.

There, for many years, the unnamed Ripper remained until, in 1959, the Macnaghten Memoranda came to light. This document actually named three suspects without firmly deciding on any of them, but the discussion of the second of these finally put a name to the man Anderson had said was definitely the Ripper. In part the passage ran, " . . . Kosminski, a Polish Jew, who lived in the very heart of the district where the murders were committed. He had become insane owing to many years indulgence in solitary vices. He had a great hatred of women, with strong homicidal tendencies. He was (and I believe still is) detained in a lunatic asylum about March 1889. This man in appearance strongly resembled the individual seen by the City PC near Mitre Square."

As if further confirmation that this man was the Ripper were needed, the Swanson marginalia appeared in 1987. These were notes made by Chief Inspector Donald Sutherland Swanson in the margins of his copy of Anderson's book, and on the back endpaper he had scribbled, " . . . after the suspect had been identified at the Seaside Home where he had been sent by us with difficulty in order to subject him to identification, and he knew he was identified. On suspect's return to his brother's house in Whitechapel he was watched by police (City CID) by day and night. In a very short time the suspect with his hands tied behind his back, he was sent to Stepney Workhouse and then to Colney Hatch and died shortly afterwards—Kosminski was the suspect."

So here we have it: A man named Kosminski was ascertained to be the Ripper, identified by a witness at the Convalescent Police Seaside Home in Sussex, and thereafter confined to a lunatic asylum, where he died soon afterward. However, when this theory is examined in detail, it is full of inaccuracies and suppositions.

The suspect was investigated by writers Paul Begg and Martin Fido, who found that his full name was Aaron Kosminski. Author Philip Sugden obtained access to closed medical records that told the full picture of Kosminski's incarceration. Briefly, Kosminski was admitted to the Mile End Workhouse on 12 July 1890 from his brother Wolf's house at 3 Sion Square. Three days later, on 15 July, he was discharged to his brother's care, but on 4 February 1891 he was readmitted to the workhouse from 16 Greenfield Street. After being examined by Dr. Edmund King, he was committed on 7 February to the Colney Hatch Asylum, where he remained until April 1894, when he was transferred to the Leavesden Asylum near Watford. He remained there until his death in 1919. He was committed in the first place because he heard voices, did no work, refused to take food from people, never washed, ate bread from the gutters, and drank water from taps. This is the man who Anderson and Swanson both claimed was Jack the Ripper. Let us now examine the case against him in more detail.

In the first place, we need to determine who the witness was who "positively" identified Kosminski. We have two clues. Anderson said the witness was "the only person who had ever had a good view of the murderer," and Macnaghten referred to "a City PC near Mitre Square." It is clear, therefore, that we are looking for a witness from the night of 30 September

1888, the night of the murders of **Elizabeth Stride** and **Catherine Eddowes**. Here we encounter our first problem. There was certainly no policeman who saw the killer with Catherine Eddowes near Mitre Square. The only man who did was Joseph Lawende. The only policeman who saw a man with one of the murdered women that night was Constable William Smith, who saw a man with Elizabeth Stride in Berner Street, but he wasn't a City policeman. Finally, in the serialized version of Anderson's memoirs he added, in reference to the witness identifying the Ripper, "but when he learned that the suspect was a fellow-Jew he declined to swear to him."

Constable Smith wasn't a Jew, so this remark narrows down the possible witness to Joseph Lawende. It is obvious that Macnaghten confused the two murders, so we can surmise that Lawende identified Kosminski as the killer at the Seaside Home in Sussex. Here again we have problems. Swanson wrote that the man was identified, sent to his brother's house, watched, and then soon after incarcerated. The Seaside Home did not open until March 1890. Admission records show that Kosminski was finally incarcerated in February 1891, but the marginalia claim that he was identified shortly before this, implying that he was identified in or around January or February 1891.

Readers will recall that Joseph Lawende stated at the inquest that he caught only a glimpse of the man he saw with Eddowes, and at that stage he thought he could not identify him again. Catherine Eddowes died on 30 September 1888. Even if the so-called identification of Kosminski was made in early January 1891, there is still a gap of 15 months. We are therefore expected to believe that after saying at the inquest that he couldn't identify the man, Lawende made an instant and certain identification after 15 months.

Kosminski's candidacy deserves further examination, but we cannot accept that he was, with any degree of certainty, Jack the Ripper. He was a shambling wreck who ate bread from the gutters, hardly the type of man we are looking for. The story of the witness identification is weak to the point of laughability. The policemen who named him erred in basic facts. Kosminski did not die soon after his incarceration but lived until 1919, and if he had been the Ripper, he would have had a period of extended inactivity before his arrest without any rational explanation for it.

Chance of being the Ripper—3

See also "The Witnesses": Lawende, Joseph; "The Police": Anderson, Dr. Robert; Smith, Constable William; Swanson, Chief Inspector Donald Sutherland; "Letters and Correspondence": The "Dear Boss" Letter of 27 September 1888; The "Saucy Jack" Postcard of 1 October 1888; "Miscellaneous": Anderson's Suspect; Anderson's Witness; *Criminals and Crime: Some Facts and Suggestions; The Lighter Side of My Official Life;* Swanson Marginalia

Langan, John

Langan's name was mentioned in the Home Office files of 12 October 1888. A letter had been received from E. W. Bonham, the British consul in Boulogne, expressing the belief that the Ripper might be Langan. There is no record of why Bonham thought so, and Langan was interviewed and cleared of suspicion.

Chance of being the Ripper—0

Laurenco, José

At the time of the murders Edward Knight Larkins was employed as a clerk in Her Majesty's Customs Statistical Office. He brought his own interpretation to the stories he read of the Whitechapel atrocities and believed that the injuries inflicted on the victims were similar to those inflicted by the Portuguese in the Peninsula War. His conclusion was that the killer had to be a Portuguese sailor.

Unfortunately for Larkins, there was no single ship whose visits to London fitted the dates of the canonical murders, so he had to stretch his theory to accommodate a sort of sailors' conspiracy. According to Larkins, sailors from three ships, the *City of London,* the *City of Cork,* and the *City of Oporto,* were guilty. **Mary Ann Nichols** had been murdered by Manuel Cruz Xavier, but the next victim, **Annie Chapman**, had died at the hands of José Laurenco because Xavier was not in England at the time.

The double-event killings of **Elizabeth Stride** and **Catherine Eddowes** were again the work of Laurenco, working with João de Souza Machado, again as copies of the first killing. When it was pointed out to Larkins that Laurenco was not on board his ship when it docked in time for the murder of **Mary Jane Kelly**, Larkins became possibly the first "Ripperologist" to bend the facts to suit himself. He first claimed that Laurenco must have been on board as a stowaway and then decided that in the Kelly murder, Machado had worked alone. Finally, Larkins put the murder of **Alice McKenzie** at the door of yet another seaman, Joachim de Rocha, the fourth he named.

The suggestions were thoroughly investigated, and not an ounce of truth was found in them. Dr. Robert Anderson perhaps put it most succinctly when he described Larkins as "a troublesome busybody."

Chance of any of these sailors being the Ripper—0

See also "The Police": Anderson, Dr. Robert

Leary, John [1]

See Arnold, John

Leary, John [2]

Leary, a soldier picked out by Constable Thomas Barrett after the murder of **Mary Ann Nichols**, was able to show that he had been out drinking with Private Law at the time of the murder.

Chance of being the Ripper—1

See also "The Police": Barrett, Constable Thomas

Leather Apron

See Jacobs; Kaminsky, Nathan; Pizer, John

Leopold II, King of the Belgians

Well, if it couldn't have been a British royal, why not a European one? This theory was suggested by the writer Jacquemine Charrot-Lodwidge, who has unearthed not a single fact to substantiate it. The notion is supposedly based on the "facts" that Leopold led a scandalous life, that he supposedly made trips to London that were unrecorded, and other such suppositions.

Chance of being the Ripper—0

Levinsky

See Levitski

Levitski

The supposed accomplice of Dr. Pedachenko, Levitski, sometimes called Levinsky, was allegedly the lookout and was also claimed by writer William Le Queux to have written the Jack the Ripper letters. His eligibility as a candidate rests on whether Pedachenko was the killer.

Chance of being the Ripper—0

Chance of being involved—0

See also Pedachenko, Dr. Alexander; "Letters and Correspondence": The "Dear Boss" Letter of 27 September 1888; The "Saucy Jack" Postcard of 1 October 1888

Ludwig, Charles

Ludwig was at one time a most promising suspect. Early on the morning of 18 September 1888, Elizabeth Burns was taken to Three Kings Court by Ludwig, who brandished a knife when they were alone. Her cries of "Murder" brought Constable John Johnson to her aid, and he saw Ludwig off. Burns did not mention the knife until after the man had left; she said she had not wanted to say anything about it while he was still there. Johnson then went after Ludwig, but he had vanished.

Shortly afterward, at about 3 A.M., Ludwig appeared at a coffee stall in Whitechapel High Street, took a dislike to the way the proprietor, Alexander Freinberg (who sometimes anglicized his name to Finlay), was looking at him, and again drew out his knife. Freinberg managed to throw a dish from the coffee stall at Ludwig and summon aid from Constable John Gallagher. Ludwig was arrested and later charged with being drunk and disorderly and threatening to stab.

As the investigation continued, the police discovered from Ludwig's landlord, who was named Johannes, that Ludwig had supposedly had bloodstained hands on the morning that **Annie Chapman** met her death. Other remands followed, and Ludwig remained in custody as the most promising suspect to date. However, he was still in custody when **Elizabeth Stride** and **Catherine Eddowes** were murdered, proving that he could not have been the Whitechapel killer.

Chance of being the Ripper—0

See also "The Police": Johnson, Constable John; "Others Who Played a Part": Burns, Elizabeth; Freinberg, Alexander

Luiskovo, Count Andrey

See Pedachenko, Dr. Alexander

Machado, João de Souza

See Laurenco, José

Maduro, Alonzo

Griffiths Salway worked for a brokerage firm in the City of London, and his business dealings brought him into contact with Alonzo Maduro, a successful Argentinean businessman. On 2 April 1888 Salway encountered Maduro in Whitechapel, and during their conversation the latter remarked that all prostitutes should be killed. Later that same year, after the death of **Mary Jane Kelly**, Salway found that Maduro had some surgical knives. These factors convinced Salway that Maduro was the Ripper, but he kept the idea to himself until the early 1950s, when he told his wife, who later told the story. There is nothing else to link Maduro to the crimes and no explanation of why the murders stopped if he was the killer, but he cannot be dismissed altogether because so little is known about him.

Chance of being the Ripper—2

Mary of Bremen

A male hairdresser mentioned in the Scotland Yard files at the Public Record Office in London, "Mary" (a nickname referring to his supposed homosexuality) had been arrested several times for assaulting women and stabbing them in the breasts and private parts with a sharp instrument. He had also attempted to rape a woman in his shop.

In their quest for the Ripper, the British police contacted their colleagues in Bremen, where "Mary" was known to have gone. Detective Baring of the German police replied that "Mary" had completed a seven-year sentence on 7 August 1888 but had been immediately rearrested, was now serving another year, and was not due for release until 7

August 1889. The fact that this suspect was in a German prison throughout the period of the murders proves that he could not have been the killer.

Chance of being the Ripper—0

Mason, Arthur Henry

Mason's name was mentioned in the Scotland Yard files in a report dated 18 December 1888 that is now missing. Two men named John Hemmings and William Schuber had complained about Mason's strange behavior to the police. Mason was interviewed, cleared, and released.

Chance of being the Ripper—0

Mason, Thomas

Stephen Knight, outlining the Masonic Conspiracy theory, suggested that the killer, Sir William Gull, was incarcerated after the murders and died in 1896. Knight looked for a suitable alias for Gull and found a Thomas Mason. What better name to use for the locked-away Gull! Unfortunately for Knight, this particular Thomas Mason was a bookbinder, not a doctor; was never incarcerated as a lunatic, as Gull supposedly was; and actually died in 1902. He had no connection with Gull or the Ripper murders.

Chance of being the Ripper—0

See also Masonic Conspiracy

Masonic Conspiracy

There are two basic versions of the Masonic Conspiracy story, but both start in the same way. The artist Walter Sickert had a studio in Cleveland Street, and an attractive young woman named Annie Elizabeth Crook worked in a florist's shop across the road at 6 Cleveland Street.

Albert Victor, Duke of Clarence, was a visitor to Cleveland Street because he frequented a homosexual brothel there. In the course of his visits he met Annie, the two fell in love, and a secret marriage took place at St. Saviour's, despite the fact that Annie was a Roman Catholic. One of the witnesses to this marriage was none other than **Mary Jane Kelly**. A daughter, christened Alice Margaret, was born to the union. At this stage Mary Kelly decided to blackmail the government.

In one version of this tale the prime minister, Robert Cecil, was given the task of silencing the troublesome Mary. Cecil was a Freemason, so whom better to give the job to than a fellow Mason, Sir William Gull, the queen's surgeon? Gull in turn demanded help from Sickert because the artist knew what Mary Kelly looked like. They needed a coachman to drive them around, so John Netley was inveigled too. The three men searched the streets of Whitechapel for Mary and her fellow conspirators, who were butchered one by one, with Masonic clues left as a warning to others. Sickert was later troubled by what he had done and painted clues to the murders into his pictures.

Others were involved too. For instance, Robert Anderson may have kept watch sometimes, and the writing in Goulston Street was erased at Sir Charles Warren's orders because he too either knew of the plot or recognized Masonic symbolism in the "Juwes" message. Of course Dr. William Sedgewick Saunders found no trace of grapes or narcotics in **Elizabeth Stride**'s body because he too was involved.

Another version of the story is that the crimes were instigated by Lord Randolph Churchill, who is also said to have involved Gull, but in this version Montague John Druitt and James Kenneth Stephen were the killers. Sickert was involved because he rescued Alice Margaret, the child born to Albert Victor and Annie Elizabeth Crook.

How much evidence is there for this fairy tale, in whatever version it is peddled? Let us examine each "fact" in turn.

The clandestine marriage was a problem because Annie Crook was a Catholic. In fact, her death certificate and other documents clearly show that she belonged to the Church of England.

The marriage took place at St. Saviour's. There is no record of any such marriage at this church, which is now Southwark Cathedral.

Annie Elizabeth Crook lived at 6 Cleveland Street just before the murders started. It is true that she lived there in 1885, but the properties from 4 to 14 were pulled down between 1886 and 1888. Afterward blocks of flats were built, and the next recorded occupant of number 6 is Elizabeth Cook. Some writers say this is the same person, who, soon after the murders, was incarcerated in order to keep her quiet. However, Elizabeth Cook remained at that address until 1893.

The "Juwes" writing was a reference to Jubela, Jubelo, and Jubelum, three masons who murdered their master, Hiram Abiff, during the building of Solomon's Temple. They were caught and put to death, and the manner of their execution was exactly the same as the manner of the Whitechapel murders. That this tale even formed part of Masonic tradition at the time has been denied, but in any case the mutilations are not identical. For instance, the tongues should have torn out of the victims, and the "Juwes" were not beheaded, though Jack tried to decapitate some of his victims.

Sickert had a studio at 15 Cleveland Street, which is why he became involved. There is no evidence that Sickert ever used this address, and that property was also demolished in 1888 after having been listed as unoccupied since 1885.

The Masonic ritual was meant as a warning to others. A warning to whom? Only the most senior members of the Masonic orders would have recognized any kind of symbolism. If the murders were meant to warn off the other prostitutes involved, such a warning would have had no effect whatsoever.

Netley, the coachman involved, made two attempts to run down the child Alice Margaret in his carriage. One attempt took place in 1888 and the other in 1892. After this second attempt Netley was chased by a mob, threw himself into the Thames, and drowned. A nice story, but in fact Netley died in 1903 after an accident in Park Road near Baker Street. He was thrown from his cab, and the wheel ran over his head.

The conspiracy was set up by Prime Minister Robert Cecil, the Marquess of Salisbury, a Freemason. Cecil wasn't a Mason.

The entire story is nonsense and is based on either the stories told by Joseph Gorman Sickert, Walter's son, who later admitted that it was pure falsehood, or the so-called Abberline Diaries, which are so obviously fake that the supposed author even got his own name wrong.

Chance of any of the protagonists being the Ripper—0

Chance of any of them being involved—0

Chance of the gullible being fooled—5

See also Albericci, Frederico; Albert Victor, Duke of Clarence; Druitt, Montague John; Sickert's Veterinary Student; Stephen, James Kenneth; "The Witnesses": Saunders, Dr. William Sedgewick; "The Police": Anderson, Dr. Robert; Warren, Sir Charles; "Miscellaneous": Crook, Alice Margaret; Crook, Annie Elizabeth; Goulston Street Graffito; Sickert, Joseph Gorman

Matthews, Oliver

Matthews was turned in to the police at Walton Street by a Richard Watson simply because he carried a black bag. He was able to prove his innocence.

Chance of being the Ripper—0

Maybrick, James

Maybrick was a Liverpool cotton merchant who died on 11 May 1889. His wife, Florence, was arrested for poisoning him with arsenic. She was found guilty of murder and sentenced to death but was later reprieved and remained in prison until 1904. The reason for suspecting James Maybrick is twofold: the Maybrick diary and the Maybrick watch.

The diary was given to Michael Barrett in May 1991 by a friend of his named Tony Devereux. Devereux, who has since died, would give no details as to how he came by the volume but stressed that it was genuine. In March 1992 the journal was taken to Doreen Montgomery of the Rupert Crew Literary Agency, and she in turn commissioned Shirley Harrison and Sally Eveny to research it. By June 1992 publication rights had been secured by Smith Gryphon, which published the diary in 1994. It immediately became the subject of intense debate, with a number of famous Ripper writers instantly claiming that it was certainly genuine and concluding that James Maybrick had been the Ripper.

On 27 June 1994 the *Liverpool Daily Post* published a report in which Michael Barrett claimed that he had forged the diary. This article was immediately refuted by Barrett's solicitors, who claimed he had been under emotional strain at the time.

More convincing perhaps was a statement the following month, July 1994, by Michael Barrett's estranged wife, who said she had possessed the journal since 1968 and had passed it on to her husband anonymously, through Tony Devereux, with a view to his basing a work of fiction on the contents. This story was confirmed by Mrs. Barrett's father, now also dead, who said the diary had been given to him by his grandmother not long before the outbreak of World War II.

As I have already said, the diary has been the subject of much heated debate. The original journal is a book with the first 48 pages missing, having apparently been removed by means of a knife. There is evidence that it was once used as a photograph album, and since it burst into public view in 1991, it has been subjected to intense scientific scrutiny. One would think that this sort of examination would establish once and for all whether the diary is a forgery. However, tests on the ink have been contradictory, with one school of thought stating that the diary is a recent forgery and others saying that it was written before the turn of the century. In the end, none of this matters in deciding whether it is really is the work of Jack the Ripper. For that one need only look at the contents of the diary.

The entire manuscript contains but one date, on the final page. It is, however, relatively easy to date some of the entries by relating them to known events. Throughout my commentary, the page numbers refer to the pages on which the original entries may can be found in the Smith Gryphon edition of 1993.

The diary refers to other murders, stating that the first was in Manchester, not London. We shall ignore those allegations for now and concentrate on what the writer has to tell us about the Whitechapel murders.

On page 210, the writer refers to an intention to visit Michael (Maybrick's brother, who lived in London) in the coming June. That particular entry can be dated, therefore, to sometime before June 1888. It is followed on page 214 by a statement that June is drawing to a close, so we can place *this* entry in June itself. Soon afterward, on page 216, the author states that he has rented a room in Middlesex Street. This, then, is the supposed home base of our killer—if the book was written by the Ripper—and would have been taken some time in July.

The first London murder referred to is that of **Mary Ann Nichols**, on page 217. She is not mentioned by name, but we may deduce that she was the victim from entries relating to the next murder. What does the author have to say about Nichols's death?

The scant information includes the statement that the author was vexed when the head would not come off. In his report of the injuries, Dr. Llewellyn stated clearly that the only cuts to the neck were one about four inches in length and a second about eight inches long that ran below this to a point three inches below the jaw on the right side. Though this incision cut down to the vertebrae, there clearly had been no attempt to actually remove the head. The diary is therefore in error.

On page 220, there is a reference to removing the head of the next victim but the writer also claims to have cut off her hands. None of the victims bore wounds consistent with an attempt to remove the hands.

The discussion of the second murder, that of **Annie Chapman**, who again is not named, begins on page 221. The entries run to page 226 and refer to, among other things, returning to the victim to remove more internal organs, not having chalk with which to write a message, leaving two farthings and Chapman's rings as clues, and wishing to remove the eyes of the next victim.

I have dealt in the "Myths and Errors" section with the pure invention of the coins and rings. No such items were left at Annie Chapman's feet, and the fact that the diary states that they were shows that again it is in error. Furthermore, there is no evidence that the killer returned to Annie's body. He may have done so, but it is unlikely.

The diary author claims responsibility for the double event of 30 September 1888. The entries begin at page 232 and continue to 235. He refers to being disturbed by a horse at the scene of the first murder, which fits with the known facts, but he then claims that he found his second victim, **Catherine Eddowes**, within a quarter of an hour. Now, the very latest time that **Elizabeth Stride** could have been attacked was a minute or two after 1 A.M. Catherine Eddowes was not even released from police custody until about the same time and was not seen talking to a man who was almost certainly her killer until 1:35 A.M. If the diary is genuine, then the killer would have to have encountered Catherine at, say, 1:20 A.M. and spent a full 15 minutes in her company until he was seen by Joseph Lawende and his friends.

On page 233, the diary states that before the next murder the author will send "another" to Central. This comment shows that the killer, if the journal is genuine, had already sent at least one letter to the Central News Agency. Later the diarist refers to the nickname Jack the Ripper, which he has given himself. This reference suggests that the nickname came directly from the letter and postcard delivered to the Central News Agency, which would imply that the "Dear Boss" letter and the "Saucy Jack" postcard were genuine and were sent by Maybrick. However, the diary itself shows that this conclusion cannot be correct. The card was posted, almost certainly, in the small hours of 1 October. By the time Maybrick was back in Liverpool and able to write his journal entries, that card would already have been delivered, so he would have been referring to another communication yet to come. The diary makes no direct mention of the postcard he would have to have just sent.

On page 241, the diary refers to the last London murder, that of **Mary Jane**

Kelly. It claims that the writer placed bits of her body all over the room, that he left her breasts on a table, and that he took the room key away with him, all of which statements are false. Furthermore, on page 245 the writer says he regrets that he did not take any of the dead woman away with him. This too is false because Mary Kelly's heart was removed. On the final page, when referring to Kelly by name, the writer says, "No heart, no heart," but the entry from the time of the murder clearly states that nothing was removed.

In effect, what little substance the diary contains is riddled with errors. To summarize: There was no attempt to remove Nichols's head; no rings or coins were left at Chapman's feet; the killer did not meet Eddowes within 15 minutes of killing Stride, if indeed he was responsible for both murders; and the description of the Kelly murder is littered with errors. If one more victim can be ascribed to the Ripper, such as **Martha Tabram** or **Alice McKenzie**, then the entire story is plainly shown to be an invention.

Let us turn now to the Maybrick watch, which came to light in June 1993 and bore scratches that read "J. Maybrick" and "I am Jack." It also bore the initials of the five canonical victims. Once again there is debate over whether the inscription is a forgery, but scientific evidence seems to indicate that the scratches are quite old. Once again, their age does not prove that they were made by the Ripper. And if the watch is intended to support the evidence of the diary, then it falls by the same arguments as that journal.

We must not forget that Maybrick does not fit the basic description of the killer. He did not have the knowledge of the Whitechapel area that the real killer did, and he was 55 years old at the time of the murders, well outside the killer's probable age range. In addition, the writing in the journal does not match that on the "Dear Boss" letter and "Saucy Jack" postcard, and neither the journal nor the letter and postcard match the writing in Maybrick's will. Finally, we are expected to believe that Florence Maybrick took her husband's life after he had told her that he was Jack the Ripper, as stated on the final page of the diary. If this were the case, would she have remained silent at the trial and risked losing her life at the end of a rope?

A book titled *Jack the Ripper—The Final Chapter* by Paul H. Feldman, published in 1997, claimed to provide further evidence that the Maybrick diary is genuine. First, Feldman argued that the writer of the diary showed his knowledge of Annie Chapman's murder by referring to removing two rings from her fingers, whereas some newspaper reports of the day mentioned three rings. This is hardly startling proof of inside knowledge because most of the press reports, and the witnesses at the inquest, mentioned two rings. It wasn't even a fifty-fifty choice because the writer plumped for the number of rings suggested by most sources.

Feldman next turned to the piece of envelope, containing pills, found in the yard at Hanbury Street and produced the startling revelation that reports of the time showed that the police were looking for handwriting that matched not only the "M" and the "Sp" on the address but also a symbol that he stated was a "J." He interpreted this character as the diary writer leaving his "mark," the initials J. M., which of course stand for James Maybrick. Feldman cavalierly dismissed the work of researchers who suggested that this "J" was in fact a figure "2."

I do not suggest that this mysterious figure was a 2—I state categorically that it was. The symbol appeared in a report from Inspector Chandler, dated 14 September 1888, and is reproduced in this book. If Feldman had sought further evi-

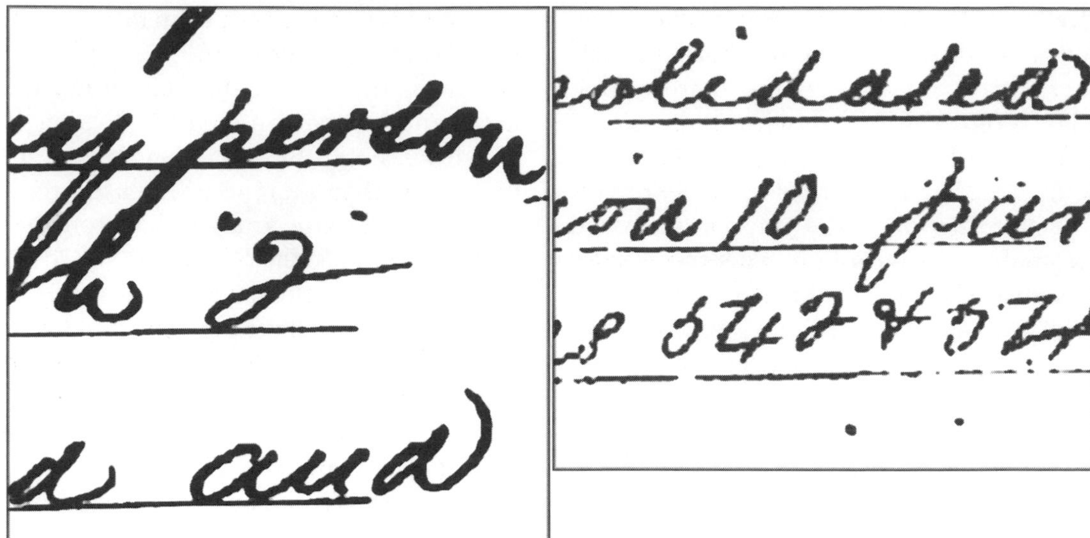

The strange symbol (left) that appears in Inspector Chandler's report of 14 September 1888 on the Chapman murder. Maybrick theorists hold this figure to be a J and dismiss any other suggestions out of hand. Compare this with the second symbol (right) that appears in an earlier report, also by Inspector Chandler. The symbol is identical to the 2 in "Page 542." It is clear from this that the symbol is correctly identified as a number 2. (Public Record Office, London)

dence, he would have found an earlier report, also from Inspector Chandler and in the same hand, dated 8 September. The top of that report is also reproduced in this book. At the top of the page on the left-hand side, Inspector Chandler wrote the details of the report and at the bottom of the three lines wrote, "pages 542 & 543." It is clear that the figure 2 in 542 is identical to the symbol in the later report. In short, in the second report Inspector Chandler was checking addresses in Spitalfields that began with a 2, and the piece of envelope found in the yard in Hanbury Street began "2 M" and had "Sp" for Spitalfields on the next line. So much for Maybrick's mark.

Feldman also argued that the mutilations inflicted on Catherine Eddowes's face were again James Maybrick leaving his mark for all to see. We are expected to accept that the two inverted V's, when put together, made an M for "Maybrick." If a clue was needed, why not cut the letter M into the dead woman's cheek or forehead? This interpretation really is stretching the facts to fit a theory. Is it not just as valid to suggest that the two slits on the eyelids form two I's, so the Ripper must really have been Inspector Izzard, who was actually in Mitre Square keeping public order after Catherine Eddowes was killed?

Another point Feldman mentioned was that Dr. Thomas Bond never stated that Kelly's heart was absent from the room, merely that it was absent from the pericardium. This distinction may be true, but earlier in that same report Bond listed where all the viscera were found. The heart was absent from that list, so it is safe to infer that Dr. Bond did not find it in the room. The killer did indeed take the heart away, and the diary writer was wrong when he said he took nothing with him.

One more piece of "evidence" in Feldman's case is the initials on the wall of Kelly's room. He claimed that F. M., for "Florence Maybrick," appeared on the wall. Depending on which reproduction one looks at, these may be seen with varying degrees of clearness. I agree that there is a mark that looks like an M, but I fail to see a letter F before it. I hold that the "letters," such as they were, were nothing more than splashes of blood that ran down and together. If the killer, whoever he was, had wished to leave his initials, or his wife's, as a clue, then why choose that particular extremely awkward spot? There must have been many easier spots to reach, for example, above the head of the bed or near the table. He would have had to lean across the bloody mess that had once been Mary Kelly in order to inscribe the initials above her right shoulder.

Finally we turn again to the letters sent to the Central News Agency. It has long been held that the name "Jack the Ripper" came from one such communication, the letter of 27 September reproduced in the "Letters and Correspondence" section of this book. Also reproduced is an earlier letter, dated 17 September, that also gave the Ripper name. Feldman stated that the diary writer knew of this earlier letter, which was not published until very recently, and hence the diary must be genuine. In my discussion of this claim, the page numbers again are taken from the original book, *The Diary of Jack the Ripper.*

The diary mentions on page 230 that all England will know the name he has given himself. This entry comes before the one on page 232 that refers to the double event and was therefore written before 30 September. It implies, therefore, that a communication has already been sent to someone, and later entries make it clear that the recipient is supposed to be the Central News Agency. I hold that this entry refers to the communication that was sent before the double event, the 27 September "Dear Boss" letter.

On page 233 the author says he hopes the authorities enjoyed his funny Jewish joke, which we assume is the Goulston Street graffito. In the same entry, he refers to sending Central another to remember him by. By "another" he may mean a communication in addition to the "Saucy Jack" postcard or the earlier "Dear Boss" letter. It does not mention a third letter and in no way can be held to refer to an even earlier communication, the 17 September letter. Finally, on page 237 the writer refers again to wanting to send another. He does not specify how many he has supposedly sent thus far.

If the diary is genuine and the 17 September letter was as important as Feldman claimed it was to his case, then the diary writer must have known about that letter and must have referred to it. We can date the entry on page 221 of the diary to on or just after 8 September because it refers to the Chapman murder. The reference to a letter to the Central News Agency just before the double event is, as mentioned earlier, given on page 232. What is there between these two entries to suggest a letter sent on 17 September?

On page 226 the writer does refer to writing "them" a clue, but this remark refers to the rhyme that follows immediately because in the fifth verse he again says, "I will give them a clue," meaning something that will happen in the future. The rhyme goes on to page 229, and then, on the very next page, just before the double-event entry, the diarist writes that he has given himself a name. This implies that he *just* gave himself that name by sending his first communication, which would be, as I said before, the letter of 27 September. Therefore, the diary writer knew nothing of the 17 September letter.

As I argued elsewhere in this book, the "Dear Boss" letter and "Saucy Jack" postcard might have been written as hoaxes and may not have come from the killer, but if that were the case then whoever did write them probably knew, through police contacts, about the 17 September letter and based his forgery upon it. I cannot accept that the genuine killer came upon the same name by accident if only the last two letters came from him. None of these details lessen the probability that the diary writer had no inkling of the first letter.

I contend that although the diary may be contemporary with the crimes or have been written soon afterward, it was not written by Jack the Ripper or the author of the letters to the Central News Agency. It is a fake, and James Maybrick was not Jack the Ripper.

Chance of being the Ripper—1

See also "The Witnesses": Bond, Dr. Thomas; Lawende, Joseph; Llewellyn, Dr. Rees Ralph; "The Police": Chandler, Inspector Joseph Luniss; Izzard, Inspector; "Letters and Correspondence": The "Dear Boss" Letter of 27 September 1888; The "Saucy Jack" Postcard of 1 October 1888; "Miscellaneous": Maybrick Diary; Maybrick Watch; "Myths and Errors": Rings and Coins Were Found at Annie Chapman's Feet

McCarthy, John

Mary Jane Kelly's landlord was suggested as a suspect by Helen Heller, a Canadian literary agent, in press reports. The fact that McCarthy was married with four children and age 37 at the time of the murders seems to eliminate him on the basis of the psychological profile.

Chance of being the Ripper—2

See also "The Witnesses": McCarthy, John

McKenna, Edward

Another initially promising suspect, McKenna fitted the general description of the murderer in that he was 5 feet 7 inches tall and had pale brown coloring. On 14 September he was arrested on suspicion, which, according to one press report, had been created after he had threatened to stab people. Questioned about the murders, he was able to prove that at the time **Annie Chapman** was murdered he was asleep in a lodging house at 15 Brick Lane.

Chance of being the Ripper—0

Merchant, Dr.

See Chapman, Dr. Frederick Richard

Miles, Frank

Miles was a painter and a friend of Oscar Wilde. He and Wilde lived together in Salisbury Street some seven years before the Whitechapel crimes. He has been put forward as a candidate by the researcher Thomas Toughill, but Miles was in a mental asylum near Bristol from 1887 onward, so he would have been in custody during the crimes.

Chance of being the Ripper—0

Monro, James

The assistant commissioner of the Metropolitan Police has been put forward as a suspect even though he was 50 years old at the time of the murders. The suggestion is without value.

Chance of being the Ripper—0

See also "The Police": Monro, James

Morford

According to a 24 September 1888 press report in the *Star,* the police received a letter, ostensibly from a pawnbroker, saying that a man named Morford who had been a surgeon and who lived in Great Ormond Street might be able to throw some light on the murders.

By 22 September detectives had failed to find any trace of the man, and he was never found. It is possible that the surname may have been incorrect; the Medical Directory for 1888 lists one John Orford, an eminent surgeon at the Royal Free Hospital on Gray's Inn Road. There is no suggestion that this man was the Ripper, but he may have been related to the suspect if the latter's surname were actually Orford.

Chance of being the Ripper—2

Murphy, John

Arrested on 13 November 1888 in the King's Cross division, Murphy was a sailor from Massachusetts who had been spotted in the Holborn Casual Ward wearing a peaked cap and carrying a knife. He was able to prove that he was elsewhere at the time of the murders.

Chance of being the Ripper—0

Netley, John Charles

See Masonic Conspiracy

Ostrog, Michael

A habitual criminal who was mentioned as the third likely suspect in the Macnaghten Memoranda, Ostrog, who had several aliases, first came to public attention in 1863 when he was sentenced to ten months' imprisonment for thefts from Oxford colleges. Not one to show preference for any particular university city, he was sentenced to three months for being a rogue and a vagabond at Cambridge in 1864. That year was a busy one for Ostrog; in addition to the Cambridge sentence, he received one of eight months, for fraud, at Gloucester in December.

He next surfaced in 1866, again in Gloucester, when he was acquitted of a fraud charge. However, a series of thefts during the rest of that year led to his receiving seven years' imprisonment in August. Released in May 1873, he was soon back to his old tricks, stealing some silver from a Captain Milner at Woolwich Barracks. He also stole books from Eton College library before going to London, where he narrowly escaped arrest. Eventually he was captured in Burton-on-Trent and in early 1874 was given a sentence of ten years.

Released in August 1883, Ostrog soon found himself a fugitive again when he failed to report, which was a condition of his freedom. He managed to evade capture for some time until further thefts in 1887 led him to the Old Bailey, where he received six months' hard labor in September. On the 30th of that month Ostrog was transferred from Wandsworth prison to the Surrey Pauper Lunatic Asylum, but once his original sentence had been served he was released on 10 March 1888.

Nothing is known of Ostrog's movements during the time of the Whitechapel murders, but he was a wanted man in October of 1888, again for failing to report to the police. It is known that he was arrested in Paris because on 18 November he was sentenced to two years' imprisonment by French authorities, again for theft. After his release Ostrog returned to England, and further prison sentences followed. He was last heard of in 1904, when he was staying at the St. Giles Christian Mission in Brooke Street, Holborn.

Beyond the mention in the Memoranda, and subsequent mentions by other authors as a possible suspect, there is nothing to connect Ostrog to the Ripper murders. Born sometime around 1833, he would have been 55 or so at the time of the murders, making him far too old for the killer. He was also too tall at 5 feet 11 inches and had dark brown hair, not the fair coloring described by various witnesses.

Chance of being the Ripper—2

Panchenko, Dr. Dimitru

Panchenko was involved in a Russian murder conspiracy and sentenced to 15 years' imprisonment. He may be the basis of the Pedachenko stories or may have been confused with the latter. What is certain is that he had nothing to do with the Ripper murders.

In 1911 Patrick O'Brien de Lacy married the daughter of General Buturlin in Russia. The bride's family was very wealthy, but unfortunately for de Lacy the fortune had been bequeathed to Buturlin's son. De Lacy decided to murder the entire family and obtained help from Dr. Panchenko, who supplied him with cholera and diphtheria germs for a fee of 620,000 rubles.

The plan was outlined to de Lacy's mistress, Madame Muraviora, but was overheard and reported to the general. De Lacy was apprehended before he could carry out his scheme and was sentenced to life imprisonment.

Chance of being the Ripper—0

Parent, Alfred

Parent was a resident of Bacon's Hotel in Fitzroy Square in the King's Cross police division. A complaint was made against him by a prostitute, Annie Cook, on 25 November 1888 because he offered her a sovereign for sex and five sovereigns to spend the night with him. Since the usual price for such services was about sixpence, Annie was suspicious and reported the matter to the police. Parent, who hailed originally from Paris, was able to prove that he was not involved in the murders.

Chance of being the Ripper—0

Pedachenko, Dr. Alexander

According to the story, Pedachenko (also known as Count Andrey Luiskovo) was originally a staff member at a maternity hospital, showing that he would have had the medical experience supposedly shown by the Ripper. Recruited into the Russian Secret Service, or the Ochrana, he was sent to England and in 1888 was living in Westmoreland Road, Walworth, with his sister.

Acting under orders from the Ochrana, he allegedly committed the murders, assisted by accomplices Levitski and Miss Winberg, in order to discredit the Metropolitan Police. Of course the plot was a brilliant success, as Sir Charles Warren was even forced to resign. Pedachenko was smuggled back to Russia but by then had a taste for killing and murdered another woman. He was then confined to a mental asylum.

The entire story is drawn from a document supposedly dictated by Rasputin and other information supplied by Johann Nideroest, a Swiss who sold information to newspapers, and Nicholas Zverieff, an anarchist based in London. It has also been stated that the Ochrana knew that Pedachenko was an alias, the killer's real name being Vassily Konovalov.

Stories of Russian plots, spies, and conspiracies should be treated with skepticism, and there is not the slightest evidence that Pedachenko even existed. Most likely the entire story is a myth based on the real-life tale of Dr. Panchenko.

Chance of being the Ripper—0

See also Konovalov, Vassily; Panchenko, Dr. Dimitru; "Miscellaneous": *Ochrana Gazette*

Pigott, William Henry

On the afternoon of Sunday, 9 September 1888, the day after Annie Chapman's murder, Pigott appeared in Gravesend,

Kent, and went to refresh himself at the Pope's Head public house. He said he had just walked from Whitechapel and spoke with hostility about women in general. This conversation led the landlady to send for the police.

When he was interviewed by Superintendent Berry, Berry noticed that Pigott had an injury to his hand that he said he had suffered when he had been bitten by a woman in the yard of a lodging house, again in Whitechapel. Retelling the same story later, Pigott said the lodging house was in Brick Lane.

His belongings were searched, and a bloodstained shirt was found in his bag. The police surgeon called to examine him thought that Pigott's shoes showed signs of having recently had blood wiped off them. Pigott was now a very strong suspect and was escorted back to Whitechapel, where he was interviewed by Inspector Abberline himself.

Pigott was then placed in an identity parade attended by Mrs. Fiddymont, Mary Chappell, and Joseph Taylor, who had seen a bloodstained man in Mrs. Fiddymont's pub, the Prince Albert on Brushfield Street, soon after **Annie Chapman** had been butchered. Only Chappell picked Pigott out as the man she had seen, but she later changed her mind and said she wasn't sure after all.

It is not known what happened to Pigott after the police satisfied themselves that he could not be the killer.

Chance of being the Ripper—1

See also "Others Who Played a Part": Chappell, Mary; Fiddymont, Mrs.

Pizer, John

There can be little doubt that John Pizer had a violent side to his nature. He was almost certainly the John "Pozer" who approached James Willis, a boot-finisher, at his work in Morgan Street in July 1887, pushed his head through the open window, and announced, "No wonder I can't get any work when you have got it all." Willis told him to go away, whereupon "Pozer" stabbed him in the hand. For this offense he received six months' hard labor. The following year, on 4 August, Pizer was again before the magistrates, charged with indecent assault, but the case was dismissed.

Pizer was a resident of 22 Mulberry Street but seems to have frequently absented himself from that address. He was certainly not staying there on the night **Mary Ann Nichols** met her death because he was instead at Crossman's lodging house in Holloway. From there, at approximately 1:30 A.M., he strolled down to Seven Sisters Road and watched a fire at London Docks. He had an excellent witness in the form of a policeman he chatted to, which of course means that he could not have been Nichols's killer.

By early September newspaper stories that the police were looking for a man nicknamed Leather Apron in connection with the Nichols murder abounded. By the sixth of that month, Pizer had returned to 22 Mulberry Street, where he stayed for the next four days after his brother warned him that there was suspicion against him and that he had been named as Leather Apron.

The only reference to John Pizer and Leather Apron being one and the same person was made by Sergeant William Thick, who said he had known Pizer for many years and that this was the nickname he had in the district. As a result, the police attempted to find Pizer, and Thick and a constable arrested him on 10 September at the house in Mulberry Street.

Pizer was taken to Leman Street Police Station and shown to Mrs. Fiddymont and Emmanuel Violenia. The latter positively identified Pizer as a man he had seen talking to a woman outside 29

Hanbury Street in the early hours of 8 September, the morning that **Annie Chapman** was murdered. However, there was no other evidence against Pizer, and after he gave the police details of his whereabouts, he was released without charge and even appeared at Chapman's inquest on 11 October to be formally cleared.

After his appearance at the inquest, Pizer was interviewed by the press and expressed surprise that he had been identified as Leather Apron. He had not known he was called by that name, and his family, friends, and neighbors said the same thing. Clearly, Pizer cannot have been the killer because he had alibis for the murders of Nichols and Chapman.

Chance of being the Ripper—0

Polish Jew

A generic term used to cover all such possible suspects as Cohen, Kosminski, and others without referring specifically to any. If one considers the writing on the wall in Goulston Street to be genuine, it is almost certain that the killer wasn't Jewish.

Chance of being the Ripper—2

See also Cohen, Aaron Davis; Kosminski, Aaron

Pozer, John

See Pizer, John

Pricha, Antoni

After George Hutchinson's description of the man he had seen with **Mary Jane Kelly** was published, the interfering Edward Knight Larkins, who also developed a theory of a conspiracy of Portuguese sailors, saw Pricha and believed that he fitted that description. Larkins pointed Pricha out to Constable Thomas Maybank, but Pricha was able to prove his whereabouts on the night Kelly was murdered and was then released.

Chance of being the Ripper—0

See also Laurenco, José; "The Witnesses": Hutchinson, George

Prince of Wales

See Albert Edward, Prince of Wales

Puckridge, Oswald

Puckridge was first named as a suspect by Sir Charles Warren in a letter to the Home Office on 19 September 1888. That note said, in part, "A man called Puckridge was released from an asylum on 4 August. He was educated as a surgeon—he has threatened to rip people up with a long knife. He is being looked for but cannot be found yet."

There is one error in Sir Charles's statement: Puckridge was not medically trained. On the certificate for his marriage to Ellen Puddle, dated 3 October 1868, Puckridge describes himself as a chemist, so it is likely that his training was as an apothecary.

Puckridge was admitted as an inmate of the Hoxton House private lunatic asylum at 50–52 Hoxton Street, Shoreditch, on 6 January 1888 and released on 4 August of the same year. Little is known of his later life beyond the fact that on 28 May 1900 he was admitted to the Holborn Workhouse in City Road and that he died there on 1 June.

There are two principal arguments against Puckridge being the Ripper. The first is that he was born in 1838, which means he was 50 when the murders began and thus far older than the likely killer. Second, Puckridge lived for 12 years after the five canonical murders, and there is no explanation for why he would have stopped killing.

Chance of being the Ripper—2

See also "The Police": Warren, Sir Charles

QUINN, EDWARD
Charged at Woolwich with being drunk and disorderly on 17 September 1888, Quinn was arrested after a constable found him in the street, covered in blood. In fact, Quinn had merely had a little too much to drink and had fallen over in the street, sustaining cuts to his hands and face.

Chance of being the Ripper—0

ROBINSON, PIERCE JOHN
Briefly suspected after the murder of **Mary Jane Kelly**, Robinson was a business partner of Richard Wingate, who lived at 10 Church Street, Edgware Road. Wingate reported to the police that Robinson had grown silent when they were discussing the murders. Furthermore, Robinson had posted a letter to his paramour, a Miss Peters who lived in Portslade, near Brighton, saying he believed "that I would be caught today."

The matter was investigated, and it was soon shown that at the time Kelly met her death, Robinson was with Miss Peters in Portslade.

Chance of being the Ripper—0

ROCHA, JOACHIM DE
See Laurenco, José

SADLER, JAMES THOMAS
Arrested and charged with the murder of **Frances Coles**, Sadler was briefly suspected of the other Whitechapel murders because Coles's death was originally held to be by the same hand as the others. Sadler was able to prove that he was at sea during some of the Ripper crimes and was also able to demonstrate that he had an alibi for the time Frances died. He was released for lack of evidence against him, but the police still believed that he had killed Coles.

Chance of being the Ripper—0

Chance of being the killer of Frances Coles—3

SANDERS, DR. JON WILLIAM
Sanders may have been confused with John William Smith Sanders. However, he did work in the area at the time of the murders as a surgeon at the Croydon Fever Hospital, the Bethnal Green Infirmary, and the St.-George's-in-the-East Infirmary. He was also a gynecologist and died in January 1889, aged 30.

Chance of being the Ripper—3

SANDERS, JOHN WILLIAM SMITH
One police memorandum at the time of the murders referred to three insane medical students; two had been traced and eliminated, but the third was believed to have gone abroad. This student was John William Smith Sanders, originally of 20 Abercorn Place, Maida Vale, who had not in fact left the country. He had begun to suffer from fits of violence and had been confined to the Holloway Asylum since February 1887. Since he was still there at the time of the murders, he can easily be exonerated.

Chance of being the Ripper—0

SAUNDERS, DR. WILLIAM SEDGEWICK
See Masonic Conspiracy

SICKERT, WALTER RICHARD
See Masonic Conspiracy

SICKERT'S VETERINARY STUDENT
In yet another story emanating from the fertile imaginations of the Sickert family, Walter Sickert is said to have taken a studio some years after the murders and

been told that the last occupant of the rooms was a veterinary student who used to stay out late at night during the period of the murders. He also burned clothing and avidly read the newspaper reports of the crimes. Finally his health failed, and his elderly mother took him home to Bournemouth. Though the name of the student was lost during the bombing in World War II, when the book containing it was destroyed, the writer Donald McCormick claimed that it sounded something like Druitt.

No doubt this was supposed to be more proof of the nonsensical Masonic Conspiracy, but the only student with a name that sounded like Druitt was George Ailwyn Hewitt, who was only 17 or so in 1888, far too young to have been the killer. In addition, the previous occupant of the room, if, as suggested, it was Sickert's studio at 6 Mornington Crescent, had been an Egyptian medical student. In short, the story carries as much weight as the rest of the Masonic Conspiracy tale.

Chance of being the Ripper—0

See also Masonic Conspiracy

Simm, Clarence

Simm came to light as a suspect only in 1989. On 20 June that year an article appeared in the *Weekly World News* in which Simm's widow, Betty, was quoted as saying that her husband had made a deathbed confession, in 1951, to having killed 14 prostitutes while he was a teenager. A lie-detector test was administered to Mrs. Simm, and the operator, Gerald Mevel, stated that there was a less than one-half of 1 percent chance that she was lying. Of course, the test did not prove that Clarence wasn't lying, or that he referred specifically to the Whitechapel murders. Furthermore, because Simm apparently committed his murders while he was a teenager, he would be under the age range of the man we are looking for.

Chance of being the Ripper—2

Smith, G. Wentworth Bell

Smith was a Canadian who came to England to represent his employer sometime in 1888. Although his office was close to St. Paul's, he lived in lodgings with Mr. and Mrs. Callaghan at 27 Sun Street, Finsbury Square.

Smith soon displayed some rather erratic behavior, including writing out large numbers of religious tracts. He announced that he had seen prostitutes parading through St. Paul's during services and that all such women should be drowned. He was known to stay out late at nights and to wear silent, rubber-soled shoes. His landlord came to believe that he was the Ripper and took his written suspicions to Dr. Lyttleton Forbes Winslow, who had made known his interest in the Ripper murders. Callaghan had written that Smith had returned home late at night on 9 August, but Winslow altered the date to 7 August, thus indicating that Smith was out and about at the time **Martha Tabram** was murdered, in order to make Smith appear to be a more likely suspect.

Beyond his somewhat strange behavior, there is nothing to link Smith to the crimes, and it must be remembered that, as a visitor to British shores, he would not have had an intimate knowledge of the East End, nor did he have a base close to the epicenter of the crimes.

Chance of being the Ripper—1

See also "Miscellaneous": Winslow, Lyttleton Stewart Forbes

Solomon, Louis

Solomon's name was mentioned in the Home Office files on 15 November 1888. A letter had been received from

Woking prison suggesting Solomon as the killer. The files go on to state that his was an ordinary criminal case.

Chance of being the Ripper—1

Stanley, Dr.

Dr. Stanley was a pseudonym given to the Ripper by Leonard Matters in his 1926 book *The Mystery of Jack the Ripper.* Stanley was supposedly a cancer specialist whose son, Herbert, met **Mary Jane Kelly** in 1886 and enjoyed a brief dalliance with her. She gave him a particularly virulent form of syphilis that killed him within two years. The doctor vowed revenge, went about first eliminating Mary's friends, and then, when he had killed her, fled to Argentina, dying in Buenos Aires in 1918.

The story has more holes than Swiss cheese. First, syphilis does not kill within two years. Second, there is no evidence that Kelly had the disease. Third, if she had, then why wasn't she too killed by it? Fourth, there is absolutely no evidence that the victims knew each other. Fifth, at the time of Mary's supposed tryst with Herbert she was actually living with Joe Fleming. And sixth, no trace of any doctor fitting the supposed details of Stanley's life can be found.

Chance of being the Ripper—0

Stephen, James Kenneth

There are various stories involving Stephen, who was tutor to Prince Albert Victor while the prince was at Cambridge. In one, Stephen and the prince had a homosexual affair, and when it ended, Stephen decided to kill prostitutes on dates significant to his former lover. In another, because he is mentioned in the discredited Abberline diaries as an accomplice, he is said to have worked with Montague John Druitt; together they left the bodies in a pattern that formed a perfect arrow pointing to the Houses of Parliament.

Stephen was around the right age, having been born in 1859, which would have made him 29 at the time of the murders. He suffered an accident at Felixstowe in 1886 that caused brain damage that eventually led directly to his premature death in 1892, and he exhibited signs of hatred toward women in some of his poems. For example, he wrote:

> If all the harm that women have done,
> Were put in a bottle and rolled into one,
> Earth would not hold it,
> The sky could not enfold it,
> It could not be lighted nor warmed by the sun;
> Such masses of evil
> Would puzzle the devil,
> And keep him in fuel while Time's wheels run.
> But if all the harm that's been done by men
> Were doubled and doubled and doubled again,
> And melted and fused into vapour and then
> Were squared and raised to the power of ten,
> There wouldn't be nearly enough, not near,
> To keep a small girl for the tenth of a year.

First, the notion that the murders took place on dates significant to Prince Albert Victor is easily discounted. The best that can be done with this nonsense is that **Martha Tabram** was killed on the birthday of the Duke of Edinburgh, **Mary Ann Nichols** was killed on the birthday of Princess Wilhelmina of the Netherlands, and **Mary Jane Kelly** was killed on the birthday of the Prince of Wales. There are no known links, however tenuous, for the double event or the murder of **Annie Chapman**. So much for royal significance.

Second, how does Stephen fit what we know of the Ripper? He had no known base in the East End, he did not fit the physical description of the Ripper, and he was clean-shaven. There is absolutely nothing linking him to the crimes, and the idea of a conspiracy is without foundation.

Chance of being the Ripper—0

See also Albert Victor, Duke of Clarence; Druitt, Montague John; Masonic Conspiracy

Stephenson, Robert Donston

The story of Robert Donston Stephenson, who styled himself Dr. Roslyn D'Onston, is alleged to have been told by the novelist Mabel Collins, who was Stephenson's lover, in confidence to her friend Baroness Vittoria Cremens. Cremens in turn dictated her memoirs to Bernard O'Donnell, during which process she outlined why she and Collins had concluded that Stephenson must have been the killer.

In her version of the story, the baroness became Stephenson's business partner in the 1890s when they set up the Pompadour Cosmetics Company, with offices in Baker Street. At the time Stephenson was a practicing black magician. He had allegedly once fallen in love with a prostitute named Ada, who had similar feelings for him, but when they announced that they intended to marry, Stephenson's father cut him off financially. As a result Stephenson got heavily into debt and finally was forced to throw himself on his father's mercy. His father said he would assist Stephenson only if he gave up Ada, which he reluctantly did. Ada, brokenhearted, threw herself off Westminster Bridge, and her death snapped Stephenson's mind and started him on the road to becoming the Whitechapel murderer.

The baroness said that at one stage she searched through Stephenson's belongings, hoping to find a clue that would prove his guilt. She found several neckties that were stained with what looked like blood. Stephenson afterward told her that he knew who the Ripper was: a surgeon named Dr. Morgan Davies who carried home the internal organs he removed from his victims by secreting them behind his necktie.

There is an element of truth in this life story. Stephenson was indeed fascinated by the occult arts, but in 1863 he took up a somewhat mundane position working for the Customs Office in Hull. Dismissed from there for unknown reasons, he married Ann Deary in 1876, but they soon parted. It is known that by July 1888 Stephenson was in London because on the 26th of that month he booked himself into the London Hospital to be treated for neurasthenia. He remained there until 7 December, so he was in the city during the canonical murders.

Stephenson was fascinated by the murders. After the double event he wrote to the police suggesting that the second word of the Goulston Street graffito was in fact *juives,* French for Jews, which would indicate that the killer was of French extraction but had lived in England for some years. He also wrote articles for the *Pall Mall Gazette* elaborating on this theory and suggesting that the murder sites formed a cross.

During his stay at the hospital he met Davies, whose demonstration of how he believed the victims had been killed convinced Stephenson that the doctor was the Ripper. He joined forces with an unemployed ironmonger named George Marsh to investigate Davies and prove that he was the killer. Unfortunately for Stephenson, Marsh came to believe, like the baroness and Mabel Collins, that Stephenson himself was the murderer and took his suspicions to the police on 24 December 1888. Two days later, on 26 December, Stephenson wrote to the police again, outlining his theory of the evidence against Davies.

Those who argue for Stephenson as the killer claim that the findings and suspicions of Cremens, Collins, and Marsh show that he was involved. Some say that as a known magician, he killed the women as part of some ritualistic practice and stopped only when he became converted to Christianity. In fact, there is no evidence at all against Stephenson, and a closer examination of the facts demolishes the case against him.

Stephenson continued to lecture on black magic after the murders had stopped, and his final conversion to Christianity did not take place until 1893. He was questioned at least twice by the police and was presumably exonerated of any involvement. Furthermore, he was too old, at 47, when the murders took place and, at 5 feet 10 inches, too tall. Finally, the idea that the killer would return to the London Hospital after committing his butchery on the streets of Whitechapel beggars belief.

Chance of being the Ripper—1

See also Davies, Dr. Morgan; "Miscellaneous": Goulston Street Graffito

Swinburne, Algernon Charles

A less likely candidate would be hard to imagine. The poet is known to have had masochistic tendencies, but the Ripper was demonstrably sadistic. In addition, at the time of the crimes Swinburne was 61 years old, far too old to be the killer.

Chance of being the Ripper—0

Szemeredy, Alois

Szemeredy was a surgeon who served in the Austrian army until he deserted and escaped to Argentina. In 1885 he was committed to a lunatic asylum, from which he was later released. His whereabouts at the time of the crimes are unknown, but he was in Vienna in August 1889 and returned in 1892 to that city, where he was arrested on suspicion of murder and robbery. While in custody he committed suicide.

Apart from the fact that we do not even know whether he was in London at the time of the murders, the strongest arguments against Szemerdy are that he would not have known the geographical area sufficiently well and was 44 in 1888.

Chance of being the Ripper—1

Tchkersoff, Olga

A "Jill the Ripper" candidate suggested by author Edwin Thomas Woodhall, Olga, a Russian, came to England with her family, which consisted of her parents and her younger sister, Vera. Vera became a prostitute and died from sepsis after an illegal abortion. This embittered Olga against the woman who persuaded Vera into prostitution and who was supposed to be none other than **Mary Jane Kelly**. The catalyst that finally tipped Olga over the edge was the deaths of her father and mother, both in 1888. This theory is best relegated to the realms of fiction, and the general argument against a female killer also applies.

Chance of being the Ripper—0

See also Jill the Ripper

Thick, Sergeant William

The Home Office files on 14 October 1889 mentioned two letters that had been received from a Mr J. H. Hazelwood giving the opinion that Thick had committed the murders. Perhaps the best summation of this theory is the comment written in the margin of one of the letters, presumably by an official: "I think it is plainly rubbish—perhaps prompted by spite."

Chance of being the Ripper—0

Thomas, Dr. William Evan

Thomas was a Welsh doctor who at the time of the murders had a surgery at 190 Green Street, Victoria Park, some distance from where the crimes took place. The only real suspicion against him is based on the tradition that he had a breakdown following the last murder, presumably that of **Mary Jane Kelly**, and later poisoned himself. These suppositions do not, however, fit the known facts. Thomas died on 21 June 1889, and if we assume that he was the killer of Mary Jane Kelly, then he would have waited more than seven months after her death before his breakdown and suicide.

Chance of being the Ripper—2

Thompson, Francis Joseph

Thompson, an English poet, was suggested as a suspect by Richard Patterson in 1998. Thompson was an opium addict, and this habit eventually led to his death in 1907. He was in London at the time of the crimes and was the right age, at 29. However, he could not have known the Whitechapel area as well as Jack obviously did, and there is no explanation of why he would have stopped killing.

Chance of being the Ripper—2

Tumblety, "Dr." Francis

Tumblety, a Canadian quack doctor, was identified as the Ripper by Stewart Evans and Paul Gainey after the discovery of the Littlechild letter that named him as a suspect. The theory lists 15 factors that indicate that Tumblety was the killer.

1. *He fits the psychological profile.* Not true. Tumblety was a strange man and was almost certainly homosexual. There was no evidence of violence in his background, and although some of his contemporaries refer to his hatred of women, others say he was incapable of the Whitechapel crimes.

2. *He was in Whitechapel at the time and knew the East End well.* There is no evidence to support this notion. The theory has it that some bloodstained shirts were found at 22 Batty Street after one of the murders and that the landlady described an American lodger she had. But there is no evidence that the blood had anything to do with the Ripper murders, and even if it did, there is nothing to show that the lodger was Tumblety. Batty Street is close to the **Elizabeth Stride** murder site but nowhere near the epicenter of the other murders.

3. *He had anatomical knowledge and collected medical specimens including uteri.* We have no proof whatsoever that he had any medical qualifications or experience. He was an accomplished liar who invented dozens of stories about himself, most of which can be shown to be rubbish. We have no proof that he had any anatomical knowledge, and even if he did, there is no certainty that the Ripper did. Either way this factor is inconclusive.

4. *He was arrested within days of the Kelly murder on suspicion of being the killer.* Not true. Tumblety was arrested on 7 November 1888 on charges of gross indecency with a number of males. The records show that he was bailed in the sum of 300 pounds on 16 November. The theorists would have us believe that he was arrested on suspicion of being the killer on 7 November but that the police didn't have enough to hold him, so he was released very quickly, meaning he was free to murder **Mary Jane Kelly**. He was then rearrested on 12 November, with gross indecency used as a holding charge, but then bailed again.

Where is the logic in this theory? We are expected to believe that the police let Tumblety go twice, knowing full well that he had butchered Kelly after the first time. It makes no sense. It is much more likely that he was bailed once only, on 16 November. Hence, he would have been in custody when Kelly was murdered and so could not have been the Ripper.

When we seek support for the statement that he was arrested on suspicion of being the murderer, we have only the American newspapers to substantiate that story. None of the British newspapers connected Tumblety with the killings, and it must be remembered that those reporters were on the spot and appeared to have access to almost everything the police knew.

5. *The murders ceased after he had been arrested and fled first to France and then to America.* This assumption can be made only if we confirm that Kelly was the final victim; as discussed earlier, Tumblety was in custody when Kelly met her death. If any of the subsequent murders can be placed at Jack's door, then Tumblety was not the killer. This same factor could be used to support the statement that any of a dozen men were Jack the Ripper.

6. *A senior police officer (Chief Inspector John George Littlechild) felt that he was the killer.* At no stage did Littlechild say Tumblety was the killer. The Littlechild letter merely stated that "Dr T" was a very likely suspect. It went on to say that he was not known as a sadist and referred to the "suspect" being bailed only *once*. Also, Littlechild wrote that he believed Tumblety to have committed suicide soon after he escaped. In fact, Tumblety did not die until 1903.

7. *Tumblety used other names.* This is no proof at all. Many people in this area used an alias at the time. One need only look at the victims to see that most of them were known by two, three, or even more names.

8. *The police were in touch with their U.S. counterparts about Tumblety before and after his arrest.* This shows only that Tumblety was under consideration, along with dozens of other possible suspects. It does not demonstrate that he was ever a strong suspect and is certainly not proof that he was ever arrested for the murders. The British police contacted more than one foreign force with requests for more information about possible suspects.

9. *A senior police officer, Inspector Walter Andrews, was sent to New York to pursue Tumblety.* In fact, Andrews was sent to Montreal to escort two criminals, Roland Gideon and Israel Barnet, from England to Canada. They were wanted for blowing up the Central Bank of Toronto. Andrews was then sent on to New York on Ripper-related business, but we do not know with certainty what his journey involved. It may well have been in connection with Tumblety, as the theory postulates, but even if it were, could it not be yet another sign that the police were simply doing their job properly? After all, Tumblety had jumped bail soon after the Kelly murder. He had been charged with gross indecency, but might not the police believe that someone arrested for such an offense who jumped bail might deserve a closer look? Like many modern-day investigations, the pursuit of the Ripper involved eliminating people just as much as the quest for the guilty party.

10. *Tumblety wasn't found in New York, so he had escaped again.* I really don't understand this point. Someone is a killer simply because he cannot be found?

11. *He was rich enough to move about and change his clothing.* This point too makes little sense. The killer was often described as shabby-genteel. Tumblety wore ostentatious clothes—and just because someone wears a different coat one day does not mean that he is a murderer.

12. *He was eccentric but shrewd.* A man who butchers at least five women

can hardly be described as eccentric! Tumblety was flamboyant, an exhibitionist, and a show-off. The Ripper was a totally different personality.

13. He probably committed other offenses for which he has not been recognized. Even if true, this point is not evidence. The Ripper may well have committed other offenses before he killed **Mary Ann Nichols**, but one cannot work back and say that because we have a suspect, that suspect must have committed other offenses. Naming those offenses and putting the suspect in that location at that time would constitute evidence. It would be only circumstantial, but at least it would be more than a supposition that such an event had happened.

14. People who knew him thought he was the killer. Some may have, but others thought him incapable of such things, and we also have to consider how many other people were thought by friends and neighbors to be the killer. Many, as detailed in this section, were exonerated.

15. It is possible that Tumblety was the Batty Street lodger. It is just as likely that he wasn't, but even if he was, there is no proof that this lodger was in any way connected to the crimes.

As if all this is not enough, we must remember that Tumblety would have stood out like a sore thumb. He was 5 feet 10 inches tall, far too big to be the killer, and he sported a massive bushy black mustache, waxed at the ends, when our killer probably had only a small brown one.

The only evidence against Tumblety is that he was mentioned as a possible suspect in a letter written in 1913 and the fact that he jumped bail on an indecency charge after Mary Jane Kelly's murder. There is stronger evidence, such as his appearance and personality, that indicates that he was not the man we are looking for.

Chance of being the Ripper—2

See also "The Police": Andrews, Inspector Walter; "Miscellaneous": Littlechild Letter

Unknown Male

Though few writers will readily admit it, there is a good chance that the real Ripper has never come to public attention. Most sensible writers accept that Jack was a local man, of the same class as those he murdered, and was someone the victims would readily have accepted as one of their own. The suggestion that after claiming his victims he vanished back into obscurity, for whatever reason, and has never been traced is much more likely than claiming a Royal, Masonic, or similar connection.

Chance of being the Ripper—5

Van Burst, Nicholai

Briefly suspected at the time, Van Burst was mentioned in the Scotland Yard files. He was a resident of Bacon's Hotel in Fitzroy Square and was taken in for questioning after he accosted several women at King's Cross. He was able to account for his movements on the nights of the murders and was allowed to go.

Chance of being the Ripper—0

Vassili, Nicholai

See Wassili, Nicholai

Waddell, William

Waddell was a convicted murderer who killed Jane Beetmoor at Birtley Fell in September 1888. At first the murder was linked to the Whitechapel atrocities, but it was soon shown that it was a local affair and that Waddell had only claimed one life. He was hanged for that murder at Durham prison on 18 December 1888.

Chance of being the Ripper—0

WARREN, SIR CHARLES
See Masonic Conspiracy

WASSILI, NICHOLAI
A Russian whose story may well be fictional, Wassili is supposed to have lived in Paris, where he attempted to reform prostitutes by murdering them. He is said to have killed five women by stabbing them in the back before being arrested and sent to a mental institution, from which he was discharged on 1 January 1888, saying that he intended to move to London. There is no proof that Wassili ever existed and, even if he did, nothing to connect him with the Whitechapel murders.

Chance of being the Ripper—1

WESTCOTT, DR. WILLIAM WYNN
An occultist and one of the founding members of the Order of the Golden Dawn, Westcott was also the coroner for Central London and was 40 years old at the time of the Whitechapel murders.

His name has been linked with the murders by those who see some sort of occult conspiracy in the crimes, claiming that the women were murdered in a graveyard as part of some ritual and that their bodies were then dumped. This scenario is clearly contradicted by the medical evidence, and the theory is without value.

Chance of being the Ripper—0

WHITE-EYED MAN
A suspect named by author Edwin Thomas Woodhall but obviously a combination of a number of factors. Woodhall stated that during the Ripper murders a man, his face painted black and with white rings around his eyes, leaped upon a woman and frightened her. The man was taken to the police station, where he managed to attack two senior men with an ebony ruler and made good his escape. Some three weeks later the man's body was found floating in the Thames, and a constable from Buck's Row who had seen the killer positively identified it as the same man. That same constable was murdered in the line of duty some time later.

This nonsense is a mixture of many tales. First, the white-eyed man was obviously Dr. William Holt, with his spectacles converted into white rings around his eyes. The so-called escape from police custody is a misreading of Sir Melville Macnaghten's comment that the killer had nearly knocked out a police commissioner and settled the hash of a principal secretary of state. He was referring not to a physical attack but to the damage done to the careers of Sir Charles Warren and Henry Matthews. The body found in the Thames was of course Montague John Druitt's, and the policeman connected with the case and later murdered was Constable Ernest Thompson, who had nothing to do with the Buck's Row murder but was involved in the **Frances Coles** case.

In short, the entire story is fiction.

Chance of being the Ripper—0

See also Holt, Dr. William; "The Police": Macnaghten, Sir Melville Leslie; Warren, Sir Charles; "Others Who Played a Part": Matthews, Right Honourable Henry, M.P.

WINBERG, MISS
Miss Winberg was said to have been sent to London by the czar's secret police to assist Dr. Pedachenko. She allegedly spoke to the victims and lulled them into a false sense of security before the doctor struck.

Chance of being the Ripper—0

Chance of being involved—0

See also Pedachenko, Dr. Alexander

Wirtofsky

Wirtofsky's name was mentioned in the Home Office files on 13 December 1888. A letter had been received from George Strachey in Dresden stating that he had been given information by one of his students, an American named Julius J. Lowenheim, that the latter had met a Polish Jew by the name of Wirtofsky in London, close to Finsbury Square. Wirtofsky had reportedly said he wished to kill a certain woman and all the others of her class, implying that he had a grudge against prostitutes.

Chance of being the Ripper—1

Xavier, Manuel Cruz

See Laurenco, José

12

The Literature

There are many books, plays, films, and videos on the subject of the Whitechapel murders. Many of these are excellent, some are less so, and others are almost worthless. This section reviews those known and, where the item is a book, will list some of the more common errors found in descriptions of the five canonical murders: Mary Ann Nichols, Annie Chapman, Elizabeth Stride, Catherine Eddowes, and Mary Jane Kelly.

Many of these books are out of print, and some are collector's items, changing hands for many hundreds of pounds. Only those likely to be found reasonably easily in book stores are given full reviews.

One minor point about these narratives: I believe that one should be wary of any "solution" that involves anagrams from messages or letters, points on a map forming patterns, or conspiracy theories.

Books

Abrahamsen, Dr. David. *Murder and Madness: The Secret Life of Jack the Ripper.* Donald Fine (United States), 1992; Robson edition, 1992.

Concludes that there were two killers: Prince Albert Victor and James Kenneth Stephen. Loaded with errors. There may be a market for the first accurate book on the crimes to come out of the United States, but this isn't it.

Achad, Frater. *Did Aleister Crowley Know the Identity of Jack the Ripper?* Pangenetor Lodge Publications (United States), 1993.

Anonymous. *Aleister Crowley and Jack the Ripper.* Private printing, 1988.

Anonymous. *Hvem Ar Jack Uppskararen?* (Who was Jack the Ripper?) Utgiuningstar (Sweden), 1889.

Examines all the murders of women in London over the preceding thirty years.

Anonymous. *Jack lo Squartatore* (Jack the Ripper). Di Donne (Italy), 1889.

Anonymous. *Jack the Ripper at Work Again, Another Terrible Murder and Mutilation in Whitechapel.* 1888.

Refers specifically to the murder of Mary Jane Kelly.

Anonymous. *The Latest Atrocities of Jack the Ripper* (Germany), 1889.

Anonymous. *The Whitechapel Atrocities: Arrest of a Newspaper Reporter.* Woodford Fawcett and Co., 1888.

Anonymous. *The Whitechapel Murders or The Mysteries of the East End.* Purkiss, 1888.

Written after the double event, the murders of Stride and Eddowes, it does not include the murder of Mary Jane Kelly.

Aronson, Theo. *Prince Eddy and the Homosexual Underworld.* John Murray Ltd., 1994.

Ball, Pamela. *Jack the Ripper: A Psychic Investigation—The Compelling Paranormal Search for the Killer's True Identity.* Arcturus Publishing, 1998.

The title says it all.

Barnard, Alan, ed. *The Harlot Killer: The Story of Jack the Ripper in Fact and Fiction.* Dodd Mead (United States), 1953.

Beadle, William. *Jack the Ripper: Anatomy of a Myth.* Wat Tyler Books, 1995.

Full-length treatment of the suggestion that William Henry Bury was the Ripper.

Begg, Paul. *Jack the Ripper: The Uncensored Facts.* Robson Books, 1988.

Covers the five canonical murders and a few of the main suspects in detail. Includes some good illustrations, including the map of the Mitre Square murder site produced at the inquest on Catherine Eddowes. Includes a curious index that can confuse by the way the names are listed in surname order but with the first initial in front. Contains the following errors:

Mary Ann Nichols
Mary Ann had two children.
Mary Ann stole clothing from her employers worth in excess of 3 pounds 10 shillings.
Annie Chapman
Annie had two children
Elizabeth Stride
Elizabeth and Michael Kidney lived at 33 Dorset Street.
Arthur Dutfield carried on business from the yard that bore his name.
There was only one house in Dutfield's Yard.
William Marshall saw a couple outside 63 Berner Street.
Edward Spooner noticed that the flower Elizabeth wore was red and white.
Mary Jane Kelly
There were two windows to the left of the door.
There was no lighting in Miller's Court.
Mary was in arrears on her rent to the tune of 30 shillings.
Mary's breasts and liver were on the bedside table.

Begg, Paul, Martin Fido, and Keith Skinner. *The Jack the Ripper A–Z.* Headline, 1996.

First-class work that lists anyone and anything to do with the crimes in alphabetical order. Well illustrated. An essential part of any library and highly recommended.

Bourgoin, Stephane. *Jack l'Eventreur* (Jack the Ripper). Fleuve Noir (France), 1992.

Probably the best foreign-language book on the crimes. Covers the facts and does not supply any particular theory.

Colby-Newton, Katie. *Jack the Ripper: Opposing Viewpoints.* Greenhaven (United States), 1990.

Colville, Gary, and Patrick Luciano. *Jack the Ripper: His Life and Crimes in Popular Entertainment.* McFarland and Co. (United States), 1999.

Not really a Ripper book as such, but it covers all the films and television shows that have featured the Ripper story.

Cory, Patricia. *An Eye to the Future.* Private printing, 1993.

Yet another reworking of the Masonic Conspiracy theory.

Cullen, Tom. *Autumn of Terror: Jack the Ripper. His Crimes and Times.* Bodley Head, 1965.

The first book to specifically name Montague John Druitt as the killer. A well-researched volume.

———. *The Crimes and Times of Jack the Ripper.* Bodley Head, 1973.

Paperback version of *Autumn of Terror.*

Desnos, Robert. *Jack l'Eventreur.* (France) 1997.

Dorsenne, Jean. *Jack l'Eventreur Scenes Vecues.* Les Editions de France, 1935.

A somewhat fanciful treatment of the story supposedly based on the recollections of a chief constable who cannot be identified.

Douglas, Arthur. *Will the Real Jack the Ripper?* Countryside Publications, 1979.

Excellent account of the crimes and theories. Brilliantly researched.

Evans, Stewart, and Paul Gainey. *Jack the Ripper—First American Serial Killer.* Kodansha International, 1995.

U.S. edition of *The Lodger.*

———. *The Lodger: The Arrest and Escape of Jack the Ripper.* Century, 1995.

Suggests that the killer was Dr. Tumblety after Stewart Evans, one of the authors, discovered the Littlechild letter. A very well-researched book. Illustrated and indexed.

Fairclough, Melvyn. *The Ripper and the Royals.* Duckworth, 1991.

Yet another version of the Masonic Conspiracy, based on further stories from Joseph Sickert that should be viewed with the same skepticism as all his other tales.

Farson, Daniel. *Jack the Ripper.* Michael Joseph, 1972; Sphere edition, 1973.

Explores the main suspects at the time and decides that Montague John Druitt was the killer. The first book to reproduce the mortuary photographs of the victims.

Feldman, Paul H. *Jack the Ripper—The Final Chapter.* Virgin Books, 1997.

A follow-up to the diary of James Maybrick arguing the case for that work being genuine. Contains no history of the crimes themselves but is, nevertheless, a book that should be on every Ripper investigator's shelf. Indexed. Some illustrations.

Fido, Martin. *The Crimes, Detection and Death of Jack the Ripper.* George Weidenfeld and Nicholson Limited, 1987; Barnes and Noble edition, 1994.

No illustrations but excellent maps of the murder sites. In addition to the canonical five murders, the book also covers the murders of Emma Elizabeth Smith, Ada Wilson, and Martha Tabram. It also includes details of murders and attacks after Mary Jane Kelly's death. Contains a good section on the police and a roundup of the major suspects at the time. Finally names the Ripper as Nathan Kaminsky. There is no index, and the book contains the following errors:

Mary Ann Nichols
Dr. Llewellyn deduced that the killer was left-handed.
Dr. Llewellyn deduced that the killer had worked from in front of his victim.
Annie Chapman
Albert Cadoche lived at number 31 Hanbury Street.
The fence between the properties was 4 feet high.
Two farthings were placed at Annie's feet.
Elizabeth Stride
Constable Henry Lamb was alerted by Louis Diemschutz and Isaac Kozebrodsky.
The doctor who attended was Dr. William Blackfield.
Elizabeth was known as "Long Liz" because of her height.
Elizabeth held grapes or stalks in her hand.
Elizabeth and Michael Kidney had lived at 38 Dorset Street.
Catherine Eddowes
Catherine had been lodging in Church Street, Spitalfields.
Bloody water was found in a sink off Dorset Street.
Catherine was 43 years old.
Mary Jane Kelly
The window was removed so that photographs could be taken.
Mary Ann Cox heard someone leaving Miller's Court at 6:15 A.M.

Fisher, Peter. *An Illustrated Guide to Jack the Ripper.* P and D Riley, 1996.

Forbes-Jones, Winston. *Who Was Jack the Ripper?* Pipeline Promotions, 1988.

Fox, Richard Kyle. *The History of the Whitechapel Murders: A Full and Authentic Narrative of the above Murders with Sketches.* Franklin Square (United States), 1888.

Fuller, Jean Overton. *Sickert and the Ripper Crimes.* Mandrake, 1988.

Another book suggesting a Royal/Masonic Conspiracy. Indexed and illustrated.

Graham, Anne E., and Carol Emmas. *The Last Victim: The Extraordinary Life of Florence Maybrick, the Wife of Jack the Ripper.* Headline Publishing, 1999.

Basically a biography of Florence Maybrick, but one chapter deals with the theory that her husband was the killer.

Graysmith, Robert. *The Bell Tower.* Regnery Publishing (United States), 1999.

Suggests that the Ripper was actually two men, Pastor John George (Jack) Gibson and his friend Pastor Jesse Gibson (no relation). Offers no real evidence and appears to be a work of fantasy. Includes supposed proof that the murders were committed to form the pattern of a patriarchal cross, but this theory requires an unrecorded attack in Rupert Street, assumes that the attack on Annie Millwood took place on the corner of White's Row, and dismisses the fact that Martha Tabram's murder was nowhere near any line. In effect, four of the murders (Mary Ann Nichols/Catherine Eddowes and Annie Chapman/Elizabeth Stride) form two lines that intersect somewhere north of Whitechapel High Street.

The following errors are noted:

In General
The killer was certainly left-handed.
The second Ripper murder was that of Martha Tabram, who died at 4:45 P.M.
In the Tabram case, Dr. Killeen stated that 38 wounds had been inflicted by a right-handed man and the 39th by a left-handed man!
Mary Ann Nichols
Mary Ann's wedding ring had been taken by the killer.
Annie Chapman
This fourth victim was attacked in Lamb Street.
Elizabeth Stride
Israel Schwartz said he saw a knife in the second man's hand.
Elizabeth's body was found by Charles Cross.
Elizabeth had been stabbed *and* her throat was cut.
The murder weapon had a rounded blade.
Catherine Eddowes
Catherine was discharged from the police station one hour before Joseph Lawende saw her.
The killer washed his hands in a sink off Dorset Street.
Dorset Street referred to as Dorsett Street.
Mary Jane Kelly
The killer had a key to Mary's room.

Harris, Melvin. *Jack the Ripper: The Bloody Truth.* Columbus, 1987.

Concludes that the Ripper was Robert Donston Stephenson. A valuable book that demolishes many of the more outlandish "solutions."

———. *The Ripper File.* W. H. Allen, 1988.

No connection with the 1975 BBC book. A reconstruction of the murders from press sources of the time.

———. *The True Face of Jack the Ripper.* Michael O'Mara Books, 1994.

Argues the case for Robert Donston Stephenson being the Ripper. Indexed and illustrated.

Harrison, Michael. *Clarence: The Life of HRH the Duke of Clarence and Avondale, 1864–1892.* W. H. Allen, 1972.

Includes comments on the suggestion that Albert Victor, Duke of Clarence, was the Ripper.

Harrison, Paul. *Jack the Ripper: The Mystery Solved.* Robert Hale, 1991.

A few illustrations, including images of many of the locations as they were when the book was written. States that the Ripper was Joseph Barnett. Covers the five canonical murders. Includes an index. The following errors are noted:

Mary Ann Nichols
Robert Paul's first name given as John.
Paul placed his hand on Mary Ann's breast to feel for a heartbeat.
Inspector Helson discovered the mutilations at the mortuary.
Annie Chapman
Both men from Bayley's ran to the Commercial Street Police Station.
Inspector Chandler found the yard full of people.
Rings and farthings were placed at Annie's feet.
Albert Cadoche lived at 31 Hanbury Street.
Elizabeth Stride
Louis Diemschutz and Isaac Kozebrodsky found Constable Henry Lamb.
Elizabeth and Michael Kidney lived at 35 Dorset Street.

Catherine Eddowes
Catherine was arrested for being drunk in Bishopsgate.
Inspector Collard sent a constable to fetch Dr. Sequeira.
The Goulston Street graffito was written in red chalk.
A sink off Dorset Street was found to hold bloody water.
Narrative accepts as fact that Catherine knew the identity of the killer.
Joseph Lawende and his friends left the club at 1 A.M.
Mary Jane Kelly
A window was removed to allow a photographer inside.
Mary Ann Cox heard someone leave the court at 6:15 A.M.

Harrison, Shirley, ed. *The Diary of Jack the Ripper.* Smith-Gryphon, 1993.

There can be few people who haven't heard of the diary that purports to be written by James Maybrick, a Liverpool merchant who confesses that he was Jack the Ripper. The book is a valuable addition to any Ripper library because it contains a facsimile of the diary itself along with a transcript for those who find reading the original somewhat difficult. Well illustrated and fully indexed.

Hayne, W. J. *Jack the Ripper or the Crimes of London.* Utility Book and Novel Company, 1889.

Hinton, Bob. *From Hell . . . The Jack the Ripper Mystery.* Old Bakehouse Publications, 1998.

A brilliant book that uses good old-fashioned logic to look at the crimes. Discounts such nonsense as conspiracy theories and looks at the evidence of the time. Deduces that the Ripper was George Hutchinson. Includes a few illustrations of the area as it was when the book was written. One map of the general location. Indexed. Highly recommended.

Howells, Martin, and Keith Skinner. *The Ripper Legacy: The Life and Death of Jack the Ripper.* Sidgwick and Jackson, 1987; Sphere Books edition, 1988.

Fanciful work that claims Montague John Druitt was the killer. One illustration (the Lusk kidney letter) but no maps. The book did provide new information but contains the following errors:

Mary Ann Nichols
Mary Ann absconded with 3 pounds of her employers' money.
No mention of Charles Cross and Robert Paul finding the body.
Elizabeth Stride
Elizabeth's maiden name given as Gustisson.
Catherine Eddowes
Narrative implies that Church Passage is 50 yards from Mitre Square.
Narrative claims that the killer cut off Catherine's right ear.
Mary Jane Kelly
The window was just to the left of the door.
Mary's nose, breasts, and ears were placed on the bedside table.
Mary's left arm was attached by skin only.
Mary's head was attached by skin only.
Mary was three months pregnant.

Hudson, Samuel. *Leather Apron, or the Horrors of Whitechapel.* Town Printing House (United States), 1888.

Jakubowski, Maxim, and Nathan Braund, eds. *The Mammoth Book of Jack the Ripper.* Robinson Publishing, 1999; Carroll and Graf, 1999.

A most useful book. Includes a chronology, the stories of the five canonical victims, and contributions from 16 authors giving their own "solutions" to the crimes. No illustrations but indexed. Recommended.

Jinko, Katsuo. *Terror in London—on Jack the Ripper and His Time.* (Japan) 1981.

Jones, Elwyn, and John Lloyd. *The Ripper File.* Arthur Barker, 1975; Futura edition, 1975.

Book intended to back up a television series that involved the fictional Z-Cars and Softly Softly detectives Barlow and Watt investigating the murders.

Kelly, Alexander. *Jack the Ripper: A Bibliography and Review of the Literature.* Association of Assistant Librarians, 1972; revised 1984, 1994, and 1995.

A masterpiece listing hundreds of sources. Essential to any library on the subject.

Knight, Stephen. *Jack the Ripper: The Final Solution.* Harrap, 1976; Panther edition, 1981; Treasure Press edition, 1984.

Illustrated and indexed. The first book to suggest the Masonic Conspiracy theory.

Locksley, John de. *The Enigma of Jack the Ripper.* Privately published, 1994.

A book with little to recommend it.

———. *Jack the Ripper Unveiled.* Privately published, 1994.

Another with little to recommend it.

———. *A Ramble with Jack the Ripper.* Privately published, 1996.

Suggests that the most likely suspect is George Chapman.

Marx, Roland. *Jack l'Eventreur et les Fantasmes Victoriens.* Editions Complexe (Belgium), 1987.

Matters, Leonard W. *The Mystery of Jack the Ripper.* Hutchinson, 1928; Arrow edition, 1964.

The first full-length English-language treatise on the case. Contains some errors that are forgivable because Matters was largely relying on secondary sources. Concludes that the killer was Dr. Stanley.

McCormick, Donald. *The Identity of Jack the Ripper.* Jarrolds, 1959; Pan edition, 1962; John Long edition, 1970.

Suggests that the murders were committed by Dr. Alexander Pedachenko as part of a czarist plot, but the entire theory is based on highly questionable documents that have not been traced by any other researcher.

Menard, Peter. *Certain Connections or Affinities with Jack the Ripper.* Nimmo, 1903.

Morrison, John. *Jimmy Kelly's Year of the Ripper Murders, 1888.* Privately published, 1983.

Booklet consisting largely of newspaper clippings of the time and photographs. It concludes that James Kelly was the murderer; hence the title.

Muusmann, Carl. *Hvem var Jack the Ripper?* (Who was Jack the Ripper?) Hermann-Petersen (Denmark), 1908.

The first book ever to suggest a name for Jack the Ripper. The conclusion is that Alois Szemeredy was the killer.

Neil, Charles, ed. *World's Greatest Mysteries—Jack the Ripper and Life in Atmospheria.* Charles Neil Publishing (Australia), 1936.

Odell, Robin. *Jack the Ripper in Fact and Fiction.* Harrap, 1965; Mayflower edition, 1966.

A very well-researched book that gives an excellent account of the murders. Does not name a specific suspect but claims that Jack was a Jewish slaughterman.

O'Donnell, Kevin. *The Jack the Ripper Whitechapel Murders* (based on the research of Andy and Sue Parlour). Ten Bells Publishing, 1997.

Highly illustrated and covering the canonical five murders. Includes a good deal of new information. Examines the main suspects well but then reverts to the hoary old theory of a Royal Conspiracy involving James Kenneth Stephen, Montague John Druitt, and others and assumes that Mary Jane Kelly was not the victim in Miller's Court. Part of the "evidence" for this theory is the supposition that the sites of the murders of Mary Ann Nichols, Annie Chapman, Elizabeth Stride, and Catherine Eddowes form an arrow that apparently pointed directly to the Houses of Parliament, thus proving a political conspiracy.

To begin with, this notion shows a misunderstanding of the basic laws of geometry. Any four points can form the four vertices of a quadrilateral, and any quadrilateral has two diagonals. If two sides and one diagonal are omitted from the drawing, then an arrow shape will be formed by the other lines. As for the "fact" that this arrow pointed to Parliament, I am sure that an accurate plotting would show that it missed that particular building. However, the same arrow also pointed to no fewer than three railway stations: Waterloo, Waterloo East, and Cannon Street. Surely this is proof that Jack the Ripper worked on the railways!

Paley, Bruce. *Jack the Ripper: The Simple Truth*. Headline, 1995.

Some good illustrations and an excellent, if rather overdetailed, map of the area. Suggests Joseph Barnett as the killer and gives much more information about him than others who name him as Jack. Some excellent historical detail. Indexed. The following errors are noted:

Mary Ann Nichols
Dr. Llewellyn said a very sharp knife was used.
Dr. Llewellyn believed the Ripper stood in front of his victim.
Annie Chapman
The house at 29 Hanbury Street was the home of 15 people.
Elizabeth Stride
Elizabeth had a bunch of flowers pinned to her dress.
Elizabeth had been living at 38 Dorset Street with Michael Kidney.
Catherine Eddowes
Catherine was one of 12 children.
Two other people saw Catherine after Joseph Lawende and his companions saw her.
Mitre Square was well lit with five lamps.
Mary Jane Kelly
A window frame was removed so that pictures could be taken.
Mary Ann Cox heard someone leave the court at 6:15 A.M.

Palmer, Scott. *Jack the Ripper: A Reference Guide*. Scarecrow Press, Inc. (United States), 1996.

We continue to await the first well-researched book on the subject from the United States.

Patterson, Richard. *Paradox: Upon Jack the Ripper, Poetry, and Francis Joseph Thompson*. Privately published (Australia), 1999.

Suggests yet another new suspect, the poet Francis Thompson.

Plimmer, John F. *In the Footsteps of the Whitechapel Murders*. The Book Guild, 1998.

A good idea spoiled by appallingly bad research. The book is a review of the five murders and seeks to apply modern investigative techniques to them. Covers a few of the main suspects. Some illustrations. No index. Among the many errors noted are:

Mary Ann Nichols
Charles Cross's first name given as George.
Robert Paul's first name given as John.
Barber's slaughter yard positioned opposite where the body was found.
Cross and Paul ran off toward the nearest police station.
Cross and Paul returned with Constable Mizen.
Dr. Llewellyn found a wine glass at the scene and handed it to the police. (This is a ludicrous statement. Any reading, even of contemporary reports, will show that the doctor claimed that the amount of blood he found in the gutter amounted to a wine glass and a half of blood. No other writer has suggested that the Ripper took a glass with him in order to measure it out!)
Ellen Holland saw Mary Ann at 2:30 A.M., one hour before the murder. This gets the time of the meeting and of the murder wrong.
Ellen saw Mary on the corner of Osborn Street and Brick Lane.
The whereabouts of Mary's father were not known.
Annie Chapman
The victim's name was Annie May Chapman.
Annie's husband was named Fred.
Annie had two children.
Implies Bayley's was opposite 29 Hanbury Street.
One of Annie's kidneys had been removed.
Brass rings and coins were placed at Annie's feet.
Elizabeth Stride
Elizabeth held grapes in her left hand.
Elizabeth met Michael Kidney early in 1888.
Catherine Eddowes
Catherine and Thomas Conway lived in the Thrawl Street area.
Bloodstained water was found in a sink in Dorset Street.
Part of Catherine's right ear was missing, implying that it was never found.
Mary Jane Kelly
Thomas Bowyer noticed the broken window as he turned to leave.
Mary's liver lay on her right thigh.

Inspector Abberline and Superintendent Arnold had to leave the room to be physically sick.

Mary's breasts, heart, and kidneys lay on a table.

Entry to the room was forced within an hour of the discovery of the body.

Mary Ann Cox was awakened by someone leaving the court at 6:15 A.M.

Raper, Michell. *Who Was Jack the Ripper?* Tabaret Press, 1975.

Richards, A. J., ed. *Ripper Roundup.* 1996.

Robinson, Tom. *The Whitechapel Horrors, Being an Authentic Account of the Jack the Ripper Murders.* Daisy Bank Publishing, 1924.

Rogers, Brian, ed. *Reflections on the Ripper: Four Accounts of the Whitechapel Murders.* Privately printed, 1999.

A short booklet covering four accounts of the crimes.

Rumbelow, Donald. *The Complete Jack the Ripper.* W. H. Allen, 1975; Penguin edition 1988.

Covers the five canonical murders and some of the main suspects in detail. Contains a few good illustrations and an index. It contains the following errors:

Mary Ann Nichols

Charles Cross's first name given as George.

Robert Paul's first name given as John.

Mary Ann was born in 1851.

Mary Ann married at the age of 12.

Annie Chapman

John Davis's mother ran the packing-case business from number 29 Hanbury Street.

Two rings and some coins were placed at Annie's feet.

Elizabeth Stride

Elizabeth's hands were folded underneath her.

Elizabeth had red-and-white flowers pinned to her dress.

Narrative implies that Dr. Phillips was the first to examine the body.

Elizabeth had been living with Michael Kidney in Fashion Street.

Catherine Eddowes

Bloodstained water was found in a sink in Dorset Street.

Suggests that Catherine was killed in one of the empty houses and then dragged out to where her body was found.

Mary Jane Kelly

Mary was three months pregnant.

Mary was in arrears on her rent to the tune of 35 shillings.

One of the windows was removed so that photographs could be taken.

Narrative makes the assumption that John McCarthy ran a vice ring from Miller's Court.

Mary Ann Cox heard someone leave the court at 6:15 A.M.

Ryder, Stephen, ed. *The First Fifty Years of Jack the Ripper* (two volumes). Ripperological Preservation Society (United States), 1998.

Reprints of various sources and articles.

Sharkey, Terence. *Jack the Ripper: 100 Years of Investigation.* Ward Lock, 1987.

Covers the main suspects and theories up to the date of publication.

Shelden, Neil. *Jack the Ripper and His Victims.* Privately published, 1999.

An interesting pamphlet-type book that gives a good deal of accurate background information on the five canonical victims. Indexed. Some modern-day illustrations.

Smithkey, John, ed. *Jack the Ripper: The Inquest of the Final Victim, Mary Kelly.* Key Publications (United States), 1998.

Facsimiles of the testimony and statements.

Spiering, Frank. *Prince Jack: The True Story of Jack the Ripper.* Doubleday (United States), 1978.

Yet another book suggesting that the royal family was involved, this time placing responsibility for the crimes on the shoulders of Prince Albert Victor. Includes "evidence" from notes supposedly found in the New York Academy of Medicine but which that establishment has failed to find any trace of.

Stewart, William. *Jack the Ripper: A New Theory.* Quality Press, 1939.

Should really be called *Jill the Ripper* because it proposes that a midwife or abortionist was the killer. This theory was originally based on reports that Mary Jane Kelly was about three months pregnant when she died. Medical reports found since this book was published show that Kelly was not pregnant, so this entire theory fails.

Strachan, Ross. *Jack the Ripper: A Collector's Guide.* Privately published, 1996.

———. *The Jack the Ripper Handbook—A Reader's Companion.* Privately printed, 1999.

Covers all the books, magazines, and other print sources that carry accounts of the crimes. Some illustrations of early and hard-to-find books. No index but nevertheless a most valuable work.

Sugden, Philip. *The Complete History of Jack the Ripper.* Robinson Publishing, 1994.

A first-class work that covers all the murders and a number of the main suspects. Though the author does not "name" the Ripper, he concludes that the best candidate is probably George Chapman, a.k.a. Severin Klosowski. Some good illustrations and maps of the sites. Indexed. Highly recommended.

———. *The Life and Times of Jack the Ripper.* Sienna/Parragon 1996.

Thomas, Lars. *Mysteriet om Jack the Ripper* (The mystery of Jack the Ripper). Gyldendal (Denmark), 1990.

Trow, M. J. *The Many Faces of Jack the Ripper.* Summersdale Publishers, 1997.

Some good historical background on Whitechapel of the time. Covers the five canonical murders and discusses quite a few of the suspects. Indexed and well illustrated. A first-class work

Tully, James. *The Secret of Prisoner 1167: Was This Man Jack the Ripper?* Robinson, 1997.

Puts forward James Kelly as the Ripper. A very well-researched work with some illustrations, some excellent maps, and an index.

Turnbull, Peter. *The Killer Who Never Was.* Clark, Lawrence, 1996.

A book that unfortunately seems to rely entirely on unreliable and inaccurate press reports of the crimes. Suggests that there was more than one killer but does not name them.

Underwood, Peter. *Jack the Ripper: One Hundred Years of Mystery.* Blandford Press, 1987; paperback edition by Javelin Books, 1988.

Contains a map of the area and covers the five canonical murders. Contains illustrations of some sites as they were when the book was written and other illustrations such as three mortuary pictures of victims. Does not really push forward any single candidate but covers the main suspects known at the time and concludes that the most likely is Joseph Barnett. Indexed. The book is loaded with inaccuracies, including:

Mary Ann Nichols

The description of the murder bears no relationship to the known facts.

Charles Cross's first name given as George.

The location of the body given as opposite Barber's slaughter yard.

Robert Paul's first name given as John.

Paul and Cross described as friends.

Paul and Cross set off toward the nearest police station.

Constable Thain's name given as Haine.

Paul and Cross accompanied Constable Jonas Mizen back to Buck's Row.

The name of Walter Purkiss, the man who lived in Essex Wharf, given as Walter King.

Annie Chapman

Inspector Chandler turned into Hanbury Street and saw men running toward him.

Chandler's first thought was that the woman was drunk.

Two rings, a few pennies, and some farthings were laid out at Annie's feet.

The envelope was postmarked 20 August.

A total of 16 people lived at 29 Hanbury Street.

Elizabeth Stride

Elizabeth had three children.

Elizabeth and Michael Kidney met in early 1888.

Elizabeth held some grapes in her left hand.

Fanny Mortimer's statement and evidence expanded into fancy, including the claim that she heard the sound of an argument, a

stifled cry, and a bump. Narrative also implies that the man with the shiny black bag was directly connected with this invented contretemps.
Dr. Blackwell stated that Elizabeth's throat had been cut from right to left.
Catherine Eddowes
Catherine was also known by the surname Thrawl.
Catherine was also known as Emily Birrell.
Catherine was 43 years old.
The name of George Morris, the watchman in Mitre Square, given as Herbert Morris.
Catherine's ovaries were removed.
The apron had not been in the spot where it was found five minutes earlier.
Mary Jane Kelly
Mary was three months pregnant.
Mary and Joseph Barnett met the night before they moved to Miller's Court.
Thomas Bowyer noticed the broken window as he went to leave.
Mary's liver lay on her right thigh.
Mary's breasts, heart, and kidneys were on the table.
Parts of Mary's body hung from picture nails about the room.
Nothing had been taken away from the body.
Mary Ann Cox heard a man leave the court at 6:15 A.M.
The funeral took place on 18 November.

Wallace, Richard. *Jack the Ripper: "Light-Hearted Friend."* Gemini Press (United States), 1997.

Seriously tries to suggest that Charles Lutwidge Dodgson, a.k.a. Lewis Carroll, was the Ripper. No useful illustrations. Indexed. Among the errors noted are:

Mary Ann Nichols
Mary Ann's age given as 42.
The current name of Buck's Row given as Durwood Street.
Charles Cross's first name given as George.
Robert Paul's first name given as John.
Constable John Neil named as the officer that Cross and Paul found.
The doctor sent for the ambulance.
Annie Chapman
Annie had two children.
Annie was seen with a foreign-looking gentleman outside 29 Hanbury Street at 2 A.M.
Annie's head almost came off when her neckerchief was removed.
Elizabeth Stride
Narrative implies that only Dr. Phillips examined the body.
Elizabeth lived with Michael Kidney in Fashion Street.
Catherine Eddowes
Mitre Square is half a mile east of Berner Street.
Catherine's body was found at 1:30 A.M.
There was a sink close to the graffito, and it was wet with blood.
The mutilations were not inflicted by the killer when he was kneeling on her right side.
Mary Jane Kelly
Thomas Bowyer's name given as Boyer
The name of Miller's Court given as Miller Court.
Mary owed 35 shillings for rent.
The window was removed to get a better view of the room.
Mary's left arm was almost severed from her body.
Mary's breasts were on the table by the window.
Mary's murder followed the only murder (that of Catherine Eddowes) in which the killer throttled his victim.

Whittington-Egan, Richard. *A Casebook on Jack the Ripper.* Wildy and Sons, 1976; Patterson Smith edition, 1997.

An excellent work that does not seek to favor any particular candidate but simply reviews the facts of each case. This book was the first to cast doubts on some long-held beliefs, such as the notion that coins were left at Annie Chapman's feet. Highly recommended.

———. *The Identity of Jack the Ripper.* 1973.

Small booklet reprint that suggests that the two most likely candidates are Dr. Alexander Pedachenko and Montague John Druitt.

Wilding, John. *Jack the Ripper Revealed.* Constable and Company, 1993.

Some good maps and illustrations. Indexed. Suggests that the Ripper crimes were committed by Montague Druitt and James Kenneth Stephen as part of a royal conspiracy. Includes such "evidence" as the fact that the Goulston Street graffito is an anagram of "F. G. Abberline now hate M. J. Druitt. He sent the woman to Hell." However, I have found another anagram, which might be more suitable: "Abberline: Note the fellow M. J. Druitt then Hogwash meant."

The book contains the following errors:

Mary Ann Nichols
Constable Neil hailed a colleague. He signaled with his lamp.
Annie Chapman
Several bright coins were placed at Annie's feet.
An apron was found partially submerged in a dish of water.
Elizabeth Stride
A corsage of flowers was pinned to Elizabeth's breast.
Catherine Eddowes
Catherine did not have a regular doss house to go to.
Bloodstained water was found in a sink in Dorset Street.
Mary Jane Kelly
Mary's rent arrears were 35 shillings.

Wilson, Colin, and Robin Odell. *Jack the Ripper: Summing Up and Verdict.* Bantam Press, 1987; subsequent Corgi editions commencing in 1988.

Few illustrations in the body of the text but a separate section with a few relevant pictures. Covers many of the important suspects of the day without finally naming a favorite. Includes a good bibliography and an index. The book contains the following errors:

Mary Ann Nichols
Charles Cross's first name given as George.
Robert Paul's first name given as John.
Mary Ann was last seen at 3:45 A.M., struggling down Whitechapel Road. A good trick because her body had been found by Cross and Paul five minutes earlier.
The name of Walter Purkiss, the man who lived at Essex Wharf, given as Walter King.
"Mr. King" slept on the first floor.
Annie Chapman
Inspector Chandler cleared people out of the yard.
The police found two rings, some pennies, and some farthings at Annie's feet.
Annie's intestines were placed on her left shoulder.
Sergeant William Thick's name given as John.
Elizabeth Stride
Elizabeth had nine children.
Elizabeth lived at 35 Dorset Street with Michael Kidney.
Dr. Blackwell was unable to say whether Elizabeth had been standing or lying down when her throat was cut.
Catherine Eddowes
Inspector Collard arrived with Dr. Brown.
Catherine had been released from police custody shortly after midnight.
Bloodstained water was found in a sink in Dorset Street.
Mary Jane Kelly
Mary owed 35 shillings in rent.
A window was removed so that photographs could be taken.
Mary Ann Cox heard someone leaving the court at 6:15 A.M.
The funeral took place on 18 November.

Wolf, A. P. *Jack the Myth: A New Look at the Ripper.* Robert Hale, 1993.

Suggests that the crimes were committed by Thomas Hayne Cutbush, except for the murder of Elizabeth Stride, which is attributed to Michael Kidney.

Wolf, Camille, ed. *Who Was Jack the Ripper?* Grey House Books, 1995.

A collection of theories from no fewer than 53 authors. An excellent book with a few illustrations. Has a picture of each author.

Woodhall, Edwin Thomas. *Jack the Ripper or When London Walked in Terror.* Mellifont Press, 1938.

Suggests Olga Tchkersoff as the Ripper, which is about all that needs to be said.

Wright, Stephen. *Jack the Ripper—An American View.* Mystery, 1999.

Another work suggesting that George Hutchinson was the killer.

Films

Amazon Women on the Moon. 1985. Starring Rosanna Arquette, Ralph Bellamy, Carrie Fisher, Steve Guttenberg, Michelle Pfeiffer, and Henry Silva.

A sci-fi parody of comic sketches. Little to recommend it.

Black the Ripper. 1975. Starring Hugh van Patten, Bole Nikoli, and Renata Harmon.

Bridge across Time. 1985. Starring David Hasselhoff, Stephanie Kramer, Clu Gulager, and Adrienne Barbeau.

Jack is reincarnated and begins killing again after a brick is brought from Britain to Arizona and placed in London Bridge. This apparently occurs because the Ripper was shot by the British police on the bridge back in 1888. Well, the United States bought the bridge, but don't buy this. Pure nonsense.

Die Buchse der Pandora (Pandora's box). 1929. Starring Louise Brooks, Fritz Kortner, Franz Lederer, and Gustav Diessl.

A woman kills her lover and then becomes a prostitute on the streets of Whitechapel. She is finally murdered herself, by the Ripper.

Dr. Jekyll and Sister Hyde. 1971. Starring Ralph Bates, Martine Beswick, and Gerald Sim.

Again not really a Ripper film; the Whitechapel crimes are nothing more than a subplot.

Die Dreigroschenoper (The threepenny opera). 1930.

Die Dreigroschenoper (The threepenny opera). 1963. Starring Sammy Davis Junior, Curt Jurgens, Gert Frobe, and Lino Ventura.

Edge of Sanity. 1989. Starring Anthony Perkins, Glynis Barber, David Lodge, Ben Cole, and Jill Melford.

Mixing Robert Louis Stevenson with the Ripper story results in a tale in which Dr. Jekyll becomes Jack the Ripper under the influence of drugs. The film is best seen while under the influence of anaesthetic.

Farmer Spudd and His Missus Take a Trip to Town. 1915.

Not really a Ripper film as such. The Spudd family merely encounters a waxwork of the killer on a visit to Madame Tussaud's.

From beyond the Grave. 1973. Starring David Warner, Donald Pleasence, Ian Bannen, Diana Dors, Margaret Leighton, Ian Carmichael, Nyree Down Porter, and Ian Ogilvy.

Based in an East End antiques shop whose owner involves his potential customers in horrific tales. One of these involves the Ripper.

The Groove Room. 1973. Starring Diana Dors.

Apparently a pornographic film that involves the Ripper. At least he isn't a Mason.

Hands of the Ripper. 1971. Starring Angharad Rees, Eric Porter, Dora Bryan, Jane Merrow, and Derek Godfrey.

Not really a story about Jack. He murders his wife in full view of his small daughter, and she, in turn, grows up to be a repressed murderess.

Here Come the Girls. 1953. Starring Bob Hope, Rosemary Clooney, Tony Martin, Arlene Dahl, Fred Clark, and Robert Strauss.

Bob Hope tries to keep one step ahead of a murderer called Jack the Slasher. A decent and amusing musical, but not one for Ripper aficionados.

El Hombre sin Rostro (The man with no face). 1950.

Jack el Destripador de Londres (Jack the London Ripper). 1971. Starring Paul Naschy.

Jack the Ripper. 1958. Starring Ewen Solon, Lee Patterson, Eddie Byrne, Betty McDowell, and John Le Mesurier.

The case is cracked by an American sleuth (surprise), and the Ripper dies when he is crushed by an elevator. Not a film troubled by a desire for historical accuracy.

Jack the Ripper. 1976. Starring Klaus Kinski and Josephine Chaplin.

Jack the Ripper. 1988. Starring Michael Caine, Armand Assante, Jane Seymour, and Ray McAnally.

Jack's Back. 1988. Starring James Spader and Cynthia Gibb.

And surprise again, it's all a Masonic plot.

A Knife for the Ladies. 1973. Starring Jack Elam.

The Lodger. 1926. Starring Ivor Novello, Arthur Chesney, and Malcolm Keen.

The first film in which the Ripper is a mysterious lodger.

The Lodger. 1932. Starring Ivor Novello, Elizabeth Allan, Jack Hawkins, Barbara Everest, and Peter Gawthorne.

Similar story to the 1926 film, but this time with sound. Also known as *The Phantom Fiend*.

The Lodger. 1944. Starring Laird Cregar, Merle Oberon, George Sanders, Cedric Hardwicke, Sara Allgood, Aubrey Mather, Queenie Leonard, Helena Pickard, Lumsden Hare, and Frederick Worlock.

Another remake of the 1926 classic.

Lulu. 1962. Starring Nadja Tiller and Mario Adorf.

The story of an attractive woman stalked and killed by the Ripper. Remake of the 1929 film. Also known as *No Orchids for Lulu*.

Lulu (France). 1978. Starring Danielle Lebrun and Michel Piccoli.

Lulu (United States). 1978. Starring Elisa Lonelli and Paul Shenar.

Lulu. 1980. Starring Ann Bennent and Udo Kier.

Man in the Attic. 1954. Starring Jack Palance, Constance Smith, Byron Palmer, Frances Bavier, and Rhys Williams.

The story of the lodger again, but Palance's performance is absolutely haunting; he is a most convincing Ripper.

Murder by Decree. 1979. Starring Christopher Plummer, James Mason, Anthony Quayle, David Hemmings, Susan Clark, John Gielgud, Donald Sutherland, Frank Finlay, and Genevieve Bujold.

Sherlock Holmes pits his wits against Jack the Ripper again and, surprise, surprise, finds that it is all a Masonic conspiracy.

Night after Night. 1969. Starring Justine Lord and Jack May.

No Orchids for Lulu. 1967.

Le Nosferat (The Nosferat). 1974.

The Ripper. 1986. Starring Tom Savini.

The Ripper. 1997. Starring Patrick Bergin, Gabrielle Anwar, Michael York, Samuel West, and Adam Cooper.

A Victorian detective comes to the conclusion that the Ripper is none other than Prince Albert Victor. Total drivel with hardly a single accurate detail throughout. Ripper purists should treat it as a comedy.

Room to Let. 1950. Starring Valentine Dyall.

The Ripper is in an asylum, but he is one of the doctors.

The Ruling Class. 1972. Starring Peter O'Toole, Harry Andrews, Arthur Lowe, Alastair Sim, Coral Browne, and Michael Bryant.

An earl's mad son, Jack, succeeds to his father's title.

A Study in Terror. 1965. Starring John Neville, Donald Houston, John Fraser, Robert Morley, Anthony Quayle, and Barbara Windsor.

Sherlock Holmes chases Jack the Ripper.

Terror in the Wax Museum. 1973. Starring Ray Milland, Broderick Crawford, Elsa Lanchester, Louis Hayward, John Carradine, Shani Wallis, Maurice Evans, and Patric Knowles.

Set in Victorian London, where the owner of the museum is murdered.

Time after Time. 1979. Starring Malcolm McDowell, David Warner,

Mary Steenburgen, Charles Cioffi, and Kent Williams.

Jack escapes from London in 1888 by means of the time machine built by H. G. Wells. He is chased by Wells, who eventually triumphs.

Das Ungeheuer von London City (The London killer). 1964.

Das Wachsfigurenkabinett (The waxwork cabinet). 1924.

Summary

A lot of books on the market seem not to rely on researching the stories from the Home Office and Scotland Yard files held in the Public Record Office; otherwise common mistakes, such as giving the name of one of the first witnesses as George Cross, would not be perpetuated. This lack of accuracy is understandable in books written before the files were opened to the public but unforgivable in any book written after 1976.

There also seems to be a dearth of accurate films on the subject. Although it may be acceptable to say that the first duty of a film is to entertain, most, if not all, of the films made thus far seem to favor a particular solution and then to tell the story with little or no regard for historical fact. Perhaps the time has come for a documentary film that does not favor a pet theory but simply tells the story, names the witnesses correctly, and does not include events that never took place.

13

Resources

Home Office Files [Held in the Public Record Office, Kew]

Most of the relevant information is in two files: HO 144 220 and HO 144 221.

HO 144 220

The file is divided into three folios:

- A49301.A—The suspects file, which includes letters, clippings, and other materials regarding, for example, John Langan, John Davidson, and Sergeant William Thick.
- A49301.B—A file concerning the offer of a reward for information leading to the capture of the killer.
- A49301.C—A file concerning the police investigations into the murders.

HO 144 221

Again, the file is subdivided:

- A49301.D—Foreign Office documents concerning information from abroad.
- A49301.E—Bloodhounds file.
- A49301.F—Very small file consisting of a letter from Sir Charles Warren to the civil servant Godfrey Lushington about the Mary Jane Kelly murder.
- A49301.G—Records of payments to and for officers brought in from other divisions to boost the local force.
- A49301.H—Concerning the murder of Rose Mylett.
- A49301.I—Concerning the murder of Alice McKenzie.
- A49301.J—This file does not exist.
- A49301.K—Concerning the Pinchin Street murder.

Internet Sites

www.casebook.org

An absolutely brilliant site with sections on the murders, suspects, documents, and other details. It even includes a chat room. Certainly worth a visit.

www.historybuff.com/library/refripper.html

A small site that reproduces some original newspaper reports, mainly from the *Times.*

www.jacktheripper.purespace.de

Titled "Jack the Ripper's Dungeon," this site appears to concentrate on the theory that Maybrick was the killer. An interesting site with some inaccuracies.

www.jack-the-ripper-walk.co.uk

Interesting site. Booking is required but can be done by e-mail from the site. The walk lasts about two hours.

www.ripper.wildnet.co.uk/main.htm

No-frames version of the Casebook site.

www.talkingtour.co.uk

A very good idea for those who wish to walk in the Ripper's footsteps, but at their own pace. There are four walks in the series, of which the Ripper walk is one. You are provided with a cassette tape that was written and narrated by Ripper expert Martin Fido.

www.walks.com/ripper.html

This long-established company has many other London walks available. One of the guides on this particular tour is Ripper expert Donald Rumbelow. The walk lasts two hours and includes a visit to the Ten Bells public house. No prior booking required. This company now has a site dedicated to the Ripper walk that can be found at www.jacktheripperwalk.com

Other sites may be found by using any reliable search engine and entering words such as *Ripper, Whitechapel, murder,* or the names of any of the victims.

Other Records

The London Hospital holds copies of the maps of Mitre Square drawn by Frederick Foster, the city surveyor, and showing the location of Catherine Eddowes's body as well as drawings of her injuries produced by Dr. Frederick Gordon Brown. It also has a copy of the "From Hell" letter that accompanied the Lusk kidney and the letter sent to Dr. Thomas Horrocks Openshaw two weeks later.

Other London resources include:

- Corporation of London Records Office—Guildhall—Coroner's Inquest Number 135, 1888—Catherine Eddowes.
- Greater London Record Office—MJ/SPC NE 1888—Mary Jane Kelly inquest.
- H12/CH/B2/2—Colney Hatch Lunatic Asylum, male admissions register, 1888–1906.

Scotland Yard Files [Held in the Public Record Office, Kew]

There are three main files: MEPO 3 140, MEPO 3 141, and MEPO 3 142.

MEPO 3 140

A very important file containing reports, statements, and other records of the murders. Some documents have been stolen by people whose idea of research is to thieve, but the following reports remain:

1. Martha Tabram
2. Mary Ann Nichols
3. Elizabeth Stride
4. Catherine Eddowes—only a photograph of the victim
5. Mary Jane Kelly
6. Rose Mylett
7. Pinchin Street Torso
8. Frances Coles

MEPO 3 141

A file of letters from those involved in the investigation. Among the more useful are a police report of an interview with Joseph Barnett and, of course, the Macnaghten Memoranda.

MEPO 3 142

A file of letters purporting to come from the killer, it includes all the letters that appear in this book except the Lusk kidney letter and the Openshaw letter. Many of the communications are obvious hoaxes.

In addition to these three files, other files contain documents relating to the crimes. These include MEPO 2 227, which mentions the police reinforcements after the Pinchin Street Torso was found.

Newspaper Reports of the Time

The following passages are excerpts from the articles cited and have been chosen to give a taste of the atmosphere of the East End of the time.

Eastern Post and City Chronicle—14 April 1888

Malvina Haynes, who received very serious injuries to her head and scalp on the night of the Bank Holiday, has been from that time until Tuesday lying quite unconscious at the London Hospital, no sounds but moans having escaped her lips. The sufferer has been under the care of Mr George E. Haslip, the house surgeon, and yesterday the patient, upon regaining consciousness was only able to briefly relate the circumstances of the outrage. On many points her memory is an entire blank and when questioned as to what her assailant was like, she replied, "I cannot remember, my mind is gone." The hospital authorities at once communicated with Detective Sergeant William New, who has charge of the case, and certain information which casually passed from the woman's lips may perhaps lead to a clue respecting the would-be murderer. Mr Haynes, the husband, who is a hard-working house painter, living at 29 Newnham Street, Great Alie Street, Whitechapel, has expressed his deep sense of unremitting skill and kindness his wife has received from the surgical and nursing staff at the hospital, and from a statement which he has made it appears that his wife, himself, and some friends spent the Bank Holiday together by seeing some of the sights of the Metropolis, and in the evening Mrs Haynes returned with them to her home. She went out later on, and screams were shortly heard in the vicinity of Leman Street Railway Station. A constable then discovered Mrs Haynes lying insensible on the ground in a pool of blood. Besides her brain being affected by the injury, Mrs Haynes is suffering from a scalp wound of rather an extensive character. A man who was said to have been near the unfortunate woman at the time of the occurrence, and who resided in the district, has since left the neighbourhood. The police hope that he may come forward, as his testimony might aid the ends of justice, by relating what he saw of the outrage.

The *Times*—14 September 1888

The *Lancet* says: The theory that the succession of murders which have lately been committed in Whitechapel are the work of a lunatic appears to us to be by no means at present well established. We can quite understand the necessity for any murderer endeavouring to obliterate by the death of his victim his future identification as a burglar. Moreover, as far as we are aware, homicidal mania is generally characterised by the one single and fatal act, although we grant this may have been led up to by a deep-rooted series of delusions. It is most unusual for a lunatic to plan any complicated crime of this kind. Neither, as a rule, does a lunatic take precautions to escape from the consequences of his act; which data are the most conspicuous in these now too celebrated cases.

East London Advertiser—15 September 1888

With all our boasted civilisation and increase of educational facilities, the morbid tastes of the poor still come to the front; or we should not hear of hundreds of persons paying a penny each to view the back-yard of the house in Hanbury Street where the poor unfortunate woman, Annie Chapman, was hacked to pieces.

The police, it is true, stopped the exhibition, but not before a considerable sum had been netted by those in charge of the house. If the police had taken possession, as they should have done, such a scandal could not have been enacted.

The *Times*—15 September 1888

The police at the Commercial Street Police Station have made another arrest on suspicion in connection with the recent murders. It appears that amongst the numerous statements and descriptions of suspected persons are several tallying with that of the man in custody but beyond this the police know nothing at present about him. His apprehension was of a singular character. Throughout yesterday his movements are stated to have created suspicion amongst various persons, and last night he was handed over to a uniformed constable doing duty in the neighbourhood of Flower and Dean Street on suspicion in connection with the crime. On his arrival at the police station in Commercial Street the detective officers and Mr Abberline were communicated with, and an inquiry concerning him was at once opened. On being searched perhaps one of the most extraordinary accumulation of articles were discovered—a heap of rags, comprising pieces of dress fabrics, old and dirty linen, two purses of a kind usually used by women, two or three pocket handkerchiefs, one a comparatively clean one, and a white one with a red spotted border; two small tin boxes, a small cardboard box, a small leather strap, which might serve the purpose of a garterstring, and one spring onion. The person to whom this curious assortment belongs is slightly built, about 5ft 7in or 5ft 8in in height, and dressed shabbily. He has a very careworn look. Covering a head of hair, inclined somewhat to be sandy, with beard and moustache to match, was a cloth skull cap, which did not improve his appearance. Suspicion is the sole motive for his temporary detection, for the police, although making every possible inquiry about him, do not believe his apprehension to be of any importance.

Regarding the man Pigott, who was captured at Gravesend, nothing whatever has been discovered by the detectives in the course of their inquiries which can in any way connect him with the crime or crimes, and his release, at all events from the custody of the police is expected shortly.

In connection with the arrest of a lunatic at Holloway, it appears that he has been missing from his friends for sometime now. The detectives have been very active in prosecuting their inquiries concerning him, and it is believed the result, so far, increases their suspicion. He is at present confined in the asylum at Grove Road, Bow.

All inquiries have failed to elicit anything as to the whereabouts of the missing pensioner who is wanted in connection with the recent murders.

East London Observer—15 September 1888

On Saturday in several quarters of East London the crowds who had assembled in the streets began to assume a very threatening attitude towards the Hebrew population of the district. It was repeatedly asserted that no Englishman could have perpetrated such a horrible crime as that of Hanbury Street, and that it must have been done by a Jew—and forthwith the crowds proceeded to threaten and abuse each of the unfortunate Hebrews they found in the streets.

Happily, the presence of the large number of police in the streets prevented a riot actually taking place. If the panic stricken people who cry "Down with the Jews" because they imagine that a Jew has committed the horrible and revolting crimes which have made Whitechapel a place to be dreaded know anything at all of the Jewish horror of blood itself, writes a correspondent, they would pause before they invoked destruction on the head of a peaceful and law abiding people. Since the return of Jews to England in 1649, only two Jews have been hanged for murder, Marks and Lipski, and taking into account the origin of many of the poor wretches who fly to this country from foreign persecution, this is a very remarkable record. That the beast who has made East London a terror is not a Jew I feel assured. There is something too horrible, too unnatural, too un-Jewish, I would say, in the terrible series of murders for an Israelite to be the monster.

There never was a Jew yet who could have steeped himself in such loathsome horrors as those to which publicity has been given. His nature revolts at blood-guiltness and the whole theory and practical working of the Whitechapel butchery are opposed to Jewish character.

The *Times*—17 September 1888

The detective officers continued their investigations yesterday, but up to a late hour last night no arrest had been made, neither is there any apparent prospect of an arrest being effected. The public of the neighbourhood continue to make statements, which are committed to writing at Commercial Street Station, and in several instances the police have been made cognisant of what the informants consider to be suspicious movements of individuals whose appearance is supposed to tally with that of the man wanted. Every "clue" given by the public in their zeal to assist the police has been followed up, but without success, and the lapse of time, it is feared, will lessen the chances of discovering the perpetrator of the crime.

The *Times*—18 September 1888

At Woolwich police court yesterday a labourer named Edward Quinn, aged 35, was placed in the dock before Mr Fenwick, charged nominally with being drunk at the police station. His face and hands were much bruised, and when charged he was much bloodstained. The magistrate was about disposing of the case briefly when the prisoner remarked that he had a complaint to make, and stated as follows—On Saturday, I was at a bar down by the arsenal in Woolwich having a drink. I had stumbled over something in the street just before, and had cut my face and knuckles as you see, and I had bled a good deal. While at the bar a big, tall man came in and stood beside me and looked at me. He got me in tow, and gave me some beer and tobacco, and then he said "I mean to charge you with the Whitechapel murders." I thought it was a joke and laughed, but he said he was serious, and pointed to the blood about me. I said "Nonsense, is that all the clue you have got?" He then dropped the subject and took me for a walk until we got to the police station where he charged me with the Whitechapel murders. Mr Fenwick—"Were you not drunk?" Quinn—"Certainly not, Sir." Mr Fenwick—"You will be remanded until tomorrow." Quinn—"This is rather rough. I am dragged a mile to the station and locked up, and now I am to wait another day with all this suspicion of murder hanging over my head." Mr Fenwick—"I will take your own bail in £5 for your reappearance." Quinn—"I object to the whole thing. Me murder a woman! I could not murder a cat." (Laughter) The prisoner was then released on his recognisance's.

Illustrated Police News—22 September 1888

The following facts which have just come to hand may furnish a clue by which the Hanbury Street murderer may be traced. On the day of the murder (the 8th instant) a man was seen in the lavatory of the City News Rooms, Ludgate Circus Buildings, changing his clothes. He departed hurriedly, leaving behind him a pair of trousers, a shirt, and a pair of socks. Unfortunately, no one connected with the establishment saw the man, or he would certainly have been stopped and questioned as to why he was changing his clothes there and leaving the old ones behind. Mr Walker, the proprietor of the News Rooms, states that he did not hear of the occurrence until late in the afternoon, when his attention was called to the clothes in the lavatory. He did not at the time attach any importance to the fact, and the clothes were thrown into the dust box and placed outside, being carted away in the City Sewers' cart on the Monday. On the following Tuesday, however, he received a visit from a man who represented himself to be a police officer and asked for the clothes which had been left there on the Saturday. Mr Walker replied that if he wanted them he would have to go to the Commissioners of the City Sewers, telling him at the same time what he had done with them. Two detectives called on Thursday, and had an interview with Mr Walker, and they succeeded in finding a man who saw the party changing his clothes in the lavatory, and he gave the police a description of him. He is described as a man of respectable appearance, about thirty years of age, and wearing a dark moustache; but the police are very reticent about the matter, and decline to give any information on the subject. They evidently attach some importance to the affair, as Mr Walker again received a visit from two detectives. The police are now trying to trace the clothes, as it is hoped they will furnish some clue to lead to the identity of the man whom they are searching for.

The *Times*—27 September 1888

No arrest has yet been made in connection with the murder of Jane Beetmoor at Birtley Fell on Saturday night, and until the police apprehend the murderer or discover his dead body, as some of them believe they will do, there is likely to be no abatement in the excitement which the murder has created in the district.

The action of the London authorities in sending Dr Phillips and Inspector Roots down to investigate the circumstances of the murder has unquestionably intensified the feeling among the public. The conclusion arrived at by Dr Phillips after his examination of the body has not yet been divulged, but there seems little doubt that the Birtley Fell murder is the work of a different hand from that of Annie Chapman, the only connection between the two probably being that the perpetrator of the former had attempted an imitation of the Whitechapel murders after brooding over the cruel details of how the bodies of the women Nichols and Chapman had been mutilated. It seems to be the strong conviction of the police that the murder has been committed by some local man, not by any stranger, and for the present they are practically concentrating their efforts on the discovery of the man Waddle, whose description has been widely circulated. Waddle is said to have been a steady man, but on Saturday he went to his lodgings the worse for drink—an unusual thing for him, and notwithstanding the discussion of his landlady, persisted in going out again. He has never been heard of in the locality since. What motive he could have for murdering the woman, whom he was courting, is a question much discussed in the neighbourhood of the crime and a statement has been made by one of the companions of Beetmoor that the latter had of late changed her mind with respect to Waddle, and had, in fact, been endeavouring to free herself from his attentions. It is fair to say, however, that beyond evidence of the disappearance of Waddle at the very time of the discovery of the murder, there is not as yet any real evidence to connect the man with the crime. The police have made a careful search around the scene of the murder for any weapon with which the crime may have been committed, but without result. The searching of the old pit shafts seems now to have been suspended, and for the present it is supposed that the police are following up certain rumours that have got about that Waddle has been seen in the neighbourhood. Many of these stories, it is needless to say, must of necessity be unfounded, for some of the places at which he is said to have been seen are in entirely contrary directions and very widely apart. Still, there is now a growing conviction that he has not committed suicide, as was at first supposed, but is still alive and in the neighbourhood; and if this be the case there should be little difficulty in effecting the capture of a man possessing such distinct personal characteristics as are attributed to Waddle.

The funeral of the deceased took place yesterday afternoon in the presence of enormous crowds of persons many of whom had travelled considerable distance. The coffin bore the plain inscription, "Jane Beetmoor. Died Sept 22, 1888." It was followed to the grave by a cortege fully half a mile long.

Note: William Waddell, to give the correct spelling of his surname, was arrested a few days later. Tried for murder, he was found guilty and executed at Durham on 18 December 1888. Before he died he made a full confession to the murder of Jane Beetmore (whose name was incorrectly given as Beetmor in the article).

The *Star*—1 October 1888

Information which may be important was given to the Leman Street police yesterday afternoon by an Hungarian concerning this murder. The foreigner was well dressed, and had the appearance of being in the theatrical line. He could not speak a word of English, but came to the police station accompanied by a friend, who acted as an interpreter. He gave his name and address, but the police have not disclosed them.

A *Star* man, however, got wind of his call, and ran him to earth in Backchurch Lane. The reporter's Hungarian was quite as imperfect as the foreigner's English, but an interpreter was at hand, and the man's story was retold just as he had given it to the police. It is, in fact, to the effect that he saw the whole thing.

It seems that he had gone out for the day, and his wife had expected to move, during his absence, from their lodgings in Berner Street to others in Backchurch Lane. When he came homewards about a quarter before one he first walked down Berner Street to see if his wife had moved. As he turned the corner from Commercial Road he noticed some distance in front of him a man walking as if partially intoxicated. He walked on behind him, and presently he noticed a woman standing in the entrance to the alley way where the body was afterwards found. The half-tipsy man halted and spoke to her. The Hungarian saw him put his hand on her shoulder and push her back into the passage, but, feeling rather timid of getting mixed up in quarrels, he crossed to the other side of the street. Before he had gone many yards, however, he heard the sound of a quarrel, and turned back to learn what was the matter, but just as he stepped from the kerb a second man came out of the doorway of a public house a few doors off, and shouting out some sort of warning to the man who was with the woman, rushed forward as if to attack the intruder. The Hungarian states positively that he saw a knife in this second man's hand, but he waited to see no more. He fled incontinently, to his new lodgings.

The *Times*—1 October 1888

Messrs, George Lusk and Joseph Aarons, writing from 1, 2 and 3 Alderney Road, Mile End, September 29, on behalf of the Whitechapel Vigilance Committee, who communicated without result with the Home Secretary with the view of obtaining, on behalf of the public at large, the offer of a Government reward for the apprehension and conviction of the assassin or assassins in the present East End atrocities say—"We shall be glad if you will allow us to state that the committee do not for one moment doubt the sincerity of the Home Secretary in refusing the said offer, as he apparently believes that it would not meet with a successful result. If he would, however, consider that in the case of the Phoenix Park murders the man Carey, who was surrounded by, we may say, a whole society steeped in crime, the money tempted him to betray his associates, in our opinion, if Mr Matthews could see his way clear to coincide with our views, the Government offer would be successful. The reward should be ample for securing the informer from revenge, which would be a very great inducement in the matter, in addition to which such offer would convince the poor and humble residents of our East End that the Government authorities are as much anxious to avenge the blood of these unfortunate victims as they were the assassination of Lord F. Cavendish and Mr Burke."

The *Times*—2 October 1888

A correspondent writes—There are most remarkable coincidences with regards to the times at which all these murders have been committed which demands particular attention. The first and third of the murders, those of Martha Turner and Mrs

Chapman, were committed on exactly the same date of two separate months—namely, the 7th of August and September, while the second and fourth murders had the same relative coincidence, both being perpetrated on the last days of August and September. If the same hand carried out these crimes, these facts seem to point to the idea that the criminal was one who had to be absent from the scene of his crimes for regular periods.

The *Star*—3 October 1888—Interview with John Kelly

When she did not come home at night I didn't worry, for I thought her daughter might have asked her to stay over Sunday with her. So on Sunday morning I wandered round in the crowds that had been gathered by the talk about the two fresh murders. I stood and looked at the very spot where my poor old gal had laid with her body all cut to pieces and I never knew it. I never thought of her in connection with it, for I thought she was safe at her daughter's. Yesterday morning I began to be worried a bit, but I did not guess the truth until after I had come back from another bad day in the market. I came in here and asked for Kate, she had not been in. I sat down on that bench by the table and carelessly picked up a *Star* paper. I read down the page a bit, and my eye caught the name of "Burrill." It looked familiar, but I didn't think where I had seen it until I came to the word "pawnticket." Then it came over me all at once. The tin box, the two pawntickets, the one for that flannel shirt, and the other for my boots. But could Kate have lost them? I read a little further. "The woman had the letters T. C. in India ink, on her arm." Man, you could have knocked me down with a feather! It was my Kate, and no other. They took me down to see the body, and I knew it was her. I knew it before I saw it, and I knew her for all the way she was cut.

The *Times*—4 October 1888

Sir, Another remarkable letter has been written by some bad fellow who signs himself "Jack the Ripper." The letter is said to be smeared with blood, and there is on it the print in blood of the corrugated surface of a thumb. This may be that of a man or a woman.

It is inconceivable that a woman has written or smeared such a letter, and therefore it may be accepted as a fact that the impression in blood is that of a man's thumb.

The surface of a thumb so printed is as clearly indicated as are the printed letters from any kind of type. Thus there is a possibility of identifying the blood print on the letter with the thumb that made it, because the surface markings on no two thumbs are alike, and this a low power microscope could reveal.

I would suggest—(1) That it be proved if it is human blood, though this may not be material; (2) that the thumbs of every suspected man be compared by an expert with the blood-print of a thumb on the letter; (3) that it be ascertained whether the print of a thumb is that of a man who works hard and has rough, coarse hands, or whether that of one whose hands have not been roughened by labour; (4) whether the thumb was large or small; (5) whether the thumb print shows signs of any shakiness or tremor in the doing of it.

All this the microscope could reveal. The print of a thumb would give as good evidence as that of a boot or shoe.

I am yours etc.,
Fred W. P. Jago.
Plymouth.

The *Times*—5 October 1888

Sir, Perhaps you will allow me to suggest that the murderer's object may be—first, by his crimes to cause a reward to be offered, and then by the accusation of an innocent man, and by the manufacture of apparent tokens of guilt against him (as by staining his clothes with blood), to win that reward. A second Titus Oates is not impossible.

I remain, Sir, your obedient servant, H. P. B., 40 Mostyn Road, Brixton, S.W., Oct 3

East London Observer—6 October 1888

At the Thames Police Court on Tuesday, William Seaman, 40, a builder of 11 Princes Street, Whitechapel, was charged with attempting to murder John Simkin, a chemist, of 82 Berner Street, Whitechapel.

Inspector R. Thresher, H Division, watched the case on behalf of the Commissioners of Police.

Prosecutor was now able to attend. He stated that on Saturday night, the 8th ult., at ten minutes to twelve, he was about closing his shop door, when the prisoner came in alone. He asked for a pennyworth of zinc ointment. Witness got the ointment and gave it to him. He then asked for a pennyworth of powdered alum. Whilst witness was serving the accused behind the counter, he was facing witness. Suddenly the prisoner struck him a heavy blow with a hammer on the head. Witness had his hat on at the time, but could not say how it got off, as it was afterwards found in the road. The blow caught him on the forehead.

Directly the prisoner hit him he rushed around the counter and again struck him with the hammer. The prisoner then dropped the hammer, and witness picked it up and gave it to a man who came in. Witness was cut at the back of the ear, and was bruised all over the body. That was the first day he had been able to get out. He had never before seen the prisoner, and he appeared to be sober. Witness was covered with blood.

By Seaman: Witness did not weigh the alum.

Prisoner: "What is it a pound?" That is what caused the dispute.

Dr F. J. Allan M.D., of 1 Dock Street, stated that when he was called to the prosecutor he found him suffering from a wound on the forehead, and one behind the left ear. The latter was also very much swollen. Both hands were very much swollen and bruised. Prosecutor had considerable difficulty in swallowing, and witness should say that he had been seized by the throat. Prosecutor was also bruised all over his body, and at one time his life was in considerable danger through the injuries he had received. The hammer produced would cause the blow to the forehead. The other wound might also have been caused by the hammer.

Henry John Smyth, a warehouseman, of 6 Chamber Street, Whitechapel, said that on the 8th ult., he was opposite prosecutor's when he heard a scream. He then saw prosecutor's daughter, who called out to witness, "They are murdering my father." Witness went into the shop and saw prisoner holding prosecutor by the throat and punching him about the face and chest. Prosecutor was covered with blood. Witness helped to hold prisoner until a constable came.

Charles McCarthy, labourer, of 11 Ellen's Place, Whitechapel, stated that about twelve o'clock on the night in question he was walking along Ellen Street. He heard a scream in the direction of Berner Street. He went into a chemist's shop at 82 Berner Street, kept by John Simkin. He saw Mr Simkin with his white beard covered in blood. He handed witness the hammer produced saying "This is what he did it with." A constable was fetched, and the prisoner given into custody.

Police Constable 85H said that when he arrested prisoner he said "I shan't say anything to you. I'll say it to the magistrate." When witness went into the shop prisoner was holding prosecutor by the throat.

Prisoner, having been cautioned in the usual manner, said he had nothing to say then.

Mr Saunders committed the accused to take his trial at the next sessions of the Central Criminal Court for attempted murder.

Daily News—6 October 1888 (Referring to the sinking of the *Princess Alice*)

Mr C. J. Carttar, late coroner for West Kent, held an inquiry, extending over six weeks, on the bodies of 527 persons drowned by the disaster, at the Town

Hall, Woolwich, the majority of whom were identified, and caused an alphabetical list of those identified, above 500, to be made by his clerk. An inspection of the list, which is in possession of Mr E. A. Carttar, the present coroner, and son of the late coroner, does not disclose the name of Stride. Whole families were drowned, but the only instance of a father and two children being drowned where the children were under the age of 12 years was in the case of an accountant named Bell, aged 38, his two sons being aged respectively 10 and 7 years. It is true that Mr Lewis, the Essex coroner, held inquests on a few of the bodies cast ashore in Essex, but it is extremely improbable that the three bodies of Mr Stride and his two children were cast ashore on that side of the river, or that they were driven out to sea and lost.

The *Times*—6 October 1888

Yesterday, at the Guildhall Police court, before Mr Alderman Stone, William Bull, 27, living at Stannard Road, Dalton, was charged on remand with having committed the murder in Mitre Square, Aldgate, on Sunday morning. The facts were given in *The Times* of Thursday. Mr Saville (chief clerk) asked Inspector Izzard if he had made inquiries during the remand.

Inspector Izzard—"I have, and the result is perfectly satisfactory. The prisoner, for several years was engaged at Messrs Ryland's, and bore an irreproachable character. Recently he has given way to drink and this is the result. His family are all highly respectable."

The Alderman—"Have you ascertained where he was on Saturday night?"

Inspector Izzard—"Yes; I have a gentleman in Court, a Mr Day, with whom the prisoner was on Saturday night till 12 o'clock."

The Alderman—"It is with great regret that I find the law does not permit me to punish you for your conduct. The statement you made to the inspector on Tuesday night was without the least foundation in fact. At a time like this your acts are perfectly inexcusable. I must discharge you and I hope you will be thoroughly ashamed of your bad behaviour."

Prisoner—"Since I have been in prison I have signed the pledge."

The Alderman—"And I hope you keep it."

Accused was then discharged.

East London Advertiser—6 October 1888

The Whitechapel murderer is still at large, and the police have frankly confessed that they have no clue. This is what was to be expected. Nothing can come from nothing, and the police have no basis to go upon. They do not even know the kind of class from which to select the criminal. They have not a single notion of his whereabouts. They do not know his motive, except so far as our guessing psychologists have enabled them to decipher it. He has left no material trace, and practically no moral trace. All the supposed guides, such as the pawn-tickets, afford no real means of discovering his identity. The articles pawned are in the hands of the police, and the pawnbroker declares that they were left by a woman. But the police cannot even trace the identity of the woman by the name on the tickets. For the rest we are absolutely in the region of surmise.

Meanwhile, perhaps, the worst feature of the murders is the manner in which the panic seems to be growing, and is being aggravated by scoundrels to whom murders of the Whitechapel order only suggest further opportunities for mischief. People's imaginations are at work, finding dangers where there are none. Every forbidding-looking man is the object of suspicion; every unfortunate in Whitechapel herself the prey of a malignant ruffian. Indirectly, perhaps the panic may lead to the discovery of the murderer. The man may be baulked of the usual prey by the extra care of the class from whom he selects his victims and getting unwary and disappointed may at length be captured. From the evidence of the police nothing, however, may be expected. It is clear that there is no detective force, in the proper sense of the word, in London at all, and that the constables are utterly unsuited for such work as is necessary to protect Whitechapel from these nightly visitations. What is likely to happen is this; there will be more murders and the ruffian's heels may be tripped by chance if not by the foresight of the police. On the other hand, detective work of a specially superior and intellectual kind can be set in hand and pushed vigorously and fearlessly may result in the discovery of the criminal.

What we have to complain of especially is the inefficiency of the surgical examinations and the coroner's inquiries which have hitherto been held. Owing to the scamping of detailed work we were led astray by the absurd theory of the American and his offer of £20 for specimens of an organ, while a whole body could be obtained for nearly as many shillings. Possibly to such a consideration may be added the off-chance that the offer of a reward of over £1,000 may stimulate the detective instinct enough to put the community fairly on the track of its enemy. The theory that the man has accomplices, is, we are afraid, too remote and improbable to produce any good results. Accomplices would only hinder a man like the Whitechapel murderer in the execution of so deadly a purpose. The success of the murderer really depends on the ability with which a single mind has been concentrated on the purpose.

Murders are generally clumsy affairs. They are committed by men who are drawn into them by circumstances, and have no time to think of a plan or suggest a means of escape. If they are done in hot blood the chances are strong of their being detected in flagrante delicto. If they are committed, say, by a burglar who is suddenly interrupted, and has no choice between his liberty and homicide, they are again liable to clumsiness of method and its consequences. Finally, if they are committed for any known or ascertainable motive there is always a probability of fixing the crime on a suspected person. But here there is no ascertainable motive, and therefore no suspected person—no plunder committed in haste, no folly which would give a clue to the authorities. The murderer has deliberately selected the most defenceless class of the community and has chosen to slaughter them under circumstances which turn his own victims into his accomplices. There is so much in this of a deeply thought out plan that we have to consider whether the murderer is a maniac in the narrow sense of the word, and is not rather a man with a maniacal tendency, but with quite sufficient control of himself and of his faculties to impose upon his neighbours, and possibly to mix in respectable society unquestioned by a single soul.

He is probably able to command solitude whenever he pleases, and that seems to be the only requisite for concealing his crimes.

The *Times*—8 October 1888

Sir—Will you allow me to recommend that all the police boots should be furnished with a noiseless sole and heel, of indiarubber or other material, to prevent the sound of their measured tread being heard at night, which would enable them to get a close to a criminal before he would be aware of their approach?

Yours faithfully, L. R. Thomson. Junior United Service Club, S.W., Oct 1

The *Times*—8 October 1888

Fears were expressed among the police on Saturday that the night would not pass without some startling occurrence, and the most extraordinary precautions were taken in consequence. It must not be supposed that the precautions taken apply only to the East End of London. It is fully understood that the murderer, finding his favourite haunts too hot for him, may transfer his operations to another district, and arrangements have been made accordingly. The parks are specially patrolled, and the police, even in the most outlying districts, are keenly alive to the necessities of the situation. Having sufficiently provided for the safeguarding of other portions of the large area under his jurisdiction, Sir Charles Warren has sent every available man into the East End district. These, together with a large body of City detectives, are now on duty, and will remain in the streets throughout the night. Most of the men were on duty all last night, and the work has been found very harassing. But every man has entered heartily into the work, and not a murmur has been heard from any of the officers. They are on their mettle, and if zeal were the one thing needed to hunt down the murderer, his capture would be assured.

Yesterday evening all was quiet in the district, and the excitement has somewhat subsided. Nevertheless, the police and the local Vigilance Committees have by no means relaxed their watchfulness, and inhabitants of the district, disregarding the improbability of the murderer risking his freedom under these circumstances, still appear to expect the early commission of a new crime. During Saturday night and the early hours of Sunday morning several persons were arrested and detained at local police stations until all the circumstances in connection with their apprehension were thoroughly sifted. Several of these were given into custody on grounds which proved on inquiry to be flimsy and even foolish, and the police have in consequence been put to a good deal of trouble without any corresponding result. It seemed at times as if every person in the streets were suspicious of everyone else he met, and as if it were a race between them who should first inform against his neighbour.

Alfred Napier Blanchard, who described himself as a canvasser, residing at Handsworth, was charged at Birmingham on Saturday, on his own confession, with having committed the Whitechapel atrocities. He had been arrested in consequence of a circumstantial statement which he made in a public house of the manner in which he had effected the murders. He now denied all knowledge of the matter, and said he had spoken under excitement, caused by reading about the murders, and heavy drinking. The Bench declined to release him, however, till today, in order to allow time for inquiries.

Up to a late hour last night no important arrest had been reported in connection with the murders at the East End at any of the City police stations. Many communications continue to be received at Scotland Yard and by the City police, describing persons who have been seen in various parts of the country whose conduct is suspicious, or who are supposed to resemble the man seen talking to the victim of the Berner Street murder on the night of her assassination.

East London Observer—13 October 1888

A reporter gleaned some curious information from the Casual Ward Superintendent of Mile End, regarding Kate Eddowes, the Mitre Square victim. She was formerly well-known in the casual wards there, but had disappeared for a considerable time until the Friday preceding her murder. Asking the woman where she had been in the interval, the superintendent was met with the reply that she had been in the country "hopping." "But," added the woman, "I have come back to earn the reward offered for the apprehension of the Whitechapel murderer. I think I know him." "Mind he doesn't murder you too," replied the superintendent jocularly. "Oh, no fear of that," was the remark made by Kate Eddowes as she left. Within four and twenty hours afterwards she was a mutilated corpse.

Daily Telegraph—13 November 1888

It was stated last night that the persons taken into custody on the previous day had been liberated, and it is doubtful if the constabulary have obtained new clues to assist their search. A circumstantial statement was made last night by a labouring man who knew the deceased, which was very minute in its particulars regarding a man seen in the company with the woman Kelly early on the morning of the 9th inst. According to this description the individual in question was of respectable appearance, about 5ft 6in., in height, and 34 or 35 years of age, with dark complexion and dark moustache curled up at the ends. He wore a long coat trimmed with astrachan, a white collar with black necktie, in which was affixed a horse-shoe pin, and he had on a pair of dark gaiters with light buttons over button boots, and displayed from his waistcoat a massive gold chain. It has not been ascertained why the witness did not make this statement—so much fuller and so different from the others that have been given—immediately after the murder was discovered.

Your Own Ripper Walk

Many years ago, when I first developed an interest in the Ripper crimes, I went on one of the Ripper walks. I hasten to add that it was not guided by any of the companies mentioned earlier in this section. The guide got the location of three of the murders wrong and stated, as an absolute proven fact, that the Ripper murders were part of a Masonic Conspiracy involving the royal family.

I am not suggesting that any company mentioned earlier is anything but careful when it comes to the facts, but you may prefer to examine the sites yourself without a guide who might possibly give a "solution" that you find difficult to accept. Or you may prefer to walk the area in the afternoon, whereas most organized tours take place at night.

So walk the area yourself, using this section as a guide. It should take about an hour and a half, but feel free to extend this time by visiting any of the pubs mentioned for a cool, refreshing drink to fortify you for the next part of the walk.

A good place to start is the Underground. From wherever you are in the capital, get on the District (green) line, take an eastbound train toward Upminster, and get off at Whitechapel station. When you reach street level you will find yourself facing the London Hospital. This is where the Lusk kidney was examined.

Turn to the right and walk past the Grave Maurice public house. Not far past it is a narrow entryway marked "Wood's Buildings." Go down the alleyway and realize that you may well be walking down the very lane Jack the Ripper used to escape from the scene of the murder of **Mary Ann Nichols.**

You will see a bridge over the railway and a large, imposing building facing you. At the time of the Ripper crimes this was a Board School, but it has been converted into private residences.

Walk over the bridge. When you reach the far end, go down the few steps back to street level, stop, and look to your right. Large gates now close off what was once was Winthrop Street, where the slaughtermen were working on the night of 31 August 1888.

Going first to your left, walk around the front of the school and take the street that runs parallel to Winthrop Street by turning right. You will see a long wall and, at the end, a small area planted with flowers. This is the spot where Mary Ann Nichols died in Buck's Row, though the street has been renamed Durward Street.

Turn around and walk back toward the bridge that brought you over the railway just a few moments before. Do not go back over it, but continue along Durward Street, passing the Whitechapel Sports Centre on your right. Walk to the end of the street, noticing as you go the two other streets on the left that pass over the railway. The Ripper might have used these streets to take him away from Buck's Row and out into the busy streets beyond.

At the end of Durward Street, turn right. You will see a zebra crossing several yards in front of you. Use this to cross this busy street safely, and you will see in front of you a street marked by two "No Entry" signs. There is a sign on the wall that reads "Hanbury Street." Take the short, narrow passageway between the two walls and walk into the eastern part of Hanbury Street itself. Go straight on, passing another school on your right. Notice the stone plaque high on the wall at the far end showing that it was built in 1895, just seven years after Jack trod these same pavements.

At the end of this part of Hanbury Street is a small miniroundabout painted onto the road with streets forking off to the left and right. Take the street to the right, and you will soon see another zebra crossing. Cross the road and continue toward the Alma public house and Spelman Street. Do not go down this street, but continue toward yet more "No Entry" signs and bear left there to remain in Hanbury Street itself. Cross over Brick Lane, a street once filled with lodging houses and now packed with Indian restaurants and businesses, but stay on Hanbury Street.

You are now approaching the location of the murder of **Annie Chapman**. Unfortunately, the exact spot is buried somewhere beneath the long wall of the brewery, which you will see on the right-hand side. Walk on to the end of Hanbury Street, passing Wilkes Street on the left. Did Jack dash down here after he claimed Annie's life?

At the end of Hanbury Street, turn left into Commercial Street. To check that you are correct, you should walk past the Golden Heart public house on the corner. As you walk slowly down Commercial Street, notice the Spitalfields Market across the road. On your left is the Ten Bells public house, where **Mary Jane Kelly** drank. Cross over Fournier Street and stop in front of the large, imposing church. This is Christ Church, Spitalfields. If this building could talk, it could tell dramatic tales of Kelly and the man who claimed her life, for Jack saw this edifice hundreds of times as he patrolled the streets looking for his next victim.

Walk on toward the three telephone boxes that are just past the church. Looking across the road again, you will see Barclays Bank on the corner of Brushfield Street, where Mary Jane Kelly's landlord had other business premises. You will see the multistory car park as well. To the right of that is what used to be Dorset Street, one of the most dangerous streets in London, and somewhere down there lay Miller's Court, where Mary was butchered. To the right of the car park is another street, White's Row. Some writers, including me, think this is where Jack made his first attack, on **Annie Millwood**, in February 1888.

Carry on up Commercial Street, crossing over Fashion Street until you come to Lolesworth Close. This was once Flower and Dean Street, where some of the victims lived, and on the corner stood the Queen's Head, outside which George Hutchinson said he saw the well-dressed man with Mary Jane Kelly on the morning that she died.

Cross over Thrawl Street and carry on until you see the City Darts public house. Stop here, for this spot has many tales to tell. The City Darts used to be called the Princess Alice, and on the opposite side of Commercial Street you will perhaps see the market stalls that lead down Wentworth Street. Look for the shop that sells luggage, right on the corner. That was the location of the Victoria Home, where George Hutchinson lived. But do not cross over yet. Stay on the same side and turn down Wentworth Street by the side of the City Darts.

Cross the road so that you are on the same side as the pub, but carry on walking away from it. Pass Attlee House on your right, and then, to your right, you will see a narrow street. This is Gunthorpe Street, and here stood George Yard Buildings, where **Martha Tabram** died.

Walk up Gunthorpe Street, noticing Toynbee Hall on your right, In the distance is an archway, and as you approach you will see a public house to your right. This is the White Hart, and below this worked George Chapman, whose real name was Severin Klosowski. He didn't arrive in this spot until 1890, two years after the five canonical murders, but he has proved to be an enduring suspect and was hanged in 1903 for three cruel murders.

Once you have passed through the archway, turn right into Whitechapel High Street and pass in front of the White Hart. Go to the main road junction, noting the Seven Stars public house across the road. Cross over and walk on, past the Seven Stars and past the entrance to Aldgate East Underground station.

After you have passed the Underground station you will soon come to Old Castle Street. This street led into Castle Alley, where **Alice McKenzie** died in 1889. Carry on walking in the same direction, though, past the National Westminster Bank on your right, until you see a subway opposite Aldgate House labeled "Exit 15." You must now walk a somewhat tortuous route in order to avoid the London traffic.

Go down the Exit 15 subway and toward Exit 11. Take this exit and turn right when you see Exit 10. Go along here and look for Exit 9, which is toward the left at the far end. When you have taken Exit 9, turn left, and you will see yet another subway on the left at the end of this short street. This is labelled "Exit 5." Go along here and leave by Exit 1. Though that route was somewhat difficult, when you leave Exit 1 you are close to Mitre Square, the scene of **Catherine Eddowes**'s murder on 30 September 1888.

Exit 1 brings you out into what was then Church Passage. To your immediate left is the spot where Catherine was seen by Joseph Lawende, talking to the man who may well have claimed her life. Turn to your right, though, and walk on into Mitre Square itself. The path you are now walking was almost certainly trodden by Catherine and the man who claimed her life.

The spot where Catherine died is in front of you, on the cobbles near the black metal gates and just in front of the bench placed close to the flower bed. If the bench is free, take a seat and ponder the terrible sight that would have been almost at your feet on that September night.

As you sit, look to your left and you will see an arched alleyway leading into Creechurch Place. Did Jack use that alley to make his escape with the bloody piece of apron he had slashed from Catherine's clothing? Or did he run down Church Passage, which is now directly in front of you?

To your left was the warehouse where Constable Watkins sought help from George Morris. When you are ready, walk over to Mitre Passage on the right and go down it into Creechurch Place. Turn right almost immediately into Creechurch Lane and walk on toward the busy main road, which is called Houndsditch. Cross Houndsditch and walk into Stoney Lane. At the end, turn right and then left into Gravel Lane. Carry on to Middlesex Street, where you cross over and head toward the public house in the distance, the Market Trader.

Go down the street by the side of the pub, which is called New Goulston Street.

At the end of this street, which may again be filled with market stalls, stop for a moment. To your left and across the road is the building where Catherine Eddowes's bloody piece of apron and the graffito were discovered. Cross the road, go left, and pass along the front of this building, which now consists of shops and businesses. At the end of the building, turn right into Wentworth Street and walk on to the junction with Commercial Street. Here again you will see the City Darts public house, and you will pass on your right the luggage shop that marks the spot where George Hutchinson lived.

Turn left now into Commercial Street and begin retracing your steps, but now of course on the opposite side of the road. Notice again as you approach the multistory parking garage White's Row, which is on your left, and what used to be Dorset Street nearby.

Walk on past the old Spitalfields Market, well worth a visit itself because it is now filled with stalls and places to eat. When you are ready, go back into Commercial Street and cross at the Golden Heart again to walk back down Hanbury Street.

Once again, you are passing the spot where Annie Chapman died. Walk on to the top of Hanbury Street, but this time take the left fork at the miniroundabout, again to retrace your steps. Pass the old school on your left with the stone plaque high on the wall and go on to the narrow passageway that first led you down here. Turn right at the top, but this time do not take the zebra crossing or go down Durward Street. Instead, stay on the same side of the road and walk on to the traffic lights at the end of the street. Cross to put yourself on the same side as Durward Street, but now pass down the main thoroughfare, Whitechapel Road, again toward the London Hospital.

Walk past the Black Bull on your left and past the Grave Maurice. The underground station you started from is on your left, and your journey is over.

You have passed the sites of the attacks upon Annie Millwood, Martha Tabram, Mary Ann Nichols, Annie Chapman, Catherine Eddowes, Mary Jane Kelly, and Alice McKenzie, the seven victims that I believe belong to the real Jack the Ripper.

14

Summary

Who was Jack the Ripper, and why wasn't he captured? Let us consider the second question first.

I do not believe, like some of my contemporaries, that the police of the day were incompetent. There may well have been some officers who did not perform their duties as well as they should have, but on the whole, the detective force and the constables on the beat did their very best. The reason they did not capture Jack was that they were looking for the wrong type of man.

These crimes were something new. They were not the results of domestic disputes and were not committed as a result of robbery or rape, so the police did not understand them. The idea of someone killing for nothing more than the pleasure of the deed was previously unheard of, and when the police realized that this was indeed the case, they looked for a slavering maniac whose mind was diseased and whose emotions were out of control. The murders were inhuman, so the killer had to be inhuman too. He had to be mad or foreign, or preferably both.

I contend that although extra constables were drafted and at times the streets must have been crawling with officers, they were all looking for someone who stood out from the crowd, someone whose behavior was suspicious or erratic, whereas Jack simply didn't behave like that. The police probably also believed that the murderer would be reeking with blood, but the method Jack usually employed was to kneel to cut the throat of his victim while she was lying on the ground and to cut in a direction away from himself. Thus, in most cases he would have escaped almost unmarked. True, he would have had blood on his hands—but how easy to thrust one's hands into one's pockets.

In summary, the police failed to catch Jack the Ripper because they did not recognize the man they were looking for. I draw parallels with the hunt for the Yorkshire Ripper, in which Peter Sutcliffe was interviewed nine times before a chance encounter led to his arrest. The police believed that the Yorkshire Ripper had a Geordie accent; Sutcliffe didn't have a Geordie accent; ergo, Sutcliffe wasn't the killer. Exactly the same kind of thinking may be seen in London in 1888.

Let us now turn to the first question. Who was the Whitechapel murderer?

This book lists more than 100 possible candidates, many of them hidden in the mists of time. Those same mists have hidden untruths, invention, lies, and some appallingly bad research so that some authors would have us believe, for instance, that the highest in the land conspired to murder prostitutes and leave their bodies in significant locations forming Masonic patterns or arrows pointing to certain buildings. Others would have our killer seeking one particular victim and eliminating her friends or those he had asked about her along the way. These theories belong in the realm of fiction.

The serial killer is nothing new to us now. He is a fact of our lives, and most countries boast (if that is the right word) the name of at least one such monster who has preyed upon the innocent. How many of these killers align the sites where they leave their victims' bodies so that they point to the White House, or the Kremlin, or Buckingham Palace, or any other famous building? How many play elaborate games in which each body is a clue to some greater mystery? Yet we are told by some to accept that this was the case in 1888. Schoolboy melodrama, nothing more.

In order to find the Ripper, we must resort to the first principles of logic and common sense. We need to look at the clues of the time and apply modern-day tools. We cannot use fingerprinting or DNA testing now, but we can use psychological profiling.

There have been profiles before, but in preparing of this book I obtained a new one from Dr. James Cook, a U.S. psychologist. He knew very little of the crimes before I contacted him, but after I sent him various inquest reports, pictures, newspaper clippings, and other materials, he came up with the following:

> This kind of pathology usually starts around the age of 15. At or before this time he had begun to kill and mutilate animals, fantasizing about them as being people. At this time too he would have begun to have an unnatural fascination with fire and may also have had a history of bed-wetting. . . . With a normal progression of his pathology he would have begun to act upon his fantasies and started killing between the ages of 25 and 35. I suspect that Jack was about 28 to 31 years old.
>
> I believe that Jack probably lived in the Whitechapel area. . . . He was probably never more than a short distance from what he considered to be a safe place. He had a demeaning job, probably as a laborer, as I believe him to have been somewhat muscular. . . . [He] lived alone, in one of the many common lodging houses that were endemic to that area, and had no close friends. His thinking was very disorganized and he may well have been schizophrenic.
>
> Since he was very disorganised, his murders were not at all well planned. His lack of organisation carried over into other areas of his life as well. His clothes were usually shabby, and his teeth may have begun to show signs of neglect. He looked like many others who lived and worked in that low-income part of the city. To the prostitutes he murdered he would not have seemed to present any threat. Jack would have appeared to them to be a nearly perfect customer.
>
> Of course, as with any newly acquired skill, Jack had to learn the art of killing. Since his thinking was so very disorganized he had given very little thought to the tools of his trade, and he was ill-prepared for his first attempt, which was unsuccessful. Here we will assume that Annie Millwood was his first attempt. She recovered from her injuries but later died of an unrelated cause. This effort left him somewhat gratified but considerably lacking in fulfilment.
>
> . . . This gave him plenty of time to rethink his needs and determine that he would need a bigger knife in addition to his pocket knife. [Referring to Martha Tabram] We see here a pattern forming with regard to Jack's targeting the abdomen and genitals of his victims. He would have to see the victims' genitals as their source of power. He may have been impotent and directed his rage on these parts out of frustration and anger.
>
> [Referring to Mary Ann Nichols] I believe that Jack was scared away from this scene, as he had no time to arrange the intestines, nor to take a body part, which as we will soon see is to become his signature. This shows again how disorganized his planning was.
>
> With these crimes behind him now, Jack is beginning to become more skilled. He now knows the best way to approach and restrain his victims. He knows how

much pressure is needed to penetrate the body with his knife. He has experienced some gratification but not yet fulfilment.

[Referring to Annie Chapman] There he went about killing Annie in his signature method. The abdominal mutilations were done after death. The uterus with the upper portion of the vagina and the posterior two-thirds of the bladder had been removed and apparently taken away by Jack. By taking away these parts, he is showing the signature one would expect of a serial killer. Some believe that the way in which the dissection was done indicated that the killer had some surgical skill or knowledge. I believe this is not necessarily the case. Jack was just cutting in a manner that felt good to him.

[Referring to Catherine Eddowes] Near the place where the piece of cloth was found was written on a wall, "The Juwes are the men that will not be blamed for nothing." Some believe this was written by Jack. I do not believe it had anything to do with him. His driving obsession was the pathological need to murder and mutilate women.

Conclusions: Jack was probably good at concealing that part of his behavior that was pathological. He was able to do his job and even socialize in a general sort of way. He may have been a regular customer at one of the pubs in Whitechapel.

Using this profile with the more acceptable physical descriptions, we can say only the following about the real Jack the Ripper.

He was about 5 feet 6 inches tall at the most and quite muscular. He had a pale, almost certainly brown mustache, had a fairly stout or stocky build, and was aged somewhere in his late 20s to mid-30s. He lived in the area where the murders took place and knew it like the back of his hand. He was a loner, and if he was employed, he had an unskilled job that may have involved his working alone. He was not surgically skilled. He was probably unmarried and possibly impotent, though he may have had sexual encounters with prostitutes. He dressed fairly neatly, or tried to, in shabby-genteel clothing. He probably possessed a deerstalker hat. He would not have committed suicide or moved away from the area, and the police may have interviewed him at some stage.

Of the candidates, who is the best fit?

It's not much to go on, but surely even this little sketch, plus some common sense and logic, indicates a much more reasonable approach than Liverpool cotton merchants with philandering wives, surgeons of the royal family aiding a Masonic cabal, a conspiracy of Portuguese sailors, famous writers leaving anagrams, the murder sites forming shapes that point somewhere, or some such similar nonsense.

We can, however, add a little more. In the "Letters and Correspondence" and "Miscellaneous" sections I have argued that, given the balance of probabilities, the Lusk kidney was probably genuine. This means that the "From Hell" letter was genuine, and by inference the letter of 17 September 1888 and the Openshaw letter may also be genuine. These communications indicate that the killer was well aware of the vigilance committees and had a particular animosity toward the Whitechapel committee chaired by George Lusk, or possibly toward Lusk himself. This conclusion of course does little but reinforce the suggestion that the Ripper was a local man, living among those he terrorized.

One other point that seems to have been largely overlooked by other authors is the significance of some of the mutilations carried out on the victims. Although it is true that, in general, the severity of the injuries increased, I find one factor most intriguing: No matter who we say was the first victim, or who we say was the last, only two were subjected to facial mutilations—Catherine Eddowes and Mary Jane Kelly. Now, it could be said that in Kelly's case, it was because the killer was able to work undisturbed, but the same cannot be said of the Eddowes case, in which Jack had only a few minutes at his disposal. How then are these mutilations significant?

Psychological profilers usually claim that facial mutilations are evidence that the killer and victim are known to each other. The stranger is an anonymous victim, so there is no need to depersonalize her, but if the killer knows his victim, then he has to destroy her personality. The closer that relationship, the more extreme the mutilations.

This concept introduces a factor that few writers have examined. True, attempts have been made to link all the victims, suggesting that a conspiracy of some kind joined them in some way and that, with the death of Mary Jane Kelly, the conspiracy ended because the goal had been achieved, but this is plainly not the case. I have given my own opinions on which attacks are most likely to be Ripper crimes, but when we look at the series as a whole, whether we include four, five, six, or more attacks, we can see that we need to establish a link between the killer and only two of his victims. I contend, then, that whoever Jack the Ripper was, he knew Catherine Eddowes slightly, possibly only by sight, and knew Mary Jane Kelly quite well. We can now add this conclusion to the available evidence in order to determine who our killer is most likely to be.

This book contains more than 140 names of those who were suspected at one time or another of being the Ripper. If we go through that list again, deleting those who did not live in the area, were not aged 25 to 35, were far too tall, had the wrong coloring, and so on, our lineup of suspects becomes much shorter. In fact, it contains just the following names:

Barnett, Joseph
Bury, William Henry
Hutchinson, George
Kaminsky, Nathan
Kosminski, Aaron
Unknown Male

Many writers have claimed in the past that Mary Jane Kelly is the key to this series of murders, and I agree that she is—not because of some secret machination but simply because we are looking for someone who knew her quite well. This criterion may be met by just two names on that reduced list. In addition, we would need to continue to include the "unknown male" in case the real Ripper remains lost in the shadows of time, but he need not be listed because he, by definition, remains unidentified. Our final list is therefore:

Barnett, Joseph
Hutchinson, George

Ideally, we now need to establish a link between one of these suspects and Catherine Eddowes. This is difficult because that link may well be tenuous and could be as simple as the killer knowing Catherine by sight or drinking in one of the same public houses she frequented. Before we continue down that avenue, we need to see whether we can identify any curious behaviour on the part of either of these men. It is my opinion that only one of this pair did something so strange that he places his own name in the frame.

Mary Jane Kelly was murdered early on the morning of Friday, 9 November 1888. The news broke later that day, and we know that vendors interrupted the Lord Mayor's Show with reports of this latest atrocity and that the newspapers were full of the crime from Friday onward. It is impossible to believe that anyone living in the Whitechapel or Spitalfields area had not heard about the crime, especially if that person lived close to the scene of the murder.

The inquest on Kelly opened and closed on Monday, 12 November, and if one reads through the testimony of the various witnesses, especially as it was reported in the newspapers of the day, there is nothing startling or surprising about any of it. Thus, we have brief medical details, witnesses reporting Mary's character and movements, and so on. Only one witness left a loose end that might have proved significant.

Sarah Lewis had argued with her husband and, as a result, stormed out of her house at 29 Great Pearl Street and walked to Whitechapel, intending to stay with Mrs. Keyler, who lived at 2 Miller's Court. She arrived at Christ Church, Spitalfields, at 2:30 A.M. Turning into Dorset Street, Sarah noticed a man, whom she described as not tall but stout and wearing a black wideawake hat, standing in an entry by Crossingham's Lodging House, which was at 35 Dorset Street, almost directly opposite to the court. It was only after that testimony was printed that George Hutchinson came forward and made a statement in which he said he had seen Kelly with a well-dressed man on the morning that she died. His statement showed that it must have been Hutchinson whom Sarah Lewis saw, giving him an ostensibly innocent reason for being in the entry near Crossingham's.

If the inquest testimony of Sarah Lewis had been the end of the matter, then we would expect that the police would have tried very hard indeed to trace this mysterious man whom she had seen. Perhaps Lewis would have been escorted around the district in an attempt to find the man, and because Hutchinson lived in the immediate area, at the Victoria Home, which was situated at 39–41 Commercial Street, on the corner of Wentworth Street and Commercial Street and opposite to the Princess Alice public house, he may soon have been spotted.

Because of the storm of publicity, it is impossible to accept that Hutchinson had not heard of the murder before the inquest concluded. Why then did he not come forward earlier to give his statement? I believe that he had no intention of coming forward until he read Lewis's testimony in the newspaper. He had been seen. If he didn't explain his presence opposite Miller's Court before the police found him, he would immediately fall under suspicion. Hutchinson finally told his story only because he had to.

Here is Hutchinson's statement again.

> About 2:00 A.M., 9th, I was coming by Thrawl Street, Commercial Street, and just before I got to Flower and Dean Street I met the murdered woman Kelly and she said to me "Hutchinson, will you lend me sixpence." I said "I can't, I have spent all my money going down to Romford." She said "Good morning, I must go and find some money." She went away towards Thrawl Street. A man coming in the opposite direction to Kelly tapped her on the shoulder and said something to her. They both burst out laughing. I heard her say "Alright" to him and the man said "You will be alright for what I have told you." He then placed his right hand around her shoulders. He also had a kind of a small parcel in his left hand, with a kind of a strap round it. I stood against the lamp of the Queens Head Public House and watched him. They both then came past me and the man hung down his head with his hat over his eyes. I stooped down and looked him in the face. He looked at me stern. They both went into Dorset Street. I followed them. They both stood at the corner of the court for about 3 minutes. He said something to her. She said "Alright my dear, come along, you will be comfortable." He then placed his arm on her shoulder and gave her a kiss. She said she had lost her handkerchief. He then

The Princess Alice public house, now renamed the City Darts, was frequented by, among others, Thomas Sadler, Frances Coles, and Leather Apron. It was also directly opposite where George Hutchinson lived. (Yvonne Berger)

> pulled his handkerchief, a red one, out and gave it to her. They both then went up the court together. I then went to the court to see if I could see them but could not. I stood there for about three quarters of an hour to see if they came out. They did not so I went away.

On the original statement the following notes appear after this passage: "Description: age about 34 or 35, height 5ft 6, complexion pale, dark eyes and eye lashes, slight moustache curled up each end and hair dark, very surley looking; dress, long dark coat, collar and cuffs trimmed astracan and a dark jacket under, light waistcoat, dark trousers, dark felt hat turned down in the middle, button boots and gaiters with white buttons, wore a very thick gold chain, white linen collar, black tie with horse shoe pin, respectable appearance, walked very sharp, Jewish appearance. Can be identified."

The detail is impossible to accept. He even described the man's eyelashes! In addition, the costume is pure theater and was likely a workingman's opinion of what a "toff" should look like. The description was false and the statement a lie given merely to provide Hutchinson with a valid reason for standing in an entry looking down Miller's Court to where Kelly lived. Only by suggesting that George Hutchinson had something to hide can we explain his presence in Dorset Street, the fact that he didn't come forward on the Friday of the murder, and the ridiculously detailed description of the man he claimed he saw.

Let us now, just for the sake of discussion, assume that Hutchinson *was* Jack the Ripper. I am *not* stating this supposition as fact but merely seeing what will fit if we begin with it.

From Sarah Lewis's scant description, we know that Hutchinson was a small, stout man. The press reports at the time gave his age as 28, and we know that he lived at the epicenter of the Ripper crimes. Furthermore, he lived almost on top of the stairwell where the apron and graffito were found on the night Elizabeth Stride and Catherine Eddowes met their deaths, 30 September 1888.

I believe that the first Ripper victim was Annie Millwood, who was attacked on 25 February 1888. It was a clumsy assault that failed in its final purpose—to kill. Hutchinson struck very close to where he lived, but the fact that his victim did not die as a direct result of his attack left him unsure, unsatisfied, perhaps even frightened.

When Annie died in March and no one came to knock upon Hutchinson's door, his confidence grew, and he decided to try again. This time he would be sure to kill. This time he would stab again and again until he was sure his victim was dead. So he carried out the attack upon Martha Tabram, again close to his home, and stabbed her so many times that she could not possibly survive. He used two knives in this case, probably inflicting the first wound with the larger one after throttling his victim into unconsciousness. Only then could he take out the other knife and allow himself the pleasure of plunging it into the helpless form again and again.

Hutchinson had struck twice now, close to his home on both occasions. It was time to spread his net a little wider. That thinking took him to the Buck's Row area, where he killed Mary Ann Nichols. Just as he was about to carry out the mutilations that motivated him, he heard approaching footsteps and had to escape, probably by rushing along Wood's Buildings and out into Whitechapel Road.

The next murder was the most satisfying for him by far. He had time to mutilate as he wished, to remove a part of the body, and to collect other souvenirs, such as Annie Chapman's rings. Mutilation of his victim was now his signature.

At the end of September he claimed the life of Catherine Eddowes. She was a woman he knew slightly, and the mutilations were aimed to depersonalize her, to remove that knowledge from his mind. Once again he mutilated and collected souvenirs, but this time he was clumsy. He got fecal matter on his hands and had to cut off part of her apron to clean himself. He dropped the scrap in a doorway on his way home or may even have gone back out to deposit it after he had cleaned himself up a little more in the privacy of his own room.

Only the following morning Hutchinson realized that there had been two murders that night; Elizabeth Stride's life had probably been taken by a disgruntled client. His name was being linked to both, and police presence in the area was increased. His act of leaving the apron close to where he lived might have backfired on him because the police were now concentrating on that area. Perhaps he was questioned as a matter of course. Whatever the truth of the matter, he had to lie low for a while. The streets were becoming too dangerous. That was why he did not kill during the month of October. Still, he did get some satisfaction from sending part of Catherine Eddowes's kidney to the interfering Lusk.

By November things had quieted down again. There were still patrols, but people were beginning to say that the Ripper was dead or had left the area. People were off guard, and it was time to strike again. Maybe he consciously decided to choose a victim whom he could claim indoors, without being disturbed. More likely Mary Jane Kelly, a woman he knew well, was in the wrong place at the wrong time. Perhaps he saw her with a client and followed her back home, or maybe she was alone and he simply picked her up.

After killing Kelly, he was delighted. He was the man all London was looking for. He was the master of all he surveyed, wallowing in the notoriety and all the talk about this latest terrible crime. Then came the inquest and the report that he had after all been seen. What could he do? If he lay low, then this damned witness might see him and point him out. He had to find a way to explain his presence in Dorset Street. Many people believed the stories of the "toff," the man with the black bag. So it was that Hutchinson came forward and told his story of the well-dressed man he had seen with Kelly. The police believed him. They were now looking for someone who bore no resemblance to him.

If Hutchinson were Jack, he may well have been a disorganized killer, but he was no idiot. The police might only have been pretending to believe him. After all, they did have detectives at his side while he patrolled the streets looking for the man who had never really existed. What if they were secretly watching him? What if they were waiting for him to strike again so they could catch him in the act? Once again he had to lie low, bide his time, curb the urges he had.

Time moved on, and every so often something rekindled public interest in the Ripper crimes. First there was that fool Annie Farmer claiming she had been attacked by Jack the Ripper. Then, a month later, there was Rose Mylett, when the police couldn't even decide whether she had been murdered! It would be best to wait until well into the new year. After all, there was no rush.

It might have been the death of Elizabeth Jackson that prompted Hutchinson to kill again. He was in total control now. Even after the scares of the double event and having been seen when he killed Kelly, he had not been carried off by the police. They were no wiser after all. And now, when pieces of Elizabeth Jackson's body were found and initially linked with the Ripper crimes, the police were quick to discount that conclusion because she hadn't been killed in the same way. Very well, then, here was a solution: If he didn't kill like the Ripper did, then people would not believe the Ripper had returned.

The murder of Alice McKenzie was once again almost on Hutchinson's doorstep. It was an opportune crime, and the police were again close to catching him, but he used his knowledge of the area to make his escape. It had been good to return to his old hobby, but not being able to mutilate as he wished had hurt him. Still, he couldn't resist one more jibe at the police and one more way of showing that this was, after all, one to be placed at Jack's door. She was the seventh woman he had attacked, so he cut the score onto her body. Once again he had outsmarted everyone. Once more he had shown that he was invincible.

If George Hutchinson were the Ripper, did he stop killing at this point? Well, he certainly stopped killing in London. By the time of the next census in 1891, he was no longer to be found in the Whitechapel area. He could have moved on at any time, of course, but I hold that he moved sometime in late 1889, or possibly early 1890. Where he moved is not yet known, but I would not be surprised to find that there were other unsolved murders wherever it was.

There is also a possibility that his family found out about the crimes and put its own restrictions on George. Bob Hinton, author of *From Hell . . . The Jack the Ripper Mystery,* discovered a very curious alteration in Hutchinson's father's will showing that George apparently simply ceased to exist as far as his family was concerned. This detail needs further investigation, not with a view to saying

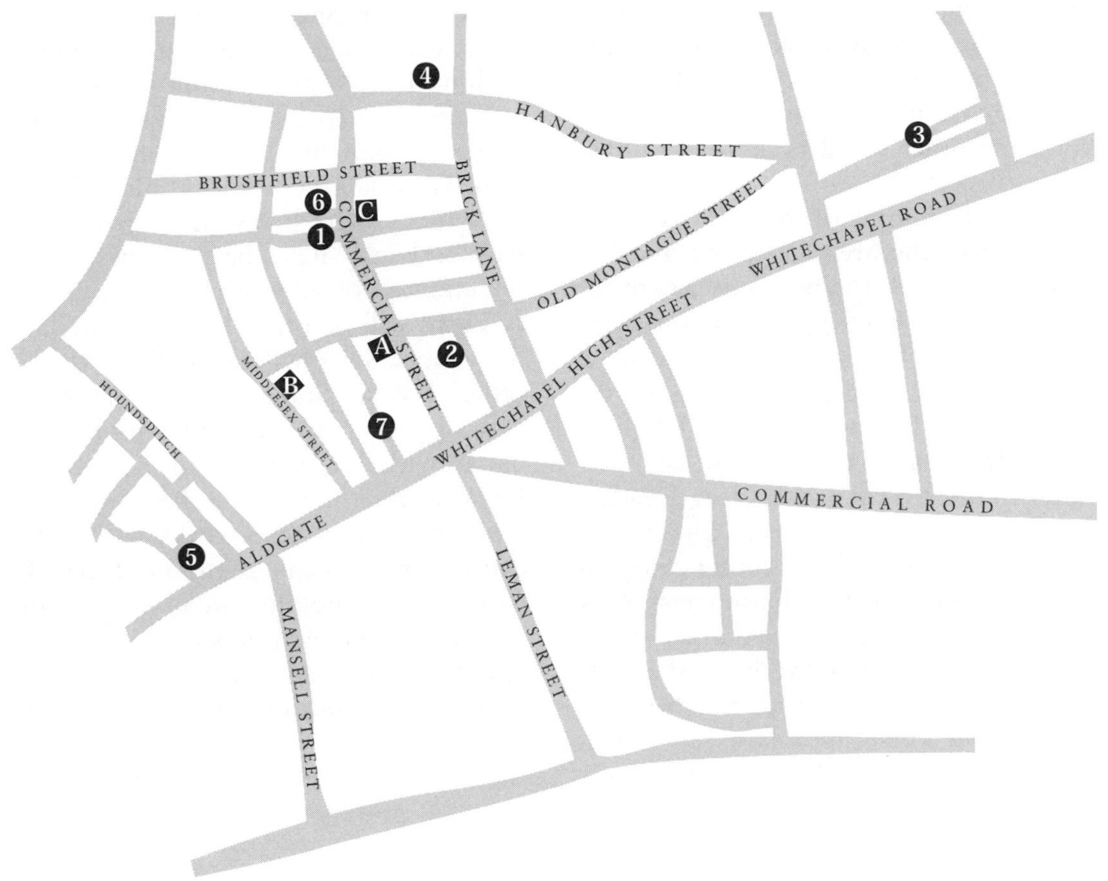

❶ Annie Millwood
❷ Martha Tabram
❸ Mary Ann Nichols
❹ Annie Chapman
❺ Catherine Eddowes
❻ Mary Jane Kelly
❼ Alice McKenzie
A Hutchinson's home
B Site of the grafitto/apron
C Queen's Head Public House

This map is similar to the first one in the book but now includes only the seven attacks I attribute to the Ripper. Also marked are the locations of the Goulston Street Graffito, the spot where the piece of apron was found, and George Hutchinson's home. Does this show a link between Hutchinson and the crimes?

that Hutchinson definitely was the Ripper and bending the facts to fit the theory but simply to trace his whereabouts to the point of his death and compare them with any other murders that might have taken place.

At the beginning of this book is a general map of the area where the murders took place, with the positions where the victims were killed marked upon it. In this section the same map has been reproduced, showing just the sites of the murders of the seven victims I believe were attributable to Jack and the location of Hutchinson's base. I leave readers to draw their own conclusions.

I repeat that I am *not* stating categorically that George Hutchinson was Jack the Ripper. All I can say is that of all the suspects named thus far, he is the only one I can accept. He fitted the "properties" of our killer, lived close to the epicenter of the crimes, knew the area well, and certainly knew Mary Jane Kelly. I would not be at all surprised if Jack proved to be someone else, but that someone must fit the physical and psychological descriptions of our killer even better than Hutchinson.

Jack the Ripper was not a raving lunatic who ended up confined to some asylum. He did not commit suicide, and we need look for no other reason for his stopping than the fact of self-preservation. He was a young local man, strong and stocky, who knew Mary Jane Kelly well and may have been a passing acquaintance of Catherine Eddowes.

There will be other books about Jack the Ripper. Some will be excellent works; others less so. Some will perhaps name new suspects, and others may look at old names with new evidence or theories. All I ask is that the reader keep an open mind and read those works with logic, clarity, and critical attention. Does the work perpetuate the myths and errors outlined in this volume? Does it rely on fanciful claims such as patterns, anagrams, and conspiracy theories? Finally, and most importantly, does the person it suggests as the killer fit the mental and physical profile that Jack undoubtedly bore?

Only when all these criteria are met will those London fogs finally begin to clear and a recognizable Jack step forward to identify himself.

About the Author

John J. Eddleston was born in Lancashire, England, in 1952 and, after a sojourn in Cambridgeshire, moved to the Sussex coast in 1987. He now lives near Brighton and in addition to writing designs websites. One of the sites he has constructed, dealing with true crime, can be found at www.murderfile.co.uk, and he may be contacted through that site.

John is the author of seven other books on true crime. In 1997 he produced a series of works detailing the stories behind all the murders ending in judicial execution in certain geographical locations in the United Kingdom. The original five works were *Murderous Sussex, Murderous Manchester, Murderous Birmingham, Murderous Tyneside,* and *Murderous Leeds.* A sixth book in the series, *Murderous Derbyshire,* covered all the death sentences handed out in that county in the twentieth century.

His seventh book and his first work for ABC-CLIO was *Blind Justice,* which covers fifty stories of someone found guilty of murder who may well have been innocent of the crime. Many of these individuals ended their lives at the end of the rope and almost certainly did not deserve that fate.

John has been fascinated for many years by Jack the Ripper and has been dismayed at the dearth of serious study on the topic, even by those who profess to be experts in the field. This book was written with a view to collecting facts in one volume, and he hopes it will go some way toward redressing the balance and applying proper research methods to the subject.

Another book, his ninth, covering the stories behind every single execution in the United Kingdom, is now nearing completion and should be available next year. After that he hopes to produce a series of books investigating particular cases of miscarriages of justice in depth with a view to having the cases reopened and the original verdicts overturned.

Index